SENTIMENTAL EMPIRICISM

Sentimental Empiricism

POLITICS, PHILOSOPHY, AND CRITICISM

IN POSTWAR FRANCE

Davide Panagia

FORDHAM UNIVERSITY PRESS   NEW YORK   2024

This book is freely available in an open access edition thanks to TOME (Toward an Open Monograph Ecosystem)—a collaboration of the Association of American Universities, the Association of University Presses, and the Association of Research Libraries—and the generous support of Arcadia, a charitable fund of Lisbet Rausing and Peter Baldwin, and the UCLA Library. Learn more at the TOME website, available at: openmonographs.org.

Fordham University Press has no responsibility for the persistence or accuracy of URLs for external or third-party Internet websites referred to in this publication and does not guarantee that any content on such websites is, or will remain, accurate or appropriate.

Fordham University Press also publishes its books in a variety of electronic formats. Some content that appears in print may not be available in electronic books.

Visit us online at www.fordhampress.com.

Library of Congress Cataloging-in-Publication Data available online at https://catalog.loc.gov.

Printed in the United States of America

26 25 24   5 4 3 2 1

First edition

For
Salim John Loxley
(May 24, 1970–October 23, 2021)
In memoriam

Contents

Introduction   1

PART I – MISSED UNDERSTANDINGS

1   Reading Political Theory in Postwar America and Postwar France   33

2   Mimesis, the *explication de texte*, and State Thinking   77

PART II – DISPOSITIONALITIES

3   Jean Wahl, Empirico-Criticism, and the Concrete   99

4   Simone de Beauvoir and the Elementary Structures of Patriarchy   116

5   More than a Unity: Gilbert Simondon's Sentimental Empiricism   149

6   Gilles Deleuze: Displacing Reflection   167

7   Michel Foucault and the Political Ontology of the *Dispositif*   184

Epilogue   211

ACKNOWLEDGMENTS   219

NOTES   223

BIBLIOGRAPHY   267

INDEX   285

I don't know whether, as the saying goes, "things which are repeated are pleasing,"* my belief is that they are significant.
[* "Bis repetita placent": a paraphrase, used in French, of Horace's saying "Haec decies repetita placebit" *(Ars Poetica)*]

—ROLAND BARTHES, "PREFACE," IN *MYTHOLOGIES* (1957)

Introduction

I do not believe an author is in the business of advising one's reader how to read one's work. But I am willing to make an exception here:

The best way to begin reading what follows is to close this book and watch François Truffaut's *Les Quatre cents coups* (*The Four Hundred Blows*, 1959). Or, if time is of the essence, to watch at least the first fifteen minutes. I refer here to the classroom scene of instruction that appears after the opening credit sequence, where the camera tracks the Eiffel Tower in a moving vehicle. The credit sequence ends with Truffaut's dedication to André Bazin, the influential French film critic, film philosopher, and editor of *Cahiers du Cinéma*, the journal of film criticism in which Truffaut had been publishing since 1953. Immediately after the dedication, the camera places the viewer at an angle above the left shoulder of a grade school student who is writing in his notebook; the viewer is in the position of a classmate who might be copying what the student is writing. We soon learn that the boy is taking a test. But we also quickly learn that the act of copying is everything to this scene, and to this film. The student pauses from his test, removes a pinup calendar from his desk drawer, and passes it to his classmates (it is an all-male classroom). Eventually the calendar lands on the desk of the film's protagonist, Antoine Doinel, who is spotted and called out by the schoolteacher—the Maître—who promptly confiscates the salacious image. Antoine is immediately disciplined and sent to stand in the corner of the classroom, behind a blackboard. The Maître announces that there are thirty seconds left for the test and then collects the papers, at which point the students exit the classroom for recess. Antoine also begins to exit, but he is instructed to stay in the corner because, as the Maître proclaims, "recess is a reward, not a right." That is, recess is a reward for those who reproduce the Maître's work well; it is not a right of classroom citizenship. The good imitators will be selected for the reward of recess, the others selected out and will not take part in the privilege of leisure time. The lesson is clear: it would be one familiar to Truffaut's generation of postwar viewers, all of whom would have experienced similar classroom scenarios. What is even more clear are the consequences of the lesson: the scene portrays a metaphysics of parsing that divides and selects those who can and cannot reproduce well. Those who can't reproduce well won't end well, and Antoine is clearly not fated to end well even if the final scene of the film leaves things undecided.

There's a reason that this film has received the accolades it has and that Truffaut remains one of the great film directors of his generation. One unique feature of his direction is the fact that Truffaut never lets the camera lie still.[1] He places the viewer in the restless line of sight of the schoolchildren. We are rarely, if ever, privy to the Maître's point of view, and in fact, the viewer is typically made to feel like a hyperactive schoolboy whose energies and attentions are being compressed and molded by the desk's rigidity, the firm tone of the Maître's voice, and the stern architecture of the classroom. The audience of the film is immersed in the lives of the schoolchildren: We hear the Maître's voice resonate throughout the classroom when, upon their return from recess, he begins the next lesson by reciting and writing on the blackboard Jean Richepin's poem "Épitaphe pour un lièvre" (Epitaph for a Hare). This is a modern Alexandrine poem, and the Maître's recitation emphasizes its somnambulist rhythm, cadence, and form in a nearly liturgical manner. In short, what Truffaut offers us in the film's initial sequence is a scene of the reproduction of and fidelity to mimesis, or what he had called "adaptation" in his famous 1954 denunciation of classical French cinema published in the pages of *Cahier du Cinéma*.[2]

The Project

This book is about the development of a genre of political and aesthetic criticism in postwar France that I refer to as "sentimental empiricism." The characteristics of this genre are that it is politically anti-authoritarian, aesthetically anti-mimetic, and metaphysically pluralist and associationist. The task of this book is to provide an account of this genre of political theorizing by appreciating how the philosophical projects discussed herein express direct political interventions on the dispositional powers of domination. To explain: The focus of such political interventions and critiques is not on an account of domination that operates arbitrarily from above nor on a republican ideal of freedom as nondomination from a master; rather, sentimental empiricism focuses on the dispositional powers of domination. By "dispositional" I refer to the work of the sentiments in arranging bodies, perceptions, attentions, and values. Dispositional powers are forces that "pose" us toward something and, in doing so, generate potential adjacencies. The transitive verb "pose" at the root of "disposition" is derived from that Latin *ponere*, meaning to place upon in a certain attitude or posture. A key contribution for research of this volume is to articulate the political, philosophical, metaphysical, and aesthetic accounts of dispositional powers central to postwar French political theory.

My specific emphasis is on the 1950s, the decade of intellectual formation and the beginning of the writerly careers of those thinkers whose writings are loosely associated with the founding of the French avant-garde literary magazine *Tel Quel* (founded in 1960) and whose works would subsequently be lumped—some twenty years later upon their arrival on Anglophone bookshelves—under the prefix of various "post-isms." None of the authors I discuss in these pages—Jean Wahl, Simone de Beauvoir, Gilles Deleuze, Gilbert Simondon, or Michel Foucault—identified themselves as sentimental empiricists (nor, for that matter, did they ever identify as post-structural or postmodern thinkers). This is a term I've cribbed and adapted from Jessica Riskin's wonderful study *Science in the Age of Sensibility*.[3] The only author that puts his empiricist cards on the table is Gilles Deleuze, who, throughout his career, remained unapologetic in his commitment to David Hume's empiricism and the account of subjectivity, of the moral sentiments, and of the metaphysics of dispositionality therein. But I use the term "sentimental empiricism" regardless, as I believe it best captures the thrust of these thinkers' theoretical innovations, which are immersed in a Western tradition of philosophical inquiry, but minor to it.

By "minor" I don't mean qualitatively inferior or quantitatively lesser. My use of the term "minor" is taken from Western music theory. The foundation of Western music theory is its chromaticism, where each musical note is a half tone. A scale has seven notes, and each note of the scale is determined by the relative distance between half-tones. There exist two half-tones between the first and second note of a major scale, and there is a distance of one half-tone between the third and fourth notes of any major scale. The eighth note of the scale is the same as the first; it is the tonal center of the key signature (or tonic). Every major key (C major, for instance) has a relative minor scale (A minor is the relative minor to C major, also known as its natural minor or the Aeolian mode). The notes of the two scales are identical. Neither C major nor A minor has sharps or flats, and if you were to look at a piano keyboard you would notice that all the white keys are the notes of the C major/A minor scales. The difference between C major and A minor is their tonal center. If you play the notes of C major with an A minor chord as your tonic, the sound-scape is completely different than if the C major chord were your tonic, even though the notes of the scale are identical. Typically, we say that the minor mode sounds more melancholic or sadder than the happier, major mode. The relative major/minor relation is one where the sameness of the notes cannot account for the difference in soundscape. In this musical sense we can say that the mode of critical thinking of sentimental empiricism is minor to the domi-nant critical traditions of Western political and aesthetic thought. It is of the same world as the major tradition of Western political and aesthetic thought—and yet, it registers a different tonality. Unlike its relative major mode, senti-mental empiricism's tonal center is not mimesis/identity but difference-in-itself. And each of the thinkers of this study begins with a metaphysics of difference-in-itself as the tonal center, though (of course) each of these think-ers innovates on that tonality in distinct ways.

I develop this minor line of research for several reasons. The first is that I wish to right a wrong that is more the result of a mis-reception or missed un-derstanding (*mésentente*, in Jacques Rancière's sense of the term) emergent from Anglophone reading practices in the discipline of political theory that treat the making of sense as a professional requirement innocent of any political ambitions. However we may adjudicate which methods are best at procuring understandings—of language, of texts, of cultural artefacts, of data analytics, or of political concepts—no one seems to doubt that the project of under-standing *is* the purview of political theory research. And yet, one of the main challenges posed by recent work in political theory from the traditions of Afro-American political thought, comparative political theory, environmen-tal political thought, and indigenous political theory is that the Western ideal of understanding is an unsettled terrain that carries with it forms of power, subjection, and claims of property and propriety that limit who can partici-pate in political speech and political action, not to mention who can participate in the activity of theorizing itself.[4] In other words, like the critical project of sentimental empiricism I present in this volume, these contemporary authors and thinkers interested in exploring matters of race, indigeneity, the Anthro-pocene, and professional standards of legitimacy question the exclusivity of mi-mesis and understanding (with its clustered morphology of adjacent ideals like clarity, transparency, meritocracy, epistemic authority, and so forth) as qualifying criteria for participation in the activities of political reflection and judgment and—*ceteris paribus*—for participation in its forms of scholarly pro-duction. In short, what these scholars offer as a critical consideration is how understanding is a dimension of cultural capital that carries with it explicit forms of political domination.[5]

One of the key features of the authors I study is their challenging of the givenness of mimesis as a credentialing standard for selection to political participation. Mimesis, as we know, is not an easy concept to define or, for that matter, to translate; and throughout I retain a capacious sense of the term that includes such possible translations as representation, reproduction, resemblance, imitation, verisimilitude, copying, identity, and so forth. This said, the critique of mimesis is one of, if not *the*, defining feature of sentimental empiricism. This critique is developed for an important political reason: in France, mimesis is a state qualification necessary for political participation, legitimacy, and authority.[6] Without competence in mimesis no French citizen would have access to offices of social and political power. Add to this the fact that throughout the nineteenth and twentieth centuries France is a settler colonial power, and we quickly deduce that at the core of French colonialism is an aesthetic and political philosophy of mimesis that grounds the operations of power necessary to maintaining and reproducing the system of values that legitimate colonial dispossession.[7] With the help of Cornelia Vismann's studies on European chanceries we can speculate how the daily tasks of colonial bureaucrats were wholly structured by practices of copying and how extensively the success of colonial rule relied on copying as an institution, but also as a philosophic, aesthetic, and political practice necessary for the successful reproduction of territorial domination.[8] It is little wonder, then, that in postwar France Herman Melville's Bartleby—a scrivener who would prefer *not* to copy—would become such a compelling political and philosophical literary figure.[9]

A key marker and site of critique for engaging the relationship between mimesis and the State is the French colloquialism "*le bon sens*," which can be variously translated as the "good sense," or the "proper sense," or simply "common sense."[10] One can say of Truffaut's Antoine, for instance, that "il n'y a pas du bon sens"; he lacks good sense in the choices he makes. But Antoine also lacks good sense—of the capacity to reproduce well—because he happily interrupts his bookish efforts to satisfy his preadolescent sexual curiosities.

Life and language are structured by "*le bon sens*"—so much so, in fact, that "*le bon sens*" are the first words of René Descartes's *Discourse on Method*: "*Le bon sens* est la chose du monde la mieux partagée; car chacun pense en être si bien pourvu, que ceux même qui sont les plus difficiles à contenter en toute autre chose n'ont point coutume d'en désirer plus qu'ils en ont." [Good sense is the most equally distributed of worldly goods; for everyone thinks himself so abundantly provided with it, that even those whose satisfactions are most difficult to acquiesce, are not in the habit of desiring more of it than they already possess.][11] Reading the passage in English doesn't render the historical psycho-acoustic resonances that would be triggered by a French reader who appreciates that "*le bon sens*" is not simply an analog to right reason and to the capacity to judge and distinguish between truth and falsehood, as Descartes explains in the subsequent sentence. "*Le bon sens*" is also a credentialing virtue for social comportment, rank, and status, as Sophia Rosenfeld has shown. In her history of common sense, Rosenfeld notes how during revolutionary times, appeals to *le bon sens* were appeals to a commoner's sensibility that stood against the infallibility of scholastic authority. The voice of *le bon sens* "was the voice of *les choses* rather than *les mots*; of sensory experience rather than philosophy, theology, or formal book learning; of commonality rather than self- interest or individuality. Speaking as "an organ of the public voice and of good sense," to the good sense of other ordinary people, became, much like speaking as a patriot, a way to suggest that what one was peddling were the shared values of the community, on the one hand, and the uncorrupted language of truth, on the other."[12] *Le bon sens* was a populist, agrarian rhetorical ideal that was also a synecdoche for the noble savage whose sensibilities were closer to nature. But as Rosenfeld further notes, by 1790–91 a more conservative reconfiguration of *le bon sens* would be underway in order to calm the enthusiasms of revolutionary fervor. After the consecration of authorship and freedom of expression established by the 1793 Declaration of the Rights of Genius, it was no longer possible to deploy state censorship to curb the revolutionary excess of words, to use Jacques Rancière's felicitous phrase.[13] Another strategy was necessary, one that would work to persuade people not to listen rather than not speak.[14] "The idea was to reverse the tide of the Revolution, if not its civil libertarian gains, through a kind of informal censorship, rooted in good sense, that would allow for the resurrection of a single national voice representative of (moderate, elite) community norms."[15]

By the nineteenth century this would be achieved by the Napoleonic reforms that established France's national system of republican education whose explicit task was to train civil servants, military personnel, and schoolteachers in the nation's political and aesthetic virtues. Crucial to that system of reproduction were the methods of reading and writing, or what in the French context is simply referred to as "literary criticism." *L'esprit français* is founded on the instruction of mimesis via a neoclassical canon of literary and philosophical humanism. In short, the postwar French critique of humanism characteristic of the sentimental empiricist tradition I study *is* a critique of state authority and the legitimacy of republican sovereignty.

Before going further we must appreciate how the claims about the tight relationship between the good sense of mimesis and the total authority of the State are part of a historical account of the relationship between politics and philosophy that would culminate with the events of May 1968 in Paris and the establishment of the *Centre Universitaire Expérimental de Vincennes* (1969), subsequently renamed the University of Paris VIII at Vincennes in 1971.[16] For the generation of thinkers I explore (many of whom would become Paris VIII professors), mimesis and the State are synonyms because mimesis lies at the heart of the French state education program, as we see allegorized in Truffaut's film. In that opening scene, the children are expected to show understanding through imitation and reproduction, and the authority of identity is manifested in the Maître's words, which are themselves reproducing a modern Alexandrine poem whose style is the epitome of seventeenth-century French neoclassicism, a marker of cultural capital indelibly bound to an *ancien régime* and its system of privileges, hierarchies, and imperial ambitions. The persistence of that form of verse as the epitome of *l'esprit français* is code for the civic virtue of "*le bon sens*" that persisted well into the Fourth Republic and beyond. The thinkers I explore pursued a definitive break from the state form of "*le bon sens*": a rupture, that is, in the technical system for the reproduction of value. At its core, that break needed to begin with a dismantling of the metaphysical edifice of mimesis as the tonal center of the colonial state's powers of authority and domination.

In short, mimesis is not just an aesthetic concept inherited from an Eleatic metaphysics of justice; it is a political metaphysic of sovereignty and authority: it holds claims about the nature of knowledge and understanding, the formal operations of representation, the criteria for the assessment of representations, and—crucially—the forces of relation and determination that legitimate the hierarchies of a system of evaluation. This political metaphysic of mimesis is also the system of thought in and through which the powers and offices of political domination are transmitted intergenerationally, from one successive iteration of the French republic to the next. To be sovereign, to have authority—that is, to have the capacity to wield power and dominion—one must be a master of mimesis and know how to copy well. This is the epitome of *le bon sens*. The only way to ensure the perpetuity of such an authoritative form of mastery—and thus the continued legitimacy of state power—is to institute a national program of training that ensures the reproduction of the State/mimesis relation through nationalized standards for accessing the meaning/understanding relation: to wit, a state program of literary criticism.[17] If I know how to copy well and thus can reproduce the universal values of the French nation intergenerationally, then I am entitled to participate in political power.

Of course, such entitlements cannot (by definition) be available to everyone. Though Descartes may begin by asserting that "*le bon sens*" is "the most equally distributed" among peoples, the project of his *Discours de la méthode* is, in fact, to provide the right principles for the application of good sense. It is worth noting that, despite the modern convention of abbreviating the title of Descartes's famous work, the full title also includes the following directive: "pour bien conduire sa raison et chercher la vérité" [to better conduct reason and search for truth]. *Le bon sens* needs method in order to conduct the mind well to dispose one's character to the search for truth in diverse fields of inquiry. Method isn't merely a formal procedure; it's a technical medium— what today we might call a format—that shapes the conduct of sense.[18] Hence the importance of instituting what Pierre Bourdieu refers to as "a programme of perception, thought and action" through such institutions as the *lycée*, the *agrégation*, and the *baccalauréat*: "Culture," Bourdieu explains, "whose function it was if not to unify at least to make communication possible, takes on a differentiating function." Bourdieu then cites the philosopher and sociologist Edmond Goblot (1858–1935), who writes that "that the bourgeoisie exists only in the practice of society and not of law. The *lycée* makes it a legal institution. The *baccalauréat* is the real barrier, the official, State-guaranteed barrier, which holds back the invasion. True, you may join the bourgeoisie, but first you have to get the *baccalauréat*. The 'liberal' culture of the humanist traditions with Latin its keystone and the social 'signum' *par excellence*, constitutes the difference while at the same time giving it the semblance of legitimacy."[19]

Bourdieu's account helps clarify why many of the thinkers that are associated with postwar French political and aesthetic thought dedicate so much time, ink, and energy to two related institutions: literary criticism and the state system of education. This also helps explain why so many of these authors are averse to the political and philosophical ambitions of humanism and, implicitly, Aristotelian and Hegelian dialectics. Unlike some conceptions of humanism that regard it as an antiseptic philosophical ideal foundational to the legitimacy of human rights, for the authors I discuss humanism is indelibly and permanently bound to a long history of state domination, colonialism, and imperialism. Moreover, classical humanism is equally bound up with the history of the Catholic Church in France and especially with the centrality of classical rhetoric and Thomist scholasticism that had as their pedagogical paragon the Jesuitical *Ratio Studiorum*.[20] Mimesis and its metaphysical, political, and aesthetic edifice of understanding are a synecdoche of the state system of domination that aligns privileges with a program of literary criticism: to wit, an aesthetic-political metaphysics of meaning and understanding. To challenge state authority means challenging the authority of understanding as both a metaphysical and political enterprise.

This latter point is, I believe, especially relevant for appreciating the political stakes of sentimental empiricist critical thought. It's not that the sentimental empiricist thinkers I study would focus exclusively on the philosophical arguments they were challenging. For them, the major mode of the history of philosophy (to return to our musical metaphor) *is* the problem, precisely because it represents a history of manners that comprises a total system of virtue training. In short, the history of philosophy is a medium for the transmission of political values.[21] Another way to think about this is to say that the cultural politics that shapes the human into a universal citizen-subject operates in such a way that a person's propriety legitimates one's right to political participation: the propriety of *"le bon sens"* ensures the right to occupancy of political offices and influence in the French republican State. All of this is oriented toward creating the type of citizen-subject who would and could fit into the institutions of national governance, including the civil service, the military, and grade school teaching. It is for this reason that I focus on the period of intellectual formation of the thinkers who interest me. That is, I wish to *overstate* their period of subject formation in their system of education because the cultural politics of pedagogical formation has been woefully ignored in the Anglophone analysis of the political philosophies of these authors' works.[22] These authors, in other words, are not just critics of the Enlightenment humanist subject for idealist reasons. Like the schoolchildren in Truffaut's film, they lived the forms of discipline, the practices of humiliation, and structures of domination expected of the kind of universalism championed by French republican citizenship. All of them were painfully aware of the fact that to enter academic life, they were expected to reproduce and thus legitimate those very same structures, institutions, and practices for the sake of the perpetuity of the French State. In other words, the majoritarian history of philosophy was for these thinkers/students a republican project of subjectification that was inextricably tied to a political metaphysics of mimesis that legitimated state domination. Here practices of reading and writing are the formal method (in the Cartesian sense) that shape the "matter" that is the student's mind.[23] The reproduction of an institutionalized mimesis thus ensures the continued legitimacy of French republican universalism and its colonial reach. Finally, each of the thinkers I study also appreciated their own complicity in reproducing that same system; hence their urgency of innovating and developing a minoritarian mode of critical thinking from within.

Here, then, is the political crux of the matter: state authority is a force of reproduction expressed in various institutional forms—and especially via the education system—that legitimates the organization, classification, and arrangement of values and hierarchies that ensures the inequalities of political domination. And now here is the theoretical dilemma: though political domination is the effect, it does not operate exclusively on the model of a top-down command. As Truffaut's classroom scene makes evident, there is the Maître's voice, but there is also an entire psycho-perceptual milieu of modalities of bodily training that dispose proper comportment (i.e., civility) for social and political benefit. Indeed, from the perspective of postwar French political philosophy, to imagine political legitimacy as anything other than the output of a technical system for the reproduction of state authority is the epitome of political alienation. From these insights two things become central: (1) Reproduction is a dispositional power not reducible to a top-down model of domination; and (2) Reproduction is a force of relation.

The site of critical attention of sentimental empiricism will thus be on dispositional powers and relations, not on identities or substances. The task for political thinking is to develop a critical apparatus that attends to the relational powers of constituency, of what holds things together or wrests them apart. The manner in which the thinkers I study address this ambition is to disown a philosophical and political system that presupposes given relations of belonging as natural. This means rejecting the system of hierarchies of social and political stratification by rupturing the adjacencies that ensure continuity. In short, sentimental empiricist thinkers disavow a metaphysics of necessary relations that become manifest in such political and normative principles like inheritance, lineage, and necessity. All these forms of relation and the metaphysical system that sustains them are perceived as carriers of an *ancien régime* of privilege and power. The politics of the philosophical project I describe is one of dismantling the organization of relations that structure this system of values and its forms of reproduction.

There is a fundamental problem, though: if there is no such thing as natural political relations, then this must also extend to that seemingly universal relation of negation in dialectics. Dialectical critique works if we assume a metaphysical dualism of identity/difference, and dialectical negation works as a mode of political critique if we accept all relations of power as reducible to a dualism of domination (i.e., bourgeois/worker, master/slave, parent/child). The mode of political and aesthetic criticism developed by the sentimental empiricist thinkers is not premised on negating identities but is oriented to disjoining the adjacencies that make social systems feel like immutable substances. Political attention will be given to the particularity of relations rather than to the negation of an identity. To dismantle a totality, one must therefore show how it is not really a substance but a dynamic system of adjacencies in process. Jean Wahl would find resources for such operations in his discovery of American pluralism and his development of a process ontology of concretization; for Simone de Beauvoir this is expressed in her life-long literary activities but also, and crucially for our purposes, in her singular and foundational articulation of patriarchy as a dispositional power of domination; for Gilbert Simondon this involved the development of a philosophy of individuation and technical thinking that was explicitly and unapologetically anti-substantialist; Gilles Deleuze developed a philosophy of sentimental empiricism that would articulate a political metaphysics of difference-in-itself; finally, for Michael Foucault, it meant developing a sentimentalist account of technical media for political governance.

To grasp the political purchase of the critique of Western metaphysics associated with postwar French thought requires our appreciating how important it was to develop a minor tradition of thought that explored a metaphysics of becoming, of difference, and of non-sense. This latter point is worth specifying because it is too often the case that postwar French thought is associated with various forms of irrationalism and is thus quickly dismissed as such. I believe this is a mistake, and thankfully I am not alone.[24] "Non-sense" here (and throughout this book) should not be read as senselessness or meaninglessness. Non-sense is a formal philosophical category that affirms that there is no standard or method for the making of sense that is independent of a set of political and aesthetic structures and institutions that coordinate the system of perception and attention for sense making. In other words, the thinkers I discuss reject the view that sense, sense-making, and meaning are innate ideas innocent of the technical media that coordinate the conditions for making sense (including reading and writing).

With these political stakes in mind, it is a curious fact about the uptake of postwar French thought in the Anglophone world that—except in a few select cases—almost no mention is made of the dynamics of cultural capital that legitimate the French system of education.[25] This is especially curious, given that most (if not all) of the authors in the pantheon of postwar French theory write explicitly about education, often recounting their own educational experiences in interviews, and most (if not all) theorize the politics of literary criticism throughout their oeuvre.[26] Upon closer inspection it also becomes clear that the attentions given to linguistic interpretation and literary criticism in postwar French thought are not part of a general twentieth-century "linguistic turn," as the frequent classification of these works in the Anglophone world would claim. The emphasis in these thinkers is not on interpretation per se, but on the practices of reading and writing, their teaching, and the instructional forms of their manifestation that shape intellectual formation and political subjectivity. The power of representation, in other words, does not come from language but from forms of articulation and perception that turn a system of signs into something readable and writeable. For something *to be* readable and writeable, a theory of meaning must be in place. The political theory of sentimental empiricism exposes and dismantles the theory of meaning of mimesis in all its philosophical, metaphysical, aesthetic, and political implications.

The conjunction of these omissions in the Anglophone reception of these literatures motivates my inquiry. In this respect I wish to disabuse the reader of a bifurcated refrain that has become a kind of facile cant that one repeatedly encounters when researching and writing about postwar French authors: "Why can't they just write clearly and simply?," I am often asked, and "How is this material actually relevant to political theory?" Such a twinned refrain marks its own complicity with the cultural capital of transparency and clarity that mimics a fidelity to established values that reproduce overtones of Anglophonism familiar to anyone whose mother tongue and national culture are not English.[27] In this regard, it might be the case that what I elaborate in this book could fall under the heading of what Emily Apter calls the "Untranslatable" that marks an "unfamiliar linguistic *nomos*" whose series of associations are not predicated upon a recognizable *ethnos*.[28] If part of this book resembles an intellectual history, then, it is not one rooted in language, concepts, words, or ideas but upon national, political, and aesthetic forms of perception and attention that structure the advenience of impressions upon the reader/ viewer. By this I mean that however we might approach the analysis of theoretical works written in the past, and however much emphasis we give to the context of their historical production, we cannot overlook the cultural capital that accompanies their reception within various national contexts. The conditions for understanding a work—what Rancière calls the partitions of the sensible—in one national culture are not the same as those of another. This may seem like an obvious and trivial point to make. But it is neither obvious nor trivial. The simple fact that there is so little work in the discipline of political theory on histories of reading practices, and the fact that the interminable methodological debates about the interpretation of works remain dependent upon a neurotypical concept of understanding, suggests that there is still much political and theoretical work to be done on the political ideal of understanding.[29]

I would add to this a further consideration: there is also much work to be done on the political theory of technical media and the ways technical media (capaciously conceived) participate in intellectual formation.[30] The stylus, the papyrus, leather binding, the printing press, photography, statistics, writing software, files, screens, the QWERTY keyboard, and so forth are not innocent tools for the transcription of ideas and beliefs. These technical media constitute an associational milieu replete with possibilities and limitations, forms of emphasis and perception, structures of attachment and circulation, and so much more; and none of these can be determined in advance by an account of understanding presumed innocent from an engagement with the technical objects of scholarly and intellectual production.[31]

For instance, it is difficult to appreciate the political and theoretical stakes of one of the most important and influential paradigms of reading emergent from postwar France—the mode of reading referred to as "symptomatic critique"—without noting the centrality of Louis Althusser's projects in *Reading Capital* and *For Marx* and the importance given to the "epistemological rupture."[32] Althusser attributes this practice of reading to Gaston Bachelard's work in the history of science and famously develops it to organize the periodicity of Marx's writings between the early (humanist) phase and the latter (scientific/theoretical) phase.[33] One might easily contest Althusser's interpretation of Marx's oeuvre ad nauseum, as well as his scientistic partition of the sensible. However, his articulation of the moral psychology of reading as a technical medium of political philosophy helps us appreciate how and why one of the most important figures in the French academy thought it crucial to develop a robust set of political claims by articulating an account of the relationship between politics, science, and reading. For Althusser and those participating in his enterprise, the political stakes of Marx's oeuvre could not and would not be available if the reader remained restricted by the established practices of reading taught within the French academy. Althusser and his students (some of whom contributed to *Reading Capital*) would need to develop a new practice of reading that would allow them to rearticulate the medium of a work as well as the political and scientific stakes of an intellectual contribution.

They were not alone. Another central figure who would attend to practices of reading in order to think politically about the world was Roland Barthes, who made reading itself a problem of political participation and action; and then, of course, there were Claude Lévi-Strauss, Jacques Derrida, Luce Irigaray, Julia Kristeva, Hélène Cixous, and many others who understood reading and readerly reception as central to intellectual formation and political participation. None of these thinkers made it into the pages of this volume, though I believe them to be exemplary interlocutors who remain footnoted throughout. I acknowledge them here, however, because a central site of my investigation is the political history of literary criticism in France and how formal methods of reading are considered part and parcel of French republicanism.

An investigation into practices of reading makes social, political, and aesthetic value palpable through the ways in which readers note their emphases and attentions in their commentaries. By citing passages, underlining text, and commenting on the writings of others we lend perceptibility to our most intimate ways of experiencing the world around us.[34] Try as we might, we are most lost when we attempt to account for the "why" of our ways of noting emphasis, of why something strikes our efforts of understanding. This is one reason the history of reading practices runs alongside the history of aesthetic and moral judgment.[35] The marking of a passage that strikes us as relevant is a judgment of value about the work we are engaging. To this I would add that such a relationship is not specific to any one discipline or division within the academy. It's not that reading in the humanities is any more or less subjective than reading in the social sciences or the natural sciences. It's simply the case that in the social and natural sciences scholars are less likely to interrogate the cultural capital of their practices of reading. But how we read and what we read for *is* formative of the ideas and values we hold.

Another conceit of this study is a wholly Humean one that I have discussed elsewhere but will rehearse briefly here.[36] As is well known, in his *A Treatise of Human Nature* David Hume offers a very compelling account of how ideas are formed. He does not believe in innate ideas; for him, ideas are derived from experience. Better put, for Hume ideas are not derived at all: they are collections of impressions adjoined in the imagination. This means that for Hume, ideas are not representations of objects but are serialized adjacencies.[37] Moreover, the imagination is not a self-legislating power that a subject commands. There is no subject that precedes the imagination because in the imagination there is no system of ordering that precedes the activity of organization. The Humean imagination is an abstract engine of association that adjoins different impressions, and there is no reason inherent to the relation that can account for why associations are made as they are. In other words, for Hume there can be no theory of self or meaning that precedes experience. In the imagination one discovers the power of relations that orchestrate the passage from one impression to the next, providing a sensation of constancy. That sensation of constancy is what gives us the satisfaction of understanding. But as Hume affirms, "Any degree of regularity in our perceptions can never be a foundation for us to infer a greater degree of regularity in some objects, which are not perceiv'd; since this supposes a contradiction, *viz.*, a habit acquir'd by what was never present to mind."[38] In other words, just because we achieve a satisfaction of understanding does not mean that there can be a theory of understanding that legitimates future events of sense making.

Hume's account of the imagination is important because it helps us appreciate how intellectual formation is shaped by habits—none of which are necessary (in a deterministic sense) to the concept of understanding. The concept of understanding is in this view a constancy resultant from practices of reading and writing. Thus, when I say that I am studying a moment of intellectual formation for the authors I engage, I mean that I am interested in how these thinkers negotiated the discontinuity between a system of intellectual formation they inherited and the political ambitions they held. The burden of the events that France endured in the immediate aftermath of the war that were part of the lived experiences of this generation of intellectuals—the Vichy regime, the Indochina war, and the Algerian war—were such that it was no longer possible to reproduce the continuities that had held things together as they had before and that a radical transformation of values, of practices, and of thinking needed to take place.[39] As Beauvoir would argue, the mimetic system that sustained state legitimacy no longer coincided with the lived experience of everyday French life.

What became politically pressing for the thinkers in this period is the realization that the power of representation, so lauded as a formal political and aesthetic medium for just democratic institutions, is also a technical ensemble that ensures the intergenerational reproduction of power relations and thus political stability.[40] This is a central political and aesthetic problem that is taken up throughout the postwar period in France and that forms the background to my investigations. Images, words, identities don't simply represent meanings; representations are a medium of political power. A representation is a technical device for the organization of values and the selection of perceptibility for who and what counts as a legitimate participant in political power. This is what is at stake in Truffaut's classroom scene, and it is what is at stake in the postwar attack on French neoclassicism via the philosophical, artistic, and literary developments that ensued. It is also what is politically at stake in those challenges posed to a humanist philosophical and literary curriculum by structuralism, deconstruction, post-structuralism, or the symptomatic readings of texts.

A political problematic I identify in these pages is quite straightforward, though neither simple nor self-evident: how is it possible to conceive of political life and collective action without relying on the identitarian conceit of a common sense or consensus that legitimates the authority of the State as the transcendental form for relating politically? Unlike their Anglophone counterparts, this generation of thinkers were not smitten with the universal ideals of liberalism, nor were they convinced by the new scientism of behaviorism, nor did their intellectual ambitions involve developing moral, political, and economic tools to arm a Cold War Armageddon against a Communist Thanos. Indeed, participation with the State was to be avoided at all costs not only because France remained, well past de Gaulle's ascendency to power, complicit in such colonial horrors as torture and rape, but also because most of the thinkers I consider had been mentored by philosophers of science—notably, Georges Canguilhem, Gaston Bachelard, and (until his execution by the Vichy regime) Jean Cavaillés.[41] These scholars were exceedingly weary of the kinds of epistemic ambitions that were being claimed on behalf of the new science of politics on the other side of the Atlantic.[42] In short, though the authors I discuss throughout were postwar thinkers, they were not Cold War thinkers in the way in which their generational counterparts in the United States and Britain were. This makes a substantial difference in terms of the philosophical attitudes and dispositions available to them. Unlike the scenario of political-philosophical development in postwar America detailed by Katrina Forrester, the thinkers I turn to do not rely on the republican liberal state and its capacity to regulate moral and political life as a viable solution to the problem of social inequality and political domination.[43] On the contrary, republican liberty is the problem because it is complicit with colonialism and imperialism.

The American postwar solution turns to the behavioral social sciences and to the invention of that medium of political decisionism (i.e., the American think tank) in order to coordinate a series of research and policy networks of influence that would, as it were, advise princes.[44] Moreover, it would treat the rational capacities of humans as the foundation for a cybernetic transformation of human worth alongside and in tandem with military expansion and nuclear deterrence. This means that a central difference between postwar Anglophone political theory and postwar French political thinking is that in the Anglophone—and especially American—case, there was a national faith (though it would perhaps better be conceived of as a national myth) in the ability of humans to strategize advantages based on individual interest. For white Anglophone political theory of the 1950s there is an imaginary outside to the powers of ideological isomorphism and political domination (of course, the same couldn't be said by Afro-American political thinkers who had no illusions about the horrors of the American settler state or the British imperial state). French postwar thinkers could not assume the same as their white Anglophone counterparts, to the point that by the time Louis Althusser pens his immensely influential notes entitled, "Ideology and Ideological State Apparatuses (Notes Toward and Investigation)" (1970) he would not hesitate to affirm that there is no reflection, no subjectivity, and no objectivity outside of the mechanisms of ideological reproduction.[45] The liberal ideal that supports the subject/object distinction and that ensures that rational choice can be a regularian solution to political injustice would not be available to this generation of thinkers precisely because the system of education that would instruct them on the history and philosophy of political and aesthetic reason was (and is) part and parcel of the imperial state power of political domination and exploitation that legitimated the reproduction of colonial dispossession. Thus, their question and motivation for philosophical experimentation: What resources are available, beyond the major tonic of Western philosophy, for the articulation, development, and deployment of a mode of critical thinking that doesn't assume the centrality of the State-form? One answer, as I propose in this volume, came in the exploration of a minoritarian mode of critical political theory I call "sentimental empiricism."

A Minor Mode of Critical Thinking

First off, allow me an explanation for what to some readers might seem like an absolute perversion of the story of postwar French thought I recount: The received consensus is that the thinkers I study—most notably Deleuze and Foucault—were left Nietzscheans, and that their critical projects are wholly and almost exclusively indebted to Nietzsche's philosophical oeuvre.[46] Contesting this truism would seem an absurdity on my part. Yet, the claim of the exclusivity of the influence of Nietzsche's writings is historically anachronistic and factually incorrect. The story is richer and more diverse than that reading allows for. First and foremost, we must note that little work on Nietzsche had appeared in postwar France prior to Deleuze's study *Nietzsche and Philosophy* (originally published in 1963).[47] That work acknowledges Pierre Klossowski's 1958 essay "Nietzsche, le polythéisme et la parodie" as an influence. But this was a one-off paper, and though Klossowski *would* dedicate the 1960s to studying Nietzsche and writing what would become *Nietzsche and the Vicious Circle*, that work would not be published until 1969. This leads us to conclude that though Nietzsche's works received much attention in the 1960s, they received little attention before then, as the various reading lists for the national *Concours* in the philosophy *agrégation* would also seem to indicate.[48]

Humean empiricism and moral sentimentalism had a significantly more notable presence in France in the 1950s. Alan Schrift makes the strong case that the weight of French sociology and the history and philosophy of science had an important effect on the content and shape of the French philosophy *Programme* and *Concours* that prepared students for the *agrégation*.[49] In this respect, a major figure who is examined and studied for the preparation of the *agrégation* immediately before and after the war is Auguste Comte. Comte's presence on the list of authors to prepare for the *Concours* had been sparse throughout the twentieth century until the ascent of Georges Davy, a sociologist, who became president of the *Concours* and presided over it from

1942 to 1956, during which time Comte and the British Empiricists (especially Hume) gained a major presence.[50] Thus, the turn to empiricism and moral sentimentalism that I trace should not be as surprising as it might appear at first glance.

As noted, I crib the term "sentimental empiricism" from Jessica Riskin's study on the conjunction of scientific inquiry and moral sentimentalism in eighteenth-century France. My adoption of the term is intended to mark a morphological exercise that delimits a genre of critical operations correlating a disparate series of resonant practices of political, metaphysical, and aesthetic theorizing.[51] Riskin's study is important to me because at its core, she shows not only how sensibility and sensation operated among the Enlightenment scientific minds she studies, but how there was an explicit engagement between diverse genres of literary forms that informed the development of the methodological innovations in scientific discovery and experimentation. "But the role of sentiment in Enlightenment empiricism," she affirms, "seems to me deeper and more pervasive. . . . Sensibility operated even in fields that studied the inanimate rather than the animate, and that took an experimental rather than a narrative view of nature. Sentimentalism characterized the methods of what are now considered the hardest sciences, physics and chemistry."[52] Riskin further notes an important correlation that structures her explorations: the intimacy of French science with English sentimental literature. This conjunction is also detailed by Roger Maioli in his important study on empiricism and the eighteenth-century novel that adds to Riskin's exploration of the "movement of the body's parts into sensory impressions of the outside world" the centrality that empiricism gives to the particular. The early-modern Aristotelian-Platonic synthesis of the *Poetics* with the *Republic*, which offered the account that poetry is the medium for the expression of eternal truths, would be upended by the novel's rejection of eternal and innate ideas in favor of the representation of the particularity of mental states. And this upheaval was, according to Maioli, a consequence of empiricism's radical ontological shift to the particular:

> From the very beginning, the driving purpose of empiricism was to rebuild our picture of the world from the ground up, allowing the multifariousness of nature to take precedence over the neat constructs of the mind. . . . This shift in ontology has direct epistemological consequences. It means that general propositions about the world, rather than truths derived from the contemplation of universals, are just fallible generalizations from our perceptions of particular things. And they must remain accountable to the latter. If our mental picture

of the world fails to account for the anomalies and exceptions of the
world of sense perception, then it is the mental picture that is flawed.
This conviction, echoed by Hobbes, Locke, Hume, and others,
reflected Bacon's belief that often enough "mean and small things
discover great better than great can discover the small." For the
empirical student of nature, particulars are the stuff universals are
made of, and through them runs the way to knowledge.[53]

In other words, what Anthony Pagden rightly identifies as the age of pity that
turned to sensationalism as a way of dismantling the classical ideal of innate
ideas and primary causes and that committed itself solely to the discovery of
secondary causes (because these were the only things knowable) was also and
correlatedly the age of the micro-segmentarity of the particular.[54] Particulars,
sentiments, sensations, and segmentations—these are some of the features of
and about sentimental empiricism that I explore in this book. That is, I look
to those elements of empiricist thinking that afford a rich morphology of manners, ideas, psychologies, and metaphysical considerations for an account of
political criticism as the transformation of particular relations. In this regard,
I do not focus on empiricism as a theory of knowledge but on sentimental empiricism as a disposition for the development of the critical sentiments.[55] By
this I mean that I consider sentimental empiricism a mode of political thinking whose claims to the primacy of experience bespeaks a commitment to an
intimacy of life and world. This commitment to intimacy finds its strongest
expression in sentimental empiricism's persistent validation of relationality as
the principal fact of existence. For the sentimental empiricist, experience is
not reducible to brute data but instead refers to a relation between life and
world.[56]

   Allow me to elaborate: I read the sensationist and sentimentalist dimensions
of empiricism as a set of contiguous observations about the social and political
effectivity of dispositional powers in everyday life.[57] The sentiments, in other
words, are powers that generate forms of intimacy among and between other
worlds, other peoples, and other times. These dispositional powers are tenden-
tial, which means that they are neither necessary nor contingent, but somewhere in between. As Rani Lill Anjum and Stephen Mumford account for
them, "Dispositions only *tend* towards their manifestations; they do not neces-
sitate them."[58] Sensations, perceptions, and sentiments aren't merely feelings
that a subject registers; they are dispositional powers that tend bodies toward
(i.e., *dispose* them toward) other bodies. The moral sentiments (sympathy chief
among these, but also envy, avarice, greed, esteem, love, hatred) are powers that
dispose bodies to come together or wrest apart. At its core, then, sentimental

empiricism is an associationist mode of thinking that looks to the interstitial dynamics of relations, and it is political in its emphasis on the powers and forms of coordination or discordance that transform micro-segmentarities into corpuscular pluralities. Finally, what distinguishes sentimental empiricism from other accounts of social and political association is that it does not rely on a transcendental theory of consciousness, nor on a specific account of human will or intention, nor on the existence of innate causes, to explain or legitimate processes and structures of association.

The principal philosophical insight of sentimental empiricism is that relations are not determined by the terms they relate; or, put slightly differently, that relations are independent of their terms.[59] This is a profound metaphysical insight that goes to the core of the sentimental empiricist theory of criticism. The political stakes of this metaphysical insight demand a focus on transforming the associative dynamics that coordinate relations in a social system—that is, to intervene in the in-between of dispositionality. In short, sentimental empiricism offers a political theory of relations that refuses the idea of necessary causality—including (and this is crucial) the necessary causal relation of negation and critique. As previously noted, sentimental empiricism is neither dialectical nor idealist, but pluralist and pragmatic. It is metaphysically pluralist in that it does not accept the idea that political and social conflict is exclusively antagonistic and that the task of critique is to resolve extant contradictions between antagonisms; it is pragmatic in that its ambition is not to achieve an understanding (or even a sharing) of innate ideas but, rather, to pursue the active work of articulating and rearticulating the forms of relating in any given associational milieu. For sentimental empiricism, the political dilemma is not how to convince a political opponent of what is or is not to be done to attain agreement on means and ends, but rather how we might imagine dispositions differently and thus how we might redispose actually existing forms of arrangement of life and world. . . . With the following caveat: neither life nor world is substance; life refers to forces that move bodies, and world refers to emergent associations.

Here then is an ecology of premises I find resonant among those I associate as sentimental empiricist thinkers throughout this book:

1. First and foremost, sentimental empiricism's site of political critique is not arbitrary power imposed from above. Rather, the political theory of sentimental empiricism hones in on how domination operates as a dispositional power of in-between-ness. Dispositional powers are those powers of association that *tend bodies toward*; they are neither wholly contingent nor wholly necessary but spontaneous

and ordering in the sense that they arrange the due order of parts. In this respect, the sentiments (e.g., sympathy, respect, admiration, hatred) are dispositional powers that arrange (or dispose) us to one another.

2. Sentimental empiricism involves a rejection of Aristotelian (and/or Thomist) substances and thus also a rejection of a metaphysics of Being. This is part of what, in the Anglophone world, would be identified as the critique of the subject and "the death of man" thesis.[60]

3. There are no innate ideas. Ideas are born of the spontaneity of dispositions and mediated through the associational power of the imagination.

4. Just as there are no innate ideas, there are also no inherent relations. Relations are external to what is being related. This means that relations are emergent from the spontaneity of dispositional powers. This metaphysical premise is especially relevant for sentimental empiricism's critique of dispositional domination because it makes available the claim that no arrangement of domination is either natural or necessary to any specific social or political order. This includes, but is not limited to, the arrangement of gender relations under patriarchy, of class arrangements under capitalism, of parental authority in the bourgeois family, and the general arrangements of privilege and inheritance that guarantee stratifications in everyday life.

5. Sentimental empiricism is not reducible to an epistemological skepticism of brute data identification. To the extent that skepticism is part of sentimental empiricism, it is not a philosophical attitude of negation but one of conjunction: not "this or that," but "this and that." Sentimental empiricism thus treats experience as a dynamic of sensorial adveniences that generate spontaneous—though incomplete—emergences of dispositions between bodies. These spontaneities of dispositions are the centripetal and centrifugal powers of the sentiments that are perpetually operant and thus denying the possibility of a settled totality or unified substance.

6. Postwar French sentimental empiricism is a genre of political, philosophical, and aesthetic experiments that develop critical practices to dismantle the political claims of universalism inherent in the postrevolutionary aspirations of the French republican state. This is especially urgent, given the immediate French postwar political milieu that is contending with a Vichy inheritance and two

colonial wars. In this milieu, it becomes nearly impossible not to associate the philosophical claims of French republican universalism with imperialism and colonialism, especially given the French state's centralized control over its educational system.

7. The first step toward dismantling the colonial state is through a radical critique of the presumed natural relation between mimesis (representation/imitation) and political authority.

8. Sentimental empiricism offers a critique of all forms of universalism, including the transcendental status of dialectical negation as the form of critical thinking. This implies that criticism (aesthetic, political, or otherwise) is not exclusively dualist and that the relation of identity/difference is not innate to critical thinking. Hence the urgency of articulating a metaphysics of difference-in-itself.

All these premises are labile. But as we shall see, they find expression in diverse and compelling ways. My ambition, however, is not to settle the matter as to what sentimental empiricism is and how it might be applied so much as to conjoin a series of political, aesthetic, and philosophical considerations that have hitherto gone unnoted in the Anglophone reception of postwar French political thought and that I believe help us better appreciate the contributions that this generation of thinkers made to contemporary political theory and criticism.

Some Adjacent Precursors

In recent years some important studies adjacent to my own have emerged, and all of these have informed my own research significantly. Among these are some recent studies of nineteenth- and twentieth-century French political culture. Most notably is the continued importance of Kristin Ross's histories of postwar French cultural politics. Two of her works are of particular relevance: *Fast Cars, Clean Bodies* and *Communal Luxury: The Political Imaginary of the Paris Commune*. The reader will find references to these works throughout because they remain so significant in helping us appreciate the entanglement between aesthetics, politics, and philosophy in French intellectual culture and how these domains of inquiry and experience—so easily parsed in the Anglophone academy—are simply not partitioned in modern French thought.

Carolyn Eichner's *Surmounting the Barricades* and Kevin Duong's *The Virtues of Violence* were also steady companions as I researched and wrote this book. Eichner's study matters because it shows how important the status and role of artisans was to the Paris Commune and how the majority of these artisans were women. The feminist socialist Communardes, as Eichner refers to them, "rejected the goal of formal rights as irrelevant within the shifting insurgent context, perceiving themselves on the brink of a new world. They sought, instead, an end to existing gender, class, and religious hierarchies and a reconceptualization of these socio-economic relations to improve the conditions of women's lives."[61] The reconceptualization of relations is, as I note, one of the central features of sentimental empiricist political thinking, especially given that the authors I study also imagined themselves on the brink of a new world.

Kevin Duong's book was published as I was in the throes of researching the educational reforms in France in the nineteenth and early twentieth centuries. What became clear to me as I read Duong's book is that the story I wanted to tell about the relationship between mimesis, democracy, and the State was a companion piece to his discovery that "redemptive violence displaced what we might call a redemptive image of the ballot."[62] That redemptive image of the ballot, I would argue, relied on a redemptive belief in the mimetic tradition as encoded and transmitted in French neoclassicism and the Jesuitical *Ratio Studiorum*. In this respect, the reader will notice my sympathy with Duong's counter-history that affirms, against the biases of liberal democratic representation, how "associations of redemptive violence with totalitarianism have provided an alibi for many critics to evade fundamental questions about the shape of the social body in modern democracies. In making social cohesion a theoretical taboo, consideration of which sets us on a path to redemptive violence, the legacies of liberal anti-totalitarianism have made us hesitant to think about the types of social bonds that democratic politics require. We would rather understand democracy as disagreement, as agonism, or as pluralism. Breaking the grip of these interpretations is therefore important because it also breaks the grip of the Cold War on our democratic imagination."[63] Not only is redemptive violence typically read in relation to totalitarianism, but so is the presumed moral relativism attached to critiques of aesthetic and political representation.[64] The latter point is, to me, especially urgent when considering how the reception of postwar French theory in Anglophone cultures further fastens "the grip of the Cold War on our political imagination."

Two other recent works are notable in this respect, both of which became available as I was completing this book. Jason Frank's *The Democratic Sublime* teaches us how democratic life is not reducible to education and enlightenment, but that "entirely new forms of democratic enchantment are required by democratic politics." I am inspired by Frank's careful study as well as his unique ability of adjoining image with political practice, especially in his chapter on "The Poetics of the Barricade." There Frank shows something at once essential but evanescent to the entirety of his project: the people are not an

Aristotelian substance but are, at best, a sublime form. Simondon's political metaphysic—as we shall soon see—would consider Frank's democratic peoples a force of individuation whose emergence is in a metastable state of perpetual *in*-formation. What is clear is that a political metaphysics of mimesis is insufficient to a radical democratic imaginary of a people bodying forth "through and beyond their mediating representation."[65]

Another work I was fortunate to have land on my desk as I completed my own is Camille Robcis's *Disalineation: Politics, Philosophy, and Radical Psychiatry in Postwar France*. More than sharing an affinity with this work, as I read each and every page I realized that Robcis and I were writing the same book about the same cast of characters—the main difference being that I was interested in radical aesthetics forms of criticism, whereas she was interested in the radical developments in and around institutional psychiatry. That said, Robcis's study does something very important that I emulate throughout my own: more than an intellectual history, her work details the transformations in thought and practices that the figures she studies developed and worked through. This leads me to one of my own central theses: the genre of philosophical experimentation studied in these pages *is* a mode of political participation intended to radically transform the relationship between mimesis and the State. It could not be otherwise. If one of the central motivations of the practitioners at Saint Albans that Robcis details was a perpetual attempt to "imagine and reimagine institutions that would produce new vectors of transference, different forms of identifications, and alternative, less hierarchical, and less oppressive social relations," then this could only occur through an intricate entanglement of theory and practice principally committed to all forms of anti-authoritarianism.[66] If nothing else, my study of the emergence and development of sentimental empiricism in postwar France traces the entanglement of politics, philosophy, and aesthetics and shares in Frank's and Robcis's attempt to further elaborate the theoretical dimensions of a radical democratic and anti-authoritarian political imaginary that is not reducible to the Cold War cant of liberal-democratic anti-totalitarianism.[67]

A final important companion study arrived on my desk in late fall of 2022 as I was preparing the final revisions to the manuscript. That study is Russell Ford's *Experience and Empiricism*, which, in many respects, parallels my own research, though the two are innocent of one another, as neither Ford nor I was aware of each other's work prior to the publication of his volume. Ford's study is more focused on Deleuze's empiricism and his direct engagements with the work and teachings of his professors Jean Wahl and Jean Hyppolite. But his analysis is, I believe, crucial for many reasons, as it provides a compelling philosophical argument regarding the themes of immanence and transcendence as central to twentieth-century French philosophy. For my own specific purposes, however, Ford's volume details something that I could not include in my own study: the importance of the sentimental empiricist critique of Hegelian dialectics and monism. As Ford rightly states, the twentieth-century French uptake of empiricism is coincident with a commitment to metaphysical pluralism (i.e., David Hume, William James, Bertrand Russell, A. N. Whitehead, and G. E. Moore) and, with the challenge in pluralist thinking, "to stay with as-yet incomplete experience and not surreptitiously appeal to the idea of completion."[68]

I mention these works because I consider them sympathetic companions to my own work, and where there are crudités, simplicities, omissions, and misappropriations in my own research, I invite the reader to turn to these other works first for possible corrections, elaborations, and further food for thought. This said, I would be remiss if I also did not mention the important intellectual sociology of professional philosophy in the French academy done in recent years by Alan D. Schrift.[69] Schrift's work is especially helpful in allowing us to grasp the centrality of the practices of reading developed through the *agrégation* and its system of examination and selection, which for the purposes of my own work is a main site of investigation.

I would be even more remiss if I were not to note the following: if the minor tradition of sentimental empiricist critical thinking is something the reader of this book finds plausible, this is because of the work that feminist scholars have done over the past seventy years.[70] It is, to me, unequivocally true that contemporary theory and criticism could not have attended to the importance of embodiment, embodied experience, and sentimentalism if it were not for the persistence and insistence of the work in feminist scholarship in the humanities and social sciences. Simply put, were it not for the work of feminist theorists over the past seventy years political theorists would still be worrying about whether liberals or communitarians had gotten justice right. Perhaps Judith Grant puts it best in her classic *Fundamental Feminism* when she explains that the story of feminist theory begins with a reaction to an ambivalence toward "the notion of Woman and woman's issues by asserting an essential connection among women as women, and by claiming that their personal and subjective experiences of oppression constituted a valid proof of the existence of the category."[71] What feminist theory and criticism have done are to show us how the body is not simply gendered and racialized, ableized and normalized; but that it is a domain for the operation of political, economic, and cultural power.

In other words, what feminist scholarship has done is allow us to note that in Truffaut's scene of instruction only male bodies are present; that the performing of mimesis is a task of reproduction that must be accomplished by boys, early on, so that they can become great leaders, all the while ignoring the crucial labor of biological reproduction and all that follows from it; that the pinup calendar circulated in the classroom is that of a sexualized female body that is the only female presence screened; and that the punishment that Antoine receives is not because he was caught with an image of a sexualized femininity but because he distracted his classmates from the lesson. In short, feminist criticism and theory allow us to note that difference and matter are always already gendered formations.[72] Moreover, it is feminist political theory and criticism that show how the work of reproduction is not merely the metaphysical work of mimesis, but the embodied labor of biological and social reproduction with which women are tasked. Finally, feminist theory and criticism allow us to not simply note these facts, but to also account for the play of dispositional powers in the arrangement of social and political hierarchies.

When I have taught seminars on the material in these pages, one objection that has been raised (both to me and to the syllabus) is why there are so few (if any) women included and why I didn't include scholarship in feminist theory and criticism.[73] The answer is shocking because it is simple and straightforward: There weren't any. Instruction in the French academic system was almost exclusively male, as were the authors studied. It is true that Simone de Beauvoir published *Le deuxième sexe* in 1949 and that parts of the writing therein had previously appeared in *Les Temps Modernes*. Moreover, it is also true that the work immediately becomes a celebrated and chastised source of feminist politics and philosophy, as does Beauvoir's life in general. But the work's celebrity status is not coincident with its status as an authoritative work, and certainly it is not a work that enters into university instruction; nor, for that matter, does she. Despite being one of the top graduates of the *agrégation* for her year, Beauvoir never pursued an academic career within the system of elite French education. It is well known that one reason for this is that Beauvoir lost her teaching license because the parents of a young female student, Natalie Sorokin, accused Beauvoir of having seduced their daughter. Notably, Jean-Paul Sartre had a relationship with the same woman, though he did not lose his license, nor was he accused of misconduct. And though Beauvoir's license would eventually be reinstated, it is nonetheless the case that her presence within the elite structure of the French education system is the singular exception that proves the rule of male elitism.[74]

Chapter Summaries

The first two chapters of this book address some differences between Anglophone scholarly reading practices in political theory and their postwar French counterapproaches. In Chapter 1 I offer a genealogy of literary reception rooted in the cultural capital of the different political ambitions of postwar American and postwar France. Chapter 2 provides a genealogy of the *explication des textes* and its political and cultural history. The central figures here are Gustave Lanson and the educational reforms that he and his Dreyfusard colleagues would implement at the beginning of the Third Republic. I give much weight to the *explication des textes* in order to corroborate and extend further Alan Schrift's sociology of the French *agrégation*, but also because the *explication des textes* is the state-sanctioned mode of articulating the normative, metaphysical, and aesthetic hierarchies that make *"le bon sens"* a central political and aesthetic virtue. The *explication des textes* is the mode of literary criticism in and through which students demonstrate their virtue in/of understanding, thus making them available for selection to various academic, political, and military offices.

The subsequent chapters are studies of Jean Wahl, Simone de Beauvoir, Gilbert Simondon, Gilles Deleuze, and Michel Foucault, respectively. Jean Wahl was an influential professor of philosophy who developed a sophisticated ontology of concreteness informed by the empiricism of William James and Alfred North Whitehead and who taught and lectured on these thinkers throughout the interwar and postwar periods. Wahl was also the thinker who made available the radical ontological pluralism of the sentimental empiricist tradition. My study of Wahl will focus on his pluralist ontology, which emphasizes a processual "towardness" of concretization. The chapter that follows, Chapter 3, takes up some recent scholarship on the political thinking of Simone de Beauvoir. My focus is on Beauvoir's articulation of patriarchy as a form of political power rooted in a system of sentiments and indirect passions structured by the sexual relation. This chapter will also outline the project of civic education in France during the Third Republic and will show how Beauvoir turns to Claude Lévi-Strauss's first work, *The Elementary Structures of Kinship*, to provide an account of patriarchy as a dispositional power emergent from concrete social practices. Neither Wahl nor Beauvoir is part of the postwar generation of thinkers that I refer to as sentimental empiricists, given that their intellectual formation predates the postwar period I examine; but both are important precursors for our appreciation of the philosophical and political innovations that ensue.

The final chapters of the book are dedicated to three archetypal sentimental empiricist thinkers: Gilbert Simondon, Gilles Deleuze, and Michel Foucault. Each of these thinkers enacts a series of minoritarian transformations that grapple with the problem of the reproduction of power and the intergenerational inheritance of the system of privileges that structure French social and political life. The more precise way of stating this is that each of these thinkers articulates a metaphysics of difference-in-itself in order to ask the question of political change: Is political change ontologically possible, and how is it thinkable? Or, as the history of the French republic seems to indicate, are we simply condemned to a reproduction of the same? Each of these writers offers different and complex answers to these questions, and often the answers they provide are wholly insufficient. My interest is less in the success of their responses than in how the concern about a political ontology of change *qua* difference-in-itself is a structuring problematic for their various intellectual projects. The Simondon I explore will broach the question of change by offering a philosophy of individuation that is in direct contrast to Aristotle's metaphysics of substances; the Deleuze I engage will turn directly to philosophical empiricism (and especially to Hume) in order to develop a political ontology of difference-in-itself; and the Foucault I explore explicitly shifts us toward a conceptual and analytic vocabulary of dispositions in order to rethink how political power operates through the arrangement and organization of associational life.

One final question needs posing: If the political problematic of these authors is rooted in a uniquely French republican form of universalism, then how do they contend with, imagine, and articulate alternative forms of associational life and—especially—of alternative modes of political belonging to those? It is the case that one of the virtues of the mimetic tradition in political theory is that it allows for recognition as a foundation for political association and unity. Given its critique of substances and of mimesis, sentimental empiricism does not afford a concept of recognition. There is no politics of recognition—or, for that matter, neither is there a politics of authenticity—that will guarantee any stable form of political attachment. Nor is there a utopian telos that stands as a beacon for an emancipatory future. Finally, as we've noted, there is no metaphysics of dialectical critique that would ensure a dualist ontology of identity/difference. In contrast to these approaches, empiricism is articulated as a philosophy of difference-in-itself where no form or practice of relating is inherent, innate, or determined prior to the emergence of the terms that enter into relation with one another; and the sentiments are articulated as forces of association that conjoin and disjoin bodies that move. With the crumbling of the Fourth Republic, of France's colonial heritage, and of any faith in republican universalism, new forms of thinking relationality and associationism beyond those proffered by the State become pressing. This book accounts for those political, aesthetic, and philosophical experiments in critical thinking that today we acknowledge in such theoretical developments as new materialism, affect theory, and a variety of other forms of postfoundational political thinking.

PART I
Missed Understandings

1

Reading Political Theory in Postwar America and Postwar France

This chapter offers an account of the missed understanding (*mésentente*) between postwar France and postwar America. In what follows I assemble aspects of scholarly production and readership that evince how each of these milieux relates the words "politics" and "philosophy" as relevant to one another.[1] This chapter thus tells the story of how a readerly culture's grasping of a word or phrase is participant in a field of scholarly reception comprised of what John Guillory refers to as "the conventions and techniques that govern how scholars write and how they read."[2]

In the first part of this chapter, I reconstruct the professional, cultural, and political conditions for what I describe as a literalist style of readerly reception in American political theory and political science. That story of the American enterprise of political science and political theory will be familiar to many, given some recent and notable publications from which I take inspiration.[3] Crucial to this genre of reading is the arrival to North America of important methodological innovations in logical empiricism and behaviorism that emphasized a specific account of meaning, science, and the verifiability of language. For all intents and purposes, that account eliminated all aesthetic and metaphysical inquiry as relevant to the study of politics, and it treated any sensationist judgment of value as subjective and therefore either meaningless because unverifiable or relativist because not objective.[4] The appeal to understanding and the invective "meaningless" became criteria of appraisal that would find synonyms in other terms like obfuscation, or unclear writing, or even esotericism. "Meaningless" did not simply mean that something is incomprehensible; it meant that the word, text, or idea in question is not relevant to political and philosophical investigation and inquiry and should be avoided.[5] Though many internecine methodological debates on the science of politics proliferated during the postwar period in the United States as a result of such developments, the political ambitions of intellectual inquiry was never up for debate.[6]

This milieu is the focus of the first part of this chapter. The second part reconstructs the political and philosophical culture of 1950s France in order to show how some aesthetic and metaphysical concerns that had been excised from the professional vocabularies of Anglophone political science and political theory were very much in play (and remained in play) as political problems of the day. The most striking difference between the two milieux is that unlike the United States, France's highly rigorous and intensely stratified university culture shows no traces of any topic of philosophical study that would or could resemble what, in the United States in the 1950s, was called political theory or political philosophy. In short, these were not professionalized academic demarcations. Moreover, logical positivism and behaviorism did not have the influence or impact in France that it had in the United States, and to the extent that it might have, by the 1950s these two traditions of inquiry had been dealt a decided blow, thanks to the works and teachings of some of the most important philosophers of science, logicians, and philosophers of mathematics of the period (i.e., Georges Canguilhem, Gaston Bachelard, Jean Cavaillès, and Jean Wahl) as well as their students (i.e., Maurice Merleau-Ponty, Simone de Beauvoir, Gilbert Simondon, Michel Foucault, and Louis Althusser).[7] What these and other thinkers made abundantly clear was that a human understanding of the order of the universe, of one's place in it, and how things are valued within any specific ordering matters to how we live our political lives, to how political societies are organized, and to how power is distributed therein. For this generation of French thinkers and authors, aesthetics, metaphysics, and even logic are expressions of political thinking: aesthetic inquiry allows us to appreciate the function and role of human perception and experience in the creation and circulation of value; metaphysical inquiry names a form of reflection that allows us to say things about how power works, how relations are made, how causality intervenes in human life, and how identity and difference interrelate; and even the science of logic, as Jean Cavaillès would argue, does not have as its telos the validity of a proof but "is demonstration through and through."[8] As such, the work done on the metaphysics of relations and the aesthetics of perception by French philosophers, novelists, playwriters, prose writers, artists, photographers, and film directors became central to a radical rethinking of the metaphysical concept of difference as a political concept, to a radical rethinking and retooling of the scholastic and Thomistic commitment to Aristotelian substances (and thus to the metaphysical concepts of identity, totality, and necessity), to a radical interrogation of the law of non-contradiction as the aporetic principle of all criticism, and to a radical rethinking of the powers, forces, and forms of association that participate in the making and unmaking of political societies. This chapter thus offers some scenes of reception and production for thinking the relation of politics and philosophy. The ambition of the pages that follow is to provide a sense of why and how the minoritarian tradition of sentimental empiricism was developed in France and how and why it was mostly overlooked once it crossed over onto North American shores.

Political Literarity in Postwar America

Siren Songs

The works variously classified under French theory, postmodernism, or post-structuralism began to receive notice among North American political theorists in the late 1970s, though it wasn't until the mid-1980s that the writings of Michel Foucault, Jacques Derrida, and others garnered exploration in academic journals and publications. Unlike the European emigres who escaped Nazi Europe and found refuge in the United States prior to and during the war (including Hannah Arendt, Leo Strauss, Hans Morgenthau, Theodore Adorno, Max Horkheimer, and others), the arrival of this other collection of foreign ideas and authors is marked by one major academic event: the 1966 "Languages of Criticism and the Sciences of Man" symposium organized by Richard Macksey and Eugene Donato at the Humanities Center of Johns Hopkins University, the proceedings of which are collected in the volume entitled *The Structuralist Controversy*.[9] Much of the debates, ideas, and issues arising from this conference remained confined mostly to literature departments for various reasons, most notably because English translations of many of these thinkers' works did not begin to appear until the late 1970s. For instance, Jacques Derrida's *De la Grammatologie* is first published in 1967, immediately after the Johns Hopkins conference, but doesn't become available in English until Gayatri Spivak's 1976 translation. Michel Foucault's work fares better with his 1966 *Les mots et les choses* being published in 1970 as *The Order of Things* by Pantheon. Though works began to appear in translation in the late 1970s in various academic presses, the University of Minnesota Press series "Theory and History of Literature" (THL, 1981–98, series editors Wlad Godzich and Jochen Schulte-Sasse) proved instrumental in making available for the first time many English translations of works in critical theory and aesthetics by such notable French tinkers as Jean-François Lyotard (most famously, *The Postmodern Condition: A Report on Knowledge*), Gilles Deleuze and Félix Guattari, Maurice Blanchot, Hélène Cixous, Paul de Man, Tzvetan Todorov, Jean-Luc Nancy, Georges Bataille, Michel de Certeau, and many others. Also significant with regard to the THL series is the fact that many of the translators and editors of these works, including Brian Massumi, Geoff Bennington, and Sandra M. Gilbert, would themselves become influential scholars of theory and criticism in the Anglo-American academy.

In 1984 at the University of Massachusetts (Amherst), William E. Connolly convened an NEH Summer Fellowship–College Teachers Seminar Program entitled "Interpretation and Genealogy in Politics." This proved an important event for the conversation between French postwar thought and American political theory, as the seminar included participants that would become notable political theory scholars in the United States, including Kathy Ferguson and Thomas Dumm (who, along with Connolly, were among the founding editors of the journal *Theory & Event*, 1997), Steven White (a future editor of the journal *Political Theory*), and William Corlett. On July 1, 1985, the editorial office of the journal *Political Theory* took up residence at Johns Hopkins University, where Connolly, the newly appointed editor, had moved to take on the Krieger-Eisenhower Professorship in the political science department.

In the February 1985 issue of the same journal, which, since its formation in 1973, had become the flagship journal for the subfield, the executive editorial committee published a summary of research that accounts for the first decade of the journal's publication history. That summary proceeds to elaborate recent developments in the field, including the fact that Karl Marx is "a clear leader in submissions." The report continues, "Thinkers such as Nietzsche, Shakespeare, Heidegger, Sade, Strauss, Foucault, Arendt, Habermas, and Sophocles either appear on the list for the first time or the number of submissions dealing with them is notably higher than before."[10] Other notable trends include the fact that conceptual analysis gives way to discursive analysis, rhetorical analyses, and literary theory; the category of the modern self as a stable subject of rights is interrogated rather than assumed; and earlier epistemological critiques of method are substituted by interest in hermeneutics, deconstruction, and genealogy. A quick scan of the table of contents of the preceding years of the journal shows that these trends were quite recent, beginning most notably with Mark Philp's essay on Foucault and power and Connolly's own essay on discipline and ambiguity (1983), followed by Charles Taylor's essay on Foucault and freedom and Fred Dallmayr's essay on Heidegger and political philosophy (1984).[11]

After this initial period, monographs and article publications influenced by postwar French thinkers proliferated, as did conversations between political theorists, literary theorists, comparative literature scholars, historians, and others in adjacent fields of inquiry.[12] Some notable and highly influential monographs of the period included Judith Butler's pivotal *Gender Trouble* (Routledge, 1990), as well as Seyla Benhabib's equally influential *Situating the Self* (Routledge, 1992), Stephen White's *Political Theory and Postmodernism* (Cambridge University Press, 1991), and Connolly's *Identity/Difference: Democratic Negotiations of Political Paradox* (Cornell University Press, 1991). Of course, this barely scratches the surface. In 1989 Michael Shapiro and James Der Derian publish a collection of essays entitled *International/Intertextual Relations: Postmodern Readings of World Politics* (Lexington Books, 1989) that would be important for the fields of International Relations as well as Political Theory, while 1992 sees the publication of the highly influential collection *Feminists Theorize the Political* (Judith Butler and Joan W. Scott, eds.; Routledge, 1992). In 1993 Bonnie Honig's groundbreaking *Political Theory and the Displacement of Politics* is published in the "Contestations" series at Cornell University Press. This volume would prove critical to a new generation of graduate students in the 1990s (including the author of this book) who were encouraged by the growth and development of the ideas presented in Honig's work.

Another influential book series to emerge in this period is the Modernity and Political Thought series edited by Morton Schoolman. That series published its first volume, William Connolly's *The Augustinian Imperative* (1993), with Sage Publications.[13] Finally, 1996 sees the publication of Seyla Benhabib's edited collection *Democracy and Difference: Contesting the Boundaries of the Political*, which boasts an impressive table of contents of Anglophone political theorists. I could go on, but I think I've made my point: The period between the early 1980s and the mid 1990s witnessed an explosion of interest, scholarship, and enthusiasm in the Anglophone world regarding a number of French authors and debates, insights and intellectual ambitions, that would have a lasting impact on the American academy throughout the humanities and social sciences, and especially on Anglophone political theory.

This proliferation of scholarly enthusiasm did not constitute a majority opinion despite its intensity and visibility. In the world of Anglophone philosophy programs, a great disturbance arose in 1992 when the University of Cambridge was to make a ballot decision (scheduled for May 16, 1992) whether to award an honorary degree in philosophy to Jacques Derrida. Some members of the discipline were outraged, so much so that a number of these individuals co-signed a letter written by Barry Smith (then editor of the *Monist*) confirming their official opposition to Derrida's work, to him even being considered a philosopher, and to the University of Cambridge's willingness to consider him worthy of an honorary degree in philosophy. The letter was published in the *London Times* on May 9, 1992—a week before the ballot vote. It was unforgiving in both tone and composure, and the matter became a cause célèbre and textbook example of disciplinary wall building. I include it in full here:

The *Times* (London). Saturday, May 9, 1992

Sir, The University of Cambridge is to ballot on May 16 on whether M. Jacques Derrida should be allowed to go forward to receive an honorary degree. As philosophers and others who have taken a scholarly and professional interest in M. Derrida's remarkable career over the years, we believe the following might throw some needed light on the public debate that has arisen over this issue.

M. Derrida describes himself as a philosopher, and his writings do indeed bear some of the marks of writings in that discipline. Their influence, however, has been to a striking degree almost entirely in fields outside philosophy—in departments of film studies, for example, or of French and English literature.

In the eyes of philosophers, and certainly among those working in leading departments of philosophy throughout the world, M. Derrida's work does not meet accepted standards of clarity and rigour.

We submit that, if the works of a physicist (say) were similarly taken to be of merit primarily by those working in other disciplines, this would in itself be sufficient grounds for casting doubt upon the idea that the physicist in question was a suitable candidate for an honorary degree.

M. Derrida's career had its roots in the heady days of the 1960s and his writings continue to reveal their origins in that period. Many of them seem to consist in no small part of elaborate jokes and puns ("logical phallusies" and the like), and M. Derrida seems to us to have come close to making a career out of what we regard as translating into the academic sphere tricks and gimmicks similar to those of the Dadaists or of the concrete poets.

Certainly he has shown considerable originality in this respect. But again, we submit, such originality does not lend credence to the idea that he is a suitable candidate for an honorary degree.

Many French philosophers see in M. Derrida only cause for silent embarrassment, his antics having contributed significantly to the widespread impression that contemporary French philosophy is little more than an object of ridicule.

M. Derrida's voluminous writings in our view stretch the normal forms of academic scholarship beyond recognition. Above all—as every reader can very easily establish for himself (and for this purpose any page will do)—his works employ a written style that defies comprehension.

Many have been willing to give M. Derrida the benefit of the doubt, insisting that language of such depth and difficulty of interpretation must hide deep and subtle thoughts indeed.

When the effort is made to penetrate it, however, it becomes clear, to us at least, that, where coherent assertions are being made at all, these are either false or trivial.

Academic status based on what seems to us to be little more than semi-intelligible attacks upon the values of reason, truth, and scholarship is not, we submit, sufficient grounds for the awarding of an honorary degree in a distinguished university.

Yours sincerely,
Barry Smith
(Editor, The *Monist*)
Internationale Akademie für Philosophie,
Obergass 75, 9494S Schaan, Liechtenstein[14]

Smith would defend his position a few years later in an interview, affirming a sentiment that would be shared by many: "Well, if you go to very many universities in North America today, including my own university, you'll find many departments devoted to 'Comparative Literature.' You will also find 'Critical Theory Institutes' and 'Humanities Centers' which contain shadows of other more traditional departments within the university. They treat works of philosophy—or it might also be works of jurisprudence, history, politics, or theological and religious works, or nowadays even medical works—not as works of philosophy, law, theology, religion, or medicine, but as texts . . . as works of literature."[15]

A similar scenario would play out exactly five years later at Harvard University. Then president Neil L. Rudenstine would veto a favorable tenure decision made by the Government Department regarding Bonnie Honig, who at the time was associate professor of Government (Harvard did not, and to this day does not, have "associate professor with tenure" positions, unlike many research universities in the United States). The event received national attention because many procedural issues regarding Rudenstine's seemingly arbitrary decision were under suspicion, especially given that Harvard prided itself as an institution at the forefront of defending the principles of liberal proceduralism.[16] And rightly so. All reports confirmed that Honig's tenure file was exemplary and exceeded Harvard's standards for tenure and that she was "a brilliant, highly productive and widely respected political theorist."[17] In the *Harvard Crimson* Jal Mehta reported that "various sources have confirmed that between two-thirds and three-quarters of the government department faculty supported the Honig nomination and that four of the five professors on the ad hoc committee supported her."[18] Strong opposition to Rudenstine's fiat was also expressed by some of Harvard's most distinguished female faculty members (including Martha Minow, professor of law; Theda Skocpol, professor of government and sociology; Carol Gilligan, professor of education; Seyla Benhabib, professor of government; Laurel Thatcher Ulrich, a Pulitzer Prize-winning professor of history; and Mary Waters, professor of sociology) who cosigned a letter to Rudenstine expressing their concern and disappointment. This was a significant gesture, as Sara Rimer reported in the *New York Times*: "At Harvard, where the senior faculty women are not known for their militance, where even tenured faculty members, men and women, are reluctant to criticize the administration, the letter amounted to a near-revolutionary act."[19] In the same article, Seyla Benhabib is quoted as saying that "the Honig affair is puzzling to us because according to all institutional criteria and criteria of scholarship, she has fulfilled Harvard's requirement for promotion and tenure."[20]

Two notable assessments of the task of American political theory would preface this incident and help shed light on it. The first is John Gunnell's foundational study of the development of the subfield of political theory (published in 1993) that concludes with the following lament: "By the end of the 1980s, the principal political theories in the United States ceased to speak about actual politics, let alone to it. To a large extent they became tributaries of the dominant academic persuasion such as postmodernism and reflections of debates such as that about philosophical foundationalism that permeated the humanities and social sciences."[21] And further: "Even when an aspect of political theory had a distinct practical-issue counterpart and constituency, it was difficult to resist the attachment to the tokens of academic authority and the sirens of esotericism and to speak in a manner that was not opaque to all outside the academy or even to those standing outside the specialized language of subdisciplines."[22]

Two years later, in the journal *Political Theory*, Jeffrey Isaac expresses similar frustrations and dissatisfactions by noting the paucity of reflections by political theorists on the events of 1989. In this provocative piece, Isaac evinces that, in the five years subsequent to the democratic revolutions of 1989 in former Soviet countries, American political theorists published "a total of 384 articles, of which a mere 2—roughly one-half of one percent—dealt with dramatic current events of earth-shattering importance."[23] The title of Isaac's piece is "The Strange Silence of Political Theory," but silence is a misnomer here. In fact, Isaac's principal concern is the strange verbosity of political theory that, like Gunnell, seemed to have fallen prey to the siren song of esotericism that betrayed an ignorance toward actual politics. Citing some recent research in the field, Isaac affirms that "the very language typifies the political theorist's aversion to first-order questions"; he further admonishes the fact that "the kind of writing that receives validation as 'serious' and 'scholarly' tends to place a premium on academic conventions—the careful and relentless citation of recent scholarship, a remoteness from colloquial expression, and, most fatefully, an avoidance of directly political themes and positions—at the expense of originality and relevance."[24]

Each of these assessments is exemplary in expressing the uniqueness of the Anglophone milieu and its initial reception of postwar French political thought in Anglophone political theory. At the core of that retort and appraisal is a commitment to a certain kind of readerly literalism (best expressed by Isaac's concern regarding the "remoteness from colloquial expression") that defines the relation between politics and philosophy as one oriented to already established and canonical terms of political reflection. Gunnell and Isaac share the judgment that the task of political theorizing is to address "actual politics" (Gunnell) or "directly political themes and positions" (Isaac). In other words, what they share is a commitment that the task of political theory is to reproduce the identity of given terms and ideas, not account for their potential transformation. Their shared professional admonition and disappointment stems from their view that a siren's song has spellbound the discipline. The particular siren in question is metaphysical speculation, though it is not named as such: rather, the coded terms for said bewitchment are the charges of linguistic obfuscation, pure speculation, and the willful evasion of "clear thinking and honest communication" alongside the avoidance of "practical" or "actual" or "directly political" matters—all expressions that, as briefly noted earlier and explained later, invoke a moral discursive economy for evaluating a genre of political reflection.[25] The demand of this literalist style of readerly reception is to expect a transparent and verifiable translation of the political meaning of a work, an event, or a practice; and it betrays, as Pierre Bourdieu notes in his studies on education, "a relation to language which is common to a whole category of speakers because it is a product of the social conditions of the acquisition and use of language."[26]

My point here is not to contest Gunnell and Isaac or, for that matter, any of the myriad of others who would also express sympathies with their concerns regarding politics and the English language—including but not limited to Sheldon Wolin's charge, in the 2004 expanded edition of his *Politics and Vision*, of "centrifugalism"; Martha Nussbaum's admonitions against the symbolic gestures of "lofty obscurity and disdainful abstractness"; Alan Sokal's *Social Text* hoax; and the editorial mandate of journals like *Philosophy and Literature*.[27] My interest, rather, is in the expectations of such a literalist style of political reading, writing, and theorizing that govern the reception of translated works in the Anglophone academy and the moral image of political thinking produced therein.

A Peculiarly American Theoretical Dispositif

The "peculiarly American enterprise"[28] variously referred to as political theory or political philosophy is not one. Like any experimental field of inquiry and scholarly production, many forces and trends can and have been identified as participant in its professional development. That said, I wish to arrange the elements of the story of its peculiarity somewhat differently than the way it is typically recounted. The innovations advanced by behaviorism and logical empiricism in the twentieth century proved foundational not simply for the methodological debates that arose between American political scientists and political theorists of the 1950s, but for the context that developed subsequent to these debates. In other words, behaviorism and logical empiricism generated a perceptual frame for studying actual politics that shaped the dispositions and readerly receptions of scholars on either side of the methodological debates and that "consistently constructed models of the world that embody the values and follow the logic of the national ideology of American exceptionalism," as Dorothy Ross has also noted.[29]

We can see this if we explore the influence of logical empiricism and behaviorism on postwar American political science and political theory that made it possible to define politics as the expression of a perceivable action that makes sense. By "perceivable action" I mean something that is empirically verifiable; and by "makes sense" I mean that it does not violate the law of non-contradiction. In short, these two disciplinary criteria provide scholars with an object of inquiry—politics—that is something other than a discontinuous set of practices or a disparate collection of beliefs. Such an articulation of the epistemic virtue of political analysis would make politics a unique and independent entity that could be studied through the specification of methods of inquiry for the verification of claims and statements. This account of the rise of the discipline of political science in postwar America is well known. But what I wish to identify—pace Gunnell—is how both the substance and epistemic virtue of the discipline were shared by political scientists *and* political theorists alike. In short, political theorists like Charles Taylor and Sheldon Wolin *and* political scientists like David Easton and Robert Dahl all concurred that the epistemic virtue of political inquiry is an Aristotelian one: to understand politics.

Meaning is an epistemic virtue in Lorraine Daston and Peter Galison's sense of the term: it becomes a technical object that operates in such a way as to respond to a fear, or set of fears, about conflicting reports and transcriptions of the world.[30] This is why value relativism is deemed something to be feared, for instance. For Daston and Galison, epistemic virtue is characteristic of the explosion of mechanical media like the pencil, mechanical levers, and chemical-based photography in the nineteenth century. "The epistemic fear was of this contradictory multiplication of representations, each of which purported to be the *urpflanze* or the equivalent in other domains. The response to that was to seek out mechanical transfer of the world to the page."[31] In photography, for instance, such a mechanical transfer occurred via a photochemical process that could transcribe an external world onto a silver plate that would almost immediately find applications in the new science of criminology. By combining photographs of faces with measurements and statistical calculations, the science of biometry takes shape, and by 1879 Alphonse Bertillon adapts his anthropometry of facial recognition for criminal identification.[32] In this period, the transcription of ideas and designs also occur on a mass scale, thanks to the industrial production of graphite pencils. In 1858 the first erasable pencil is invented that enables not only the mechanical transfer of thoughts and images on an unprecedented scale, but their immediate editing and correction. Notably, pencils proved even more transportable than ink pens, which wouldn't become a self-sustaining device until 1867 with the invention of an automatic ink delivery chamber.[33]

There are many more relevant examples that help us appreciate how the rise of logical empiricism and its commitment to verifiable meaning (i.e., the logical proof) develops as a practice of epistemic virtue, but the point is this: the second half of the nineteenth century saw an explosion of media for the technological reproduction of the world—thus the need, the task, and the virtue of developing technologies that could confirm the validity of any representation of reality. For the logical empiricists, the ambition was straightforward: invent a genre of transcription (i.e., a symbolic logic) that could automatically (i.e., mechanically) verify the validity of a proof and in doing so transcribe an empirical world onto a page. The epistemic virtue of transcription would stay the fear of misrepresentation. Metaphysics at least since Aristotle had attempted to make sense of things.[34] After thousands of years and innumerable metaphysical speculations, it had failed. But now the possibility of creating a new way of making sense and verifying its facticity was possible (and necessary), thanks to some important discoveries in the fields of mathematics and physics. From their training in physics and mathematics the innovators of logical empiricism—and more precisely, the members of the Vienna Circle—would learn to apply mathematical notation to verify the empirical reality of a mental universe that cannot be observed directly but can be measured and calculated. They applied this insight to the concept of meaning, which, like the universe and its forces, is impossible to observe but can be measured, calculated, and recorded.

Logical empiricism is not a uniform system of thought, and its participants diverged on many counts. But it does offer a theoretical *dispositif* in its method and commitment to verifiability. Verifiability is a technical and—importantly—automatic device that mediates between the production of phenomenon and the production of evidence. The application of symbolic logic is key here because that techne of transcription would allow proponents of logical empiricism to collapse the distinction between empirical verifiability and objective meaning. A meaning can be proven to be both objective and empirical because there is a theoretical *dispositif* that secures the indexical relation between statement and world, by demonstration, via a deductive proof. Like the microscope, the telescope, the photographic plate, and the CERN supercollider, the notations of symbolic logic constitute the material culture for the experimental practices of the Vienna Circle's philosophical laboratory.

Many of the founding members of the Vienna Circle, notably Rudolph Carnap and Hans Reichenbach, are counted among the interwar emigres that came to the United States as a result of the spread of Fascism and Nazism in Europe. Carnap was a physics student, though he also had an interest in philosophy, and especially in Immanuel Kant's *Critique of Pure Reason*. After three years of service during World War I, he began his studies at the University of Berlin, where Albert Einstein had just taken up a post (1917–18). According to his "Intellectual Autobiography," Carnap notes having attended courses given by Frege in 1910 and then again in 1914. After completing his doctoral studies in 1921, he pursued research in the foundations of physics until 1926, when his friend Moritz Schlick invited him to join him in Vienna. What he, Schlick, and Reichenbach all had in common was a foundation in physics that would source their pursuit of the philosophical foundations of scientific inquiry within the Vienna Circle. As Carnap notes,

> The task of fruitful collaboration, often so difficult among philosophers, was facilitated in our Circle by the fact that all members had a first-hand acquaintance with some field of science, either

mathematics, physics, or social science. This led to a higher standard
in clarity and responsibility than is usually found in philosophical
groups, particularly in Germany. Also, the members of the Circle were
familiar with modern logic. This made it possible to represent the
analysis of a concept or proposition under discussion symbolically and
thereby make the arguments more precise. Furthermore, there was
agreement among most of the members to reject traditional metaphysics. However, very little time was wasted in a polemic against metaphysics. The anti-metaphysical attitude showed itself chiefly in the
choice of the language used in the discussion. We tried to avoid
the terms of traditional philosophy and to use instead those of logic,
mathematics, and empirical science, or of that part of the ordinary
language which, though more vague, still is in principle translatable
into a scientific language.[35]

What we learn from Carnap's account is of three unique features of logical
empiricism: the first is a familiarity with modern logic and, notably, the work
of Frege, as well as Bertrand Russell's and Alfred North Whitehead's *Principia
Mathematica* (1910–13). From these logicians they learned that philosophical
statements could be subject to logical proofs and thus be susceptible to a principle of verification. The second is a rejection of the validity of metaphysical
and/or theological speculation. The possibility of eliminating metaphysics rests
on a specific account of empiricism that establishes a claim of property and
propriety about *how* a sentence can have meaning. The third principle follows
from the previous two: it is possible to transcribe thought onto a page (Daston
and Galison's studies on the graphite pencil show it to be an essential medium for the development of logical empiricism). The possibility of such
graphite transcriptions guarantees verification that stands as the empirical
proof of meaning. Meaning is verifiable in the same way that the existence of
atoms is verifiable. The notational system in question is a technical instrument, a *dispositif* of clarity, that can transcribe meaning into precise symbolic
propositions.

It is worth noting that while Carnap was studying physics prior to receiving Schlick's call to come to Vienna, Einstein and Henri Bergson had participated in a debate in Paris on the nature of time (April 6, 1922). That famous
encounter produced an equally famous rift between philosophers and scientists that would be renewed and reinvigorated seven years later in Davos, Switzerland (March 30, 1929), when Carnap would meet Martin Heidegger and
would attend the latter's debate with Ernst Cassirer.[36] Among the many things
that emerged from the first debate was Einstein's infamously incendiary and

fork-tongued statement: "Il n'y a donc pas un temps des pilosophes" (the time of the philosophers does not exist).[37] From the Davos meeting would emerge Carnap's equally provocative and incendiary "The Elimination of Metaphysics through Logical Analysis of Language" (1932; translated into English in 1959) that described the difference between a statement and a pseudo-statement.[38]

Logical empiricism's philosophical manifesto had been written in 1929 ("The Scientific Conception of the World: The Vienna Circle"), but Carnap's 1932 essay could be read as an addendum to that earlier work. In both instances we sense Carnap's (and the Vienna Circle's) famous interpretation of the last sentence of Ludwig Wittgenstein's *Tractatus Logico-Philosophicus*: "Whereof one cannot speak, thereof one must be silent" (*Tractatus* 7). That final sentence is, of course, among the most mystical and diversely understood phrases in twentieth-century philosophy, which is part of its ironic charm. Is Wittgenstein claiming the existence of a domain about which silence is the only mode of engagement? Or is he denying the validity of any such form of thought, experience, or mode of existence? For the Vienna Circle—and especially Carnap—that phrase, and the *Tractatus* as a whole, were "a warrant for the central claims of their scientific conception of philosophy and their articulation of the fact/value problem."[39] This, even though there was some reservation that Wittgenstein held silence and the mystical in too much regard.

Such reservations were no doubt also fueled by Wittgenstein's own behavior when he met with the Vienna Circle. According to Ray Monk, "To persuade Wittgenstein to attend these meetings Schlick had to assure him that the discussion would not have to be philosophical; he could discuss whatever he liked. Sometimes, to the surprise of his audience, Wittgenstein would turn his back on them and read poetry. In particular—as if to emphasize to them, as he had earlier explained to von Ficker, that what he had not said in the *Tractatus* was more important than what he had—he read them the poems of Rabindranath Tagore, an Indian poet much in vogue in Vienna at that time, whose poems express a mystical outlook diametrically opposed to that of the members of Schlick's Circle."[40] Monk also cites Carnap's own impressions of Wittgenstein: "His point of view and his attitude toward people and problems, even theoretical problems, were much more similar to those of a creative artist than to those of a scientist; one might almost say, similar to those of a religious prophet or a seer . . . the impression he made on us was as if insight came to him as through a divine inspiration, so that we could not help feeling that any sober rational comment or analysis of it would be a profanation." And finally, here is Carnap again: "When we were reading Wittgenstein's

book in the Circle, I had erroneously believed that his attitude toward metaphysics was similar to ours. I had not paid sufficient attention to the statements in his book about the mystical, because his feelings and thoughts in
this area were too divergent from mine. Only personal contact with him
helped me to see more clearly his attitude at this point."[41]

Personal impressions and suspicions aside, the Vienna Circle's reading of
the *Tractatus* remained central to their pursuits of clarity and verifiability
and to their goal of eliminating metaphysical speculation from philosophical
inquiry—as we can see in Carnap's 1932 essay. Carnap's essay is a reaction and
response to the events of 1929: the Davos meeting, the publication of Heidegger's
lecture "What Is Metaphysics?" (1929, which he had written after Davos), and
the penning and publishing of the Vienna Circle's manifesto.

Carnap begins his essay by connecting his ideas with previous attempts in
the history of philosophy to eliminate metaphysics.[42] These efforts, he tells us,
have been successful, but have ultimately failed, given that metaphysical inquiry is still being practiced. We should note, however, that "metaphysics" is
a catch-all term (despite Carnap's focus on Heidegger's work in this essay). For
him, metaphysics includes "all philosophy of value and normative theory."[43]
This is notable, as it includes theology, aesthetics, ethics, and normative
philosophy. Carnap's claim for the importance of logical empiricism is not a
defense of truth. That's not possible for him, given that he's eliminating metaphysics and thus any claim to a transcendental truth. The anti-metaphysical
position is simply a claim about procedures for the verifiability of meaningful
statements. The focus and task of first philosophy will, for Carnap, be the derivation of a proof.

As Galison has shown, there were strong relations—both personal and
professional—between Logical Empiricism and Bauhaus: "The Vienna Circle bestowed an aura of scientificity on the Bauhaus and the Bauhaus conferred
an image of progressivism and postwar reform on the Vienna Circle."[44] But
more importantly was their shared commitment to the rationalization of life
through the mechanization of architecture for one and the mechanization of
verifiability for the other. "Both were attempts," Galison explains, "to interior-
ize an image of the machine world they saw on the outside, one through
language and logic, and thought, the other through color, geometry, and architecture. Personal and collective forms of life would be reformed by the
same means."[45] By showing us the connection between logical empiricism
and Bauhaus, Galison makes clear the extent to which they are both participant in a modernist aesthetic that takes the idea of a mechanical device as
method and ideal for "a 'modern' way of life, freed from ideology and grounded
on a vision of the machine age, if not its reality."[46]

Logic is thus the mechanical *dispositif* for the automated derivation of a proof via the removal of pseudo-statements in language: today's analog or, better put, inheritor of this insight is the algorithm. Here is Carnap: "In a strict sense, however, a sequence of words is meaningless if it does not, within a specific language, constitute a statement. It may happen that such a statement of words looks like a statement at first glance; in that case, we call it a pseudo-statement. Our thesis, now, is that logical analysis reveals the alleged statements of metaphysics to be pseudo-statements."[47] It is too easy to read such phrases normatively and, as I suggested earlier (borrowing from Daston and Galison), there is clearly an effort at delimiting a kind of epistemic virtue here. But since so much has been written on the normative status of such scientific claims, I'm more interested in the act of medial transformation that the philosophical *dispositif* is doing. Carnap's delimitation between a statement and a pseudo-statement is not to be read as a distinction between truth and falsity. This is not the point of the operation. The point, for Carnap, is to transform the task of philosophy into a practice for empirical (or scientific) derivation of proofs. The only thing that can be said to have meaning is a language. A painting— for instance—cannot have meaning because it is nonlinguistic. The only way in which we can imagine a painting to have meaning is that someone has said something about that painting, and that expression can now be analyzed, and its truth may be derived. But then what we're analyzing in analyzing the statement is not the meaning of the painting but the meaning of the statement about the painting. This delimitation of what can be said, and only this, is the task of the new philosophy. "Since the meaning of a word is determined by its criterion of application (in other words: by the relations of deducibility entered into by its elementary sentence-form, by its truth-conditions, by its method of verification), the stipulation of the criterion takes away from one's freedom to decide what one wishes to 'mean' by the word. . . . The meaning is implicitly contained in the criterion; all that remains to be done is to make the meaning explicit."[48]

The characteristic lucidity of Carnap's statements hardly requires further explanation. They stand on their own. That's the point of the project: automated verifiability (via symbolic logic) procures autonomy (of meaning). On this view, language does not represent a world, it is a world; and just like the natural world, there are criteria that operate independent of human perception or feeling. These criteria are like the laws of physics that work regardless of our freedom to decide whether they should or should not work. Language produces meaning like the steam engine produces work. Our wish to make meaning is all well and good, but it is not philosophical; it is, as he will go on to say, artistic. Hence, the terms that Carnap lists in his essay—"the Idea," "the Absolute," "the Unconditioned," "the Infinite," "the being of being," "non-being," "thing in itself," "absolute spirit," "objective spirit," "essence," "being-in-itself," "being-in-and-for-itself," "emanation," "manifestation," "artic-ulation," "the Ego," "the non-Ego," etc.—are all pseudo-statements. And they are pseudo-statements not because they bear no relation to a truth, but because they "have no sense, assert nothing."[49]

The rhetorical move here is important, especially since it is the exact same rhetorical move that outlines the epistemic virtues of political theory in the Anglophone academy's castigation of postwar French thought discussed earlier (i.e., Gunnell, Isaac, Nussbaum, Smith): For Carnap to affirm that pseudo-statements have no sense and assert nothing means that they are not philo-sophical. This is at once a play on Heidegger's own metaphysical speculations on "non-being" but also on Carnap's (and logical empiricism's) prima facie acceptance of the law of non-contradiction. Carnap's position is clear: pseudo-statements are epistemic vices not only because they are unverifiable and mean-ingless, but because a pseudo-statement presupposes an interstitial domain of contradiction where something can be true and not true at the same time. Thus, for Carnap the possibility of excising or eliminating metaphysics rests on the law of non-contradiction, which is indisputable.

In the subsequent sections of his essay, Carnap comes clean by telling his reader that all the pseudo-statements he cites are taken from one work, Hei-degger's *Was ist Metaphysik?*, but "our results," he says, apply with equal valid-ity to any other metaphysical statement such that "most metaphysicians since antiquity have allowed themselves to be seduced into pseudo-statements by the verbal, and therewith the predicative form of the word 'to be,' e.g. 'I am,' 'God is.'"[50] For Carnap, then, the task of the new philosophy is to do away with metaphysical inquiry altogether, because, as he says quite explicitly, it is the form of inquiry and form of thought that are themselves meaningless: "But in the case of metaphysics we find this situation: through the form of its works it pretends to be something that it is not. The form in question is that of a system of statements which are apparently related as premises and conclu-sions, that is, the form of a theory. In this way, the fiction of theoretical content is generated, whereas, as we have seen, there is no such content."[51] Unlike Carnap and his style of writing, which transcribes propositions as valid state-ments, the metaphysician (which at this point refers to any person who claims to make statements of value that can both be true and not true at the same time) fools him- or herself into believing a pseudo-statement is, in actuality, a statement: But in reality the metaphysician "has not asserted anything, but only expressed something, like an artist."[52]

Among the many things at stake for Carnap is the relation between me-dium and form. The claim to method is a claim about a technical mentality grounded in the automatic functioning of a theoretical *dispositif*. This is what

Carnap means by "form" throughout the essay—a term that, as Galison notes, must be read as an instance in a series of intercalated practices of the modern. And form is precisely the hinge on which his assertions about pseudo-statements rest. Metaphysicians make pseudo-statements because they make claims and because their only mode of expression is theoretical. But what the new philosophy of logical empiricism and its method of verification have shown are that the theoretical form is not amenable to the metaphysician's mode of expression. That metaphysicians wish to express an attitude in "the medium of the theoretical" is the actual mistake that Carnap's essay elaborates.[53] The fault is in the bad choice of medium, which is why Carnap both admires and celebrates Nietzsche's oeuvre, which he praises for being historical and thus "predominantly empirical." When Nietzsche does decide to venture into the metaphysical, "he does not choose the misleading theoretical form, but openly the form of art, of poetry" and writes *Thus Spake Zarathustra.*[54] The expression of an attitude is what happens in art whereas the making of clear statements is what happens in science and philosophy. "Metaphysicians," he famously concludes, "are musicians without musical ability."[55]

Again, my interest in working through this material is not to offer an assessment of its normative or intellectual validity.[56] On the contrary, it is to show how "the medium of the theoretical" *is* the innovation of the Vienna Circle's new philosophy and how this new philosophy transforms philosophical reflection into an operation of validity assessment or, to use the name that would stick and would cause so much vitriol in American political science, "method." "Method" becomes the term of art that describes the analysis of validity claims based either on a logical tautology or an empirically verifiable matter of fact (i.e., what Charles Taylor would refer to as "brute data")[57] and not on a transcendental concept of truth or subjective meaning. In fact, what Carnap shows in his effort to eliminate metaphysics is that a logical proof is derivable by deductive reasoning, and this proof *is* the empirical evidence (or datum) of meaning. Logical empiricism is literally the conjoining of the new methods in deductive logic with a literalist reading of Davide Hume's famous condemnation of Aristotelian scholasticism: "If we take in our hand any volume; of divinity or school metaphysics, for instance; let us ask, Does it contain any abstract reasoning concerning quantity or number? No. Does it contain any experimental reasoning, concerning matter of fact and existence? No. Commit it then to the flames: for it can contain nothing but sophistry and illusion."[58]

This new theoretical *dispositif,* I submit, would prove central for a culture of readerly reception and translation at work in the peculiarly American idiom of political science *and* political theory that would attest to the empirical validity of "actual politics" as both a collection of discrete practices and a topic of scientific investigation. Anything that isn't verifiable as "actual politics" would be deemed, following logical empiricism's interpretation of validity criteria, either sophistry or illusion, lacking clarity and professional seriousness.

On June 22, 1936, Moritz Schlick was murdered on the steps of the University of Vienna by a former doctoral student, Johann Nelböck.[59] The year before, Carnap (a socialist and a pacifist) felt his commitments put him at risk with the rise of Nazi Germany and thus immigrated to the United States. In 1936 he took up a post at the University of Chicago, where he would remain until 1952, subsequently moving to UCLA. The story of the reception and proliferation of logical empiricism in the United States is well documented, and, despite its eventual softening in the 1950s, it remains one of the most important and influential philosophical movements of the twentieth century. As Jeremy Arnold argues in *Across the Great Divide*, "The disciplinary history of 20th century analytic philosophy has shaped the methods, problems, and philosophical concerns of analytic political philosophy."[60] Katrina Forrester also shows how the 1950s was a time of profound and renewed investigation in the human sciences in order to develop new conceptual tools for American liberalism in light of the totalitarian threat: "Anti-totalitarian democracy required a new kind of "objective ethics"—a universal but not absolutist moral theory."[61] For Forrester, this project and its complications and intricacies laid the groundwork for the emergence of John Rawls's monumental contribution to American political theory, *A Theory of Justice* (1971). And for John Gunnell and Eric Lee Goodfield the 1950s is the period when the methodological and disciplinary debates in American political science, and between political scientists and political theorists, would prove critical in redefining the discipline's research mandates. As Gunnell (especially) notes, "The University of Chicago was a crucial nexus for American political science and the émigré perspective— with respect to both the defense and the critique of scientism."[62] I would hazard the claim that such work could not have been possible without the lasting influence of the innovations of the Vienna Circle, and especially of Rudolph Carnap's influence on Anglophone philosophy and social science. What Carnap brought to North America was a theoretical *dispositif* that would give the human and social sciences a method for transcribing the validity of statements. This proved to satisfy an important political need, as we will shortly see: America was in the throes of the Cold War against an enemy who was, by definition, a secret infiltrator on the virtues of American life, a deceiver, a propagandist of false liberties and pseudo-statements. More urgently still, such a theoretical *dispositif* would prove essential for educators and academics under McCarthyism. They could deploy and champion it to show that their research, their ideas, and their souls were not those of the *Red-Ucator*. This theoretical *dispositif* thus quickly became the gold standard in professional qualification, licensing scholars and researchers to make actual statements and not mere pseudo-statements. With such an exceptional (in Dorothy Ross's sense) social science methodology in place, a democratic polity (as well as an academic discipline) can achieve scientific legitimacy and, ultimately, victory in the battles ahead.

The Operant

If logical empiricism would lend American political science and political theory a theoretical *dispositif* for reading the meaning of politics, then the combination of behaviorism with McCarthyism during the totalitarian scare of the Cold War would further assist in giving political science criteria for what counts as perceivable action, and especially perceptible risk. This is the second aspect of the milieu of readerly reception for the arrival of postwar French thought.

Decisive to this aspect of Anglophone—but especially American—intellectual formation for the reading of politics would be the publication and enthusiastic reception of David Easton's *The Political System* (1953), which became a kind of manifesto for the behavioral revolution in political science and political theory. It is here that we can access an archetypal definition of "actual politics"—namely, the formulation of policy for the purpose of advising future state outcomes and decisions (i.e., state ends). Easton's work and his subsequent development of behavioral social science inquiry and systems theory rested on the distinction between value theory and causal theory. These two approaches are for him inseparable, but they are distinguishable. E. F. Miller describes this best: "The distinction refers only to different types of propositions that are to be found in any comprehensive political theory, including the great political theories of the past. Descriptive or factual propositions refer to observable facts; causal propositions to the assumed relations between facts; value propositions to the state of affairs that the theorist would like to bring into existence; and applied propositions to the conditions whereby given ends can be attained. Even to speak of different kinds of propositions is deceptive, he adds, since these propositions do not, in practice, exist in a pure form: 'Strictly speaking, we ought to say that these are several logical aspects of propositions since no statement can ever refer exclusively to facts, values, or theories.'"[63]

There is a decided distance from Easton's readerly distinction between value statements and causal statements and Carnap's distinction between statements and pseudo-statements. For the latter, there is no question of the empirical difference between facts and values. But Easton is not a philosopher interested in the verification of meaningful statements. He is a political scientist interested in "developing a general causal theory that would bring politics, and the future, under rational human control";[64] and he is considering this in relationship to American postwar exceptionalism and the mounting concern over the spread of Soviet totalitarianism—a predictable risk that demands policy solutions.[65]

It was Easton's good fortune that "a general causal theory" (i.e., a "systems theory") for controlling politics and the future was in reach, given the wartime development of cybernetics that in 1948 Norbert Wiener, one of its founders and most vociferous spokespersons, would define as the "science of control in communication in the human and the machine"; "cybernetics" is a term famously derived from the Greek *kybernētiké*, meaning to steer or to govern.[66] At the core of this innovation was the idea of negative feedback, which is the basis for understanding the meaning of the term "control," which does not mean "domination" (in the manner that one might imagine totalitarian control to mean something like an authoritarian constraint on individual freedom).[67] Indeed, the opposite is true. "Control" here means the regulation of movement in space and time to attain a future goal whose achievement is predictable but undetermined. The classic cybernetic example is anti-aircraft machine gun fire. A cybernetic system has a control mechanism (which Wiener and his colleagues call "negative feedback"). This mechanism sends signals back and forth (hence "feedback") between missile and the moving target in order to correct the trajectory of the missile's movement (hence "negative") so that it might eventually hit its target. Negative feedback is possible, given the development and innovations in twentieth-century behaviorism, information theory, and engineering that, alongside the new philosophy of logical empiricism, would offer postwar American political science and political theory a way of perceiving and defining political action as a measurable quantity that, once measured, can be rendered calculable and thus predictable.

Like meaning, action is inordinately difficult to identify. "Behavior" is the name that Q. R. B. Skinner would give to perceivable action. It is an especially persuasive account for those interested in empirically verifying what a right or wrong action is, especially when one's professional ambition is to advise national policy vis-à-vis a foreign government that presents the threat of both spiritual and geopolitical annihilation. Communism threatened the destruction of the American way of life *and*, with the development of a Soviet nuclear program, the annihilation of American lives. In postwar America both of the king's two bodies risked total destruction.[68] To protect American lives, it was (and still is) necessary to predict the future actions of an opponent (in this case the enemy) with the caveat that we do not know what the opponent is *really* thinking or believing. All we know is what we can observe—namely, that the opponent is (like us) moved to complete a task. We know that the Soviet Union's task is total domination, the precise definition of "totalitarianism"; and Marx, Lenin, Stalin, and Chairman Mao are all explicit about this. Thus, it is essential that we observe the actions of the opponent and, on the basis of those observations, condition our responses accordingly.

The great thing about the concept of behavior as a science of action is that it does not require any metaphysics of consciousness, soul, or faith; this is one of the crucial elements that the behavioral social sciences will take from logical empiricism. Behavior is simply a way of accounting for the coordination and manifestation of discreet and empirically observable actions, thereby offering an account of action that is both measurable and predictable, in a logically empirical way, without having to rely on anything other than observation. This is because the moment you remove internal motivation as a dependent variable, then all you have are independent variables that can be correlated to yield a predictable outcome.

In short, we don't need to know what the aircraft pilot believes, if they take Communion on Sundays, or if they kneel facing west while praying. All we need to know is what the plane can do and what the pilot can do; that is, *how* the physics and engineering of the machines enable the motion and thus the trajectory of the aircraft. Similarly, we do not need to know why a voter believes what one believes; all we need to know is how that voter will vote in a future election. And to be able to determine that, we don't ask voters what they believe; rather we ask them about their choices on issues like abortion, or housing, or immigration. The answers we collect in surveys count as perceivable action that informs the potential outcome of a future decision. A survey poll is a classic stimulus/response experiment designed to isolate specific, observable behavior for the purpose of predicting the likelihood of a future outcome.

Importantly, the outcome is not a certitude, it is a likelihood; this is what the cybernetic component of the behavioral social sciences insists on. You can have higher or lower accuracy, greater or lesser probability, but this will depend on the accuracy and quantity of your data sample: You can never be certain that your missile will strike its target 100 percent of the time; but with the stimulus/response dynamics of negative feedback, you can correlate a high likelihood of yield. The expectation of certitude belongs to the believer, not to the scientist, because certitudes require what both logical empiricism *and* behaviorism deem at once illogical and irrelevant: namely, a metaphysical theory of truth or meaning. The project of the behavioral social scientist, however, is not the expression of a metaphysical truth (just like it wasn't for Carnap and the other members of the Vienna Circle). Rather, the project is one of the verifiability of meaning through the derivation of a logical proof that will yield the predictability of actual politics.

This behavioral account of action as well as the logical empiricist account of verifiability would prove decisive in the postwar efforts to redefine and reconceptualize the ambitions and disciplinary responsibilities of American political science and political theory. It is on the basis on these two elements, along with the associated innovations of cybernetic negative feedback systems, that a new science of politics emerges, promising America and the world an empiric of actual politics. Thus, studies on voting practices, policy analysis, and the comparative analysis of political institutions, *as well as* the political theories of meaning and understanding (i.e., hermeneutics, historical analysis, speech action theory, and phenomenology)—all these innovations would participate in delimiting the intellectual milieu of a theoretical *dispositif* set on affirming the empirical fact of actual politics. During the American "Cold War university," Katrina Forrester explains, Western Civilization courses were designed to reinvent liberalism as an anticommunist and antitotalitarian "fighting faith." "Social scientists had grand ambitions, both intellectual and to serve the interest of the State. The behavioral, cybernetic, and systems sciences were flourishing, while tools of modernization and rational choice theories were taken up across disciplines."[69] With the science of physics America had won the war and defeated one strain of totalitarianism; and with the new science of politics, itself a genetic offshoot of physics, it would defend itself from the encroachment of another strain of totalitarianism—Soviet Communism.

A Science of and for the State

Perhaps the most simplistic way of understanding the theoretical *dispositif* that marries logical empiricism with behaviorism and cybernetics is to point to the implied equivalency between political theory and state thinking. In a world where, as Gunnell and others have observed, interdisciplinary competition loomed large, the possibility of determining a specific area of influence and operation was at once necessary and vital. The American Cold War university's anticommunist mission had competitors, including, for the first time in U.S. history, a military division of research and development in the RAND Corporation. Founded in 1948 as a nonprofit organization, RAND had direct access to leading physicists, mathematicians, and chemists, as well as technical innovations and data, that would have a privileged and lasting influence on U.S. domestic and foreign policy. Central to this was the development of a series of game theoretical models of thinking and calculations that would be used to assess and predict ballistic outcomes, or what would be baptized "rational choice theory." The "peculiarly American" science of the State during the postwar period would thus eventually betray a certain sentimentality. The two fundamental dispositions that conditioned its ambitions were vulnerability and strategic analysis that would shape the field of expertise that became what Thomas Medvetz calls the "space of think tanks."[70]

The year 1953 was crucial in confirming America's sense of its own vulnerability. That summer RAND physicists, in constant communication with their Los Alamos counterparts, learned that the physics of the hydrogen bomb was not only feasible but efficient. They had discovered that "a relatively small amount of fissile uranium or plutonium was all one would need to trigger fusion implosions of hydrogen isotopes" that would produce an explosive yield equaling 500 kilotons of power in a device significantly smaller than the bomb dropped over Nagasaki.[71] This proved significant because, beyond its superior power of annihilation, the smaller device could also be implanted into an intercontinental missile and thus would not require airplane transport. Such missiles were still a theoretical object, but the building of them was deemed possible. Simultaneously, on August 8, 1953, the Soviets set off their own hydrogen bomb, which, though analyzed as less powerful, had the advantage of using lithium as the basis of its refrigeration system. The American H-bomb was small, but its cooling system was impractical and untransportable, either by missile or by airplane. In short, the Soviets had an advantage on the American H-bomb, and this meant U.S. vulnerability.

The result of the summer of 1953's activities are now the stuff of military, political science, and cinematic history (see Stanley Kubrick's *Dr. Strangelove; or, How I Learned to Stop Worrying and Love the Bomb,* 1964). What emerged from the flurry of these events is what today we recognize as postwar American foreign policy—in part thanks to an important figure at RAND, Albert Wohlstetter. Wohlstetter had been put in charge of studying the vulnerability of America's Strategic Air Command (SAC) devising a highly successful plan for the development of overseas American bases. His project was complex and based on a series of mathematical models, but what it ultimately offered was a technical system for verifying the claim that the U.S. (and especially SAC) was vulnerable to ICBMs and that the solution to such vulnerability was strategic analysis (first) and military follow-through (second). "The Wohlstetter study set the model of what strategic analysis should be," Fred Kaplan explains. "It was the study that, for years after, almost everyone in the quantitative quarters of RAND would instantly cite when asked to name the most impressive systems analysis they had produced. It imposed a much higher premium than had previously existed on the claim that good strategic analysis meant quantitative analysis with elaborate calculations and "hard" data. And since most of this data came from Air Force Intelligence—which, curiously, this group of analytic skeptics accepted without much question—quantitative analysis tended to paint a very scary picture of the Soviet threat."[72] In short, and once again, we arrive at the definition of "actual politics" as a system of uncertain outcomes that may be analyzed according to logical calculations based on empirically verifiable data.

The RAND corporation and other similar policy institutes were competitors with the American Cold War university, which, unlike these other institutes, had the further responsibility to educate a citizenry. While RAND et.al. were decidedly not a threat to U.S. security, these universities, their faculty, and their students could be. They housed *Red-Ucators*, many of whom were foreigners who could undermine American values from within. Vulnerability and insecurity in the face of nuclear destruction (at best) or totalitarian invasion (at worst) were the most palpable political sentiments during the reinvention of the liberal university in the 1950s, and McCarthy's Red Scare would lead a singular charge to exploit such vulnerabilities.

Just a few miles down the street from RAND's Santa Monica headquarters, UCLA and other campuses of the University of California were debating whether to enact the Loyalty Oath (1949–51) put in place because of the Levering Act (passed in California in 1950) requiring all state employees to disavow radical beliefs.[73] At the time, the State of California's constitution held that no oath should be required of its citizens. The Levering Act was intended to replace that law by classifying public employees as civil defense employees and thus requiring them to swear an oath that would denounce any allegiance to radical activities, especially Communism. A clear effort to purge *Red-Ucators* from the UC system, what it also emphasized in no uncertain terms was that part of the reinvention of the liberal university in postwar America included an agreement (or, at least, ought to include an agreement) that the university was in the service of the State and was responsible for preserving national policy.

This state of affairs is exactly what Sheldon Wolin famously denounces in his attack on the behavioral social sciences in "Political Theory as a Vocation." Throughout the pages of that 1969 *APSR* article, Wolin would argue that the absence of a utopian critical impulse in political theory and political science inquiry was characteristic of what he referred to as the appliance model of theorizing: "Theories are likened to appliances which are "plugged into" political life."[74] The metaphor is at once devastating and accurate, as we have seen, given the prevalence of machinic thinking during the postwar period. It dramatizes the point, as all good metaphors do. But in its hyperbole, it makes evident the emphasis on applicability, technicity, and automation that was so important to the modernist machinic aesthetic of postwar American political science. By developing techniques and insights that rendered action perceptible and calculable, the Red Scare's marriage of logical empiricism and behaviorism made it so that the only thing that could and *should* count as relevant to political inquiry is actual politics. Such an entity did not require an account of consciousness or interiority, let alone an explanation of the order of the universe and humanity's place in it or, for that matter, an intellectual canon of concepts and ideas. Such metaphysical speculations only increased the risk of American vulnerability by producing pseudo-statements that, under the threat of totalitarianism, betrayed a kind of mystical thinking that could (and likely would) produce siren songs of moral relativism.

These strands help us reconstruct what it means to read and understand the word "politics" in postwar American political science and political theory. Far from being a value-neutral enterprise, American political science extends its exceptionalist ambitions in defense of the importance of state power, thereby generating a theoretical *dispositif* that assembles a series of anxieties and impressions in such a way as to make politics readable as a meaningful term (as Carnap recommended) that identifies an operant. That operant in this case is "political action" that is at once perceptible and calculable. The importance of reading politics in this manner and with this meaning was not simply a matter of disciplinary formation, but also one of national security. To read and write in a transparent way, in clear English, and thus to distance "the sirens of esotericism"[75] means that the political science and political theory in America can access a verifiable meaning-statement whose sense could adequately be assessed, controlled, and, if need be, corrected . . . in exactly the same way that a missile guiding system could assess, control, and correct the trajectory of its ballistic load in order to achieve its target. The Cold War university was thus not only instrumental in developing a new science of politics, but instrumental in developing a new literary field: political communication. By combining the insights and innovations of logical empiricism, behaviorism, and cybernetics, such a literary field shapes scholarly research to achieve (1) citizen education and (2) policy advice.

Readers and writers in postwar France would not attend to the relation between "politics" and "philosophy" in quite the same way.[76]

Political Literarity in Postwar France

Reading Texts Closely

What logical empiricism and behaviorism in postwar America promise are a new legibility and transcription of the political, thus requiring new practices for social scientific reading and writing. This is made possible by a series of innovations and inventions in the philosophy of language and social science inquiry that procured a new science of politics: if statements could be logically verifiable, then the language of politics, policy, and strategy can and must also be. Add to these innovations a new type of war fought on the communication and information front with mathematical calculations and the modeling of games, and what you have is an intellectual milieu that partitions new forms of attention and distraction, new sensibilities about how one reads the word "politics," and thus new epistemic virtues about disciplinary dispositions.

I wish to further elaborate my story of the arrival, adoption, and reaction to postwar French thought by continuing to focus on the cultural politics of reading and suggest that a major (and highly controversial) innovation that French theory offered American political theory was not just the rediscovery of a philosophical tradition of critical thinking indebted to the modern masters of suspicion (Marx, Freud, and Nietzsche) that had been displaced (to use Bonnie Honig's felicitous term) during the postwar period, but also the discovery of close reading as a professional form of attention available to the Western canon of political thought. I take American political theory's encounter with practices of close reading to be what the 1985 executive editorial committee of the journal *Political Theory* meant when it noted that among recent submissions, "earlier techniques of empiricism tend now to become critiques of the primacy of method of epistemology; hermeneutics, genealogy, and deconstruction make appearances in these latter essays."[77]

In the Anglo-American academy, close reading is and was the purview of English departments for some time, certainly at least since the foundational work of I. A. Richards in *The Principles of Literary Criticism* (1924) and *Practical Criticism* (1929). It seems that political theorists and political scientists had not encountered this practice of reading before; at the very least, they had not acknowledged it as a way of reading works in political theory. And the same might be said of Anglo-American philosophy if we consider Barry Smith's letter denouncing Jacques Derrida's status as professional philosopher. Given this, it should be of little surprise that what eventually became known as French theory would find its home in humanities and literature departments in the United States whose already well-established disciplinary ambition was instruction in and of close reading.

Among the many things that made the presentation and arguments in works of French theory at once compelling, puzzling, and at times unreadable was the fact that the historical works of philosophy discussed by these French thinkers, though shared and known to North American scholars of political theory, were not described and presented in familiar or even recognizable ways. One of the main reasons for this is that with the arrival of French theory also came exposure to the well-established (in France) practices of the *lecture linéaire* and *explication de texte* that were unfamiliar and even untranslatable to Anglophone readers in the social sciences. The way in which one makes an argument in a *lecture linéaire* or an *explication de texte* will not look like a logical derivation or analytic proof. Part of the difference rests on the fact that these close reading practices begin by interrogating the status of the literary work and not with a concept of the statement. For French readers, a "work" (or *oeuvre*) is an aesthetic term that refers to a cultural product (i.e., "the work of art"). This category of objects had been codified into law on September 2, 1793, by the "Declaration of the Rights of Genius."[78] A foundational moment in the history of copyright law in the West, the declaration "gave authors, musical composers, painters, engravers, and draftsmen the exclusive lifetime right to sell, resell, distribute within the French Republic, and cede all or part of their property. Article 7 of the law, granting heirs a ten-year copyright, added a phrase to include 'all other productions of mind or genius that belong to the fine arts.'"[79] The law thus makes it so that a work of art can have the status of property: it is the product of labor ("of mind or genius") that belongs to someone, a complete whole, with a discernible boundary, contour, or outline—just like a fence or a wall might contain the territory of a state or a frame contains the surface of the painting. The readerly expectations of the French *lecture linéaire* and *explication de texte* thus proceed by accepting the work as a complete aesthetic object that may be parsed or divided (i.e., *partagé*) in the same way that land can be divided up into plots. Such a parsing exercise requires that students be able to construct an argument about the meaning of the work based on how they understand it and its constituent parts to work together as a composition. (I offer a genealogy of the *explication de texte* and its political history in Chapter 2.)

Both the *lecture linéaire* and *explication de texte* are part of the French grade school curriculum that are examined for the *baccalauréat* exam at the end of high school. In the case of the *lecture linéaire* the student is examined orally and is first required to read one's chosen text out loud. Then the student must make an oral argument about the meaning of the text based on the passages one has chosen to prepare for the exam. This requires the student to situate the text in its historical context, discuss the author, explain what kind of work it is, and—crucially—to give an account of the system of enunciation at work in the text. The student is expected to execute a *lecture linéaire* in twenty minutes; this is then followed by a ten-minute oral examination.

Unlike the *lecture linéaire*, the *explication de texte* does not require a presentation of the text but an analysis of it. By mastering the *explication de texte* the student learns how to identify and engage the *problematique* of the work. A *problematique* differs from either the theme of the work or the thesis of the author, though the student is responsible for the analysis of these also. The *explication* requires an engagement with the whole work (not just a se-lection, as in the case of the *lecture linéaire*). But just as with the *lecture*, the *explication* is oriented toward articulating the value of the work. The work's meaning is not derived from the logical analysis of its statements but from an explanation of *"l'enjou"*—literally, the playfulness—of the text. Central to the exercise of the *explication* is a capacity to explain not just what the author is saying but what the work itself wishes to fortify as its ambition(s). The one type of reading protocol (*lecture*) evinces a capacity to explain and analyze how the components of a work fit together (and is typically best suited for poetic works), whereas the *explication* is best suited for philosophical works and is a required component of the Philosophy *baccalauréat* exam. Finally, both the *lecture li-néaire* and *explication de texte* are not simply readerly conventions; they are educational requirements that belong to France's education minister's portfo-lio of responsibilities.[80]

These practices of reading and textual criticism are part of the intellectual milieu of post-Revolutionary France that have as large a role to play in the development of postwar French theory as does the theoretical *dispositif* of logical empiricism within the context of postwar American political science and political theory. But as one might imagine, the sentimental dispositions and expectations of the French practices of reading are decidedly different from their Anglo-American counterparts. The principal difference lies in the nature of the unit of analysis. French close reading reads passages with the status of the work in mind and explores the juxtaposition between the particularity of the passage and the *problematique* of the whole work. Anglo-American social science reads statements with their verifiability in mind and for the purpose of parsing statements from pseudo-statements. Whereas the former interrogates the integrity of the work, the latter verifies the integrity of the statement.

The pedagogy of close reading finds its origin in early twentieth-century re-forms of the French university system (1902), and especially in the development of Gustave Lanson's literary sociology. For all intents and purposes, Lanson was the innovator of the *explication de texte* and the person that successfully advocated for its centrality in the French curriculum in his role as education reformer, but also (later) as director of the École Normale Supérieure (ENS). For Lanson, a text was a composite object that was part product of an author's ideas, part product of its historical setting, and part product of the reader's reading competence.[81] In a 1935 *American Scholar* memorial, Jean-Albert Bédé (a former student and professor in the Department of Modern Languages at Princeton University) writes that "in Professor Gustave Lanson, who died recently in Paris, France lost not only her ablest literary scholar but a personality whose strong influence permeated the French University system from the Sorbonne to the smallest college town."[82]

Lanson became director of the École Normale Supérieure (ENS) after World War I and held that post until 1927, when Jean-Paul Sartre effectively got him fired: An ENS student at the time, Sartre had developed a personal and professional disdain for Lanson and often partook in lampooning him. In 1925 Sartre wrote, directed, and starred in a play that ridiculed Lanson, Durkheim, and other defenders of Cartesian objectivism in the social and human sciences. Sartre portrayed Lanson as a bearded sycophant of bourgeois wealth. But the coup de grâce came in 1927, when Sartre and his classmates (including Georges Canguilhem) developed an elaborate prank. Sartre called local newspapers and other media outlets in Paris informing them that Lindbergh, who had just crossed the Atlantic, would be fêted as an "Honorary Student" at the ENS. More than five hundred members of the press showed up that morning to find Sartre walking around the rue d'Ulm with someone dressed up like Lindbergh; on some reports the Lindbergh impersonator was Canguilhem. Once the scandal was exposed, Lanson was forced to resign because of his apparent inability to maintain a certain decorum among the students of the rue d'Ulm.[83] Despite the misfortune of having to try to manage Sartre during his student years, Bédé is right to insist on Lanson's indelible influence on France's education system. With the institutionalization of the *lecture linéaire* and *explication de texte* as foundational elements of France's secondary and postsecondary education system, he taught the country how to read and write and how to write about what one read.

The Programme de l'Agrégation

In an important book and accompanying series of articles, Alan Schrift demonstrates the central and consistently unacknowledged importance of the institution of the *Agrégation de Philosophie* for twentieth-century French philosophy. Schrift's point is straightforward but crucial: any attempt to make sense

of postwar French philosophy or, for that matter, any comparative analysis between it and its American, British, German, or Austrian counterparts must
consider the foundational role of the institution of the *agrégation* to the intellectual formation and career development of virtually every academic educated
in France. "The failure to acknowledge the role of the *agrégation de philosophie*," Schrift affirms, "leads to a failure to understand what, at a profound level,
distinguishes *all* French philosophers—whether Derrida or Deleuze or Bouver-
esse or Descombes—from their German, British, and American counterparts,
namely, the thorough grounding in the history of philosophy prior to 1800,
that has been throughout the twentieth century a necessary condition for employment as an instructor of philosophy in France."[84] And, one should add, this
is the case not simply for university instruction, but for all middle and high
school instruction of philosophy. In short, the *agrégation* and the corresponding exam represents the central credentialing institution for French philosophy
in the twentieth century, and as such, it is the most significant site of social and
pedagogical reproduction and "pedagogic authority," as Pierre Bourdieu also
shows in his *Reproduction in Education, Society and Culture*.[85]

The *agrégation*, Schrift details, was established in 1766 under Louis XV as
an exam to certify secondary school teachers in philosophy, letters, and grammar. But it wasn't until 1830, under the July Monarchy, that the *agrégation*
became an independent philosophy exam "with the appointment of the
philosopher Victor Cousin (1792–1867) as president of the *jury d'agrégation* and
the change of language for the written essays from Latin to French."[86] The
modern form is directed by the Ministry of Public Instruction (as is the case
with the *baccalauréat* exam that tests for excellence in the *lecture linéaire* and
explication de texte). The exam is based on the *Programme* (or syllabus) determined the preceding year. As noted, this is a rigorous and competitive exam.
Consider what Schrift states is a typical example for the first half of the twentieth century: In 1913 sixty students registered for the exam and seventeen
passed the written portion, while only seven of these seventeen passed the oral
portion and were admitted as *agrégés*.[87]

Two other aspects of the *agrégation* are noteworthy: The role of the *agrégé-
répétiteur* (or *caïman*) and the constitution and content of the *Programme*
itself, and both of these indicate that "not only the work of the advanced students but also much of the work of the professoriate is determined in response to the *Programme* of the *agrégation*."[88] The *agrégé-répétiteur* is an instructor assigned to prepare the future *agrégés* students for their exam. These
instructors, some of whom have been among the most distinguished professors
of philosophy in France (including Jean Cavaillès, Maurice Merleau-Ponty,
Louis Althusser, and Jacques Derrida) are tasked not only with helping stu-

dents study the material of the *Programme*, but to train them and initiate them into the culture of sensibilities of the exam. This is at once an academic and intellectual preparation *and* a training in bodily comportment, attunement, attention, and so forth. It is, quite literally, a pedagogical state institution designed to reproduce knowledge through repetition (hence the relevance of Louis Althusser identifying the education system as a pillar of the Ideological State Apparatus).[89] Here is Derrida commenting on the role of the *agrégé-répétiteur*:

> A repeater, the *agrégé-répétiteur* should produce nothing, at least if to produce means to innovate, to transform, to bring about the new. He is destined to repeat and make others repeat, to reproduce and make others reproduce: forms, norms, and a content. He must assist students in the reading and comprehension of texts, help them interpret and understand what is expected of them, what they must respond to at the different stages of testing and selection, from the point of view of the contents or logico-rhetorical organization of their exercises (*explication de texte*, essays, or *leçons*). With his students he must therefore make himself the representative of a system of reproduction. . . . Or, rather, he must make himself the expert who, passing for knowing better the demand to which he first had to submit, explains it, translates it, repeats and re-presents it, therefore, to the young candidates.[90]

Such a description of the role of the *agrégé-répétiteur* helps explain the near constant presence of the philosophical themes of the reproduction of the same (i.e., mimesis) as sources of social and ideological suspicion in so much postwar French philosophy, and it also assists us in better appreciating the political stakes of Deleuze and Guattari's sentimental empiricist definition of philosophy as "that art of forming, inventing, and fabricating concepts."[91] The function of representation as a site of social reproduction (and thus of the reproduction of credentialing exclusions and inequalities) is not an abstract concept or philosophical ideal: it is an office of instruction sanctioned by the State; it *is* the State. Thus, when one reads the writings of French authors on or about repetition (as in the case of Deleuze's 1968 *Différence et Répétition*, or Michel Foucault's treatment of the repetition of the Same in his 1966 *Les mots et les choses*, or Simone de Beauvoir's description of the mundanities of French domestic life) without appreciating these institutional and pedagogical conditions, we miss the political stakes of their philosophical expositions. For a reader of philosophy trained to read philosophy or political theory in the United States, any of these works could seem like metaphysical speculations devoid of actual politics and unredeemable based on their lack of clarity or analytical rigor; or, at best, they could only be read as a collection of philosophical statements that required explanation and/or application, but not political treatises that offered theories of and about politics. And yet, they are.

One final aspect about the *agrégation de philosophie* is worth noting: the content of the *Programme*. As noted, the *Programme* for the *agrégation de philosophie* is a general structure of examination that accredits students for teaching philosophy at the secondary and/or post-secondary levels. The oral and written phases of the exam require that the student have a high level of competence in both the *lecture linéaire* and *explication de texte*—that is, in the literary analysis and close reading of philosophy. Prior to 1968, the student had to be able to do this in Greek and Latin as well as French and in either German or English. After 1968, the Greek and Latin requirements were dropped, and a student could opt to offer an *explication de texte* in either German, English, or Arabic. The content of the *Programme* changes from year to year, but one thing remains almost a constant: most of the major French philosophers of the twentieth century were prepared at the École Normale Supérieure, which is, de facto, the hub of French philosophical training.[92] This means that most of what counts as French theory in North America is a product of ENS training.

Between 1900 and 2000 there were ninety-five *Programmes* published; because of the wars, none occurred between 1915 and 1918 or in 1941 or 1945. "Plato appears on the written *Programme* 36 times, Aristotle 31 times, Kant 31 times, and Descartes 28 times. The only others to appear more than twenty times are the Stoics (25 times), Spinoza (22), and Leibniz (22). The only eighteenth-century figure to appear more than ten times is Rousseau (11); the only nineteenth-century figures to appear more than five times are Nietzsche (8, first appearance in 1970) and Hegel (7, first appearance in 1968); and the only twentieth-century figure to appear more than two times is Bergson (6, first appearance in 1951)."[93] For the *Programme* there is, of course, also the oral component, about which Schrift notes something provocative and interesting: Whereas Nietzsche appears on the writing *Programme* for the first time in 1970, his *On the Genealogy of Morals* appears on the reading list for the first time in over thirty years in 1958. That there would be an immense attention to, writing about, and engagement with Nietzsche's work from the late 1950s onward (noting as before that the first book written on Nietzsche in France after the war is Deleuze's 1962 monograph)—so much so that we can talk about Nietzsche as being foundational to postwar French theory and, indeed, to poststructuralism—should not surprise us in the least.[94] This is not to say that the *Programme* is determinative of the form and content of modern French philosophy, but it is to say—in concert with Schrift—that it is of enormous impact to a student's intellectual formation and to one's future scholarly production.

Political Relations

At the May 4, 1959, Cannes Film Festival, François Truffaut screened his directorial debut and one of the crowning jewels of French New Wave cinema, *The 400 Blows (Les Quatre cents coups)*. The English translation of the title doesn't capture the sense of the French, which is an idiomatic expression that means "to raise hell." The film is a coming-of-age story that recounts the troubled youth of Antoine Doinel, a fourteen-year-old boy who is a lightly veiled alter ego of Truffaut himself. The film's accolades and successes are well deserved, in part because it affords us a snapshot into Parisian life in the 1950s. And what Truffaut screens for us, perhaps unsurprisingly, is a stark contrast between pre- and postwar France as embodied by the clash between adults and youth, between the old and the new. At the core of the plot is Antoine's total rejection of the established system of authority embodied, once again, by the abusive schoolteacher and the equally abusive and dismissive parents. And the movie ends, famously, with Antoine escaping the juvenile detention center where he had been sent after attempting to steal his stepfather's typewriter and running toward the ocean. The final shot is a freeze frame close-up of Antoine as he breaks the fourth wall, turns to the camera, with the ocean as his backdrop: a visual metaphor, no doubt, of a country needing to escape the constraints of its immediate past, embrace its moment of newness and the ocean of possibilities—and no doubt dangers—at its feet. The new France's future is an ocean of uncertainty.

What is certain is a profound desire to break out of the enclosures of the past. "Many who witnessed the suffering, humiliation and powerlessness of the defeat and Occupation wanted to draw a line through the past and were ready to usher in a new beginning," write Gilles Bousquet and Alain Pessin.[95] More to the point, the break with the past also required a break with the philosophies of historical progress and idealism. What the new France shared with America was a rejection of totalitarianism. But unlike America, in France it was a decidedly leftist ambition. In the immediate postwar period, France did not suffer the pains of a Red Scare. On the contrary, the figures of the French Resistance that were able to survive would ensure that the placid intellectuals of the prewar period who acquiesced and retreated from political involvement out of either fear or sympathies with Vichy would not persist. As is well known, Sartre championed the figure of the engaged intellectual and did so by developing a philosophical career that shunned academic specialization or, indeed, disciplinary constraints. Trained by the best schools and the best readers and writers and having a demonstrated record of disdain of the bourgeois establishment that date back to his ENS days, Sartre would create a cultural empire of writers and publication venues, salons and lecture halls, conversations and rumors, as well as a distinguished and prolific collection of his own writings. He never joined the French Communist Party, nor would he ever declare himself a Marxist; his philosophical orientation toward self-authenticity wouldn't allow it. But that didn't stop him from championing the dismantling of the bourgeoisie, as is evident throughout the pages of the in-augural issue of *Les Temps Modernes*. With *Les Temps Modernes*, Beauvoir and Sartre recruited as part of their editorial collective some of their most cher-ished and longest-standing classmates, including Raymond Aron, Maurice-Merleau Ponty, and Albert Ollivier. But Sartre is not the focus of my story. My focus is how the dispositions of the political resistance found expression in the intellectual milieu of postwar France. And though Sartre is often deemed a central figure in this regard, as Sunil Khilnani's *Arguing Revolution* shows, his philosophical commitments of individual authenticity, political action, and intellectual engagement also quickly became that to which many postwar French thinkers would turn away. It is an odd twist of fate—or perhaps the price of international fame and success—that the figure most associated with the critique of France's bourgeois establishment would quickly become the one most strongly attacked for his bourgeois humanism.

The project of *Les Temps Modernes* was to create a venue for the public intellectual to engage in perpetual resistance through an exacting *lecture lineaire* of society. This was its editorial intention: "While *TM* (*sic*) is mani-festly to be a literary and political journal, its uniqueness is to reside in the fact that the two designations are to be taken as interdependent."[96] It was an immediate success that lasted until its recent closing in 2018. It was also one of the first publications (the other was the magazine *Esprit*) that would con-sistently voice its opposition to France's colonial atrocities in Vietnam and Algeria, evinced in the decision to run an article entitled "L'Algerie n'est pas la France" in the November 1955 issue.[97] To this, one must add its impressive se-ries of articles between 1946 and 1950 on the French war in Indochina.[98] As noted, it is difficult to underestimate the effect of these two colonial wars on the philosophical and political imaginary of postwar France. Simply put, im-mediately after the Occupation of Vichy and of the horrors that came of that, France was tasked with starting the country anew. And just as those efforts got underway, the country was forced to contend with a further reconfiguration and reimagining of its nationhood, which already had a fragile legitimacy.

Kristin Ross's discussion of the familial metaphor as a dominant trope in articulating the relationship between France and its colonies, and especially Algeria, is noteworthy. As Aristotle warns, metaphors are tricky things; and given the kinds of attentions to language that accompany France's official instruction on reading and writing, it's not surprising that one of the most prominent philosophers of language in postwar France, Paul Ricoeur, would eventually compose a magnum philosophical treatise on metaphor.[99] The problem of metaphors and their interpretation—as Ricoeur shows—is not so much a matter of the meaning of the metaphor, but a matter of how the two different terms in a metaphor (the tenor and the vehicle) relate to one another in order to generate an understanding: how can two things that have no business relating actually produce a comprehensible meaning? In the case of the relationship between France and Algeria the dominant metaphor used by statesmen and the press alike was the marriage metaphor: these are two countries that belong together despite being different and, indeed, far away from one another. Here is Ross: "What Jacques Soustelle called 'the great rupture between the Sahara and France,' the national divorce whose violence and tensions defined the entire period, was transpiring in the midst of a massive postwar French reaffirmation of the couple as standard-bearer of the state-led modernization effort and as bearer of all affective values as well."[100] The France/Algeria marriage was going through a divorce and, unlike the paternalistic metaphors used to describe the relationship between France and Indochina just a few years earlier (where France is the clear parent and Indochina the child), France viewed Algeria as a young bride who would benefit from a communal cohabitation among *near* equals. "The marriage metaphor's representation of a free but indissoluble union was reasserted by Edgar Faure" in February 1955, explains Ross. "Algeria composes a unity with the Metropole that nothing can compromise," he said.[101] In all of this, what was clear and what Ross rightly stresses is how the political, the economic, and the sentimental are all interrelated. Such national sentiments would eventually be put into full view not just in the magazines and the newspapers of the period that regularly ran photographs of events on the ground producing a visual colonial archive that was well on its way to becoming unbraided, but also in the publication of Saadi Yacef's 1962 *Souvenirs de la Bataille D'Alger*, which would be turned into Gillo Pontecorvo's masterpiece, *The Battle of Algiers* (1966).

So much for the immediate postwar political landscape that was the milieu during which all the thinkers that would arrive onto American soil in the 1970s received their intellectual and political formation. Central to that moment of impression are several things: the status of authority and its relationship to idealist philosophies of the State; the matter of the relationship between identity and difference as made manifest in the violent political struggles of anti-colonialism; the validity of state-imposed forms of reading and writing; the issue of credentialing standards in relation to state authority; *and*, most importantly, the various events of dismantling that transformed not just the identity of France as a political union but the metaphysics of relations, the very fact that *how* things relate—the structures, forces, and intensities of a relation—are not natural to the objects related. Many political and philosophical insights emerged from this period; but the most important (and not just for the purposes of this book) is a palpable, legible, and visible sense that no unity or totality can constitute a natural relation. This, I want to stress, is not simply a metaphysical proposition (though it is *also* and very much that); it is a *political* metaphysic born of actual politics that informs the political imaginary of sentimental empiricism.

Catholic Substances

When considering the development of the cultural and political structures that participate in framing the intellectual milieu of postwar France, it is difficult to overlook the function and role of the Catholic Church. Philip Nord has traced some dynamics of the Catholic cultural renaissance in the interwar years, especially in the 1930s—a timeframe Nord refers to as a "golden age" of Catholic culture in France. There was a strong Catholic presence in the arts that saw the rejuvenation of sacred pictorial art, as well as in prose and the musical arts. The standard story of religious decline as a result of Renaissance humanist paganism was part of the discourse of rejuvenation: "What was needed," Nord explains, "was a new age of faith, and there were examples in the past to look to: Golden Age Spain and the French Middle Ages. Then faith burned with unparalleled intensity. Saints and knights strode the earth, but they served in obedience to a wider purpose, to the human collectivity of which they were a part, to the will of God whose instruments they were."[102] The villains of this story of remaking are humanism and secularism and the accompanying relativism that follows any defense of value pluralism. This is, of course, not an unfamiliar story, which was also available in postwar America, as Forrester notes.[103]

All this laid the groundwork for the Catholic embrace of Vichy. Vichy "beckoned to Catholics."[104] "The Church's enemies were also the regime's enemies: liberalism, parliamentarism, Freemasonry, 'excessive' Jewish influence, communism. Not least of all, Vichy proclaimed its determination to reeducate the nation's youth."[105] And Catholic leadership was also Vichy leadership, especially regarding youth education led by the Catholic scout movement with the founding of the Fédération national catholique des Scouts de France (SdeF) in the 1920s, which promised and delivered on a robust combination of militarism and clericalism. In short, the successful rejuvenation of French Catholicism in the interwar years helped institute the virtue and value of heroic idealism that, especially given the success of the scout movement, was strong among young French men and would be amplified with the popularity of Hergé's (penname of Georges Remi) *Tintin* Belgian comic series.

Tintin was a Catholic scout who pursued adventures in the Soviet Union and the Congo to help defeat communism and support African imperialism. The comics (created between 1929 and 1939) appeared in the Catholic Fascist newspaper *Le Vigntième Siècle* (The Twentieth Century), whose director, the Abbé Norbert Wallez, instituted the children's version of the newspaper *Le Petit Vingtième* in 1928 and made Hergé (who had begun working for the magazine the year before) director. But it was Wallez whose conservative Catholicism and admiration of Mussolini dictated the geopolitics of Tintin.[106] Wallez had himself published a book of political philosophy in 1923, *Bélgique et Rhénanie: Quelques directives d'une politique,* in which he "devoted a section of his book to an anti-Semitic diatribe in the polemical mode of the extreme right; he pilloried the financiers of the stock market. Also, in the pure Germanophobic tradition of the old Belgian right, he exalted the Catholic Rhineland, damning the militaristic Prussian heretics and calling for a Belgian-Rhineland Federation."[107] All of this to say that Catholic culture in twentieth-century France was fervent.

During World War II, Catholic activists and resisters ultimately dismayed by Vichy turned to competing currents of thought—communism, Gaullism, and of course republicanism. At the core of this about-face remained the strong presence and influence of the Catholic youth and the associated dominance of the ideal of Catholic action characteristic of a Paulinian engagement with and in the world and whose core values included Christ-centric community building practices and public charity. Young Catholic farmers were responsible for France's so-called silent revolution through the formation of agricultural syndicalism as well as agricultural modernization; all the while, the leading figures of the Christian ideals of heroic action, Le Cid and Jeanne d'Arc, retained their place of privilege in the cultural imaginary.[108] This meant that even after World War II, Catholicism retained its place of privilege in French culture. "The Catholic reawakening, born of the interwar decades," Nord concludes, "changed the face of France, and indeed, as has been hinted, how France looked to the wider world."[109]

Students and young scholars of the *agrégation* in the postwar years would have grown up immersed in such a renewed Catholic culture with the fortitudes of its dogmas and educational practices well ensconced, including the metaphysical and theological status of transubstantiation; in short, they were fully immersed in the Scholastic metaphysics of Aristotelian substances, and not just as part of their *Programme* preparations. The significance of this will be discussed in greater detail in the chapter on Gilbert Simondon, who is the postwar thinker who most committedly articulates a critique of Aristotelian hylomorphism and, *ceteris paribus*, of metaphysical essentialism and human exclusivity. The infamous critique of identity or anti-essentialism associated with postwar French thought was received in the United States as a form of Nietzschean moral relativism and anti-humanism. But within the French context, the critique of essences is a metaphysical critique of the political authority and power of church and state that, despite its various permutations, never abandons its Thomist commitments.

St. Thomas Aquinas relied on Aristotle's metaphysics to successfully defend the impossible: the Christian faith (which is a precondition for salvation) is sustained by the *intellectus fidei* (understanding of faith), which is that element of faith (the second is divine revelation, or *principia revelata a Deo*) that protects the intellect from deception, and this is based on received (i.e., objective) reality. This reality is received in and through the Eucharist whose mystery of transubstantiation remains, for Aquinas, a mystery of faith (in that he does not explain the mechanisms of transubstantiation in order to "prove" the process of conversion of substance). But what Aquinas's metaphysical adoption and elaboration of Aristotelian essences allow him to do is to defend the mystery as a possibility. Thus, "instead of elevating the mystery from the level of mere imagination to an allegedly higher plane of a truly conceptual comprehension, along the lines of Hegel's *Begriff* (concept), in its very metaphysical contemplation the *intellectus fidei* will preserve the utterly simple, literal sense of the dominical words 'This is my body which is given for you' (Lk 22:19; RSV), more familiar to Aquinas in its Vulgate rendition, 'Hoc est corpus meum quod pro vobis datur.'"[110] Simply put, by making received, objective reality an element of faith, Aquinas gave a metaphysical justification for why the Eucharist (and thus transubstantiation) is necessary to Christian salvation by relying on Aristotle's metaphysics of essences. Such a Thomistic Aristotle remained at the core of Catholic dogma and would be reaffirmed in Pope Pius XII's encyclical *Fidei Donum: On the Present Condition of the Catholic Missions, Especially in Africa* (April 21, 1957).

For French intellectuals critical of the Algerian war, the appearance of this Papal Encyclical, a year before the collapse of the Fourth Republic, that proclaimed the church's mission of giving the gift of faith through the evangelization of the Eucharist, could not have seemed coincidental. Couple this with the metaphors of marriage and sacred union that accompanied the political discourse around Algerian independence, and one can't help but conclude that a metaphysics of essences was at the core of the political imaginaries *and* the "actual politics" of postwar French thinkers and writers. A theological doctrine founded on Aristotle's metaphysics of substances that was premised on the law of non-contradiction (the *tertium non datur*) was in every meaningful sense a political metaphysics. Or better, what it meant was that metaphysical dispute (and not simply its dismissal) was and is the site of deep and profound political contestation on and about the nature of political equality, political freedom, power, and authority.

The soul is the substance upon which church power and authority are exercised: the soul is the immaterial essence of human existence whose telos is the afterlife, which (as we know) can go either way. The possibility of salvation comes only through the access granted by the church and its power of the sacraments, the most important of which is the sacrament of the Eucharist that allows the soul to commune with the transubstantiated body and blood of Christ. Thus, an attack on Aristotelian metaphysics as would begin to be formulated in this period meant two things: the need to articulate an alternative metaphysics that was neither substantialist nor teleological, and thus not exclusively grounded on a consequentialist account of deed, action, and spiritual health; *and* the need to rely on a readerly intellectual milieu that understood how and why the articulation of a new metaphysics is also a political critique of extant theories of power, order, and social organization. In short, the dissolution of the metaphysics of essences *is* a critique of political authority and—especially—a critique of the totalizing power of church/state authority over everyday life.

All of this, it should be noted further, was exacerbated, given that the main advisor to Pope Pius XII's penning of *Fidei Donum* was the ultraconservative French archbishop Marcel Lefebvre, a defender of Catholic exclusivism, a future leader in the conservative bloc of the Second Vatican Council, and a devout partisan of Vichy who would eventually be excommunicated under Pope John Paul II on July 1, 1988, for his "schismatic act by the episcopal consecration of four priests, without pontifical mandate and contrary to the will of the Supreme Pontiff."[111] *Fidei Donum*, or "gift of faith," begins with the following statement: "The gift of faith, which through the goodness of God, is accompanied by an incomparable abundance of blessings in the soul of the Christian believer, clearly requires the unceasing homage of a grateful heart to the divine Author of this gift."[112] The document goes on to defend the importance of "Apostolic zeal" in ensuring that the multiplication of African nations is accompanied by a multiplication of lay and ordained missionaries that will go to Africa and teach its population how to overcome internal strife and look to the church as the great unifier. A classic document of Catholic evangelicalism, this is also a geopolitical treatise that insists on the fact that, despite the internal wars of a continent, unification is possible through the church and Christ's Apostolic mandate. Through the missionaries, the document affirms, "the fullness of the apostolic dignity resides, which as St. Thomas Aquinas testifies 'is the chief dignity in the Church.' That apostolic fire which Jesus Christ brought upon the earth must issue from their hearts and inflame the hearts of all Our faithful children and arouse in them fresh zeal for the missionary tasks of the Church everywhere."[113]

When Hume penned his famous invective, which threw to the flames the textbooks of Scholastic metaphysics, he was not denouncing metaphysical philosophy tout court, as the Vienna Circle logical empiricists understood he had. He was, in fact, referring explicitly to the Scholastic defense of Aristotelian substances (and, *ceteris paribus*, transubstantiation) as inherited from a Thomist commentary and defense of *intellectus fidei*.[114] Hume had no time for substances, of this there is no doubt. But this doesn't translate into affirming a general dismissal of all metaphysics. In fact, and as I argue throughout, sentimental empiricism appreciates the metaphysics of relations in its commitment to the sentiments understood as the dispositional powers of union and disunion that coordinate adjacencies. French thinkers of the 1950s would discover that sentimental empiricism *does* offer an anti-essentialist metaphysics as the basis of a critique of authoritarian power and rule.

Engines, Turbines, Factories, and Washing Machines

We have looked at education, religion, and politics as elements in and of the intellectual milieu of postwar France. As with our genealogy of postwar America, our focus has been on how the various composite parts collected here stage the scenes of perceptibility and attention that render the actuality of politics readable. Our structuring conceit has been that institutional and cultural practices of reading carry with them epistemic virtues. Both milieux thus evince a concerted effort to rethink the relationship between professional academic life and political life. America substitutes the idea of the engaged public intellectual with the policy analyst and advisor exemplified in the figure of the RAND researcher who produces policy reports that function as advice to princes' literatures.[115] In France, "public" is not reducible to "policy" but is, instead, expressed in the explosion of a literary culture (and publication industry) that gives the politically engaged intellectual places to disseminate their critical denunciations of colonial rule and authoritarian power. The possibility of such forms of written prose having political influence was aided by the fact that many presses and publications had direct ties to political parties, as did the authors, editors, and reviewers therein; Anna Boschetti refers to this as the literary field of *Les Temps Modernes* that includes the ever important and coalescing role of the *agrégation*, whose function, as we noted, was not only pedagogical but also sociocultural in that it united many of the key figures of the period, most visibly Simone De Beauvoir, Jean-Paul Sartre, Raymond Aron, and Maurice Merleau-Ponty, all of whom had been classmates at one point or another.[116]

I would now like to proceed by looking at one other shared element that is taken up in very different ways: the experience and subsequent analysis of technical objects of the everyday variety. It is a remarkable fact about French postwar reconstruction that "French people, peasants and intellectuals alike, tended to describe the changes in their lives in terms of the abrupt transformations in home and transport: the coming of objects—large-scale consumer durables, cars and refrigerators—into their streets and homes, into their workplaces and their *emplois du temps*. In the space of just ten years a rural woman might live the acquisition of electricity, running water, a stove, a refrigerator, a washing machine, a sense of interior space as distinct from exterior space, a car, a television, and the various liberations and oppressions associated with each."[117] Kristin Ross notes two cultural-political themes emergent from this period that are coincident with the explosion of everyday technical objects (and the factories that produced them): cleanliness and speed. Not surprisingly, these are thoroughly gendered themes: the former belongs to the household and is associated with the explosion of magazine advertising promoting cleaning detergents, while the latter is coupled to male mobility, thanks to new and affordable cars, motors, and car factories that employed the men who built the motors (i.e., like the Citroën "Deux Cheveux" and the Renault Frégate).

It is not surprising, then, that someone like Roland Barthes would develop a theory of criticism through a series of essays published in the mid-1950s for the literary magazine *Les Lettres Nouvelles* on engines, soap bubbles, detergents, wrestling, the new Citroën, billboard advertising, plastic, margarine, and many other newly arrived and lived objects of French modernization. These critical vignettes would, in 1957, be published as *Mythologies*, a founding text of French structuralist criticism that introduces the use of Saussurean linguistics for the semiological critique of everyday life. Technical objects are the coded symbols of a culture. These codes can be analyzed in a systematic way to produce an account of the political myths of a people.

Like the American intellectual milieu of the Cold War university, the French postwar theoretical *dispositif* is one imbued with science and physics, logics of relations, geopolitics of domination, cybernetics and information theory, and a drive to resist totalitarian forms of power. Again like the American context, these elements are all imbued and interrelated with one another. There are, however, three notable differences: the first is that France's political culture is primarily preoccupied with its colonial heritage that is the fulcrum upon which political issues and public debates pivot; the second is that the French Communist Party, though never a majority party, nonetheless has an active presence in French politics and intellectual life throughout the postwar period; finally, religion, especially French Catholicism and its accompanying *intellectus fidei*, plays a significant role in the political and educational milieux of postwar French life. To these differences we must also add a series of important intellectual developments that have not been discussed in this chapter but are worth noting (though they have been treated with much care by other scholars): the rise and growth in the interwar years of French Hegelianism, especially after Alexander Kojève's Paris lectures on the *Phenomenology of Spirit* (1933–39) and the highly influential discussion of the master/slave dialectic therein and Edmund Husserl's equally influential Paris lectures (1929 and published in 1931 under the title *Cartesian Meditations*) that, for all intents and purposes, mark the birth of French phenomenology.[118] To all this I would also add the publication of Maurice Merleau-Ponty's first book, *The Structure of Behavior* (1942), that offers a trenchant critique of reflex behavior and introduces a phenomenological discussion of perception into the larger concerns of Gestalt psychology. This work had begun as a research proposal (in 1933) when Merleau-Ponty for the first time "emphasizes the significance of the perception of one's own body for distinguishing between the 'universe of perception' and its intellectual reconstructions, and it gestures toward the 'realist philosophers of England and America' (presumably William James and A. N. Whitehead, as presented in Jean Wahl's 1932 *Vers le concret*) for their insights into the irreducibility of the sensory and the concrete to intellectual relations."[119] Finally worth noting is the immense and immeasurable influence of three important philosophers of science who had a lasting impact not just on the intellectual development of French postwar thought, but on the structure and content of the research of their students: Georges Canguilhem, Jean Cavaillès, and Gaston Bachelard (Bachelard is the one who introduced the concept of "epistemological break" that would be central to Louis Althusser's reading of Karl Marx's work as well as for Thomas Kuhn's development of the idea of paradigm shifts in scientific revolutions). It is thanks to these three philosophers of science that a rich program of research develops in and around what Michel Foucault (a student of Canguilhem's at ENS between 1946 and 1951) would call the modern episteme.[120]

Conclusion: Political Theory, Reading, and *Mésentente*

The point of my reconstructions is not to decide which intellectual milieu is better, but to emphasize the divergent ways of imagining the relationships between politics and philosophy and how these divergencies were emergent from different practices, and thus different expectations, of scholarly reading and writing. The expectation of scholarly reading for the American intellectual milieu is one that understands a text as having identifiable properties and that values the goodness of a work in terms of the transparency, legibility, and verifiability of meaningful statements. Hence the association between the expectation of clarity in writing (and thus the suspicion toward siren songs and other esoteric mysticisms) and scholarly excellence. The good scholarly work is one that is clear and well argued; it has integrity and sincerity, where everything is in full view: nothing is hidden behind ornament, just like the Quaker Testimony of Simplicity that adheres to the principles of plainness in speech. This enables clear communication between participants to ensure the smooth coordination of interests through various technical means, including contracts.

In the French intellectual milieu, politics is not reducible to orchestrated agreements but is a problematic that demands articulation, just like the student articulates the problematic of a work when preparing for one's *agrégation* exam. The literarity of politics—its visibility and its perceptibility through the activities of reading and writing—is not a matter of identification, transcription, and verification. Rather, the literary expectations require one to attend to the architectural composition of the work and to the relation of the parts therein. The knowledge produced by this formalist reading practice (which, it goes without saying, is thoroughly consistent with Aristotle's account of literary criticism in *Poetics*) is oriented toward an explanation of the relationship between parts and whole. Meaning is not established through the derivation of a proof, nor is it presupposed as the necessary property of an object; it is what the reader produces by handling the various parts of a work. Therein lies the founding *mésentente* that helps us appreciate how the two intellectual milieux discussed in these pages think the relationship between "politics" and "philosophy" differently.

2

Mimesis, the *explication de texte*, and State Thinking

In this chapter I wish to lay out the cultural politics and pedagogical history of the *explication de texte* in order to give greater access to the claim I'm making regarding postwar France's entanglement in and with a political metaphysics of mimesis. By a political metaphysics of mimesis I mean a system of judgments, practices, hierarchies, and privileges that prioritizes the reproduction of the same through time in order to guarantee political stability and order.[1] "The same" is the English translation of the French *le même*—a moniker for mimesis if ever there was one—that also encapsulates such terms as "identity," "the given," and "common sense"; it is a term that interrogates the political claim that belonging demands identity. A political metaphysics of mimesis relies on the idea that relations (in language, in society, in nature) are fixed and determined; these relations include the criterial hierarchies that organize the reigning order of things. Such an edifice appears, at first glance, to stand as an abstraction. But it isn't. What seems like a conceptual abstraction actually refers to an established and institutionalized set of practices, conventions, laws, and sentimental and aesthetic dispositions that establish the criteria and qualifications for selection into various national political, military, and educational offices. More than what we might conventionally identify as a branch of state bureaucracy, what I am referring to is a technical system—or political *dispositif*—for the adjacency of value with rank that offers access to political authority and power, but whose legitimacy is never questioned (i.e., never *needs* defending) because systemically automated through mechanisms of its own reproduction from one generation of students to the next.[2]

To begin to have a sense of these institutionalized practices, I ask the reader to imagine teaching a university course and not being able to choose which authors or works will be the basis for the examination of that program of study.[3] Now imagine that the administrative entity that decides the content of the exam syllabus is not housed in the university where the program of study is taught, but is directed by the national ministry of education. Next, imagine that part of the expectations for qualification are not only the content of the material you may be required to prepare, but also a specific style and form of knowledge presentation and exposition. And finally imagine that in all of this, the entity responsible is the most powerful and most well-funded of all the ministries in the government's portfolio.[4] From a North American perspective this sounds like a nightmare scenario that violates all sorts of real or imagined norms of academic freedom. But in France, it is the case that the Ministry of Education is the largest funded government agency, whose 2015 budget for grade school education stood at 65 billion Euros, with an additional 23 billion Euros for higher education and research. This, as M. Martin Guiney notes, is more than twice the budget of the French Ministry of Defense, which stood at 31.4 billion Euros in 2015.[5]

Ezra Suleiman's *Elites in French Society* is unrelenting in elaborating how, since its inception in the Napoleonic reforms at the beginning of the nineteenth century, France's education system and curriculum have had one objective in mind: the maintenance of political stability through the formation of elites. Suleiman cites Napoleon, who is unequivocal on the matter: "I want to create a corporation not of Jesuits who have their sovereign in Rome, but of jesuits (*sic*) who have no other ambition than that of being useful, and no other interest than the public interest."[6] One of the cornerstones of Napoleon's reforms was uniformity—of dress, of curriculum, and of method of instruction. The unofficial template (unofficial, albeit acknowledged as the aforementioned passage suggests and as I will discuss further) was the Jesuit's 1599 *Ratio Studiorum*. The purpose for this regimentation was (and still is, according to Suleiman, who published his book in 1978, ten years after the May 1968 student revolts) that of training and instilling in future elites "*le sens de l'Etat*" (the sense of the State).[7]

Again following Suleiman, it is important to stress that in France the education system is two-tiered: there are universities, and then there are the *grandes écoles*. These latter are exclusively responsible for training French elites, and they have "a direct link to the major corporate organizations of the elites: the grands corps."[8] These latter institutions are tasked with carrying out functions on behalf of the State. One enters the *grands corps* by graduating at the top of the class of the corresponding *grandes école*. For instance, a student must graduate at the top of one's class and pass the requisite exams (the *concours*) at the École Normale Supérieure (ENS) in order to receive the license to teach. But access to that trajectory is partitioned at multiple levels, not the least of which is the fact that the ENS is in Paris, thus making it nearly impossible for someone who hasn't grown up and pursued one's education in Paris to participate in the rigors of the ENS. As France's former prime minister and then president Georges Pompidou once declared without irony, "One is a *normalien* as one is a prince by blood."[9]

As I present it, sentimental empiricism finds expression as a series of critical dispositions responding to this system of adjacencies, hierarchies, and segregations of political authority and elite formation; that is, it is a response to the authority and legitimacy of knowledge as a state-sanctioned institution. As Pierre Bourdieu notes, "Inquiring into the conditions of possibility of reading means inquiring into the social conditions that make possible the situations in that one reads."[10] When thinkers like Deleuze, or Beauvoir, or Foucault, or Althusser, or Irigaray, or Bourdieu, or Rancière, or Derrida read works of philosophy and, in doing so, decry the presence of state power and domination therein, they are addressing a specific set of state-sanctioned practices, institutions, and conditions of reading, writing, and political-aesthetic judgment formation that are necessary to elite formation. It is in this sense that the generation of authors I discuss imagined their enterprise as a "science" of criticism. Theirs is a response to extant critical operations available via the *explication de texte*. The *explication de texte* is a formal method of literary criticism championed by Gustave Lanson, one of France's most active educational reformers at the turn of the nineteenth century. The *explication* extolls a formal method of reading necessary for passing the *Concours*. But to iterate a point already noted, "literary criticism" in this national context is not siloed to the professional qualifications of literature departments, as we like to imagine it might be in the Anglophone academy and certainly, as we learned in Chapter 1, Barry Smith imagined in his invective to the *Times*.[11] In France's national and pedagogical milieu, literary criticism simply refers to practices of reading, writing, presenting, and the public performance of understanding of what one knows. In other words, literary criticism is what one does in and through any act of reading and writing. It is through practices of reading, writing, and the presentation of one's understanding that both the student and the Maître demonstrate a capacity to reproduce what is learned *and* the formal knowledge procedures through which learning is achieved.

The critical impulse of sentimental empiricism is formalist. Recall the labile premises I outline in my introductory remarks. It is notable that none of those premises is oriented toward a critique of the meaning or content of terms. Rather, the focus is on the formal system that arranges and adjoins terms in such a way as to produce criteria for knowledge and understanding. In other words, sentimental empiricism is a mode of criticism that looks to the intersections and adjacencies in and through which elements participate and coordinate with one another. It is in this sense that I spoke of sentimental empiricism as oriented toward forms of political participation and solidarity. The sentimental empiricist thinkers I study consider the political metaphysics of mimesis as a dispositional power of social and political arrangement operationalized in the *explication de texte*. This technical operation is never named as such simply because it would have been understood by any reader in France to be the site of attack, though Roland Barthes is the one thinker who is most explicit in his refutation of the fallacies of "Lansonisme."[12] For these thinkers, the critical task is not one of dismantling or negating the content of any specific work. Instead, what sentimental empiricism offers critical theory is an attention to the particular manifestations of adjacency, coordination, and forms of partaking that extend throughout the systems of authority. The question of how to introduce and exact political change is thus directed toward altering particular forms of partaking and nodes of adjacency within the system and *is not* directed at changing another's system of beliefs, preferences, or ideas. In other words, sentimental empiricism is not liberal-democratic if, by this, we understand political change to occur via the modification of beliefs or opinions of others. Sentimental empiricism understands political change as transformation—or, indeed, as an ontological rupture—of the modes of adjacency and forms of relation that orchestrate political access and legitimate authority.[13] Beauvoir, for instance, does this by exploring the forms of adjacency that coordinate gender as a system of power, especially in and through the sexual relation as a structuring mimetic regime of gendered power; Wahl does this by introducing the radical empiricist idea of the irreducible plurality of being into an account of concreteness so that any account of unity can only be a metastable becoming toward concreteness; and Deleuze, Simondon, and Foucault each have their ways of attending to the particularity of adjacencies as a mode of critical political theorizing.

I follow Alan Schrift, Kristin Ross, John Guillory, Ezra Suleiman, and Pierre Bourdieu in noting the centrality of France's education system to the innovations of postwar French political thought.[14] In this respect, tracing the cultural politics of reading and writing addresses a principal conceit of my research: mimesis *is* the political theory of the modern state that contains within it a system of hierarchies for judging and selecting the good or true representation from the false one. This is so because the State demands the reproduction of knowledge through institutionalized forms of imitation that become the credentialing standards for the dissemination of French republican universalism.

There is one final point I wish to add that I consider crucial to our appreciation of sentimental empiricism: As we noted in Chapter 1, the thinkers we associate most prominently with postwar French thought arrived in the English-speaking world through the Anglophone university's literature programs. This makes some sense, given the emphasis on literary criticism in their works, and especially on the formal practices of reading and writing as sites of political and ethical contestation. As I argue in this chapter, such attention to literary criticism is better understood as an attention to a political metaphysics of mimesis that operates as a state-authorized *dispositif* of social reproduction. But what is often missed in this story is the central role that developments in the philosophy of science played in France immediately preceding, during, and after the war. Though I do not discuss them in any detail, I would be remiss if I did not note the central importance and insurmountable influence of the published works *and* teachings of Georges Canguilhem, Jean Cavaillès, and Gaston Bachelard.[15] To the extent that sentimental empiricism is a critical theory, it is born of the work and influence of the French philosophy of science that will focus on operations of discontinuity and rupture in systems of knowledges.

The Institution of "*le même*"

Education as a principal responsibility of national government had been the official policy in France since the reforms to the *baccalauréat* (the degree required for university admission) recommended by Alexandre Ribot in 1902. This said, those reforms need to be considered in reference to a longer history of the development of the modern French education system throughout the nineteenth century and to the Dreyfus Affair of 1894. Central to this story, I would add, is the establishment of copyright laws. The 1793 "Declaration of the Rights of Genius," Carla Hesse shows, were "a Jacobin effort to abolish the vested interests of inherited privileges, to consecrate the bearers of enlightenment, and to enhance public access to the ideas of the Enlightenment."[16] In short, the history of the modern French state, and of French republicanism more generally, is importantly a story about French readership and how the legitimacy of state authority is embattled around criteria of a literary education.

The modern development of French intellectual formation began with the Napoleonic education reforms instituted with the May 1, 1802, decree. Key among these reforms was the establishment of thirty *lycées* whose principal function was the education of future military and civic elites. This further resulted in a series of standardized norms that were not just pedagogical but also cultural and organoleptic. Teachers were expected to remain celibate and live in common housing, standard clothing for teachers was obligatory and included military-like decorations (i.e., epaulettes to indicate rank), and "classes began and ended not at the sound of a bell, but to the role of a military drum."[17] Moreover—and perhaps most importantly—the 1801 Concordat between Napoleon and the papacy (that remained in effect until 1905) reinstituted religious education in France and made it so that the Catholic Church, and especially the Jesuits, could continue to control the education system by applying the rigors in literary competence and classical rhetoric of the 1599 *Ratio Studiorum*.

By the end of the nineteenth century, in other words, there was a highly rigorous and intensely segregated, two-tiered educational system in France that was designed to differentiate between social classes. "What distinguishes the primary and secondary school system was the social origin of their pupils and the social status of their teachers on the one hand, and on the other hand the type of career and place in society which their pupils could aspire to."[18] Only the pupils of the *lycées* and *collèges* were given permission to sit for the *baccalauréat*, which is the exam that selects students for entry into the *grands écoles*. The education system thus revolves around the selection function of the examination system (i.e., the *concours*) that guarantees the cultural capital necessary for socioeconomic and political mobility.[19]

By the end of the nineteenth century forces advocating educational reform were making their way throughout France. Though nineteenth-century social stratification was hardly stultified, what became clear throughout the closing years of the Second Republic was that if any change was to be instituted, then the Jesuitical control over education needed to be curtailed. This intensification of educational reform produced what amounted to yet another battle between the ancients and moderns that was galvanized around the Dreyfus Affair and the political dissensions it generated. Chief among these is the emergence of the Dreyfusards, who would give evening lectures to working-class audiences as part of what were referred to as *les universités populaires*.[20] More capacious than this, however, was the general sentiment against the Catholic education of the masses that would culminate with the educational reforms of 1902 that removed the qualification in Greek and Latin for the *baccalauréat*, and thus for entry into the university system. That is, a way to satisfy the Dreyfusard appeal to *laïcité* would be to eliminate ancient languages from the curriculum, since these were explicit doctrinal tools of the Catholic Church (recall that Catholicism remained a Latin-based faith throughout the twentieth century, until the 1965 reforms of the Second Vatican Council).

As is well known, the charges against Dreyfus proved to be the result of a pervasive anti-Semitism prevalent among the military elites, all of whom had received a classical Napoleonic/Concordat education. The reason some of France's intellectuals became Dreyfusards was, no doubt, for all the noble liberal and anticlerical reasons one might consider. But it is also the case that the Dreyfus Affair presented a strategic occasion to, once and for all, take the power of education, and especially the power of literary formation, away from the Catholic Church. Retiring the Latin and Greek requirement for the *baccalauréat* didn't simply mean retiring two strongholds of ancient letters; it meant retiring an apparatus of knowledge production that determined that Latin and Greek were the foundations of grammatical and linguistic understanding—that is to say, of reading as such.[21] This was accomplished by substituting the traditional program of the "*humanités classiques*" with that of the "*humanitées modernes.*"[22] And all of this was done in the name of *laicitée* as the supreme value of the French Republican universalism.

As Guiney notes, the 1902 reforms "symbolized the Republic's attempt at democratization, at taking literature out of the hands of an elite and placing it at the center of the process of civic instruction."[23] At the same time, they didn't offer a clean break with their Jesuitical past. It is true that eliminating the Latin and Greek requirements for the *baccalauréat* enabled a shift from the ancient humanities to a modern humanities, but the mode of learning and the privilege given to mimesis as a credentialing standard of pedagogical accreditation and selection into the civil service of Maître(sse) did not change. This said, and before I proceed to my treatment of Gustave Lanson's contribution to the 1902 reforms, I wish to make one thing clear: the critique of humanism, the critique of knowledge, the critique of consciousness, and the critique of mimesis that have become cornerstones for identifying some of the critical emphases of postwar French thought have as their primary point of reference the educational debates and reforms of 1902 and the appeals to *laicitée* that emerged through these reforms and in relationship to the Dreyfus Affair. In other words, for France at the turn of the century (but really, throughout the twentieth century), the terms "humanism," "consciousness," and "mimesis" were (and are) essentially contested terms of political discourse and not just specialized literary and/or philosophical concepts. They comprise a morphology of the State Apparatus because they are tools for the dissemination of French republican universalism.

On the 1599 *Ratio Studiorum*

The Society of Jesus received formal institution in 1540, but it wasn't until 1599 that the *Ratio Studiorum* would be codified and established as the manual that would instruct the principles of education for all Jesuit schools throughout

Europe as well as the mission of the Jesuitical ministry in the New World. The success of this system of pedagogy, and of the Society's mission, is not to be overlooked or underestimated. With A.M.D.G. as their motto (*Ad majorem Dei gloriam*, "for the greater glory of God") the Jesuits quickly established a reputation for excellence in academic preparation and instruction as well as a phenomenal track record for the building of schools. As one historian notes, within the first century of its institution the Society of Jesus established more than 300 colleges throughout Europe, and in France alone, 40,000 students were registered in seventy-five academic centers.[24]

More than a manual for scholarly instruction, the *Ratio Studiorum* remains a classic work of Renaissance humanism that aims at the education of the mind for the purpose of the beatification and salvation of the human soul. It is, as one historian of French education notes in 1910, "the Magna Carta of the order to-day, and the youth are still taught under the influence of the Jesuitic humanism of three hundred years ago."[25] It is not possible to go into a close reading of the *Ratio Studiorum* here. But it is worth noting that the *Ratio Studiorum* is a source code for the transmission of Aristotelian scholasticism as well as classical Latin and Greek literature. These remain a constant in Jesuitical education (the *Ratio* was modestly amended in 1832, but not in scope, direction, or content) because of the conviction that scholasticism and classical literatures "offer abiding and universal values for human training," as Allan Peter Farrell notes. He continues:

> Through close and inspiring contact with classical culture, students will have high human standards by which to appraise not only works of art and of literature but also social and political theories and movements. . . .
> Scholastic philosophy, particularly scholastic metaphysics, crowns the training in the liberal disciplines by laying a sound foundation for an adequate understanding, interpretation and application to human life of the sciences, both natural and social, and by providing a rational basis for faith—becoming the handmaid of religion, which is the proper and supreme integrating principal of knowledge.[26]

Farrell's description, though penned in 1938, needs little updating or explanation. For all intents and purposes, this is how most French citizens were educated throughout the nineteenth century, including those military and civic leaders that were directly involved in the Dreyfus Affair and the ensuing crisis of the Third Republic. But more to the point, whether they were educated by Jesuits or not, this classical humanist pedagogy remained the gold standard of France's *esprit d'état* that, as Bourdieu notes, demands *"une pensée d'État"* (a thinking of the State).[27] The composition of individual taste, of class consciousness (through taste), and of national excellence all pivoted around the education of the soul through the dictates and precepts of a classical, scholastic, humanist curriculum: the perfection of the soul could only happen through the State.

Key among such precepts—and central to the *Ratio Studiorum*—were the three rhetorical dictates of prelection, disputation, and emulation. The prelection (or *praelectio*, taken from Quintillian's *Institutio Oratoria*) was a preferred element of Jesuitical instruction. As the word indicates, prelection (or "pre-reading") refers to practices of reading that are intended for all topics (not just literature). Students were expected not only to read works on their own, but to read them together in class. To this day, prelection finds expression in the development of course syllabi that assign readings that both students and professors are both expected to complete before class. In the case of the instructor, the *Ratio* is explicit in chastising any form of improvisation or impromptu reflection. Indeed, the development of taste should not be based on impressionism but on sound study and on the simultaneous development of ratio and will, mind and soul. As such, any attempt at extemporaneity must be avoided at all costs. The prelection also has an order of explanation that must be followed and that will allow for correct understanding. Here is Farrell, once again, offering a helpful summary of the order of prelection:

1. Give the argument or theme of the whole work.
2. Show the connection between one assignment and another, sometimes between one passage and another.
3. Explain some of the more difficult sentences of a passage; not many, nor verbatim, using the author's own words, but ordering them in a simpler fashion.
4. Occasionally resolve a complicated sentence into parts, and comment on a word here or there whose meaning may be doubtful. If such a word can be explained with fair exactness using another Latin word, well and good; if not, then use the vernacular.
5. Comment briefly on certain points of syntax or propriety of word and phrase, or figures of speech and the structural qualities of the work.
6. Occasionally cite similar turns of expression from other reputable authors. This should be done only rarely in the grammar classes, and not often in the prelection.
7. In the prelection of a poetic work, obscurities should be clarified by giving a prose rendition, not of individual words, but of one or more verses.

8. In the upper class of grammar, the teacher may now and again employ the vernacular if he feels that it will make the meaning of some Latin word or phrase clearer. But he is not to dictate such vernacular renderings to the student, nor allow them in the repetition.

9. Finally, the teacher should accommodate his explanation to the grade and progress of the class, omitting details that are no longer necessary to help the students understand the text.[28]

The pedagogical centrality of prelection makes several things clear. At the heart of the *Ratio Studiorum*'s enterprise isn't simply a classical humanist commitment to ancient texts, but a scholastic metaphysical commitment to the project of understanding, married to the activity of reading understood as repetition and imitation. Criticism is an art of reading to the extent that it is tasked by the directives of prelection. Finally, all of this is possible if we concede—in a quintessentially Aristotelian fashion—that the integrity of the work is premised on the right relation between parts and whole, and that any unity regards the formal arrangement of parts that are composed according to the laws of causation.[29] The task of the reader is to understand the work by elaborating the natural relations between parts through explanation, through referencing, through definition, and so forth. Another way of saying this is that what the *Ratio Studiorum* dictates is the primary importance of mimesis and, especially, of the formal procedures in and through which understanding is achieved. Finally, the publicity of prelection produces a shared common sense. Understanding is exercised publicly, as it were. All of this, taken together, will shape the student's mind, will, and soul and provide for them "high human standards by which to appraise not only works of art and of literature but also social and political theories and movements."[30]

For the Dreyfusard reformers of the French education system, Gustave Lanson chief among these, the possibility of taking power away from the Catholic Church's stronghold on civic education and the moral shaping of middle-class souls and minds lay in the development of a new, more modern, humanist education that wrested literary criticism away from scholastic rhetoric and introduced to it the modern methods of positive science. Hence the innovation and development of the *explication de texte* that remain wholly within the readerly conventions of the prelection but are updated and given a more secular, anti-clerical twist. Now it is the nation's republican soul—not the Christian soul—that must be instilled in the student through formal conventions of reading and understanding. This is not exactly the imbibing of the nation through the mother's milk that Jean-Jacques Rousseau had advised in the "Education" chapter of *The Government of Poland*, but it is a very close second.[31]

Gustave Lanson and the *explication de texte*

When we speak of national educational reforms in France, we might be persuaded to consider France's national borders as our referent. But France is unique in that the stratification and segmentation of education that we are addressing makes it so that those who belong to the class of instructors all coexist within a very circumscribed 2.5 square kilometer area of Paris—the fifth arrondissement on the left bank of the Seine River—known as the Latin Quarter. It is not an exaggeration to say that "the fifth" was the epicenter of French education, national education policy, and public intellectual life. The Latin Quarter is so named because this is where Latin was taught, studied, and spoken by the students walking its streets. In short, the Latin Quarter's soundscape projected a classical humanist curriculum.

Consider also the geography of the Latin Quarter: The Collège de Sorbonne was founded in 1253, and the Sorbonne buildings still house several university structures managed by the Chancelleries de l'Universitées de Paris, including the Sorbonne University. A fifteen-minute walk away from the doors of the Sorbonne (1.5 kilometers away) one finds the imposing structures of the Rue d'Ulm, otherwise known as the École normale supérieure (ENS), the most prestigious academic institution in France, known for having graduated a number of famous "normaliens," including Henri Bergson, Simone Weil, Maurice Merleau-Ponty, Jean-Paul Sartre, Michel Foucault, Louis Althusser, Émile Durkheim, Pierre Bourdieu, and Jacques Derrida, to name a few (Simone de Beauvoir attended the Sorbonne, as did Gilles Deleuze, both passing the *agrégation*; in Beauvoir's case, she came second in the *agrégés* rankings to Jean-Paul Sartre, though she was, at the time, the youngest student ever to pass her exams). Finally, the fifth is also where the French Ministry of Higher Education, Research, and Innovation is housed. French intellectual culture in the twentieth century was centered in a geographically and architecturally circumscribed area whose confines (628 acres, making it slightly larger than the University of California, Los Angeles's 467 acres) control the State's system of epistemic legitimacy. This is both why and how Louis Althusser and Michel Foucault (to name two famous instances) would account for education as a quintessential Ideological State Apparatus (Althusser) or disciplinary structure (Foucault).[32] In no uncertain terms the Latin Quarter (as cultural myth, geographic territory, and architectural space) is the site and source for the marriage between state power and mimesis.

Gustave Lanson was in every way a product of and reformer of this intellectual milieu. His innovations were explicitly directed at restructuring French literary criticism, but by the 1950s and 1960s Lanson became the site of critical attack by the proponents of the nouvelle critique. What Roland Barthes would call "Lansonisme" had attained the status of a renewed scholasticism, with its unequivocal and unapologetic commitment to a scientistic literary history married to the positivistic psychology of Théodule Ribot. Tellingly, a 1968 American reviewer of Roland Barthes's work notes that in Barthes's view of Lanson "to write is always to imitate, to copy, to reproduce. The work has models and the only accepted relation between work and its models is that of analogy. The major labor, then, of the academic critic is that of searching out biographical traits (or, now the Freudianism has become respectable in the French university, psychological traits) in the author's life which match those personages, actions, and sentiments which occur in his (sic) works. Thus, academic criticism is always an attempt to set work, piecemeal, in relation to something else and represents a premature flight from the work into the world of the author."[33]

As we note in this description of Lansonisme, there is very little that would distinguish it from the nineteenth-century French adherence to the *Ratio Studiorum*, especially given the emphasis on the Aristotelian mimetic relation of model/copy via imitation and analogy; to wit, *le même*. Indeed, the description of Barthes's view of Lansonisme is a striking analog to Truffaut's opening scene in *The 400 Blows*. More than a set of instructions, pedagogical demands, or aesthetic concepts, it is important to appreciate the model/copy relation as a union that marries mimesis with sovereign power. This aesthetic and political concern is easy enough to trace in Gustave Lanson's reform ambitions, which are unapologetic in their denunciations of the nineteenth century's continued adherence to the pedagogy of l'ancien régime and "the absurdity of using only monarchic and Christian literature to train the future members of a democracy where state religion does not exist."[34] And yet, through the form of instruction and the literary practices established and instituted via the *explication de texte*, it is also possible to appreciate how, by the mid-1950s and beyond, France's nouvelle critique would reject Lansonisme and its Jacobin ambitions on exactly the same grounds that Lanson had rejected the *Ratio Studiorum*. What we see in these debates in and around literary criticism is the expression of the fundamental problem of political difference. Crudely put: How is political change possible, given a social and cultural milieu designed to reproduce values? This, as we noted, is *the* problem of political and aesthetic criticism that is taken on by postwar sentimental empiricism.

Lanson was a committed Rousseauvian and Dreyfusard who adhered to the belief that a secular left must educate France's children if the country were ever to extricate itself from the clutches of Catholic dogmatism and the social hierarchies of l'ancien régime. By the time he became involved in the educational reforms of 1902 he had been teaching in the *lycées* for nearly two decades and was clearly fed up with the predominance of classical rhetoric as the model of literary education. His solution was to provide a secular pedagogy rooted in a positivist literary history that would teach the French nation how to read and write *l'esprit Français*. At its core the *explication de texte* would reject the classical humanist ambitions of the *Ratio Studiorum* for what Lanson would champion as *"les humanitées modernes."* This meant that he was fully on board with removing the mastery of classical Latin and Greek from the *baccalauréat* curriculum in the hopes that a literary culture could develop beyond the classical humanism currently taught in the classroom. This was crucial because throughout the nineteenth century France's literary curriculum remained entrenched in a Louis XIV imaginary of *"le Grand siècle,"* and by 1880 the eighteenth-century authors—including the leading philosophes of the revolution like Voltaire, Diderot, Rousseau, Buffon, and Montesquieu—remained mere excerpts to the literary curriculum of the *lycées*, "so that no single work of theirs acquired legitimacy as a whole, with the selection of passages serving as filters."[35] Even the selections that were chosen were not taken from either the political or literary writings of these authors but mainly from their correspondences or their histories, as in the case of Voltaire, whose "masterpiece" was considered to be his *Le siècle de Louis XIV*.[36] By the late nineteenth century, the seventeenth century was still considered the golden age of French culture, both in terms of literary identity and its pedagogy: *l'esprit Française* remained royalist.

Thus Lanson's dilemma (as articulated by D. S. Watson): "How is it that a nation which for the most of the last century has included the word 'equality' in the national motto, can still provide a state educational system which perpetuates hereditary inequalities?"[37]

Lanson's answer was to reinvent the French literary canon by reinventing the formal practices of reading and writing. This was the first monumental step. The next one was to make this new form of literary criticism the foundation of the Dreyfusard reforms by instituting it as a national requirement. It was in this respect that the production of meaning and understanding became a national project through the reproduction of formal reading practices. Key to both these elements was (once again) imitation, the tool through which learning would happen. Lanson's contributions to the educational reforms of the Third Republic provided a national program of mimesis.

This is somewhat ironic. As Guiney notes, the "standards of literariness inherited from the Jesuit tradition, understood as mimesis both in the sense of restricting the literary canon to works that claim fidelity to the outside world, and imitation of classical style, continued to define literary studies in the *lycée*, long after the Ministry had declared them irrelevant."[38] And Lanson fought hard to fix this. But at the same time, the *"psittacisme"* (Fr. parroting) of the classical humanist system that Lanson so vehemently condemned remained. The *explication de texte* demanded it, especially given that Lanson wanted to shift literary studies away from what he referred to as an "impressionistic" historiography to one rooted in a positive history. This meant that science and literature were at the heart of Lanson's ideal of civic instruction, which was intended—in good Dreyfusard, republican, and militantist fashion—to implement the ideals of *laïcitè*.

But classical repetition and imitation proved impossible to excise from pedagogy. This, because the *explication de texte*—which, after 1902, did successfully become the basis of all literary instruction in France—remained modeled on the older system of philological exegesis.

Here's how it works:

The *explication de texte* is comprised of two stages. The first stage requires the student to perform a grammatical/philological explication of the literal meaning of a work. This is the work of "analysis" that explains a text's grammar and structure. The next, equally important, step is the explication of the historical significance of the literary work.[39] This is where positivistic observation enters the fold, to the extent that the work is observed as an empirical datum of history. In its historical context, a work's importance is established in relationship to other great writers. Hence the insistence on literary history, and especially French literary history, in Lanson's own published works (*Histoire de le Litérature Française*, 1896, and *Corneille*, 1898, among nearly thirty other monographs published throughout his lifetime). Both of these steps establish the genius of the author, but also do the work of situating the author within a canon of minds that evince *l'esprit française*.[40] Here is Lanson on precisely this point: "The work undertaken by M. Brunatière is a necessary preparation for this history of French literature that we lack (and that I hope he gives us one day): a history in which, in general, broad, and continuous movement drives all literature, each genre follows its own movement, in which, from the environment of all the circumstances that determine and condition works of art, the incommensurable power of individual originality emerges brilliantly."[41]

Lanson would repeat this civilizing sentiment throughout his ambitious career as educator. In 1925, in one of his many entries in the professional publication *Études françaises*, he would assert that "the *explication des textes* is identical in essence to the practical exegesis in the religious sciences and ancient Greek and Latin philology" (L'explication des textes est identique en son essence à l'*exégèse* pratiquée dans les sciences religieuses et dans la philologie grecque et latine).[42] And again in 1909 he would specify the function of grammatical analysis thusly:

> The basis of all French explication ("de toute explication française"), it is well understood, is the grammatical analysis of the text. There is no greater and more dangerous error than to eliminate or execute poorly the labor of the grammarian under the distant pretext we are making literature. The exact intelligence of the vocabulary and syntax of the author, in the page that we have chosen, is not only necessary to fix the literal sense but it prepares the subtle knowledge of the nuances of the idea.[43]

Despite his efforts to avoid Jesuitical parrotism in the name of a universal *laïcitè*, Lanson recapitulated the habitudes of classical humanism: to whit repetition and imitation. Simply put, the emphasis on philological and grammatical analysis presupposes the close study of grammar and philology taught on a thoroughly repetitive and mimetic basis. It is true that in the *explication de texte* one does not mimic the stylistics of classical rhetoric; but it is also true that through it one mimics the grammatical analysis of philology that was always part of the classical rhetorical tradition. The only difference here is that a science of grammar replaces a rhetoric of style.

The same holds for the status of positive history, the second pillar of Lanson's methodological innovations in literary criticism. If the literariness of a work is established by public acts of reading (or what Jacques Derrida would years later refer to as "acts of literature"), the empirical fact of a literary canon, and thus of national taste, would be established. "The history of each masterpiece," Lanson will affirm, "contains within it an abbreviated history of taste and of the sensibilities of the nation that produced it and of the nations that adopted it."[44] The science of literature, as manifested in the practice of literary history, offers a scientific form of criticism that annotates national excellence and civic virtue. More than this, what the *explication de texte* enables is a public display of intelligence through acts of literature that establishes the mastery of the student and the illocutionary power of taste as a credentialing standard for selection in the national corps of educators. "The Lanson method of literary history," one scholar notes, "was a hybrid theory caught somewhere between positivist historiography and classical philology."[45]

After the 1902 reforms Lanson shifted careers, moving from his role as *maître de lycées* to becoming the director of the Sorbonne. It is here that Lanson was able to institute his program of literary criticism at the level of university instruction. During this period he not only wrote some of his most important works in literary history of the time, but he also penned many articles and gave many lectures on the importance of literary history and the *explication de texte* in the modern humanities. This is not to say that Lanson remained unchallenged in his ambitions and reforms. On the contrary, though the Sorbonne may have been dubbed "the Dreyfusard university" and, after Lanson, renamed the "nouvelle Sorbonne," other Parisian universities were not as quick to accept the shift from the ancients to the moderns that the nouvelle Sorbonne championed. Charles Péguy, for instance, would not hesitate to direct his ire against Lanson; this, to the point of challenging Lanson's sincerity by accusing him of instrumentalizing the Dreyfus Affair to his advantage for professional and academic promotion.[46] Regardless, Lanson would remain at the helm of the Sorbonne until his forced retirement in 1927 after a media prank by Jean-Paul Sartre, Georges Canguilhem, and others resulted in a public outcry against his mismanagement of student affairs.[47]

Conclusion

In *Communal Luxury* Kristin Ross explains how pedagogy underwrites France's modern political culture "from the end of the eighteenth century through its consolidation after the demise of the Commune in the Third Republic, all the way up to its panicked reiterations in recent years in the face of schoolgirls in scary head-scarves." She then goes on:

> The pedagogical vision of politics works, broadly speaking, in two ways: first, it conceives of teaching as forming the society of the future. And second, it conceives of politics as the way to instruct the world (parts of which, as we are repeatedly told, "are not ready for democracy"). The right to education is thought throughout to be the condition for the formation of political judgment. One learns to become a citizen. A system of education must be established whose task is essentially one of uplift and integration through knowledge: the worker or peasant is raised to the status of a sovereign citizen—raised, that is, to a dignity he or she possesses by right but not in fact. The peasant must be uprooted from his provincial soil just as in our own time the new arrivals, the immigrants or the newly poor, must be separated from their social or cultural difference by offering them the keys to the country: political access through education.[48]

Uplift and integration were, without a doubt, Lanson's ambitions with his *explication des textes*. By training students how to read, Lanson (and others) believed that they could train students how to make judgments; not just aesthetic judgments, but political and philosophical judgments, too—that is, good republican

judgments. Attending to the form of the work, to its grammar, and to its structure would allow students to learn how to articulate taste in relationship to the
work itself, to the author's genius, and to a history of taste that was a national
history but also a universal one. In other words, literary criticism provides a
dispositional attachment to reading as an expression of national character. This,
in turn, would result in the production of a common sense (*le même*) through
ritual participation in the "acte de lecture" that is, in no uncertain terms, a
political act of aesthetic prelection. The *explication de texte*, however, would
not be constrained to the study of literature. This is a crucial point to keep in
mind. On the contrary, it would be the method of reading and understanding
in philosophy, sociology, and many other disciplines. Lanson's "*humanités
modernes*" and their Dreyfusard ambitions would be augured by this new formal method of reading and criticism that conjoins aesthetic perception,
philosophical understanding, and national greatness.

The result, as many have noted, is the reproduction of a homeostatic
system of social and political selection through practices of mimetic competence—to wit, the establishment of cultural capital as a credentialing power
for access to political power and authority. As Roland Barthes would note, the
emphasis on erudition in reproducing the legitimacy of mimesis as a system
of institutional qualification and national excellence was both politically and
aesthetically inadequate, given "stubborn adherence to a determinist ideology
which holds that the work is a 'product' of the 'cause' and that exterior causes
are more 'causal' than others"; and he continues: "Perhaps too because to shift
from a criticism of determinations to a criticism of functions and significations
would imply a profound conversion of the norms of knowledge, hence of
technique, hence of the academic critic's very profession . . . we can understand that the university hesitates to convert its requirements."[49] It is in this
sense, then, that we can appreciate the political metaphysics of mimesis as a
republican episteme.

The problem of selection, mimesis, and the model/copy relation as requirements for knowledge and understanding are at the heart of the sentimental
empiricist thinkers I study because, as we have seen, this dynamic is at the
heart of the political culture they inhabit and, as *agrégés*, are expected to reproduce. For them, the task of political thinking is to develop a form of criticism rooted in a metaphysics of difference-in-itself that responds and rejects
the political metaphysics of mimesis. The generation of thinkers I study could
no longer adhere to the national aesthetic and civilizing mission of *l'esprit
Française*, given the traumas and horrors of Vichy, of the war in Indochina,
and of the Algerian war. For them the matter was one of radically rethinking
the history of philosophy as the history of criticism and judgment via an

interrogation and rupturing of the artifices that hold adjacencies together. Born of their shared tutelage by prominent philosophers of science (Canguilhem, Cavaillès, and Bachelard chief among these), the postwar French thinkers I study would articulate theories and practices of political and aesthetic criticism oriented toward rupturing the links that adjoin determinations. In this regard, it should be of little surprise that one of the great public literary achievements of the engaged intellectual would be baptized "*Les Temps Modernes*" after the 1936 Charlie Chaplin film, where Charlot's corporeal tics and twitches rupture an industrial system of machinic reproduction by frenetically tinkering with joints, gears, pulleys, and levers. Chaplin's Charlot would no doubt seem to these postwar cinephiles like the embodiment of "a criticism of functions and significations" whose bodily spasms fracture the powers of adjacency that ensure technical reproducibility.[50]

PART II

Dispositionalities

Preface

In Part II, I move away from a focus on the political aesthetics of literary criticism in postwar France and concentrate on the thinkers that form the foundation of this study: Jean Wahl, Simone de Beauvoir, Gilbert Simondon, Gilles Deleuze, and Michel Foucault. I treat each of these thinkers as making significant contributions to the political theory of sentimental empiricism, and I do so by providing accounts of their philosophical and aesthetic writings as explicit political interventions. That is—and to be clear—I read their philosophical and aesthetic discussions as *explications des textes* that generate their political philosophy. I reiterate this point because—as I note in my introductory remarks, and as the preceding pages make evident—the sentimental empiricist critique of the dispositional powers of domination that I take to be a common thread in the writings of these authors occurs not only through the arguments, descriptions, debates, observations, and interventions contained and referenced in the philosophical writings of these authors, but also in the selection of sources and the theoretical topics addressed and studied in those writings.

The texts discussed in the following chapters participate in various writerly and aesthetic genres, including film, literature, science and technology studies, and theater, among others. The political intervention, however, is not always indexed as such but can be acknowledged if one attends to the selection of texts, the philosophical topics, and *"l'enjou"* (i.e., problematic) that compose the formal reading practice of the *explication de texte*. For example, Deleuze's *La logique du sens* (*The Logic of Sense*, 1969)—a study on the role and function of meaning and meaningless in philosophy—is not generally classified as a work of political philosophy, nor do the arguments within it have any prima

facie political implications. But if we appreciate that the category of meaning had important political stakes in the context in which Deleuze wrote
this text, we can quickly appreciate how his selection of and focus on the
concept of "paradox" throughout the work (beginning with his treatment of
Lewis Carroll's nonsense literature) was itself a political intervention. The
ability to "make sense" (the capacity for and ability to engage in rational
meaning-making, in the making of meaningful arguments) was central to
republican virtue training at every step of the French educational system,
and it was only by successfully navigating that educational system that one
could gain entry to France's Grands Corps. Thus, the capacity to make
sense was a necessary condition for political participation. Deleuze's choice
to engage in a careful treatment of "non-sense" has political ramifications,
implicitly challenging the privileged status of meaning and the exclusivity
of dialectical criticism. A paradox, in other words, is not a contradiction that
may or may not be resolved via the linear operations of reason; it is an im-
passe to thought—an intermediality in which the inherent dualist relation
of dialectics (the mode of thought prescribed and recognized as the exclusive mode of legitimate argumentation in the French educational and
political culture) cannot work as a procedure for thinking. "Paradox," he
affirms at the outset of the book, "is initially that which destroys good sense
as the only direction, but it is also that which destroys common sense as the
assignation of fixed identities."[1] Deleuze publishes this in 1969, but the sentimental empiricist seeds that express the radical pluralist ambitions of this
passage and the desire to pluralize the metaphysics of critique beyond a
dualist model of dialectical thinking begin to take hold in the immediate
postwar period.

In this example, one can see how, by keeping the political aesthetics of the
prevailing reading culture in mind, it is possible to appreciate how the texts
addressed in the following chapters—all examples of postwar French scholarly production—contain and enact political interventions, even when discussing topics not obviously related to political themes, and do so in ways aimed
at illuminating the dispositional powers of domination.

What connects Part I of this book with Part II is an attention to (a) how our
authors each engage with the perspective and insights of sentimental empiricism as outlined in the Introduction and (b) how these authors use these tools
in their efforts to describe domination as something more complex than a dualist antagonism.

For these authors domination does not require a unitary and inherent relation (e.g., master/slave) necessary to operationalize its effectivity. It can also
operate between entities on a parallel footing who make no explicit claim to

holding power because they don't have to, since the systematic mores and manners of good sense and propriety work to arrange social and political segrega-
tion. The dispositional powers of domination don't oppress and constrain; they
partition the orders of things. This—as I suggest in Chapter 4—is what Simone de Beauvoir discovers and innovates in her account of patriarchy: To appreciate the systematic domination of patriarchy requires that we do away with
the exclusivity of a hierarchical model of domination. Patriarchy is a form of
domination, no doubt; but its form is manifest as a pervasive system of dispositional arrangements of gendered bodies (e.g., the feminine body belongs at
home, the male body belongs in the workplace).

Through its appreciation of the sentiments as dispositional powers of arrangement, sentimental empiricism innovates an analysis of systematic domination by which is meant domination through a system of affects, judgments,
sensibilities, and perceptibilities that organizes and orders social and political
partitions. When domination operates dispositionally, neither non-interference
nor negation are available options for political critique, because the locus of
power is not singular, but plural and distensible. The sentimental empiricist
authors that follow will thus develop experiments in critical thinking that are,
themselves, born of the dispositionality of the sentiments with a view to dismantling the pervasive effectivity of the dispositional powers of domination.

3

Jean Wahl, Empirico-Criticism, and the Concrete

Within the framing of this study, but really within the context of twentieth-century French philosophy, Jean Wahl stands as a towering figure. His list of publications is colossal, as is his list of "firsts." He was one of the first French philosophers to write and lecture on Nietzsche, Hegel, Kierkegaard, and Heidegger. His philosophical monographs and essays are to this day regarded as foundational sources that introduced French philosophy to ideas and trends throughout Europe, America, and Britain not canonized in the *Programme*. Most importantly for our purposes, Jean Wahl made available to France and French philosophy the radical empiricism of William James as well as the metaphysical empiricism of Whitehead, Hume, and many other English-speaking thinkers. The minor tradition of sentimental empiricism in postwar French thought exists thanks to Wahl's work: his writings, his teachings, and the circle of intellectual camaraderie he nurtured throughout his life.

Wahl's influence extends even beyond traditional academic settings, whether book or classroom. The Collège Philosophique is a case in point. Inaugurated by Wahl in 1946, this was a non-institutional and unofficial philosophical forum that would meet three times per week, often in Wahl's home, and that provided an audience for many thinkers who would not appear in the official *Programme*. Most famously (though this is far from the only such incident), Wahl was a great friend to, sustainer, and admirer of Emanuel Levinas, whom he supported throughout the difficult years when Levinas was not affiliated with any formal academic institution. The Collège Philosophique would provide Levinas with a home and an audience during this time. When Levinas was despairing that the academic press Éditions Gallimard had refused to publish his magnum opus, *Totality and Infinity*, and was on the brink of jettisoning it, it was Wahl who reached out to him and insisted that he defend the work as his primary thesis for his *doctorat d'état*, which Levinas did in 1961 in his mid-fifties "before a committee comprised of Wahl, Marcel, Vladimir Jankélévitch, Paul Ricoeur, and Georges Blin, as well as an audience that included Maurice Blanchot."[2] It is reported that Wahl began his comments at Levinas's defense by affirming that "We are here to evaluate a thesis about which other theses will be written."[3]

Wahl's work has received little attention in the English-speaking world.[4] On the North American side of the Atlantic he remains relatively unknown, except among scholars of Gilles Deleuze's work, as Wahl was the person who introduced Deleuze to Anglophone empiricism and literature. It is also very likely that Wahl encouraged Deleuze to write his first book on Hume.[5] This said, recent work in political theory, English literature, and media studies has turned to many of the themes found in Wahl's works as well as some of the authors Wahl discusses in his writings. Kennan Ferguson, Melvin Rogers, Steven Shaviro, Erin Manning, Alexander Livingston, Jane Bennett, William Connolly, Brian Massumi, Jairus Grove, and Antoine Bousquet have all revisited the writings of William James, Alfred Whitehead, and other empiricist authors to reconsider a realist metaphysics of pluralist becomings.[6] In France, too, there is a resurgence in interest in the thinkers that Wahl introduced and made available; notably, Bruno Latour, Isabelle Stengers, and David Lapoujade all engage the British and American empiricism Wahl curated throughout his academic career.[7] Given this impact, it is difficult to imagine recent scholarly developments in posthumanism and affect theory without Wahl's direct or indirect contributions.

In this chapter we will focus on one of Wahl's more important works, at least for our purposes: *Vers le concret* (1932). This work remains untranslated, though an excellent translation of its preface has recently been published. We will also engage his 1920 doctoral thesis, which Wahl wrote under Henri Bergson's supervision, *The Pluralist Philosophies of England and America*, published in English in 1923 and currently available as a public domain work (no new editions have been issued since the original Open Court Company edition). In my reading of Wahl's works, I wish to elaborate what he identifies as empirico-criticism, whose main threads include a rejection of the metaphysics of substance as well as a pluralist ontology of the concrete.

One of Wahl's fundamental theses in *Vers le concret* also extends throughout his many writings—namely, the recuperation of the concrete in light of philosophical idealism's rejection and denunciation of it. "The idealist," he affirms in the first paragraph of the Preface, "will always say that what is claimed to be concrete is only an abstraction or a fiction."[8] He goes on to explain that the real problem is that such claims confuse that inadequacy of language in grasping the concrete with the fact of concrete experience; this because the concrete is not graspable as a totality available to representation, but is an incomplete but real (in the sense of felt) experience. The task is neither to explain, justify, or define the concrete, but to account for its manifestation. To do so, one must acknowledge the impact of the concrete in the interconnections that assemble it, or what Wahl refers to as the "quasi-continuity of assembled weaves."[9] Existence for Wahl is not Being, nor is it a final synthesis in reason; it is a *towardness*. In this chapter we will explore Jean Wahl's studies of empiricism and pluralism with a view to unpacking this sense of *towardness* of the concrete that structures his pluralist metaphysics and that informs so much of sentimental empiricism's attention to the dispositional powers of domination.

Wahl and Simone de Beauvoir are pivotal figures in this study. Whereas in Chapter 4 we will elaborate Beauvoir's contribution to sentimental empiricism through her articulation of the dispositional power of patriarchy, Wahl provides sentimental empiricism with an account of empiricism "defined by its affirmation of the nondeducibility of being, by its affirmation of the datum, that is, its affirmation of something immediate, which is welcomed, received."[10] Wahl understands that the empiricists he studies (James and Whitehead chief among these) discovered a "feeling of the given" that denies the intelligibility of Being.[11] "Being for them is feeling rather than idea, something that rebels against reason; it is not at all the essence of reason."[12]

I begin this chapter with a portrait of Wahl's life. I then proceed to discuss his empirico-critical philosophy. Mine is a partial and circumscribed study of Wahl's oeuvre, given how prolific he was.[13] Moreover, I only focus on his philosophical writings and merely mention some of his internment camp poetry. Further than this, I do not comment on his historiographical approach to philosophical exposition, which Emanuel Levinas rightly describes as an "inexhaustible exploration of the thought of others."[14] Though I do consider these as crucial to Wahl's philosophical enterprise, it is simply not possible to take responsibility for all these elements within the limits of this chapter. This said, as we approach our considerations of Wahl's works, it is important to note one thing: The development of his philosophical insights, especially those that matter to us here, is provided in and through his commentaries of other thinkers. In other words, when studying Wahl, we study his acts of reading—his *explications de texte*—and the transcriptions of these readings that are his writings.

Jean Wahl: The Interwar Years

Wahl never wrote about politics, though his life was decidedly marked by the political turmoils of twentieth-century Europe. He was born in Marseille in 1888 into a secular Jewish family. His father, Edmund, relocated the family to Paris when he became a professor of English at the Lyceé Janson de Sailly, occupying the post previously held by Stéphane Mallarmé.[15] In a postface to the Italian edition of *Vers le concret* his daughter, Barbara Wahl, notes Wahl's life-long dedication and love of American literature, and especially the poetry of Walt Whitman.[16] Levinas too remarks on Wahl's "precocious bilingualism," which helps explain the facility he had throughout his life with English authors whose works were not readily available in French translation and that made his philosophical enterprise, especially *Vers le concret*, "outside the protective enclosure of the system."[17]

Wahl entered the École Normale Supérieure in 1907 and graduated at the top of his class in 1910, passing the *agrégation* and beating out his friend Gabriel Marcel as the top student. Several years later, he would be part of the *agrégation* commission that would evaluate Sartre's and Beauvoir's results and, "according to Maurice de Gandillac, Wahl later told him he had a hard time deciding to whom to give the first prize."[18] After a decade, during which period he taught in various secondary schools, he received his *doctorat* under the direction of Henri Bergson, submitting both a principal and complementary thesis; the first of these was "The Pluralist Philosophies of England and America," while the second is entitled, "The Role of the Idea of the Moment in the Philosophy of Descartes." He then took university posts in Nancy and Lyon before accepting a professor's chair in the history of philosophy at the Sorbonne in 1936.

What we know next of Wahl's life is thanks in large part to a typescript account based on conversations between Wahl and Elizabeth Alden Green, a professor of English at Mount Holyoke College, as well as a 1945 *New Yorker* profile.[19] The day before the German invasion of Paris (June 14, 1940), Wahl escaped the city, thanks to the assistance of three Chinese students who helped him join his parents in the south of France, where they had taken refuge. He returned to Paris that fall to begin teaching at the Sorbonne but was forced to retire in December upon the passage of the first Vichy Statute on Jews of October 3, 1940, which prohibited Jews from participating in many professions, including the professoriate. Nonetheless, he remained in Paris and would meet with students regularly but unofficially for the rest of the academic year. In July of 1941 he was arrested by the Gestapo and tortured at La Santé prison, where he remained for thirty-six days on the charge of "impertinence."[20] Moore and Schrift's Introduction remarks that "although conditions at the prison were difficult, he was allowed to keep the English edition of Shakespeare his brother had given him; he read three plays a day and translated some of the sonnets into French, and although refused access to a pencil, he managed to write several poems by means of scratching on packaging paper with a needle."[21] These would be the first of what would eventually be collected as *Poèmes de circonstance* (Lyon: Confluences, 1944). One of these was published in the *New Yorker*:

> **Evening in the Walls**
> You are with me this evening, all my
> friends.
> I hear your voices in the dark, I see your
> faces.
> My power is made of all your little
> powers.
> And as I think of you I gather strength.

The bulk of his poems, however, would be written during his imprisonment at the Drancy internment camp.[22] Notoriously more brutal than La Santé, Drancy nevertheless allowed its prisoners pencils and the possibility of congregating. This meant that Wahl was able to write over one hundred poems while there and even deliver a lecture on Bergson.[23]

Wahl's escape from France and his arrival in the United States is not unlike many other émigré Jewish intellectuals of the time: at once serendipitous and daring, given the reality of imminent death. In 1933 the Rockefeller Foundation had set up a fund to help deposed scholars around the world, and in 1940 it established an emergency program for European scholars whose lives were threatened by the Nazis. Wahl was placed on this list, along with Georges Gurvitch, Alexandre Koyré, Claude Lévi-Strauss, and Karl Löwith.[24] The core of what would become the École Libre des Hautes Études at the New School for Social Research in New York was being formed during the time of Wahl's imprisonment in Darcy. His inclusion on this list enabled him to be officially appointed a professor of philosophy at the New School, which was the first step necessary for him to receive an invitation to an American teaching post.

Wahl was informed of his appointment, as well as of the official letter from the New School, by the head nurse of the Drancy prison. More official confirmation would come in a letter from his brother. But Wahl rightly seemed apathetic about the news, given his imprisonment and what felt like an unlikely outcome. This is where serendipity intervened. Drancy camp was struck by a dysentery epidemic, and to minimize the contagion on the soldiers, the

Nazis elected to release a handful of prisoners. Thanks to the intervention of the head nurse and the camp doctor, Wahl was among the few who were released from Drancy, after sixty-four days. He remained in France for a year after his initial arrest, escaping Paris and living in Lyon—then still part of unoccupied France. He had no intention of leaving France, but it became clear in early 1942 that the partial German occupation would soon be total. In June of that year, he received the documentation he needed and boarded a Portuguese ship that left Marseille and arrived in the United States on June 30.[25] In the United States he took up his post at the École Libre at the New School. While there, he also accepted the invitation from Helen Elizabeth Patch (then chair of the French and Literature departments at Mount Holyoke) to organize a series of symposia, which he did in the summer of 1942. These were a huge success and resulted in his being hired as faculty at Mount Holyoke, where he taught until 1945 and where he kept company with other emigres, including Hannah Arendt, Roman Jakobson, and Claude Lévi-Strauss, as well as Wallace Stevens and other leading American intellectuals. After the war Wahl promptly returned to France and resumed his position at the Sorbonne in 1945. This is the period when he founded the Collège Philosophique, which he directed for twenty years, as well as directing many philosophical journals, including the eminent and influential *Revue Métaphysique et de Morale*.

Wahl died on June 19, 1974. By then he was regarded as one of the most admired and important philosophers of twentieth-century France. An active member of the Collège de Sociologie and the *Acéphale* group, he was central in introducing France to such figures as Nietzsche and Kierkegaard at a time when they had no presence whatsoever in the *Programme*'s canon. In a review published in the French journal *Critique*, Noël Laurent comments on Wahl's stature thusly:

> More discreetly than by Jean-Paul Sartre, living philosophy in France is represented by Jean Wahl. Wahl has the advantage over Sartre in possessing an almost incomparable mastery in the knowledge of the history of philosophies. Yet he is also no less an original philosopher, even a poet-philosopher, one who is rather remote from the professorial tradition. . . . If the word hadn't become so muddled in the public mind, [Wahl's] thought could be characterized as existential: yet, being pragmatic, it is above all and voluntarily fluid and ungraspable. Its profound difference from Sartre's thought is perhaps expressed at a fundamental level if we distinguish, within the existential tradition, between Kierkegaard and Nietzsche, on the one hand, and the philosopher-professors of contemporary Germany (Husserl, Heidegger),

on the other. Wahl is preoccupied above all with Nietzsche and
Kierkegaard, Sartre with the phenomenologists.[26]

Laurent's commentary helps us formulate different intellectual inheritances
of French existence philosophy and allows us an initial sense of the difference
between Sartre and Wahl. But in making his point, Laurent also slightly misses
the mark. No doubt, Nietzsche and especially Kierkegaard were important to
Wahl's articulation of human existence, but it was his discovery of concrete
experience in the writings of the radical empiricists he studied, taught, and
encouraged others to study and teach that would offer the postwar French intellectual milieu an alternative account of a philosophy of existence than
what was available in the phenomenological tradition of contemporary Germany that, by the interwar and postwar periods, had a strong hold on French
existentialism.

Vers le concret

Levinas notes that Wahl's philosophy of human existence refers us to the metaphysical experience of a concrete tension "de l'être au-delà de lui-même"
(i.e., of being beyond itself): "Toward the concrete" for Levinas "is the return
to the 'metaphysical experience' that overflows the static 'adequation to the
thing,' beyond all positioning of being, because it is beyond any position or
condition of members of the establishment."[27] I do not wish to rely too much
on Levinas's commentary in my discussion, but his formulations do offer us a
crystalline insight into the centrality of pluralism to metaphysical experience
in Wahl's oeuvre that is important to our current enterprise: "Its [Metaphysi-
cal experience's] irreducibility to synthesis, to unity, is the mark of transcendence and the extraordinary. The pluralism of this philosophy does not refer
us to a regrettable fractioning of totality, but to the multiplicity of the modes
of transcendence that human persons are."[28] In short, Wahl's concrete is neither a synthetic totality nor a disaggregated monism, but an oscillation between
pluralities in the immediacy of experience. To unpack this primary thesis,
I wish to explore three interweaved themes in *Vers le concret*: (1) the independence of relations and the presentation of concreteness in the relation; (2) the
critique of dialectical synthesis; and (3) metaphysical pluralism.

Vers le concret begins by interrogating the idealist rejection of the particular and the concrete. Prior to this work, Wahl had completed a study on Hegel
(entitled *Le Malheur de la Conscience dans la Philosophie de Hegel*), as well as
a study on Plato's *Parmenides*. In both earlier works, Wahl shows the struggle
of idealism in subsuming the particular to the general. This struggle, he goes

on to explain in his Preface to *Vers le concret*, betrays the fact that idealism cannot ignore the impact of the concrete as occasion for investigation: "Whether one calls it a thing-in-itself or a kind of impact [*choc*], the idealists are forced to grant it."[29] The difference between the realist and the idealist is less one that regards the validating norms of their respective systems of thought but, more primoradial than this, a difference in their respective acknowledgment of the validity of the experiential occasion as such. The realist will accept the claim that any particular experience might connect back to a general; but they will also ask whether this impact and this occasion are also not a reality without a general; "he will ask whether, at the same time they race to link up with the intellectual whole under the impulse of the scientific spirit, they are not composed with other occasions and other impacts to form this picture that is the sensible world."[30]

By posing the question in this way and so early in his Preface we are afforded the empiricist stakes of Wahl's project. These are not epistemological stakes but a shift in philosophical attitude from one that tries to make sense of and explain the particular in relation to the general to one that wishes to acknowledge the granularity of experience that remains uncomposed (that is, ungeneralizable) in its immediate presentation. The empiricist, for Wahl, is one who must acknowledge the presentation of the concrete first and foremost and independent of any pre-existing system that would link it up with a general whole. If Wahl is a philosopher of human existence, he is one who wishes to account for the impactful experience of existence that—as he confirms in a footnote to the passage previously cited—is a sensation that "will present itself for the realist as contact, participation, communion."[31] The task for the empiricist is thus not that of explaining the presentation, but to account for the conjunctions that present themselves in the immediacy of experience. It is in this sense that the philosophers he will write about—James, Whitehead, and Marcel—"claim the right of the immediate."[32]

Wahl's turn away from idealism and his suspicions regarding the adequacy of the idealist critique of the immediate are directed at the structure and form of the dialectic. He begins with the irreducibility of the concrete, but not its absolute knowability. For Wahl the claim of experience—and the immediate— is not a claim about the facticity of the datum. "The concrete," he affirms, "will never be something given to the philosopher. It will be what is being pursued."[33] Existence is experience, but experience happens regardless of a knowing or an understanding subject. The movement of dialectical thinking—and Wahl singles out Hegel's dialectic in this regard—is one that must admit a division between subject and object to overcome said division. Overcoming is necessary to achieve understanding; that is, in dialectical thinking the subject/object distinction is presupposed so that the movement of overcoming can move us toward understanding. But for Wahl the challenge lies in accepting this dialectical metaphysics of movement for all thinking. "Movement is not immanent to the idea," he asserts. And this is key for him. What is necessary, in fact, is to think beyond the movement of the dialectic, since we know that that is not the only form of movement that exists in the universe.

For Wahl, the problem with idealism and dialectical thinking lies in its claim to the universality of dialectical movement that implies a universality of contradiction as the structuring relation, and thus also of the subject/object division as a structuring partition for human existence. Recall that this was one of the fundamental premises of sentimental empiricism I articulate in the introduction, and that is an important element in the sentimental empiricist account of the dispositional powers of domination. Wahl insists throughout *Vers le concret* that the universe—or at least our understanding of it—has changed; and it has changed in a manner that we can no longer assume space and time to cohere to the metaphysical conditions of dialectical thinking. For Wahl to thus claim that movement is *not* immanent to the idea is to assert that ideas are not things in themselves, that they are not substances, and that no idea comes equipped with an innate order. The movement of thought is not reducible to negation and the overcoming of the negation. Even if we do concede that movement is immanent to the idea, Wahl will go on to affirm, then it "comes from what the idea tries to do in relation to something other than itself."[34] This "in relation to something other than itself"—the element of difference in itself—will be the core focus of Wahl's empirico-criticism. But we must appreciate how unstructured and undetermined difference is for Wahl. The concrete is, for Wahl, difference-in-itself as "the relation to something other than itself." The concrete is thus neither substance, nor thing, nor inherent relation: "The dialectic today does not suppress oppositions but holds them before itself. It is an oscillation rather than a dialectic, an active and tense oscillation of ideas."[35]

In the Preface to *Vers le concret* we begin to familiarize ourselves with elements of Wahl's contributions to sentimental empiricist thought as I am accounting for them throughout this volume; and indeed, we can see throughout those pages (and also in the *Pluralism* book) nascent formulations of the labile premises I articulate in the Introduction. Central to Wahl's appreciation of the empiricism of (especially) James and Whitehead is the conceit that thought is not determined by a general law of relation. For the empiricist to "claim the right of the immediate" means that in the immediate there exists a pluriverse of possible compositions of any one event or object such that the concrete always exists in the condition of towardness in multiple relations.

The problem with contradiction as *the* form of relation of dialectical think-ing, and of thinking difference in opposition to identity, is that it subsumes all possible modes of relating to that one, singular form. Hence Wahl's insistence that the movement of thought is not contradiction but oscillation, "an active and tense oscillation of ideas."

The influence of Whitehead in Wahl's critique of dialectical thinking is especially notable and is more fully expanded in the chapter on Whitehead's speculative philosophy in *Vers le concret*. This is a difficult chapter to sum-marize, and, given its length, it reads more like a treatise than a book chapter. Importantly, the chapter (which originally appeared as a stand-alone article) was France's first and only introduction to Whitehead's speculative metaphys-ics, as none of Whitehead's works had yet been translated.[36] Wahl, being fluent in English, is thus operating at three different levels in this chapter: interpreter, translator, and disseminator. A few considerations are worth making in light of this. First and foremost is the fact that Whitehead for Wahl stands at the anti-pode of Immanuel Kant (Whitehead, he affirms, is "totally opposed" to Kant's theory of the subject), as well as to Thomist Scholasticism, especially as regards the claims of the intelligibility of being: "The being that is the essence of rea-son is entirely different from being such as they [i.e., James, Whitehead, and Marcel] conceive it. The theory of being that we discover in the background of these philosophies is opposed to that of Saint Thomas as well as that of Des-cartes."[37] But Whitehead's empiricism is also well beyond that of Hume, accord-ing to Wahl. Though indebted to and appreciative of his empiricism, Hume's sensationism remains too atomistic and too tied to a Newtonian and Cartesian mechanistic universe. Hume's world is a disconnected one that does not allow us to grasp the concrete as a mode of extension. Humean impressions are punc-tilious, and though vivacious, they do not extend or associate on their own. The work of association occurs in the imagination. Whitehead's metaphysical em-piricism moves us further along than Hume precisely because, after the discov-eries of quantum physics that Whitehead takes on in his process philosophy, it is no longer possible to assert the monism of the concrete, nor is it necessary to rely on any account of subjectivity to think relationality. In short, the movement of oscillation is a force in nature that denies the punctiliousness of disconnected impression. Here is Wahl addressing this matter while discussing Whitehead's metaphysical empiricism:

> Space is thus an ensemble, a volume, a quality of events. It is not juxtaposition of points, but interfusion of volumes. This will make us understand what Whitehead means by the negation of simple localization.

An event is no more at a given point than a smile that is drawn on a figure is at that point in that figure. Localization in space (understood as an abstract pattern) is always an ideal of thought and never a fact of perception (N. Kn., p. 166). A concrete event cannot be enclosed in a definite place in a space that is abstraction. How can the volume that is an event be fixed in points?

In fact, the relation of situation is something far more complex than we ordinarily believe. Where is your toothache? The dentist to whom you showed the tooth that hurts, told you that it was perfectly healthy and healed you by treating another tooth. What is the tooth and where was the toothache located? Where is the flame that you see in this mirror, where is the star that you see right now? Where is the very person that I believe I see at this moment, and what is his situation in relation to the molecules that compose him? (C. N., p. 147). Science and philosophy have adopted a naïve theory "whereby an object is in only one place at a definite moment." In reality, an object is in all its neighborhood, is ingredient in all its neighborhood, to use Whitehead's expression, and its neighborhood is indefinite.[38]

It is difficult to read this passage and not consider the extent to which for Wahl, the concrete is a form of energy rather than an objective substance. He takes this insight from Whitehead's philosophy of the organism that, he believes, allows us to appreciate Whitehead and James in conversation with one another: the concrete (or what James calls pure experience) is unfixable and unlocalizable energy. As ensemble and interfusion of volumes, space is nonlocalizable and thus cannot be determined as a fixed point. Like Henri Bergson's account of duration (which Wahl repeatedly invokes throughout), space is not a thing but a force. Thus, a situation is not simply some*thing* that has happened, it is a relation that is "far more complex than we ordinarily believe." The concrete is evental because both time and space are relational forces. Neither space nor time counts as mere context. Wahl signs on to Whitehead's critique of the bifurcation of subject and object and proceeds to rearticulate the evental nature of the concrete as extension. When Wahl invokes Whitehead's language of neighborhood, he is not appealing to an account of context or environment as referee for understanding something whose parameters are stable and well defined. Rather, "neighborhood" refers us to a metaphysics of the indeterminate that Wahl's Whitehead describes as the nature of the concrete itself. This is why science and philosophy remain naïve when unwilling to move beyond the metaphysics of bifurcation: by retaining the subject/object distinction, they are unable to account for the energetic extension of all reality that perpetually reaches beyond itself to such a degree that any claim to a punctilious determination is insufficient to the realism of experience.

The claim developed in the chapter on Whitehead, and throughout *Vers le concret*, is that empiricism is a philosophy of the concrete qua difference-in-itself. This is a claim that isn't so much asserted as it is articulated in Wahl's substitutions of terms, which move us decidedly away from any bifurcated dualism of identity/difference. What I mean is that for Wahl, the concrete is not in any necessary relation to anything, it is pure difference; that is, the concrete *is* relation. What empiricism teaches is that experience is not a complete datum with inherent relations, but a movement of extending beyond—or, better put, a movement of towardness. This is a fundamental innovation instituted by Whitehead and James, according to Wahl, that supersedes Hume's empiricism.[39]

Allow me to expand on these points further, as I consider them important to the whole of our investigation. If empiricism is a philosophy of difference-in-itself, it is also (and by extension) a philosophy of associationism that articulates the concrete as a dispositional power of adjacency. This is the fundamental difference for Wahl between positivist accounts of the real qua datum and an empiricist metaphysics of the concrete, especially after James and Whitehead. The concrete is not an object or a substance, but a reaching-outward-and-beyond. This also coincides with the empiricist account of experience. Experience is not datum; it is the outward extension of bodies.[40] The dispositional movement of extension implies a multiplicity of relations in concreteness; hence the "towardness" (i.e., *vers*) in the title of Wahl's book. It's not so much the case that the thinkers Wahl discusses are orienting us toward a form of concrete thinking; on the contrary, in their own way they each articulate the concrete as an indefinite movement of towardness. *Vers le concret* does not name a direction or an end point; it names the nature of human existence as such: existence is not essence but a movement toward the concrete, toward the indefinite, toward adjacency, toward "the fact of multiple relations."[41]

I return once again to the aforementioned passage and note how Wahl is consistently renaming terms and reformulating our sense of their function: space is volume—he doesn't think in terms of juxtapositions but in terms of interfusions; a situation is a complex relation and not a point in time; the example of the toothache borrowed from Whitehead suggests that a localization is a reverberation; and finally there is the reformulation of neighborhood as an ecology rather than, say, a locality with a postal code. What we witness in these rearticulations—indeed, in this empiricist creation of concepts—is a reconceptualization of associationism beyond a Euclidian geometry of point and line: "The error once again derives from the conjoining of Renaissance mechanical science with the theory of attribution in Aristotelian logic. One does not want to take into account the fact of multiple relations. And thus one necessarily arrives at an inevitable monadology, at a view of the universe as made up of separate objects (C. N., p. 150). In fact, if we see a blue object, there is here a very complex relation, into which the color, the percipient event, the situation, and intermediate events enter."[42]

All of this suggests that at the core of Wahl's empiricism is a critique of Aristotelian substances; this is what he means when in the Preface he refers to "the empirico-criticist school" and describes the empiricist thinkers he presents as "anti-substantialists."[43] In James's theory of consciousness there is no ego/non-ego relation, "nor is there an unchanging substrate of the ego."[44] James's account of consciousness (here Wahl cites James's "Does Consciousness Exist?" from *Essays in Radical Empiricism*) offers us no stability of identity, nor does it provide us with an account of independence.[45] Rather, James and Whitehead both dismantle the substantialist account of identity *and* the unitary account of the subject. From them we learn that for the empirico-critic there can be neither inherency nor totality but pluralism and associationism through and through.

Wahl established the philosophical inheritance and foundations of the empirico-critical position ten years earlier in his *The Pluralist Philosophies of England and America*. This is a work in the history of philosophy that traces the origins of Anglophone pluralism in America and Britain, of course, but also in Germany (i.e., Fechner and Lotze), in France (Renouvier), and in Poland (Lutaoslawski). Upon reading it, however, it becomes clear that Wahl's philosophical history is oriented toward his in-depth study of William James, whose radical empiricism is the topic of Book III of that work. In *Vers le Concret* Wahl returns to James and focuses on James's correspondence from 1842 to 1910. Each section of the chapter is devoted to a period of correspondence, and at each stage of his discussion Wahl interfuses James's philosophical psychology with his biography, putting on display James's intellectual journey "towards the concrete." Wahl offers us an account of James's empirico-criticism and his metaphysics of towardness by recounting a lifetime of epistolary writing, communication, and the interlacing of experience with ideas that never omit James's discussions of his own struggles with ideas, but also with mental and physical suffering (fevers, fatigue, weakness), that anguished him throughout his life. What we discover as a narrative arch of this epistolary empirico-criticism are discrete moments of transformation of ideas that aren't simply overcomings of previously held positions, but what Wahl refers to—retaining the English—as an "over-lapping" of preoccupations; an overlapping that he then translates as a "chevauchement des préoccupations les uns sur les autres" ("this overlaying/overlapping of preoccupations the one with the other").[46]

The chapter of *Vers le concret* entitled "William James d'après sa correspondence" isn't so much an intellectual biography as an account of the pluralism of the concrete through the incompleteness of epistolary evidence that offers Wahl a way of reconceptualizing the human: "The life of a thinker like James," Wahl concludes, "is oriented towards the search for the direct and the immediate." In this search, we have the irresolvable tension that he described in his Preface of "an active and tense oscillation of ideas."[47] But ideas are now no longer abstractions; they are compact densities. In his narrating the trajectory of James's philosophical development Wahl is able to expound and expand upon his empirico-critical orientation: "Transcendence is the idea of a beyond by means of which knowledge has a direction toward which it directs itself, from which it draws its nourishment. Immanence is the idea of this compact density in which no element is absolutely transcendent in relation to any other."[48]

I read Wahl's formulation of a transcendental immanence as a synonym for the towardness (i.e., "beyond") of the concrete (i.e., "compact density") discussed earlier. While it is the case that *Vers le concret* allows us to retrieve a full sense of this empirico-critical metaphysics in all its complexity and richness, I would be remiss in my account if I did not point the reader to Wahl's *The Pluralist Philosophies of England and America*, where these ideas first began to take shape. Like Kennan Ferguson's study of James's pluriverse, Wahl's chapter on James shows how pluralism isn't a set of precepts, or an epistemological postulate, or a policy orientation.[49] Pluralism is not a system because "the world cannot be formulated in a single proposition."[50] Indeed, pluralism for Wahl is an anti-systematic disposition at the core of empiricism: "Pluralism may even appear to us only as a new name given to empiricism, since empiricism is above all a philosophy of parts in contrast with a philosophy of the whole."[51] In *Vers le concret* this overlapping of empiricism with pluralism will be further intensified as a result of Wahl's encounter with Whitehead's speculative metaphysics and the latter's philosophy of the organism. But this sense of a conjunction between empiricism and pluralism finds its first expression in Wahl's discovery that there are no inherent relations and that all relations are external to their terms.

Wahl locates this empirico-critical insight in Bertrand Russell's neo-realism, which he outlines in his *Pluralism* book. Referring specifically to Hegelian teleological monism, Wahl affirms that the idea of an inherent relation is an unproven postulate. "Russell shows what difficulties we encounter if we accept the monistic conception of truth," he says, and then continues, "We must reject the axiom of the internality of relations and refuse to speak of a nature of terms made up of relations, we must no longer believe that true judgments regarding a thing form part of that thing. Indeed, we shall be able to say that we know a thing without our knowing its relations, and that the knowledge of certain of its relations does not imply a knowledge of them all."[52]

If the oscillation of immanence and transcendence is at the core of Wahl's investigations in *Vers le concret*, this is because he had first encountered this metaphysical insight in his study of pluralist empiricism. As we have already noted, immanence and transcendence aren't contradictions in Wahl's empirco-critical approach; they are forces between which human existence—and experience in general—oscillates. The concluding pages of *The Pluralist Philosophies of England and America* makes this metaphysical oscillation available to the reader by showing how we might think Russell's logic of relations and James's pluralism adjacent to one another:

> Radical empiricism is partly the affirmation of relations without internal foundations in the terms. It was natural that the pluralism of James, the more it unfolded its presuppositions, should prove to be fairly similar to the realism of Russell. James showed, Perry tells us, that there are relations other than those of logical implication and organic unity, emphasized by rationalism. No doubt this theory, to James, is no logical theory but observation: *there are* relations external to their terms.[53]

Readers of Gilles Deleuze's book on David Hume, *Empiricism and Subjectivity*, will recognize this exact sentence, almost verbatim, from Deleuze's discussion of Hume's theory of spontaneous relations. It is the insight that is a foundational premise of sentimental empiricism.[54] What we discover in Wahl's investigations is a commitment to articulating an empiricist account of criticism rooted in a pluralist metaphysics of relations. *Vers le concret* and *The Pluralist Philosophies of England and America* are an attempt to introduce into France a way of thinking about subjectivity and human existence that requires neither necessity nor inherency to define the nature of Being. Wahl's empirco-critical orientation is anti-systematic because it rejects the idea that relations must be coordinated according to conditions, or terms, or ideas that pre-exist the impact of the immediate. At the same time Wahl's empirico-critical orientation is anti-authoritarian because it rejects a metaphysics of inherent relations necessary in order to account for the continuity of authority through time: If relations are not inherent, then authority (whether the authority of reason, or the moral law, or the State) can't be transcendental because the continuity of power from one temporal phase to the next is neither guaranteed nor securable. This means that any system of relation like kinship, or privilege, or domination is an arbitrary relation.

"The pluralist theory begins with a refutation of monism," Wahl affirms in 1920, by which he means that pluralism rejects all claims to unity that assume necessity as a condition of belonging.[55] There are experiences, and then there are relations, and the relations between experiences are themselves experiences that "are themselves essentially diverse."[56] In short, what Wahl discovers in this oscillation between empiricism and pluralism is a metaphysics of difference-in-itself that exists independent of identity: "An irreducible multiplicity underlies this unity, and radical empiricism, which at first appears as the affirmation of identity between thought and being, also appears as the affirmation of an essential multiplicity. The world is so diverse that we cannot even say that its wholly diverse, that it is solely multiple, discontinuous, and heterogeneous; here and there are to be found continuous currents, homogeneous masses, unities."[57] In affirming this, Wahl is not asserting a contradiction; instead, he avows the irreducible indeterminacy of the concrete as both immanent and transcendent. That is, he avers a towardness of the concrete.

Conclusion

As disseminator, mediator, interpreter, and intellectual translator—not to mention teacher and author—Jean Wahl did not give up on the empirico-critical orientation he develops throughout the interwar period. Upon returning to France after the war, he would establish the Collège Philosophique as a place where these and many other minoritarian works, ideas, and authors not canonized in the *Programme* could be posed in oscillation with one another. What is also clear, moreover, is the extent to which Wahl's influence would enable a series of intellectual experiments that take as a central point of consideration the human condition of *aisthesis*—the undetermined impact of an external world upon sensing bodies. This condition of aiesthesis advenes the towardness of the concrete in its multiple relations. The move away from theories of unity and identity in Wahl's writings and in his reflections on the writers he studies brings us to an encounter with a radically pluralist and indeterminate sensing body, one whose conditions of experience and possibility of knowledge are not constituted by any absolute idea (Being) or inherent relation (contradiction/teleology).

What we also find in Wahl's writings, and the reason he is such a central figure to this study, is all the elements I articulate as characteristic of the minor tradition of sentimental empiricism in postwar France. Wahl does not express these as political insights, nor are their stakes for postwar political theory ever formalized. But in Wahl's treatment of the empirico-critical disposition we see the grounding of Gilbert Simondon's theory of individuation and concretization, as well as his critique of Aristotelian hylomorphism; in Wahl's appreciation of the externality of relations in Russell, James, and Whitehead, we find Deleuze's transcendental empiricism and his metaphysics of difference-in-itself; and in Wahl's account of the concrete, we find a philosophical grounding for Foucault's analysis of the microphysics of power. To appreciate these other thinkers' innovations requires our considering their work alongside Wahl's empirico-critical metaphysics of the concrete. For the thinkers we'll study, Wahl's critique of a unitary metaphysics with inherent relations will become crucial to developing an analysis of the dispositional powers of domination. The task of political thinking and criticism for these writers will not be reducible to the dialectical negation of contradictions. Rather, the task will be to show how within any unity there proliferates a dynamic system of relations that are neither total nor inherent but multiple and in perpetual oscillation. In short, the task of sentimental empiricist criticism is that of "affirming relations without internal foundations in the terms."[58]

Simone de Beauvoir's treatment of patriarchy takes on this empirico-critical insight. Her innovation is to show the political stakes of the critique of inherent relations for everyday life, and her point, in all its apparent simplicity, is devastating: the metaphysics of power that structures gendered relations is concrete and real, but not an inherent relation internal to human existence. Beauvoir's articulation and subsequent critique of patriarchy show that there are no internal foundations in the terms "man" and "woman" that would and could legitimate the purported naturalness of patriarchal domination. By acknowledging the multiplicity of encounters that diurnal life affords—what she refers to as "lived experience"—Beauvoir offers us a founding moment in the sentimental empiricist analysis of the dispositional powers of domination—to which we now turn.

4

Simone de Beauvoir and the Elementary Structures of Patriarchy

On December 11, 1945, prior to beginning her research on what would become *The Second Sex*, Beauvoir delivered a lecture entitled "The Novel and Metaphysics" at the Club Maintenant in Paris. That lecture was revised and published in the April 1946 issue of *Les temps modernes*.[1] Not surprisingly, engagements with this essay have focused on the claims Beauvoir makes on behalf of the novel, its relationship to the enterprise of philosophical systems building, and her own experiments in philosophical literature, as well as those of other writers of the period.[2] What I find striking about Beauvoir's remarks, however, is less her conviction or contributions to the existential novel than her appreciation of the novel as a source of concreteness that gives access to the concreteness of metaphysical experience. She begins the essay by confessing her life as one of readership, something she also does throughout her autobiographies: "When I was eighteen, I read a great deal; I would read only as one can read at that age, naïvely and passionately. To open a novel was truly to enter a world, a concrete, temporal world, peopled with singular characters and events. A philosophical treatise would carry me beyond the terrestrial appearances into the serenity of a timeless heaven."[3] The "and" that relates literature and metaphysics will, for Beauvoir, allow her to think the simultaneity of immanence and transcendence as a concrete, situated experience; or, what she refers to in that essay as "lived experience."[4]

In this chapter, I wish to show the uniqueness and originality of Beauvoir's articulation of patriarchy as a dispositional power of domination. As I have been indicating throughout, the articulation of the dispositional powers of domination is one of the major contributions to political thinking of sentimental empiricism. It is an account that indirectly relies on what David Hume's sentimental empiricism describes as the indirect passions in Book II of the *Treatise*. Whereas Hume emphasizes the ways in which the indirect passion produces sociality, Beauvoir shows how they also produce a distensile force of domination that is independent of any appeal to hierarchical relations or, indeed, to a sovereign bearer of power.[5] In her account, patriarchy is a system of domination without sovereignty.

I read Beauvoir as one of the principal innovators of the sentimental empiricist commitment to thinking about domination as more than a dualist and hierarchical system of oppression. For her, patriarchy is a dispositional power because it orders relations through a range of non-inherent practices in tandem with a system of perceptibilities and evaluations that disposes the right order of things. Hence the pervasive (though not always explicit) thematic of propriety and decorum throughout Beauvoir's writings, but most notably in her autobiographical works. Manner, decorum, and style, as the modern sentimental novelists made abundantly clear (i.e., Jane Austen, George Elliot, Louisa May Alcott—all of whom are cited throughout Beauvoir's *The Second Sex*), shape personhood by disposing bodies and arranging their movements. Beauvoir's discovery and articulation of the dispositionality of the powers of patriarchy offers us a political physics of the indirect passions by showing how those passions constrain, shape, and concretize lived relations.

I sidestep more conventional interpretations of Beauvoir's phenomenology and existentialism and consider her sense of existence, of lived experience, and of situatedness in company with Jean Wahl's empirico-critical metaphysics of the concrete. No doubt, my approach may seem odd in relation to traditional readings of Beauvoir's work that consider her account of gender relations in light of Hegel's phenomenology, especially Alexander Kojève's infamous and highly influential Paris lectures on the master/slave dialectic.[6] But if the "Literature and Metaphysics" essay is any indication, Beauvoir was not wholly enamored of Hegel's philosophical system.[7] We also know that Beauvoir never attended the Kojève lectures, and, as Meryl Altman argues, "Beauvoir's initial engagement with Hegel was closer to the intellectual generation formed by the First World War, and had remarkably little to do with questions of solidarity, responsibility, or political life."[8] The July 6, 1940, entry of her autobiography, *The Force of Circumstance*, confirms this. Her first encounter with Hegel was not accompanied by Kojève but by Jean Wahl, who had just escaped Paris a few weeks earlier: "I worked through Hegel for two hours with the Wahl [book] on *Le Malheur de la Conscience dans la Philosophie de Hegel*. At the moment I understand almost nothing.'"[9]

Wahl had been a principal interpreter of Hegel's thought in France throughout the interwar period, though his account of Hegel and his sense of the viability of Hegel's metaphysics of consciousness were less than optimistic. As we noted in Chapter 3, Wahl thoroughly rejects Hegelian idealism and articulates instead a metaphysics of concrete existence that is not reducible to Hegel's synthetic ideal. Here is how Bruce Baum explains this point: "In order to preserve the concreteness of a reality that is not to be assimilated to thought, Wahl cannot allow thought and being to be united in a synthesis, at least not through reason. Reason can achieve a synthesis in thought, but it lacks the power to mediate between opposites or achieve a genuine synthesis in being."[10] It seems that Beauvoir took this insight to heart in her account of patriarchy throughout *The Second Sex*—an account that identifies patriarchy as a concrete dispositional power that regulates and reproduces the partitions of gendered inequality and domination despite the absence of any natural or causal principle for their execution.

The contributions of feminist scholarship—and feminist movements more generally—over the past century have made it possible to acknowledge how the political life of bodies is entrenched in systems of power that directly and (most importantly) indirectly submit bodies to evaluations that arrange the common sense (*le bon sens*) of social life. This political insight would not have been as readily available without Beauvoir's analysis of the elemental structures of patriarchy that she elaborates in *The Second Sex* and that she shows to be a system of perceptibilities rooted in the everyday governance of style, manner, and social evaluation. Lori Marso makes this point best: "We might say that patriarchy works as a complex assemblage of affects keeping us emotionally, psychically, materially, and bodily captive to the falsely created hierarchy of sexual difference."[11] This chapter unpacks just *how* Beauvoir discovers and subsequently articulates patriarchy "as a complex assemblage of affects" that governs social sentimental life and that shapes the positions, the capabilities, and the comportment of female bodies. For the purposes of my larger project, Beauvoir stands as one of the first scholars in the postwar period to appreciate how sentimental empiricism can offer an analysis of the indirect passions as a system of political power.

To appreciate this contribution more fully, it is important that I briefly turn our attentions to Hume's discussion of the indirect passions and to his account of sympathy therein. But why Hume? Certainly, I don't turn to Hume to understand Beauvoir's critique of gender, nor do I presuppose Hume's moral sentimentalism as a shibboleth for unlocking the truth of Beauvoir's oeuvre. Rather, I share Annette Baier's consideration of the importance of Hume's innovation of the science of human nature, which was radical in his time and, as we shall see, remains radical for us today. "By turning philosophical studies towards human persons, instead of towards God and the universe,"

Baier explains, "Hume took himself to be giving 'a different turn' to philosophical activities."[12] Part of that "different turn" involved reflecting on humans as creatures moved by their passions rather than by their reasons or their souls. For Hume, in other words, it is the direct and indirect passions that motivate bodily movement and corporeal agility in the world, which means that it is the passions that motivate lived experience. Hume's new science of human nature will be a human science not in the sense of providing an inviolable truth about human subjectivity, but in the sense that it offers an account of the importance of social evaluation for human experience and collective association. Such an account must begin with forgoing any belief in the human subject as a stable substance with inherent relations that maintain it as an identity through time. In other words, this "different turn" acknowledges the externality of relations and their concretization through an encounter with the world and those other bodies that occupy it.[13] For Hume and for the science of human nature he initiates, human sentiments ground relations as concrete experiences: that is, experiences are lived because they are felt.

Turning to Hume helps us appreciate the sentimental domain of concrete relations that Beauvoir articulates as the dispositional powers of patriarchy. Patriarchy is Beauvoir's term for that form of dispositional power that Hume calls sympathy. But "sympathy" as Hume uses it is not reducible to empathy or a felicitous feeling of disinterested caring. Sympathy describes a force of outreach into the world that allows us to virtualize the pleasures *and* pains of others. Understood as a form of sympathy—that is, as a dispositional power—Beauvoir shows how patriarchy structures social partitions and gendered divisions.

The account of the dispositional powers of patriarchy matters for several reasons, but especially these two: the first is that it materializes a form of power in the concreteness of everyday lived experience; the second is that the new form of power can be studied and analyzed observationally by looking at said concrete relations. This is especially important if we turn to the French manuals of civic instruction used for the daily teaching of morals in French primary and secondary schools. In the second part of this chapter, we examine one such manual closely: Poignet and Bernat's *Le livre unique de morale & d'instruction civique* is a work that does not demand much interpretive prowess, and so our approach to the manual will be mostly descriptive. This said, the manual is significant for its form and purpose, which orient the child to a sophisticated system of mores and manners that forms the playing field for the dispositional powers of domination to do their work. This system shapes the child's sympathetic attachments to one another, to their elders, and to the nation; that is, the explicit purpose of the manual is to develop in the child the proper decorum that will procure *"le sens de l'État"* (the sense of the State).[14] The diurnal attention given to the instruction of mores and manners in this slight volume is, in no uncertain terms, evidence for a domain of evaluation that allows Beauvoir to analyze the concreteness of patriarchy as an indirect system of sentiments.

The third section of this chapter will show how Beauvoir articulates patriarchy as a dispositional power of everyday life. My effort does not offer an exhaustive analysis of her treatment of patriarchy in *The Second Sex* but focuses instead on her 1949 review of Claude Lévi-Strauss's *The Elementary Structures of Kinship*. I look at Beauvoir's underappreciated and unexplored debt to Lévi-Strauss's analysis of exogamy that, as she admits in her introduction to *The Second Sex*, made it possible for her to provide her readers with her analysis of the sexual relation in patriarchy.[15] *The Second Sex* shows us how patriarchy holds the same status as the incest taboo in Lévi-Strauss's study: in both cases we are offered an account of a sentimental system of evaluation that organizes social hierarchies as if they were natural because they were emergent from the exchange logic of exogamy. More importantly, however, "patriarchy" is the term Beauvoir will use to account for the sexual relation as a dispositional power of domination. The articulation of dispositional domination expressed through the indirect passions of patriarchy is Beauvoir's crucial contribution to the development of a political theory of sentimental empiricism throughout the postwar period.

Simone de Beauvoir: A Political Thinker

I share Lori Marso's, Toril Moi's, and Elaine Stavro's consternation regarding the reception and treatment of Beauvoir's work.[16] Given all of the secondary literature available that discusses Beauvoir's contributions to philosophy, and especially to feminist philosophy and criticism, it is surprising how *The Second Sex* is not appreciated as a study of political manners, conduct, and comportment but is, instead, treated as a prescriptive treatise that attempts to identify and define the nature of woman as such. Whether right or wrong, adequate or inadequate, the champion of feminist philosophy or its failure, the principal mode of reading Beauvoir's *The Second Sex* rests on attending to it as a work composed of propositional statements that attempt to pin down the status of women.

My contributions in this chapter are limited and should be considered as an addendum to the recent resurgence of scholarly interest on Beauvoir's contributions as a political thinker.[17] I put the matter this way precisely because it seems at once odd and alarming. As Marso, Moi, and Stavro all note, much

academic engagement with Beauvoir is directed at her philosophical formulations, especially around questions of identity and subjectivity. Marso is most
explicit and unapologetic about this. In her entry on Beauvoir's *The Second
Sex* in *The Oxford Handbook of Classics in Contemporary Political Theory*, she
states the following: "Simone de Beauvoir's 1949 masterpiece, *The Second Sex*,
is rarely considered a canonical text worthy of being studied within the history
of political thought. Even within feminist scholarship, although it is often
cited or acknowledged, only short excerpts, usually the introduction, are read
carefully."[18]

Toril Moi confirms Marso's claim that Beauvoir's work is rarely read with
an eye to its political ambitions: "If many feminist critiques of Beauvoir strike
me as fundamentally flawed," she explains,

> it is not so much because they misread Beauvoir's position on differ-
> ence (although some do), as because they utterly fail to grasp that
> Beauvoir's political project is radically different from their own. Taking
> for granted the assumption that effective feminist politics presuppose a
> theory of female identity, such critics fail to consider alternative
> positions. And so, measured against such an alien standard, *The
> Second Sex* is bound to be found lacking; the premises of such debates
> virtually assure the misrecognition of Beauvoir's project.[19]

For Moi what gets lost in the debates around gender identity is Beauvoir's consistent articulation of a theory of freedom that affirms how, as a result of patriarchy, freedom is unavailable to women. Beauvoir's articulation of concrete
freedom, on Moi's reading of *The Second Sex*, cannot take place without economic independence. But economic independence does not simply mean allowing women access to the workforce or receiving equal pay. Freedom and
economic independence, Moi explains, cannot exist without sexual liberation
and the abolition of the expectation to repress a woman's sexual needs:

> Whole, autonomous human beings are sexual beings: "Man is a
> human being with sexuality; woman is a complete individual, equal to
> the male, only if she too is a human being with sexuality," she writes.
> "To renounce her femininity, is to renounce a part of her humanity"
> (SS691–2; DSb601). Sacrificing their sexual needs and desires to the
> pressures of social conventions, women mutilate themselves, since
> freedom includes the right to sexual expression. For independent
> women in France in 1949, however, such freedom was hard to find. As
> we have seen, contraception and abortion were illegal. To give birth
> out of wedlock usually amounted to professional suicide, while

marriage, on the other hand, might well mean the end of any real independence for the woman. Even assuming that the woman some-how solved the problem of contraception, she could not simply pick up a man in the street without fear of venereal disease and violence.[20]

What Moi's reading of Beauvoir's politics makes clear is that for Beauvoir, "secondness" means unfreedom; but it is a kind of unfreedom that will not be easily solved by policy reform because the centrality of sexual expression and liberation to Beauvoir's account of freedom cannot occur without the trans-formation of the sensibilities and mores that sustain the system of political eval-uation that includes this "secondness" as a legitimate and perpetual category of social standing. In other words, the title *The Second Sex* doesn't simply re-fer to women, it also refers to the system of dispositional powers that allow for an entire class of persons to be arranged as "second."

Elaine Stavro echoes Marso and Moi in her dissatisfaction with Beauvoir scholarship, especially as regards the continued inattention given to her political theory, but also to her active political engagements. Stavro's work un-packs the complexity of Beauvoir's oeuvre by emphasizing Beauvoir's bricolage style; for Stavro Beauvoir's political theory combines bricolage and complexity to express an account of lived subjectivity at once embodied and situational. This view of subjectivity is both reactive and engaging, in that it expresses conviction to one's situation but does not rely on any general set of conceptual, cognitive, or normative tools to inform action. In other words—to use a lan-guage that is consistent with the sentimental empiricist tradition I sketch out in this book—in Stavro's reading, Beauvoir is neither an essentialist nor a uni-versalist, but is instead a particularist: "Beauvoir does not rely upon the tran-scendental capacity of will and free choice, but presumes that in creatively synchronizing with the concrete situation we can contribute to broader social and political forces." In doing so, "Beauvoir knits together domains of the political that often remain separate."[21]

What I wish to add to these scholars' formidable studies is an account of how Beauvoir's analysis of the manners, mores, and sentiments of patriarchy (her naming it, but also her identifying it as an anthropological fact) allows us to appreciate the indirect passions as a dispositional system of power and ar-rangement. By giving perceptibility to the power of patriarchy and by provid-ing us with its distensile dynamics, Beauvoir opens the door for the kind of political analyses of the effects of social judgment through sensibility and sen-timent that will subsequently find expression in the French school of ideology-critique (notably Althusser's study of ISAs, Bourdieu's field theory of sociology, and Rancière's political aesthetics) as well as the analyses of technologies of power one finds in Foucault's work of the 1970s as I analyze them in Chapter 7. Focusing on her reading and her adoption of Lévi-Strauss's *The Elemental Structures of Kinship*, I will show how Beauvoir goes beyond Lévi-Strauss's structural analysis of incest and exogamy by evincing how these norms and practices are the expression of dispositional forces that organize propriety and decorum as inherent to civic life because dependent on the *bon sense* of the (hetero)sexual relation.[22]

Patriarchy and the Indirect Passions

The term "patriarchy" (fr. *patriarchie*) originates as a mixed term, part Latin (*patri*, meaning father) and part Greek (*archy*, meaning rule). It refers to a system of rule through the father's lineage. Lineage and inheritance are more relevant for our purposes than the fact of rule or its locus in any one figure, as it is precisely the matter of the inheritance—both the act of inheriting that is governed by a system of rules and of inheriting that system of rules—and its apparent naturalism of the rules that govern it that matter most to the sentimental empiricist analysis of the dispositional powers of domination. Both lineage and inheritance are themselves dispositional arrangements.

The term's political history is tied to the Christian church and to diverse forms of ecclesiastical organization that share the attribute of casting the father as the head or ruler of a territory and whose task it is to administer the system of privileges and inheritances therein. In French the term possesses a further nuance not available in English: *patrie* is not only the French word for "father," but the word for "nation," "fatherland," and more literally "home."

According to various usage indicators (including the Oxford English Dictionary and Google's NGram), patriarchy doesn't acquire its contemporary meaning as a term identifying a general system of sexual domination until immediately after the postwar period, coinciding with Beauvoir's publication of *The Second Sex* and its English translations. All of this indicates two things: (1) In using the term "patriarchy" in *The Second Sex*, Beauvoir is not drawing on a common term in regular usage but is rather coining a term of political discourse to describe a system of privilege and dispositional domination structured around the sexual relation; and (2) She does not consider patriarchy merely as a hierarchical operation for the imposition of a sovereign will but, instead, articulates its power within a general system of affections that arranges social standing and political privileges.

Throughout the book, Beauvoir invites her reader to appreciate how patriarchy is a pervasive and generalized system of value that organizes social relations in such a way as to generate impressions and mental images that arrange bodily movement—specifically, the movement of female bodies. This is Beauvoir's fundamental insight about the dispositional power of patriarchy and one that is often taken for granted because it has become so foundational. This attention to affections and evaluations is also the contribution to the analysis of moral sentimental life that David Hume introduces in Book II of his *A Treatise of Human Nature*. Of course, Hume is not addressing patriarchy per se. But what Hume does do in Book II is outline and defend the position that everyday life is motivated by a dynamic system of affections that articulate and arrange bodies. In other words, Hume's radical insight in Book II of the *Treatise* is to show how human motivation is sentimental and thus corporeal; that it is responsive to a complex interlacing of biophysical reactions and mental impressions that comprise "those violent emotions or passions."[23] This dynamic system of affections is what he calls the direct and the indirect passions.

In this section, I wish to provide an account of the indirect passions in Hume in order to better appreciate how Beauvoir innovates on the dispositional powers of patriarchy as an indirect and distensile system of power.[24] To reiterate something I stated further, I do not intend my inclusion of Hume to be a shibboleth for getting at the truth of Beauvoir's account of power. However, as is the task of the overall project of this book, I do intend to introduce Hume and the sentimental empiricist tradition to our appreciation of Beauvoir's innovations because it is a tradition of thought that—as I hope to have shown—was both pressing and active throughout the interwar and postwar period, especially during Georges Davy's direction of the *Concourse* (between 1942 and 1956). In short, what this sentimental empiricist milieu affords is a way of thinking about domination as a sentimental force, and thus as systematic and distensile; or, as Lori Marso refers to it, as "a complex assemblage of affects."[25]

For our immediate task we must recall that Hume ends Book I of the *Treatise* with his famous discussion of personal identity, a treatment that I have analyzed elsewhere and return to in Chapter 7 when assessing Gilles Deleuze's contributions to postwar French sentimental empiricism.[26] Hume's treatment of personal identity makes it impossible to account for human motivation toward action as rooted in anything like a human soul or, in today's parlance, a conscious mind. Rather, human movement in the world will be the result of reactive forces (i.e., the passions) that stimulate and engage one's attentions. Hume's account also affirms that invariability is not a quality of self, by which he means that we cannot confirm in any meaningful way that self-identity is a constant that persists through time: "Thus we feign continu'd existence of the perceptions of our senses, to remove the interruption; and run into the notion of *soul*, and *self*, and *substance*, to disguise the variation" (T 1.4.6.6).

No doubt, such affirmations are what garnered Hume the reputation as a man of "impious principles" that made it impossible for him to secure stable employment.[27] More than his denunciation of miracles, the fact that Hume denies that humans actually possess anything that resembles a divine soul is a devastating conclusion. If humans do not have a soul, how do they move, and how can they be responsible for their actions?

Hume had a gift for expressing incredibly sophisticated ideas in bombastically devastating formulations. The claim that the soul or identity or substance—that is, a metaphysics of Being—is a mental fiction is not mere anticlerical provocation, however. Hume is instead trying to get at the idea that our experiences of external reality cannot achieve the ultimate confirmation of constancy we at once expect and have become accustomed to assume. Another way of saying this is that Hume is a thinker of variability and difference who begins by accounting for things like constancy or custom as a consequence of a human need for invariability. Invariability, he goes on to explain, is a necessary fiction that finds fortune in the mind's inability to sense change:

> A change in any considerable part of the body destroys its identity; but tis remarkable, that where the change is produc'd *gradually* and *insensibly* we are less apt to ascribe to it the same effect. The reason can plainly be no other, than that in the mind, in following the successive changes of the body, feels an easy passage from the surveying its condition in one moment to the viewing of it in another, and at no particular time perceives any interruption in its actions. From which continu'd perception, it ascribes a continu'd existence and identity to the object. (*T* 1.4.6.10)

Let us take some time with this passage. Hume begins with a basic conceit: one of the most difficult things to do is to observe change. It's almost as if he's suggesting that humans are incapable of doing so, or at the very least he's affirming that the human mind struggles to register difference, especially if and when variability is gradual and slow. The reason for this is not that humans are mentally deficient but that the mind is part of the body and thus feels, and what it feels is fluid passages from one moment to the next. In other words, minds do not register substances; instead, they sense the "easy passage" from one state to another that sources our feeling of the continued existence of an object.

That the "body destroys its identity" is one of those devastatingly bombastic assertions Hume is so good at penning. The challenge in appreciating this assertion beyond the violent dismissals it might provoke (which is Hume's point: the mind doesn't reflect, it reacts passionately) lies in the fact that Hume collapses

Descartes's mind/body dualism by conferring onto the mind the bodily powers of sensation. Thus the mind feels easy passage from one moment to the
next, and in doing so, it ascribes continued existence to an object. By making
the mind part of the system of affections, Hume inverts the Eleatic and
Christian metaphysics of Being and treats reflection as a sensorial activity
that may or may not register variability well. The mind, in other words, cannot observe identity; it "feels an easy passage." Such a feeling of fluidity means
that the mind is not actually conscious of substances but operates in an interstitial domain of relations where movements like transition and passage make
themselves felt. Any claim to identity or substance or soul is actually an expression that registers an "easy passage" between various phases of interruption and not an empirical observation of something real in the world. Not all
such passages are easy, of course. There are times, as in the death of a close
acquaintance or a loved one, when we experience profound variability, and
we may be vividly impacted by this. But Hume's concern is less with addressing these cases than with accounting for invariability and identity as a subset
of these events. Within the context of our appreciation of Beauvoir's dispositional account of patriarchy as both systematic and persistent, we can say that
Hume's position allows us to appreciate the mechanisms in and through
which patriarchal privileges are inherited from one generation to the next,
and always attributable (as if it were natural for us to do so) to a specific gendered subject formation.

There is one further point worth raising before moving further. Hume's
discussion of the sensing mind doesn't simply deny the possibility of soul as
the seed of human action; it also treats the operations of mind as natural in
the sense of automatic and unintentional. Consciousness is not born of the
rational soul but occurs in the imagination, which is a dynamic system that
assembles impressions and ideas. It is in the imagination that variability is
transformed into constancy via various powers of relation that include resemblance, contiguity, or causation. This, in fact, is what Hume affirms he
will set out to prove throughout the *Treatise*; namely, "to show from daily
experience and observation, that the objects, which are variable or inter-
rupted, and yet suppos'd to continue the same, are such only as consist of a
succession of parts, connected together by resemblance, contiguity, or causation" (*T* 1.4.6.7). This includes, in no uncertain terms, the conventions for
participation and cooperation that coordinate social activity. The hard work
that Hume sets for himself with the development of his experimental mode
of thinking is to put on display a mode of inquiry and reflection that is not
oriented toward the discovery of eternal truths or inalterable identities, but
to the perpetual and unyielding engagement of bodies with one another.

In other words, his fundamental question is not what is the nature of something, but what are the forms of relation and succession such that we can perceive anything as continuous.

Having dismantled any possible consideration of soul, will, or consciousness as the invariable source of action in the world, Hume proceeds in Book II to ground human motivation in a system of direct and indirect passions. He begins by distinguishing between original and reflective impressions (the former being the source of bodily pain and pleasure, whereas the latter are the passions), and then he further distinguishes between calm and violent reflective impressions. Violent reflective impressions include love and hatred, grief and joy, and pride and humility; they are violent not because they necessarily cause harm but because their intensity is so strong that they affect people powerfully. Admitting that he's unhappy with this facile distinction, Hume considers a more precise distinction of the violent passions between those that are direct and those indirect. Whereas the direct passions are those that affect individual bodies independently of others (i.e., desire, grief, aversion, joy, hope, fear, and security), the indirect passions are what we have come to consider social affections or social powers—that is, those passions that presuppose other bodies and refer to how bodies interact and affect each other. This includes such passions as "pride, humility, ambition, vanity, love, hatred, envy, pity, malice, generosity, with their dependents" (T 2.1.1.4), as well as an emergent system of social evaluation born of these.

Hume's delineation and study of the indirect passions do two very important things: first (and perhaps most importantly), it generalizes action as human movement and motivation, and in doing so it raises to a level of noteworthiness what today we might call the everyday and what Beauvoir, in volume II of *The Second Sex*, identifies as the domestic sphere.[28] By attending to the indirect passions that affect bodily movement and motivation, Hume is suggesting that everyday activities, affections, and desires are worthy of philosophical reflection and attention. The second (related) contribution that emerges from Hume's analysis of the indirect passions is that he effectively desanctifies a classical schema that assigns absolute normative value to heroic action and great deeds. Hume's analysis of motivation is uninterested in the idea of human action as normatively superior to everyday activities. On the contrary, he attends to the indirect passions because he is interested in the powers of bodily interaction and their intermingling, regardless of any transcendental hermeneutic of meaningful action. The entirety of Book I of the *Treatise* and the critique of invariability therein suggests that an abstraction like a theory of meaning has little purchase as to how we move about in the world. The best that we can do is look and see how bodies interact to create meaning (i.e., artifice) in the world; and the way this is done is not by applying a concept of meaning as an interpretive guide but by developing an understanding of how relations like resemblance, contiguity, and causality assemble diverse impressions. As he affirms, "'Tis difficult for the mind, when actuated by any passion, to confine itself to that passion alone, without any change or variation. Human nature is too inconstant to admit of any such regularity. Changeableness is essential to it" (T 2.1.4.3).

A study of the indirect passions will allow Hume to develop an analysis of social-political relations and the allocation of resources therein and thus provide us with a way of analyzing a system for allocating social benefits. Everything here revolves around the shift in philosophical orientation I have been emphasizing: from thing in itself to the relations that assemble diverse parts to form impressions in the mind. Hume's analysis of the indirect passions of pride and humility is a case in point. In contrast to Hobbes, for instance, he begins his analysis by suggesting that we can't rely on definitions to arrive at an understanding of these passions but must, instead, focus on the concrete circumstances in which the passions make themselves apparent. The manifestation of pride and humility betray the fact that their object is "that succession of related ideas and impressions" we call the self (T 2.1.2.2). Thus the indirect passions of pride and humility work to generate a sense of self. But like all the passions, pride and humility are not inherent. They arise as a result of a body's interaction with an external world, which means that they have an external object as their cause.

From this Hume will conclude that, though one can generalize and say that all humans, regardless of "tempers and complexions" (T 2.1.3.4), share in their capacity for pride and humility, at the same time one cannot assume that the causes of these passions are not natural "but are the effects of art, and arise partly from the industry, partly from the caprice, and partly from the good fortune of men" (T 2.1.3.5). While Hume is perfectly comfortable in affirming the generality of human nature, this claim to generality does not translate into a dogma of universal applicability. This is because, for him, what is general about human nature is not a specific identity or essence or quality, but the varying set of operations that interact to generate impressions and ideas. Human nature for Hume names the ability to experience sensation. Sensation arises from the passionate, sensing body. All humans have the capacity to feel pride and humility. And the objects that cause those sensations are various and variable. But that's only part of the point of Hume's analysis of the indirect passions. The further conclusion is that it is precisely because we generate experiences of pride and humility from an external world that we can create social life among and between us. In other words, sociality is what emerges from a body's passionate encounter with the world.

Hence the importance and centrality of sympathy to Hume's analysis of social relations. Though a first sustained account of sympathy is found in *Treatise* 2.1.11.1–8, I do not think I am overreaching when I say that the entirety of Hume's sentimental empiricism is dependent on the technical operations of sympathy, by which I mean that it is not possible to appreciate the contributions of Hume's analysis of the indirect passions to our understandings of social power without his account of sympathy. Indeed, I would go so far as to assert that for Hume, sympathy is the passion of human kinship. In this regard I am in complete agreement with Jacqueline Taylor's description of sympathy as a "technical term for Hume, referring not to any particular emotion, but to a principle that allows us to communicate our passions, sentiments, and opinions to others."[29] Taylor's appreciation of Humean sympathy describes it as a dynamic system of passionate interactivity, whereby any body can extend beyond the immediate physical reach of its physical situation. Another way of stating this is that sympathy is the power of the imagination as expressed in the external world. If the imagination works to associate ideas and impressions to produce "easy passage" from one thing to the next, sympathy operates in exactly the same way between and among other creatures in the world. Sympathy is the social power for the association of differences, which is why Hume will assert that "no quality of human nature is more remarkable, both in itself and in its consequences, than the propensity we have to sympathize with others, and to receive by communication their inclinations and sentiments, however different from, or even contrary to our own" (*T* 2.1.11.2).

In her book *Politics with Beauvoir: Freedom in the Encounter*, Lori Marso shows that "Beauvoir insists that to understand how freedom is grasped or missed, we must bring the bodies of the parties into view. Emphasizing situation, she adds that we must consider the structural, social, historical, and political conditions in which the embodied Self "looks" and whether and how the embodied Other "looks back."[30] The possibility of Beauvoir's doing so rests on a sentimental empiricist mode of analysis of the indirect passion of patriarchy, which she treats as a dispositional power grounded in the sexual relation. To better grasp the full force of Beauvoir's innovation and of her analysis of the concreteness of patriarchy, we must return to the matter of education and look at the pedagogy of civic mores and manners during France's Third Republic.

The Sentimental Powers of Arrangement

A notable aspect of Beauvoir's early childhood autobiography, *Memoirs of a Dutiful Daughter*, is how much of it is organized around her experience as a reader and how Beauvoir subsequently relies on her readerly development as

synecdoche for her childhood development. More than accounting for a literary education or an initiation into language, those moments when Beauvoir
discusses her readerly activities are almost always linked to reflections on various forms of social evaluation, and especially on norms of propriety. A dramatic instance of this is when she describes her having stumbled upon a copy
of Paul Bourget's *Cosmopolis* while working at her father's desk. Beauvoir's recollection of the incident is placed at the end of Part One of her autobiography
and is prefaced by the following reflection:

> There was one phrase grown-ups were always using: "It's not proper!" I
> was rather uncertain as to what the true significance of this expression
> could be. At first I had taken it to have a scatological connotation. In
> Madame de Ségur's *Les Vacances,* one of the characters told a story
> about a ghost, a nightmare ending in soiled sheets which shocked me
> as much as it did my parents. It was not proper. At that period of my
> life I associated indecency with the baser bodily functions; then I
> learnt that the body as a whole was vulgar and offensive: it must be
> concealed; to allow one's underclothes to be seen, or one's naked
> flesh—except in certain well-defined zones—was a gross impropriety.
> Certain vestimentary details and certain attitudes were as reprehen-
> sible as exhibitionist indiscretions. These prohibitions were aimed
> particularly at the female species; a real "lady" ought not to show too
> much bosom, or wear short skirts, or dye her hair, or have it bobbed, or
> make up, or sprawl on a divan, or kiss her husband in the underground
> passages of the Métro: if she transgressed these rules, she was "not a
> lady." Impropriety was not altogether the same as sin, but it drew down
> upon the offender public obloquy that was infinitely worse than
> ridicule.[31]

Beauvoir's childhood mind associates customs of propriety with abjection, ex-
crescence, and the soiling of sheets, only to then appreciate that the sense of
disgust extends to the whole body, and especially to the female body. And then
the revealing insight: impropriety is not the same as sin, for which one's soul
might be condemned, but it is the apotheosis of public condemnation. The
mores of impropriety are an indirect passion, in Hume's sense, aimed almost
exclusively at female bodies.

I have noted the importance of the relation between mimesis and propriety in previous chapters, usually emphasizing the ways in which propriety is
used to dictate what and how to read to induce proper imitation. In this case,
though, the mores of propriety are just as clearly used to dictate what *not* to
read to *not* induce *im*proper imitation. "Impropriety to my way of thinking was

related, though only extremely vaguely, to another enigma: 'unsuitable' reading matter," Beauvoir tells her reader shortly after the aforementioned passage.
She explains this by recalling her mother's reaction when she is discovered
innocently browsing her father's copy of *Cosmopolis*. "What are you doing?"
her mother exclaims. She stammers something to her. Then her mother re-
plies in a pleading voice full of anxiety, "'You must not!' she cried, 'you must
not touch books that are not meant for you.'" However common and/or innocent such a scene may be, for Beauvoir it made an impression—a violent,
physical impression, as well as a mental one. She tells her reader that she would
forever associate her mother's reaction to her reading *Cosmopolis* with another
childhood experience of sticking her finger in a light socket:

> The shock had made me cry out with surprise and pain. While my
> mother was talking to me did I look at the black circle in the middle of
> the porcelain plug, or did I not make the connexion until later? In any
> case, I had the impression that any contact with the Zolas and the
> Bourgets in the library would subject me to an unforeseeable and
> thundering shock.[32]

That there is an association between reading and the system of indirect passions that is "propriety" should not surprise the reader of Beauvoir's memoir
because, by the time that the episode recounted by Beauvoir occurred, France
already had a well-established system of civic education that included daily
lessons and instruction manuals and a robust and coordinated system of
inspectors and inspections that ensured the proper instruction of public mores. That system had been proposed and defended by Jules Ferry after the
educational reforms of 1882. In a famous letter addressed to educators and
instructors, Ferry outlines the importance of a civic education of public morals that will create a common civic understanding for all French schoolchildren. The letter is a founding text of French *laïcité* that remains, to this day,
relevant to contemporary debates around the *affaire du foulard*. The letter
begins by affirming that the most important mission of all instructors is that
of imparting to the schoolchildren an understanding of civic moral virtue.
This is, as Ferry points out, a new regime of instruction heretofore not practiced in France. Whereas religious morals should be taught at home and at
church, during school, children will learn about civic morals. The new regime, Ferry goes on to explain, is intended to clarify something that has, for
too long, remained confused: namely, the separation of church and state.
"Without a doubt, its first object was to separate the school from the Church,
to ensure the freedom of conscience of both teachers and students, to distinguish at last between two domains that had been confused for too long: that

of beliefs, which are personal, free and variable, and that of knowledge, which is common and indispensable to all, as everyone admits."[33] But, Ferry goes on to affirm, the law of March 28, 1882, does something more than provide license to distinguish between private beliefs and public knowledge, "it affirms the will to found a national education in our country, and to base it on the notions of duty and right that the legislator does not hesitate to include among the first truths that no one can ignore. For this capital part of education, it is on you, Sir, that the public authorities have counted. By exempting you from religious teaching, they did not think of relieving you of moral teaching; that would have been to take away from you what makes your profession dignified. On the contrary, it seemed quite natural that the teacher, at the same time as he teaches children to read and write, should also teach them those elementary rules of moral life which are no less universally accepted than those of language or arithmetic."[34]

The rest of Ferry's letter reads like a series of suggestions on how to best engage this new responsibility of the instruction of civic mores through reading and writing. Central to this are examples, many real-life examples, as are found in the literary vignettes students will have available in the manuals they have been assigned. But one must not rely on these manuals as if they offered formulas or wrote abstractions. The manuals are mere tools, Ferry declares: "It is not the book that speaks, it is not even the civil servant who speaks; it is, so to speak, the father in all the sincerity of his conviction and feeling."[35] Indeed, Ferry is insistent—almost to the point of betraying an anxiety—that the manuals not be treated like a catechism book or, for that matter, a Bible: "The book is for you, not you for the book, it is your advisor and guide, but it is you who must remain the guide and advisor par excellence to your students."[36]

In her study of the role of inspectors in French civic moral instruction between 1880 and 1914, Delphine Mercier notes that the main themes of civic morality map well along conventional Enlightenment mores of national progress, individual freedoms, and a moral consensus.[37] This is, she notes further, an innovation on the churchly moral instruction that had preceded these, which allows us to conclude that it is actually at the turn of the century, rather than immediately after the Revolution, that France begins to self-identify as a post-Enlightenment nation. "The fundamental objective of primary moral training, the relationship to work, first at school and then at work," Mercier goes on to analyze, "thus forges the social bond that justifies patriotism. Adaptation to school life and the standardization of behavior that it implies constitute, for all pedagogues, a prelude to the integration of the child into society. Redefining the daily attitudes of the pupil is tantamount to forming model pupils, in the hope of making them, later on, free and useful citizens because they are educated and enlightened. Since obedience remains the main school virtue, the attitudes required of the pupil are therefore often stated in the form of precepts to which the child must conform, in a mechanical and docile manner."[38] This of course goes against Ferry's stated wishes of imposing blind obedience to abstract principles, but the result is almost inevitable: imitation and fidelity to reproduction go hand in hand, especially when one pairs moral instruction with an educational culture in literary criticism as the one innovated by Lanson during this time. What these manuals thus afford is an insight into what a consensus on Enlightenment norms and republican values looks like and how it is that through a rigorous system of literary education (which emphasizes competence in reading and writing via the *explication de texte*) it is possible to produce and reproduce mechanisms of propriety that ensured the inheritance of privileges.

But what are these manuals? What do they look like, and how do they operate? First and foremost, we must imagine these little books on the desk of every schoolchild in France from the first grade onward. Their appearance is both slight and unimposing. Poignet and Bernat's *Le livre unique de morale et d'instruction civique* was perhaps the most popular, the first edition of which was published in Paris in 1898 (we are examining the tenth edition of this work published in 1911—see Figure 1). The Avant-Propos of the manual charts the advantages of the work, it describes the kind of work that it is, and it outlines a method for instruction that, as is immediately evident, analogizes itself to a civic catechism (this, despite Ferry's hope to not think of civic morality as catechistic). The rest of the book is comprised of various lessons intended to cultivate the student's civic sensibility. The title page specifies its civic imprimatur and the book's conforming with the Inspector General's 1893 directives. But it is the title page's epigraph from the seventeenth-century French poet Jean de La Fontaine that speaks volumes: "Une morale nue apporte de l'ennui; le conte fait passer le précepte avec lui." [A naked morality brings boredom; the tale brings the precept with it.][39] The volume in fact compiles several morality tales, reflections, and reading exercises that create what Hume had called a "gentle passage" of precepts and rules of conduct. The authors further specify that the book is several things more: it is a guide for practical instruction, it is a book of moral narratives, a book that contains exercises for reciting mores, a book of moral dictation, and a book that models good writing and penmanship (given the many accompanying lithographs of proper penmanship students were expected to copy).

At every moment, then, the Avant-Propos betrays a commitment to maximum access and maximum utility, both of which will ensure maximum pleasure in learning. Before the actual exercises and lessons are presented, the

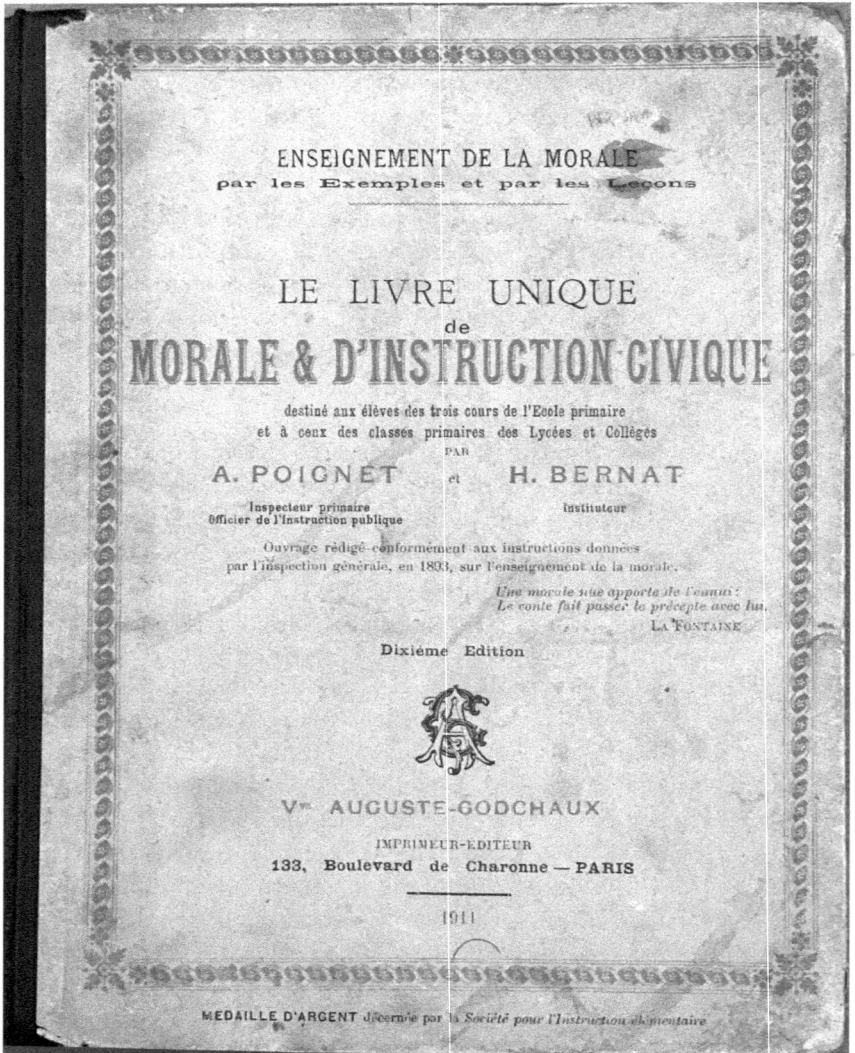

Figure 1. Title page of Poignet and Bernat, *Le livre unique de morale et d'instruction civique* (photo by author)

authors offer an extended account of the method of instruction that emphasizes the literary example as the means in and through which moral learning will occur. "If well chosen," they declare, "the examples may suffice to form the moral conscience of the child and lead him to virtue."[40] More importantly, however, the authors insist that their book should not simply be an instruction manual, but should become the means in and through which the child learns to internalize civic virtue so that the book's spirit is part of every element of daily instruction and not just the hour or so dedicated to civic education. This is why there is such a strong emphasis on practical learning through reading and writing, they affirm. Once the child learns how to acquire a moral lesson from the literary examples given, one will quickly be able to transpose and extend (i.e., imitate) such attentions and dispositions to other times during the school day and in other subjects. The vignettes and readings, moreover, are not mere children's stories or morality tales. They are taken from the many great authors of modern France, including Victor Hugo, Voltaire, Stendhal, and Diderot, and they even include a prominent American's (Thomas Jefferson's) view of France. The manual thus doesn't just aid in the communication of a general culture of values, but also works to generalize its own applicability.

The Avant-Propos ends with an address to the children. "The time will come," the authors assert, "when you will have to leave school for good. If, by that time, you have learned the three paragraphs of each lesson well, if you are deeply imbued with the precepts they contain, if you feel disposed to imitate the good examples contained in the readings, this book will have contributed to making you good sons, good citizens, good Frenchmen."[41] Upon flipping the last page of the Avant-Propos we discover the first lesson: on family relations. Subsequent to that is a series of lessons on schooling, on the duties of servants and laborers, on "la Patrie," followed by a section devoted to one's duties toward oneself. This lesson is divided into two parts: one's duties toward one's body, which include tidiness and cleanliness, and then one's duties toward one's (civic) soul, which includes lessons on individual liberty, responsibility, conscience, and the moral law. The manual concludes with a final section on one's duties toward others.

Lesson 3 (see Figure 2) is dedicated to the child's duties toward one's parents and is especially relevant within the context of our reading Beauvoir's memoir and *The Second Sex*. The lesson tracks along what today we would recognize as wholly predictable gender roles. The lesson begins with a passage from Compayré's *Eléments d'éducation morale et civique* entitled "Une fille affectueuse" (An affectionate Daughter) followed by the moral lesson addressed to boys entitled "Le Meilleur fils" (The Better Son). The affectionate daughter is one because she is able to give her mother a gift on her birthday despite not having money to buy her a gift. Instead, the child takes the time to pick flowers, demonstrating emotional maturity and perseverance in seeking out a gift even though she does not have the means to purchase it. The lesson inadvertently acknowledges Beauvoir's reading of Lévi-Strauss (as we shall soon

Amour — Respect — Reconnaissance

LECTURES

1. — Une fille affectueuse.

Marie Carpentier est devenue une institutrice célèbre sous le nom de Mme Pape-Carpentier. Elle avait sept ans quand, le soir du 13 mars 1822, elle s'était rendue accompagner de sa petite camarade Louise. « Qu'as-tu donc, lui demanda Louise, à l'air si triste? — Je vais te le dire, Louise : c'est aujourd'hui la fête de maman, et je n'ai rien à lui donner, pas même des fleurs. — Eh bien je vais te dire où tu en trouveras de belles fleurs. Tu sais là maison qui est au bout du village, où il y a un grand jardin? Tu es sûre que Mme X. y demeure, et tu es sûre qu'elle te donnera toutes les fleurs tu voudras. — Marie courait déjà à la grille du jardin. Il lui semblait qu'on n'aurait rien refuser à une petite fille demandant quelque chose pour sa mère. — Entrez, dit une voix sèche, Marie, au peu déconcertée, entra, se trouva en présence de la maîtresse de la maison. Elle osa cependant, non sans rougir cette fois, exposer le but de cette visite. « Je le souhaite une bonne fête. » — Et elle se jeta dans les bras de sa mère qui, les larmes aux yeux, la couvrit de caresses et la félicita de s'être montrée si bonne fille aussi affectueuse.

2. — Le meilleur fils.

Un fameux négociant de Babylone était mort aux (*Éléments d'éducation morale et civique.* — Belapion, édit.) « Votre père n'est point mort, il est guéri de sa dernière maladie, il revient à Babylone. — Dieu soit loué! qui me rende cher! » Zadig dit ensuite la même chose au cadet. « — Dieu soit loué! répondit-il, je vais rendre à mon père tout ce que je lui ai donné. — Vous ne rendrez rien, dit Zadig, et vous aurez les trente mille pièces; c'est vous qui aimez le mieux votre père. »

VOLTAIRE.

Maxime

L'amour filial est le premier des devoirs.

Amour — Respect — Reconnaissance

LEÇONS

Une fille affectueuse.

> 1. *Personne au monde ne nous aime autant que notre père et que notre mère : personne ne nous voudra aussi fort plus de bien qu'eux : c'est notre tout, nos devons les aimer; c'est là le premier et le plus sacré de tous nos devoirs. L'enfant qui n'aime pas ses parents est un véritable monstre.*

2. — Nous devons encore les respecter. Nos parents sont nos supérieurs, il ne nous est pas permis d'agir avec eux comme avec des camarades et de leur montrer trop de familiarité. Nous leur parlerons donc toujours poliment et respectueusement. Plus tard, nous ferons preuve de respect à leur égard en leur donnant la première place dans notre demeure et en faisant tout ce qui dépendra de nous pour honorer leur vieillesse.

3. — Nous leur témoignerons enfin une reconnaissance infinie pour tous les soins dont ils nous entourent et pour les bienfaits dont ils nous comblent. Nous devons tout à nos parents qui, pour nous élever, pour nous rendre heureux, s'imposent les plus grands sacrifices. Montrons-nous reconnaissants en les aimant, en les respectant, en nous appliquant bien à tous nos devoirs et en témoignant envers les parents et la plus noire des ingratitudes.

Récitation

Amour filial

Toujours, ô mon père, ô ma mère,
Je veux tendrement vous aimer.
Ma mère, oh! combien vous m'êtes chère!
Des mots ne sauraient l'exprimer.
Parmi de cruelles alarmes
C'est toi seule qui m'as nourri;
Si tu m'as bien des fois souri,
J'ai dû te coûter bien des larmes.
Longtemps, ô mon père, ô ma mère,
Soyez mon exemple ici-bas;
Longtemps vous pourrez, je l'espère,
Veiller sur les deux sur mon pas.
Vous qui protégez ma faible enfance,
Je saurai peut-être, à mon tour,
Par mon tendre et pieux amour
Vous faire une heureuse vieillesse.

MAURICE BOUCHOR.

(Chants populaires des écoliers, Hachette et Cie, édit.)

Questions orales ou écrites

1. Quelles sont les personnes qui nous aiment le plus? — 2. Quel est notre premier devoir envers elles? — 3. Pourquoi devons-nous les aimer? Quel est notre second devoir envers nos parents? — 5. Comment devons-nous leur montrer notre respect? — 6. Quel est notre troisième devoir à leur égard? — 7. Que font pour nous nos parents? — 8. Comment pourrons-nous leur témoigner notre reconnaissance?

Rédactions

I. — LE RESPECT. — Ce que c'est que le respect en général. — A qui le devons-nous? — Il faut rendre aux nièces de le témoigner. — Respect dû aux parents. — Manière de le leur témoigner.
II. — Expliquez cette pensée : « La reconnaissance est la mémoire du cœur. »
III. — Commentez ces deux vers de Pacis : *Je recommanderai à mon père et comprendre; Cromme* [?] *pour tout autre, si ne l'est pas pour moi.*

Figure 2. Third lesson of *Devoirs* and *Respect*, la leçon moralisante de manuel s'adressant à un écrivain (el ark [?] ...)

see), which focuses on the intricacies of sexual relation and the female Other than a gift exchanged between males. The affectionate daughter demonstrates a capacity to care for her mother through her gift of flowers but also by becoming a gift; that is, she gifts and is a gift through her labors of gifting.

The "better son" is a passage selected from Voltaire's novella *Zadig*. It recounts a test between two sons who are to inherit a fortune from their father. The story is a secularized version of biblical wisdom stories: the test will decide which of the two children is the rightful inheritor, given the virtuous choices he can make. What is compelling about this story is its paratactic relation to the previous one. Whereas the girl's morality tale is about giving a gift, this story is about receiving a gift. Here the better son demonstrates civic virtue by protecting the well-being of his sister and making sure she is well cared for. He opts to forgo his inheritance once he finds out that his father hasn't really died but asks that his sister keep the money he had given her. In doing so, he is allowed to keep all the money because he has shown that he will continue to care for the family, and specifically his sister, once his father has truly passed.

These are not especially revealing stories. For a contemporary reader they track well along stereotypical gender roles. The daughter's duty (both moral and civic) is to show care toward the family through the sentiments. The son's duty is also to provide care, but his care is expressed by showing wisdom in managing finances. Fair enough. But Beauvoir is not writing in our time, and our own capacity to note these lessons as corresponding to traditional gender roles is possible because of Beauvoir's analysis of patriarchy, which was neither available nor (as noted) a term in circulation at the time. Moreover, what we must appreciate is the extent to which for Beauvoir the moral virtues of patriarchy could not be ascertained and analyzed according to a direct set of rules or instructions. What is clear from these civic manuals—indeed, what is on the title page as their motto—is that moral instruction cannot occur through the direct inculcation of normative precepts, but rather can only occur through indirect means—the induced training of the sentiments that occurs through reading of morality tales. In other words, that the instruction of consensus—the basis of political stability in the Third Republic's principal gamble as imagined and instituted by Jules Ferry, Gustave Lanson, and the many inspectors and Maîtres—was not an instruction of rules and precepts but an instruction of sentiments and sensibilities through reading and writing. As much as this is a manual of civic morality, this is also a manual that evinces a system of social evaluation and classification that puts into practice how reading and writing—that is, literary criticism—are intrinsic to state formation *and* to political stability. What the manual also evinces, after reading

Beauvoir's *The Second Sex*, is an elemental structure of patriarchy that operates as a concrete system of indirect passions.

The Indirect Passion of Patriarchy

Beauvoir would no doubt have been one of the many students with Poignet
and Bernat's *"livre unique"* (or something similar) as a textbook on her school
desk. This would have been in addition to her copy of *The Imitation of Christ*
that she would have been expected to memorize by the time of her First Communion. Her childhood education was characterized by a devout Catholic
piety coupled with all the accoutrements of bourgeois propriety. The prestigious Catholic Istitut Adeline Désir (commonly known as the Cours Désir)
that she attended for elementary school was also a prep school for Catholic
girls. Its end-of-year school prizes were not academic but, as one of Beauvoir's
biographers describes, awarded "for piety, devotion to duty, and deportment."[42]
Moreover, teaching was done by lay women who had adopted and adapted the
Jesuit's *Ratio Studiorum* for their teaching purposes.[43] In short, Beauvoir's childhood education was one that ensured a marriage of church and state, which
helps explain why the title of her 1958 memoir, *Memoirs of a Dutiful Daughter*,
is *Mémoires d'une jeune fille rangée*—"*rangée*" meaning dutiful, but also "order"
(as in "in good order") as well as "line" or "row" (as in "well aligned" or even
"well arranged"; "*rangée*" being the etymological root of the English "arrange"). Beauvoir's memoir, published the year before the publication of *The
Second Sex*, has as its principal concern a system of passions as well as the practices and activities that constituted her becoming a dutiful woman.

There are two further considerations worth making before proceeding further. The first regards the status of the family and family law in France; the
second regards the status of French universal suffrage. As Camille Robcis has
argued, one of the central features of French political life and culture since
the revolution is the social question and, more specifically still, the family as
an answer to the dilemmas raised by the social question. This includes laws
about marriage, inheritance, natality, abortion, and the funding of family benefits.[44] Neither claims about individualism nor abstract nationhood were
enough, according to Robcis, to sustain a national consensus of and about the
legitimacy of the French state. Thus, the family (defined, exclusively, as the
heterosexual family) was a major locus of policy throughout the nineteenth
and twentieth centuries. The Napoleonic Code instituted marriage and sexual reproduction as the first stage toward guaranteeing political solidarity,
which helps explain why the lessons of the *livre unique* begin with a child's
duties toward the family and ends with the duties one has toward oneself. One's
sense of self comes after one's social sense as first and foremost a member of a

family (notably, there is an entire lesson in the *livre unique* devoted to orphans and their role/place in social unification). This emphasis on the heterosexual family extends throughout the Second and Third Republics and well into the Vichy regime with the voting into law of the July 29, 1939, Family Code (*Code de la famille*). As Robcis concludes,

> Family policy was not on the agenda of a specific political party or religious group but rather constituted a key component of French social policy, just like health insurance or pension funds. It had become a unit to organize social distribution and for thinking about solidarity. In the fall of 1946, the constitution of the Fourth Republic mirrored this consecration of the family by stating that "the nation will provide the family with the means necessary for its development." The family was at the heart of the Republican social contract.[45]

The family was indeed at the heart of the Republican social contract, but women were not given the vote in France until the measure was signed into law on April 21, 1944, under the provisional government led by Charles de Gaulle. This is a compelling point worth pondering further: how is it that a society so set on defending the status of universal rights and, especially, the virtue of social and political solidarity with the French state, could not and did not recognize nearly 50 percent of its population as participants in the ultimate political expression of its republican virtue? The answer, again following Robcis, lies in the fact that the system of indirect passions and its policy expression in French family law operated in such a way as to not allow women access to the claim to universalism necessary to assert the right of suffrage (or, indeed, any universal right). The relevant universal in this case was not woman, but the family, of which women were members, no doubt; but they didn't possess the status of universalism that would grant them access to the right to vote. "French-style universalism constituted . . . an obstacle to women's suffrage: women were denied the right to vote because of their particularity, because they were not true abstract individuals, because they remained too marked by the determinations of their sex."[46] In other words, the central obstacle to women's suffrage in France was the system of indirect passions coordinated around the family/political solidarity relation that remained bound to an Aristotelian/Thomistic account of political society as rooted in the ius naturale of the family and heterosexual procreation.[47]

It is of little surprise, then, that Beauvoir would develop what would appear to Anglophone interpreters as a universalist and essentialist account of woman in *The Second Sex*. However politically and theoretically distasteful such an account might seem when it is viewed through the lens of the past half century of critical feminist thought, I suggest that in a political culture in which political participation was articulated through and conditioned on a such universalist and essentialist conception of the family, adopting the same universalist/essentialist frame may have been a necessary move to make if Beauvoir's interjection was to be heard in a civic culture that had never granted women access to the status of a universal. Thus, even if one acknowledges a certain essentialism in Beauvoir's answer to "what is a woman?" in *The Second Sex*, it would seem unwarranted to transform that acknowledgment into a condemnation without, at the very least, considering the ways in which the choice to adopt such a universalist position may have been forced by the political context in which it was written—a context dominated by the political theory of republican universalism and the French Family Code, both systems that had consistently denied the possibility for women to claim the status of universality necessary for access to universal rights.

The strength of *The Second Sex*'s analysis of patriarchal power and its importance as a work of political theory lie in its ability to show how a universal both exists within and emerges from an intricate system of the indirect passions as laid out in manuals like Poignet and Bernat's *Le livre unique de morale & d'instruction civique*. In short, Beauvoir's identification and analysis of patriarchal authority is an identification and analysis of a system of sentiments for the production of political consensus formation and solidarity. What also becomes clear upon a rereading of *The Second Sex* is how patriarchy will be shown to be the form of political solidarity that operates in a manner analogous to the incest taboo in Claude Lévi-Strauss's account of kinship formation—that is, as a mediator between nature and culture, both universal and particular.

For Lévi-Strauss the prohibition of incest is the conceptual kernel that explains the passage from nature to culture, not in any literal or historical sense, but in the sense that any account of culture relies on an ideal-typical account of nature. To be wholly reductive (as mine is not a study on Lévi-Strauss's structural anthropology), Lévi-Strauss's basic insight is to show that if men are not able to have reproductive intercourse within the family because of the incest taboo, they must look outside of the family and develop social relations. This injunction initiates a system of sexual exchange that is the foundation of any form of group solidarity. Thus, he concludes, in his *The Elementary Structures of Kinship*, by invoking Marcel Mauss's anthropology of potlatch, "the prohibition of incest is less a rule prohibiting marriage with the mother, sister or daughter, than a rule obliging the mother, sister or daughter to be given to others. It is the supreme rule of the gift."[48]

Beauvoir and Levi-Strauss had known each other for most of their adult lives, having met in 1929 when studying for the *agrégation*. They had a common friend in Maurice Merleau-Ponty, to whom Lévi-Strauss dedicated his

Savage Mind and who was, during the time of her writing *The Second Sex*, a close collaborator and contributor to *Les Temps Modernes*. She recalls some of this in her childhood memoir: "My fellow-pupils were Merleau-Ponty and Lévi-Strauss; I knew them both a little. The former I had always admired from a distance. The latter's impassivity rather intimidated me, but he used to turn it to good advantage. I thought it very funny when, in his detached voice, and with a dead-pan face, he expounded to our audience the folly of the passions."[49] The two remained at some distance from one another until after the war, at which point Lévi-Strauss expressed great admiration about several essays by Beauvoir that appeared in *Les Temps Modernes* and that were a prelude to *The Second Sex*. We have no textual evidence that I am aware of that might account for Levi-Strauss's engagement with Beauvoir's work; however, we do have substantial material on Beauvoir's engagement with Levi-Strauss's work in this period, including her *Les Temps Modernes* review of *The Elemental Structures of Kinship* as well as her acknowledgment, in the fourth footnote in the Introduction to *The Second Sex*, where she thanks "Claude Lévi-Strauss for sharing his proofs of his thesis, which I drew on heavily, particularly in the second part."[50]

We shall rely primarily on her review of Lévi-Strauss's study of primitive societies. My purpose for doing so is to show how Beauvoir introduces to political theory and to the intellectual milieu of postwar France an account of dispositional powers of patriarchy that is neither institutional nor explicitly legal, but at once elemental, concrete, and dispersive. The way she does this is by showing how an account of social relations like the one we find in Lévi-Strauss's structural anthropology of familial relations is also an account of a political system of domination rooted in the indirect passions of masculine pride and the fear of the loss of power. In doing so she makes the sentiments and manners we found in such things as the manuals for civic instruction crucial to the analysis of domination, social consensus, and the inheritance of political privileges.

It is clear, upon reading Beauvoir's review of Lévi-Strauss's *The Elementary Structures of Kinship*, that she is taken not just with his research but with his central insight that there are elements in social structures that are both universal and culturally specific. The point for either thinker is not to establish once and for all the metaphysical standing of these structures but to show how social relations assemble around the ambiguous standing of such normative markers. In this regard we can see how Beauvoir is influenced by Lévi-Strauss when, in *The Force of Circumstances*, she recounts how "since the beginning of May [1948], my study on *La femme et les mythes* had begun appearing in *Les temps modernes*. [Michel] Leiris told me that Lévi-Strauss was criticizing me for certain inaccuracies in the sections on primitive societies. He was just finishing his thesis on *Les structures de la parenté*, and I asked him to let me read it. I went over to his place several mornings in succession; I sat down at a table and read a typescript of his book; it confirmed my notion of woman as *other*; it showed how the male remains the essential being, even within the matrilineal societies generally termed matriarchal."[51]

Lévi-Strauss—like many of his generation—was interested in reviving and revising French sociology from what was imagined to be an intellectual stasis since Émile Durkheim's contributions. Like Jean Wahl, he had spent most of the war period in the United States to escape Nazi and Vichy persecution, having been stripped of his French citizenship because of his Jewish heritage. He was in exile at the New School for Social Research, where he befriended the American anthropologist Frank Boas at Columbia University, as well as developing close intellectual relationships with other French emigres, especially Norman Jakobson. Shortly after his return to Paris in 1948, Lévi-Strauss submitted his major and minor dissertation work at the Sorbonne, the latter of which was *The Elementary Structures of Kinship.* The central thesis of this otherwise difficult work is to show how a seemingly universal injunction like the incest taboo doesn't emerge from anything instinctual in humans but is a consequence of marital relations—the arrangements of bodies—within social systems that are, first and foremost, formal systems of exchange relations. The prohibition against incest, according to his research and analysis, is not based on a natural repugnance to sexual relations with sisters, daughters, or mothers; it is a rule that licenses marriage alliances. At the center of this system is the woman as the object of exchange. If the incest prohibition betrays a logic of the gift, then women are the entity for whom the rule is established as relational objects of gift exchange. In this respect, Lévi-Strauss concludes, the incest taboo is both negative and positive: it is negative as a normative prohibition, but it is positive/productive as the source of the transition from family to society.

Beauvoir begins her review by announcing that Lévi-Strauss's book hearkens a new awakening of French sociology. But she does not dwell on the book's contributions to the general field of sociology for long. Rather, her review delves immediately into the stakes of the work as an event of thinking. Key for her is how Lévi-Strauss introduces us to the foreignness of thought: "Thus he gives us back the picture of a universe that does not need to mirror heaven in order to be a human universe."[52] In other words, Lévi-Strauss does not offer a mimetic operation but rather—to return to Lori Marso's lexicon—an *encounter* of nature and culture as "encountered in the field of sexual life, since sexual life, while a matter of biology, immediately involves others [*autrui*]."[53] Beauvoir then goes on to note something of importance not only to Lévi-Strauss's oeuvre, but to her thinking as well: "The fundamental structures on which human society as such is founded are expressed and accomplished through the incest prohibition."[54] Thus, Beauvoir suggests, the story of human society does not begin with economic development or scientific progress, but with sexual relations first and foremost.

The sexual relation, however, does not belong to the private sphere but is rather of the collective; it is the basis of social solidarity. There is no sexual relation without an Other, but there is also no private sexual relation. The incest prohibition and the norm of exogamy are evidence of the fundamentally collective character of all sexual relations: "The very first concern of the collectivity," she affirms, "will be to prevent the establishing of a monopoly of women. This is the underlying meaning of the incest prohibition which affirms that women should not receive a social usage based on their natural distribution."[55] It is this fact of distribution traced by Lévi-Strauss, identified by Beauvoir in Lévi-Strauss's work, and further elaborated by Beauvoir herself throughout her review and then in *The Second Sex* that establishes the political force of the sexual relation as the foundation of patriarchy. In other words, and this needs to be made clear, what Beauvoir is doing in her review and in *The Second Sex* is establishing once and for all and without equivocation the political dimensions of the sexual relation as the validity structure of social solidarity. By affirming this, she is also able to show how patriarchy is a concrete system of political authority. Finally, and this follows from our earlier discussion, once patriarchal authority is established as a concrete formation grounded in the fact of exogamy, then the indirect passions stand as political forces in the reproduction of social cohesion and political consensus of legitimate rule. Thus Beauvoir asserts, "A profound asymmetry between the sexes exists and has always existed. The 'Reign of women' is an outdated myth. Whatever the mode of filiation may be, whether children are included in the father's group or the mother's, women belong to the males and are part of the various prestations they grant each other. All matrimonial systems entail that women are given by certain males to other males."[56] Beauvoir thus extends and innovates on Lévi-Strauss's study of the incest taboo and the norm of exogamy by showing that sexual relations constitute the foundations of political authority through the gift dynamic of reciprocity: "The exchange is always found at the basis of matrimonial institutions."[57]

If Beauvoir's review of Lévi-Strauss is important to us in showing how she develops the indirect passions of patriarchal authority in her own thinking and writing, it is also crucial for appreciating one further element: namely, her assertion that unintentional acts have meaning. This is a direct inversion of the

Aristotelian and scholastic conceit that actions have causes and therefore intentions. "However," she asserts in the third-to-last paragraph of her review, "the premier merit of this study is precisely to challenge the old dilemma: either human acts are intentional or they are devoid of signification. The author defines them as structures whose whole precedes the parts and whose regulating principle possess[es] a rational value even if it is not rationally conceived."[58] By "rational value" I take Beauvoir here to mean a systematic logic (i.e., a regulating principle) that can be traced, classified, and evaluated in exactly the same way that Hume analyzes the governing powers of the indirect passions that distribute dispositions and social valuation. The indirect passions, we recall, were neither willful nor intentional, though they created dynamics perceived as intentional. More specifically, any regulative principle cannot be universal but is endogenous to the dynamics of the system itself. The incest taboo is general, but not natural. It is born—for Beauvoir—from the need to institute order and authority. "The sexual act," she confirms, "instead of closing in on itself, opens a vast system of communication. The incest prohibition merges with the institution of human order. Everywhere men have sought to establish a matrimonial regime in which women figure among the gifts by which the relation of each [man] to the others is expressed and social existence, as such, is affirmed."[59]

Beauvoir published her review of Lévi-Strauss's *The Elemental Structures of Kinship* in the July 1949 issue of *Les Temps Modernes*. That same year *The Second Sex* appeared as a single collected monograph in two volumes. It is clear, after reading her review, that her intent in the first volume (especially in Part II of volume I) is to develop a political theory of patriarchy that relies on Lévi-Strauss's anthropology of exogamy. This is coupled with a second element—the study of myth—that is part and parcel of the project that identifies patriarchy not simply as a mythic structure but as the founding myth of all political authority. It is in the pages of Volume I of *The Second Sex* that Beauvoir is unequivocal in her contribution to modern political thought: "Thus, the triumph of patriarchy was neither an accident nor the result of a violent revolution. From the origins of humanity, their biological privilege enabled men to arm themselves alone as sovereign subjects; they never abdicated this privilege; they alienated part of their existence in Nature and in Woman; but they won it back afterward; condemned to play the role of the Other, woman was thus condemned to possess no more than precarious power: slave or idol, she was never the one who chose her lot."[60] And then, a few pages further on:

> At the moment when man asserts himself as subject and freedom, the idea of the Other becomes mediatory. From this day on, the relation-

ship with the Other is a drama; the existence of the Other is a threat
and a danger. The ancient Greek philosophy, which Plato, on this
point, does not deny, showed that alterity is the same as negation,
thus Evil. To posit the Other is to define Manichaeism. This is why
religions and their codes treat woman with such hostility. By the
time humankind reaches the stage of writing its mythology and laws,
patriarchy is definitively established: it is males who write the codes. It
is natural for them to give woman a subordinate situation; one might
imagine, however, that they would consider her with the same benevo-
lence as children and animals. But no. Afraid of woman, legislators
organize her oppression. Only the harmful aspects of the ambivalent
virtues attributed to her are retained: from sacred she becomes unclean.
Eve, given to Adam to be his companion, lost humankind; to punish
men, the pagan gods invent women, and Pandora, the firstborn of these
female creatures, is the one who unleashes all the evil that humanity
endures. The Other is passivity confronting activity, diversity breaking
down unity, matter opposing form, disorder resisting order. Woman is
thus doomed to Evil.[61]

In these two passages from *The Second Sex* I read an entire agenda of political,
philosophical, and critical analysis that would occupy French thought for years
to come. The "triumph of patriarchy" is neither revolutionary nor heroic in
the Arendtian and Aristotelian sense of political action; it is wholly ordinary
and mundane—one could even say domestic. Its triumph is the triumph of a
system of power expressed in everyday—in this case, sentimental-sexual—
relations, exactly the kind of everyday relations that Hume had analyzed in
his discussion of indirect passions in Book II of the *Treatise*.

The reference to Pandora in the second passage reveals this. Pandora isn't
just the one who "unleashes all the evil that humanity reveals"; she is the embodiment of the gift exchange as a divine curse (*Pan-dora* from the Greek
meaning "all" [i.e., *pan*] "gift" [i.e., *dōron*]). From Hesiod's poem *Works and
Days*, we learn that Pandora is the gift of evil whose *pithos* (jar) unleashed the
plague of the passions. But she is also the gift as universal; her Sisyphean function is to at once be a gift and to give. As gift, Beauvoir affirms, woman is
doomed to difference qua Other. But since Plato we know that alterity is the
same as negation, and thus evil: "The Other is passivity confronting activity,
diversity breaking down unity, matter opposing form, disorder resisting order."
In other words, the structure of critique as negation that marks the necessary
conditions of *le bon sense* (i.e., good sense) *is* the patriarchal form of thought
that denies alterity—that is, woman qua difference—legitimacy and authority

as anything other than that which must be negated. Woman is passivity, diversity, matter, disorder; in short, woman *is* the fluid and unintentional exchange of the indirect passions.

Conclusion

If the formulations of Beauvoir's ideas I laid out in this chapter seem familiar or even rote, it is because similar formulations have been persistent across much of the research in postwar philosophy, political theory, and aesthetic criticism since Beauvoir's penning of them. For this reason alone, we owe an immeasurable debt to Beauvoir for her unique and original insight that the indirect passions delimit a domain for the operation of the dispositional powers of the sentiments.

Moreover, Beauvoir establishes two points that are central to the sentimental empiricist approach to theory and criticism that forms the focus of this book: the first is that sentiments matter to our political understandings; the second is the elaboration of the beginnings of a philosophical, metaphysical, and aesthetic tradition that takes seriously the politics of alterity and the conceit that difference is negation. Beauvoir's account of patriarchy includes—at the very least—an awareness of the Eleatic and Parmenidean assumption that Being and order ought to be privileged over becoming and disorder. Better put, Beauvoir's account of the elemental structures of patriarchy does not just sensitize us to the political dimensions and operations of authority in the ordering of the sexes. It also contextualizes that patriarchal authority within a broader philosophical tradition that privileges identity over difference and that understands difference exclusively as a negation of identity, and thus—to use her words—Evil. Woman, then, is doomed to Evil, not because of some circumstantial or mistake of the passions, but because at a metaphysical and societal level she is understood as difference—the negation of man. Woman is doomed to Evil, in other words, because she is difference, and difference is doomed to Evil. This is not simply true as a metaphysical speculation, but it is evident at every turning of the page of Poignet and Bernat's *Le livre unique de morale et d'instruction civique*, whose task it is to arrange (i.e., fr. *ranger*) young minds and bodies so that they will be disposed to the *bon sens* of French republican universalism.

The challenge and task of political thinking after Beauvoir's intervention are to think relations and critique differently, to think bodies differently, to think politics beyond the boundaries of heroic action and statecraft, and to look to the granular and domestic entanglement of the indirect passions. For Beauvoir and a generation of thinkers after her, it is in these granular spaces that the dispositional powers of domination are most intense and effective. Simondon, Deleuze, and Foucault—the next authors we will study—all take Beauvoir's thesis and expand on it, as will other (mostly male) thinkers who emerge in the 1950s and who will begin to enter the echelons of the Grands Écoles professoriate.

The recent revival of interest in Beauvoir's work over the past two decades has emphasized her contributions as a political thinker. Toril Moi's work allows us to focus on the importance Beauvoir gives to practices of reading, but also to acts of literature and how her own forms of writing are important to how we think about gender and sexuality as acts of composition; Elaine Stavro's work shows us the intricacies of Beauvoir's political engagements and how these are not distinct or easily abstractable from her philosophical elaborations and commitments; and Lori Marso's work shows the ways in which Beauvoir sets up the event of feminist thinking and political engagement as an encounter with the world and others—that is, as a constant condition of politics as such.

In this chapter, I have endeavored to add a further dimension to this revisiting of Beauvoir's oeuvre by looking at how she reformulates the domain of politics from one that is exclusive to the state form to one that attends to political authority as a system of indirect passions emergent from sentimental encounters. Our cursory examination of the civic manuals that Beauvoir had to internalize in order to become a well-disposed and dutiful (i.e., *rangée*) schoolgirl provide concrete evidence for the existence of such a system of passionate instruction intended to sustain and perpetuate French Republican universalism and the system of social virtues and criterial hierarchies it professes—a system that, after Beauvoir, we can comfortably characterize as patriarchal. By having at her disposal early drafts of Lévi-Strauss's work while crafting the pages that would become the first volume of *The Second Sex*, she was able to add a corrective to his exogamy thesis and show how the indirect passions are established as a system of political authority and social control that grants legitimacy to the exercise of state power. Such a form of authority does not originate in state institutions and its arrangements. Rather, state institutions are an expression of the indirect passions that generate patriarchy. In short, after Beauvoir, political analysis—and political theory—could not ignore the sexual relation and its grounding political effects: the family, childbearing and childrearing, and what we would eventually come to understand as the becoming of gender identity. More than a matter of social policy as enshrined in the *Code de la famille*, the family is political at conception. At the same time, postwar French philosophy and criticism could no longer ignore the fact that the forms of social reproduction that ensured state legitimacy were saturated with intentional but, more importantly, unintentional effects procured by the elemental structures of patriarchy. After Beauvoir's politicization of Lévi-Strauss's thesis regarding the exchange relations of exogamy and her insistence that sentiments constitute political relations, Western political thinking writ large was confronted with the sexual relation—and thus the family—as a source for the expression of unfreedom. Simply put, one of Beauvoir's many contributions to contemporary political theory is to show—both empirically and philosophically—how the sexual relation is the foundation of all forms and manifestations of state legitimacy and thus *is* a political control on the French republican ambition of universal freedom.

The first of the labile premises I outline in the Introduction to this book is that sentimental empiricism is anti-authoritarian. Beauvoir's political anthropology of patriarchy gives us some insight into how "authority" is neither represented nor representable by any one figure or symbol. It is, rather, a distributed system composed of well-trained indirect passions and quotidian social evaluations that all combine to establish and consistently reaffirm woman as Other and thereby as essentially associated with negation, disorder, and evil. This is the grounding gesture of all political authority to the extent that, as she shows, political legitimacy is born of the sexual relation. Though we have, we can, and we will no doubt continue to debate the precision, exactness, or even earnestness of Beauvoir's experimental thinking on these issues, it is impossible to deny her profound contributions to the political thinking of postwar France (first), and to the Western tradition of political thought more generally.

5

More than a Unity

Gilbert Simondon's Sentimental Empiricism

Gilbert Simondon published two major works during his lifetime: *On the Mode of Existence of Technical Objects* (1958) and the first part of his magnum opus, *Individuation in the Light of the Notions of Form and Information* (1964).[1] Neither of these are what we would classically recognize as political treatises, but both works are recognized as central to understanding the developments in political and aesthetic thought of postwar France. Despite his documented influence on subsequent thinkers—including Gilles Deleuze, Bernard Stiegler, and Bruno Latour, not to mention Brian Massumi, Erin Manning, Alberto Toscano, and many others—Simondon's works, his thinking, and his philosophical oeuvre remain underexplored and understudied.[2] More to the point, and save one important contribution,[3] his relevance to the innovations in *political* thinking of postwar France remains underappreciated.[4] As Andrea Bardin notes, "The very absence of an explicit political position in his [Simondon's] writings helps explain the lively debate surrounding the political questions that appear to emerge from both his philosophy of individuation and his philosophy of technics."[5]

Even more to the point, the tradition of sentimental empiricism that I am tracing would not have been as robust without Simondon's philosophical contributions. One of the principal tasks that he engages in his writings is that of elucidating a metaphysics of difference-in-itself as its own force rather than— thinking back to our discussion of Jean Wahl—as inherently related to the concept of identity. Simondon does this by challenging the Eleatic law of the excluded middle (*tertium non datur*) that affirms the law of non-contradiction: that law states that something either "is" or "is not" but cannot be both.[6] Simondon proposes a middle passage between being and non-being in his efforts to think

difference as pure relation, and he offers a rebuttal to the hylomorphic metaphysics of substance. In doing so, he advances the following propositions:

1. The relation of difference and identity is not prior to any other
   relation;
2. Relations are not substances;
3. How difference relates is undetermined; and
4. Identity names one of many possible ways that differences relate,
   but it is not prior to any other mode of relating.

In short, by taking away the necessary priority of identity qua substance
Simondon also takes away the need to adhere to a philosophical project committed to either resolving or dismissing contradictions. In this regard, philosophical thinking is no longer oriented toward problem solving but, instead,
to exploring and articulating the associative milieus of differences; to wit,
philosophical thinking is oriented to exploring a metaphysics of transformation and change.

This chapter highlights two features of Simondon's thought to appreciate his
contributions to postwar French sentimental empiricism. The first is his critique
of Aristotelian hylomorphism as expressed in his metaphysics of individuation.
For this part of the discussion I will rely exclusively on the paper entitled, "The
Position of the Problem of Ontogenesis," which is the first part of the Introduction to Simondon's *Individuation in the Light of the Notions of Form and Information* (this translation was originally published in the pages of the journal
Parrhesia).[7] The second element I discuss is Simondon's philosophy of technical
objects, which relies on his account of individuation to develop a relational philosophy of technics. In this respect, Simondon is greatly influenced by the
philosophy of science of Bachelard and Canguilhem, and especially Bachelard's critique of substantialism, as we see expressed in this crucial passage
from Bachelard's 1934 *The New Scientific Spirit*: "There are no simple phenomena; every phenomenon is a fabric of relations. There is no such thing as a simple
nature, a simple substance; a substance is a web of attributes. And there is no
such thing as a simple idea, for as Dupreel has pointed out, no idea can be understood until it has been incorporated into a complex system of thoughts and
experiences. Application is complication."[8]

The Sentimental Empiricism of Gilbert Simondon

It is difficult to underestimate the extent to which an Aristotelian account of
substances remains integral to our contemporary thinking of and about media.
Most of us are committed to the idea that a medium is what it does and that

what it does is to influence or effect human psychology and behavior. That is, most of us are committed to an instrumentalist account of technical media that understands the essence of media as determined by their function and purpose—both of which are inherent in their design. This view is at the core of many accounts of technology inspired by Martin Heidegger's famous essay on technology, as well as his studies of "movedness" in Book II of Aristotle's *Physics* (1939).[9] Briefly, Heidegger's concern in *The Question Concerning Technology* (1954) is that modern technology's mode of being releases a standing reserve of energy that Heidegger calls "enframing," which he characterizes negatively as a form of control or "ordering": technology "banishes man into a kind of revealing that is an ordering."[10] Further to this, one of Heidegger's concerns (as expressed in the essay on Aristotle's *Physics*) is that "for us today, space is not determined by way of place; rather, all places, as constellations of points, are determined by infinite space that is everywhere homogeneous and nowhere distinctive."[11] This concern over homogeneity and indistinction and his account of modern technology's essential movement as enframing suggest a normative dilemma of modern technology: its nature is exploitative (and specifically exploitative of natural resources) because having rendered all space indistinct, modern physics is not in a position to provide the normative differentiation of space necessary to safeguard certain substances (say trees, or topsoil, or human *poiesis*).

Though too brief, this recollection of Heidegger's position on technology is in stark contrast to Gilbert Simondon's studies. Simondon's philosophy of individuation challenges the inherited intuition that thinking begins with substances and goes further in also challenging the substantialist account of technical objects tout court. *On the Mode of Existence of Technical Objects* first appears in 1958, four years after the German publication of Heidegger's *Question Concerning Technology*; and though, as Andrea Bardin notes, references to Heidegger are quite rare in the work and mainly concern Heidegger's reductionist account of technicity as instrumentality, it is clear that Simondon's concern with technics is distant from either Heidegger's technophobia or even the cybernetic technophilia of his time.[12] *On the Mode of Existence of Technical Objects* was Simondon's first book and what established him in France as a thinker of technics. "Individuation in the Light of the Notions of Form and Information" was his doctoral thesis, which he defended in 1958, and it elaborates a robust and (admittedly) difficult philosophical project that we will barely dip into. These works together comprise an impressive and lasting intervention into a sentimental empiricist metaphysics of relation that we saw both Jean Wahl and Simone de Beauvoir develop in their distinct ways.

Recall how Aristotle claims that any substance can only become what it is; it cannot become other than what it is, and it cannot transform, alter, or change its essence. This is what *genesis* (the Latin translation for the Greek γίγνεσθαι meaning coming-to-be) means for Aristotle. Thus, essence precedes genesis; or being precedes becoming. But, Simondon will ask, how can we assume the existence of being prior to genesis? Is it not the case that we must rethink the process of genesis itself as independent of substance—that is, *as* process that is undetermined by essence? Moreover, why is it that we presuppose substance/identity as prior to genesis/transformation/difference? Pursuing these metaphysical questions anew (especially in light of the discoveries in physics, cybernetics, and information theory of the time) allows Simondon to think becoming as process rather than as the property of a pre-constituted essence.[13] Simondon's explicit task, then, is to distance our thinking from both an atomistic *and* an Aristotelian metaphysical tradition that conflates "being as such from being as individual."[14] He is thus not interested in privileging the constituted term or identity as the basis of philosophical inquiry into the nature of being because "in privileging the constituted term, it has ignored the *operation* constituting the individual, that is, *individual as process*."[15] This process of formation (or *in*-formation) of any individual term is what Simondon means by the term "individuation." It is also what he calls "allagmatics" (taken from the Greek *allagma*, meaning change, vicissitude, or what is given in exchange).[16] Here, then, is Simondon's primary thesis: "The true principle of individuation is genesis in itself in its process of operation, which is to say the system in its coming-to-be of actualizing energy." And further: "The principle of individuation is an operation."[17]

In the Introduction to his *Individuation* book Simondon affirms that both the atomistic and the hylomorphic account of Being are problematic in that they "both presuppose the existence of a principle of individuation that is anterior to the individuation itself."[18] That is, both hylomorphism and atomism affirm that Being's concreteness precedes any process of formation determining Being as a cause rather than an effect. Thus, when we ask, "What is X?" (say, gender identity or human consciousness), we assume X to be prior to our question. By conceding that substance exists, neither atomism nor hylomorphism is in a position to account for ontogenesis (i.e., the becoming of existence) that is the operation of individuation. His objective, then, will be to focus his inquiry on what he calls "pre-individual being":

> We would like to show that the search for the principle of individuation must be reversed, by considering as primordial the operation of individuation from which the individual comes to exist and of which its characteristics reflect the development, the regime and finally the modalities. The individual would then be grasped as a relative reality,

a certain phase of being that supposes a preindividual reality, and that, even after individuation, does not exist on its own, because individuation does not exhaust with one stroke the potentials of preindividual reality. Moreover, that which the individuation makes appear is not only the individual, but also the pair individual-environment. The individual is thus relative in two senses, both because it is not all of the being, and because it is the result of a state of the being in which it existed neither as individual, nor as principle of individuation.

From the get-go we learn that Simondon's investigation is not one into the existence of reality but is—in sympathy with Wahl's empirico-critical metaphysics of the concrete—an inquiry into the towardness of formation (indeed, we can think Simondon's theory of individuation as a force of "towardness" in Wahl's sense of the term). These processes are replete with undetermined developments, amorphous oscillations, and plural relations. If there is concretization in the operation of individuation, such concreteness is not a substance (again echoing Wahl); it is a metastable phase. For Simondon, in fact, there are not stable essences but only metastable concrescence. There is thus a preindividual reality that is a dispositional power of assembly formation that he will refer to as "dephasing": "The opposition between being and becoming can only be valid within a certain doctrine that supposes that the very model of being is a substance. However, it is also possible to suppose that becoming is a dimension of being corresponding to a capacity of being to fall out of phase with itself, that is, to resolve itself by dephasing itself."[19]

Existence is a process of dephasing, which is to say that existence is neither being nor becoming, but both together.[20] Emphasizing this operation is the work that Simondon's language of metastability accomplishes. Forms coalesce; the condition of existence is not one of either substance or change; existence is the pulsation of dispositional power that (de)phases. In short, Simondon's philosophy of individuation challenges the Eleatic privileging of the law of non-contradiction as the first principle of being: either being or non-being, either substance or process, either stable or unstable, either identity or difference. In its stead, Simondon's dispositional process of dephasing oscillates (Wahl again) between terms—stable *and* unstable, identity *and* difference, being *and* becoming. Moreover—and I take this to be central to Simondon's intervention—the incapacity to think individuation is merely a habit produced by repetitions that consistently generate the relation of contradiction as a primary metaphysical relation.

Recall, in this respect, how Aristotle's account of substances throughout the *Physics* and *Metaphysics* is grounded in the Eleatic contention that being and non-being cannot both be said of the same thing—that there is no middle position (*tertium non datur*) between being and becoming. For Aristotle, it is not only the case that a substance is a totality, as we have seen, but the understanding must only think in terms of unities. All understanding, in other words, is oriented to complete wholes. The radicality of Simondon's sentimental empiricism is to show how the Eleatic principle of totalization (the either/or implicit in the *tertium non datur*) is itself a metastable dephasing emergent from a preindividual reality "that is more than a unity."[21]

Simondon's appeal to the "more than a unity" is, in an ironic sense, consistent with Aristotle's own project, even though it is wholly inconsistent with the latter's metaphysical premises. By this I mean that like Aristotle, Simondon founds his investigation on recent (for him) discoveries in the field of physics, and specifically quantum mechanics and the second law of thermodynamics. These innovations were, of course, not available to Aristotle and the Eleatics, and Simondon readily affirms that this is exactly why it has not been possible until now to think the force of individuation:

> Individuation has not been able to be adequately thought and described because previously only one form of equilibrium was known— stable equilibrium. Metastable equilibrium was not known; being was implicitly supposed to be in a state of stable equilibrium. However, stable equilibrium excludes becoming, because it corresponds to the lowest possible level of potential energy; it is the equilibrium that is reached in a system when all of the possible transformations have been realized and no more force exists. All the potentials have been actualized, and the system having reached its lowest energy level can no longer transform itself. Antiquity knew only instability and stability, movement and rest; they had no clear and objective idea of metastability. In order to define metastability, the notions of order, potential energy in a system, and the notion of an increase in entropy must be used. In this way, it is possible to define this metastable state of being—which is very different from stable equilibrium and from rest—that Antiquity could not use to find the principle of individuation, because no clear paradigm of physics existed to help them understand how to use it. We will try therefore to first present *physical individuation as a case of the resolution of a metastable system*, starting from a *system state* like that of supercooling or supersaturation, which governs at the genesis of crystals. Crystallization provides us with well-studied notions that can be used as paradigms in other domains; but it does not exhaust the reality of physical individuation.[22]

In contrast to Greek antiquity, recent discoveries in physics allow us to consider physical states as both stable and unstable, and this allows us further to posit the living individual not as a hylomorphic substance (i.e., an identity) but as an individuating system of dispositional powers. Prior to this moment, Simondon wants to say, object and energy were independent of one another; it was an either/or scenario. Something was either a particle or it was an energy wave. But as Gaston Bachelard taught and developed, and as Jean Wahl's introduction of Alfred North Whitehead into this conversation also shows, recent findings in physics reject both the atomist and the hylomorphic conceit that there is a distinction between simple and complex substances. It is this insight that allows Simondon to posit that atoms are not the basic unit of existence and that we can no longer think any individual entity as a stable form but, rather, need to think individuation in terms of metastability.

Metastable dispositions are how Simondon accounts for the towardness of concretization in individuation. To explain: An entity forms; but the process of formation (i.e., individuation) does not stop just because an entity appears. Any apparent entity cannot be considered stable, as its process of formation is never complete; or rather, the physical nature of the universe is such that we cannot assume stability as an inherent property of anything. The best that we can say is that any individual substance is a metastable entity to the extent that the dispositional powers that crystalize the elements and compose that concretization are forces of adjacency that are not inherent to the entity but external to it. The dispositionality of individuation does not rest. An individuation is thus a "more than a unity" to the extent that it is always in a state of dispositional concretization. Existence for Simondon thus "defines a condition of equilibrium in complex systems, the stability of which can easily be broken by the intake if a little bit of energy or information and, conversely, needs a continuative and regular energetic support to counter its tendency to entropy."[23]

Simondon's philosophy of individuation confirms the sentimental empiricist commitment to thinking of entities as relations. This means that to think anything in particular, one must think that particularity as a dispositional dynamic. This is what he means when he affirms the "more than a unity" of being. Hence, Simondon says in the Introduction to his *Individuation* book, it is possible to put forward the hypothesis that is an analog to that of quanta in physics and to that of potential energy in entropy:

(1) That individuation does not exhaust all of the preindividual reality, and that a regime of metastability is not only maintained by the individual, but carried by it, so that the constituted individual transports

with itself a certain associated charge of preindividual reality, animated by all of the potentials that characterize it. (2) An individuation is relative, just like a structural change in a physical system; a certain level of potential remains, and further individuations are still possible. (3) This preindividual nature that remains linked to the individual is a source for future metastable states from which new individuations can emerge. (4) According to this hypothesis, it would be possible to *consider every true relation as having the status of being, and as developing itself within a new individuation.* (5) The relation does not spring up from between two terms that would already be individuals; it is an aspect of the *internal resonance of a system of individuation,* it is part of a system state. (6) This living, which is both more and less than unity, carries *an inner problematic and can enter as an element into a problematic that is larger than its own being.* (7) Participation, for the individual, is *the fact of being an element in a greater individuation,* via the intermediary of the charge of *preindividual reality that the individual contains,* that is, via the potentials that the individual contains.[24]

I have taken the liberty of numbering each of the sentences to spend some time with them (in the original passage they are not numbered), as I take this paragraph to be one of the most compelling articulations of Simondon's contributions to sentimental empiricism. Let's break down this passage:

1. Individuation is a process that is neither wholly necessary nor wholly contingent. An individuation may reach a metastable phase but its metastability is premised on the dispositional powers of concretization that persist in their dephasing; hence individuation's status as *in*formation (Simondon defines information as a "prise de forme" that translates as a "part-taking of form")[25] and Simondon's wholly Humean insistence that "being does not possess a unity of identity, which is that of the stable state in which transformation is possible; being possesses a *transductive unity,* which is to say that it can dephase itself in relation to itself."[26]

2. Individuations are undetermined by a telos because dispositional. Simondon's philosophy of individuation is neither dialectical nor teleological. The dispositional powers of individuation mean two things further: first, that being is difference; and second, that "the notion of form must be replaced by that of information."[27] By this, Simondon does not mean information as data but a coming-to-be of form. The causal principle here is once again dispositional, by which I mean neither wholly necessary nor wholly contingent.[28]

Unlike the view proposed by information theory, Simondon's dispositional account of information is not reducible as either signal or message because information is not a substance.[29]

3. The *in*formational condition of a transductive unity suggests that the potential for transformation is ever-present, which is why the preindividual condition never dissipates when a dephasing occurs. This means that change is a constant and not an achievement brought about by the overcoming of a contradiction.

4. No concretization is a necessary substance but a metastable individuation.

5. In a transductive unity the potential for change is "part of a system state." Muriel Combes observes that Simondon is less concerned with dismissing traditional hylomorphic terms like form and matter than he is in revising them. The terms "form" and "matter," she explains, "are now connected to an understanding of being as a system in tension, and are seen as operators of a process rather than as the final term in an operation consigned to the shadows."[30]

In expressing these postulates, Simondon concludes that a philosophy of individuation requires a new type of modal logic that is not dependent on the ancient law of non-contradiction: "The method consists of not attempting to compose the essence of a reality using a *conceptual* relation between two pre-existing extreme terms, and of considering all veritable relations as having the rank of being. The relation is a modality of being, it is simultaneous to the terms for which it ensures the existence."[31] The task, in short, is to pluralize logic it-self, which is one of the major tasks that the *Individuation* book sets out for itself.[32] To do so requires not only transforming the status of the law of non-contradiction, but also transforming the dispositionality of thinking itself.

6. In this respect, the expression "inner problematic" (in sentence 6 from the previous block quote) is decisive and returns us to the emphasis on "l'enjou" in the *explication de texte*. To recap briefly: given the metastable phasing of any individuation, a transductive unity remains unresolved because it is (a) dispositional and (b) in a process of formation. More to the point, an individuation does not exist prior to the transductive operation; an individuation is "pos-ited" as emergent, as is the case with the formation of crystals in a supersaturated solution.[33] The crystal is an "inner problematic" (which is both more and less than a unity, as he says, and thus more and less than a problem) to the extent that it exists in an unresolved tension with its milieu. And this condition of the crystal qua "inner

problematic" makes it inordinately difficult to affirm that the crystal is the telos of supersaturation. It can't be. The crystal is a metastable individuation that exists because of a dispositional relation to its milieu. In short, it is an emergence.

Finally:

7. Participation does not regard the collaboration of discrete and stable units in the procurement of a consensus that resolves conflict or disagreement. The "inner problematic" of individuation requires a rethinking of participation as an interactive element in a preindividual reality whose disparate phases persist.

The challenge posed by the "inner problematic" is that neither an orientation to consensus nor to recognition are adequate intellectual and/or political responses to the dispositional dephasing of individuation. As individuations we don't participate by expressing a consensus or by affirming a recognition because neither the stability of a solution nor the concreteness of an identity is available. Participation is thoroughly interactive and dynamic, irresolute and fundamentally associative and relational. To return to a passage already cited from Alberto Toscano's discussion of Simondon, "The originary disparateness of preindividual being forbids any totalization"; and this includes the totalizations posited in a politics of consensus *and* a politics of recognition.[34] The "inner problematic," in other words, is the dispositional powers of the "preindividual reality that the individual contains." This inner problematic never dissipates but remains as the force of participation for any and all individuations.

At this point in my presentation of Simondon's contributions to sentimental empiricism, I wish to pause for a brief summary before moving onto, and returning to, the discussion of technics and the parallels between his account of technical objects and his philosophy of individuation. As we have seen, Simondon's crucial contribution is to extend Wahl's discovery of a radical pluralism in the tradition of sentimental empiricism by articulating a "more-than-a-unity" of individuation. An individuation is thus not a substance but a perpetually operant system of metastable relations. Like the sentimental empiricist of the eighteenth century who understood the sentiments as dispositional powers of conjunction and disjunction that provisionally stabilize existence, so does Simondon affirm the power of individuation as a process of adjacency that can only persist. However, the dispositional power of dephasing within any metastable individuation also persists, which means that any metastable formation is persistently subject to transformation.

For Simondon, it follows that his philosophy of individuation is not just an ontology of the dispositional powers of associationism (as Toscano correctly shows) but also, and crucially for our purposes, a metaphysics of perpetual participation. Simondon in this sense inverts Aristotle by affirming that substances are not primary, but participation *is*. "Participation" here refers to a technical operation ("*l'opération technique*") of mediation in itself ("*la mediation elle-même*") that does not give priority to form over matter. Here is Simondon:

> Mediation is prepared by two chains of preliminary operations which bring together material and form in a common operation. Giving a shape to clay is not imposing a parallelepiped shape on the raw clay: it is the compacting of prepared clay in a manufactured mold. If we start from the two ends of the technological chain, the parallelepiped and the clay in the quarry, we have the impression that, in the technical operation, a meeting between two realities of heterogeneous domains is achieved, and that a mediation, by communication, is instituted between an inter-elementary, macrophysical order, larger than the individual, and an intra-elementary, microphysical order, smaller than the individual.[35]

The account of mediation in these first two sentences undermines the more conventional accounts of mediation Simondon recounts in the latter part of the passage. The first account is wholly Aristotelian and assumes that form is active and matter is passive, that the mold shapes the clay. But the former, allagmatic, account insists otherwise. Here the operation regards a common participation between two heteronomous series, neither of which is active and/or passive. This is what's at stake in the description of shaping as a "compacting of prepared clay in a manufactured mold." Neither the prepared clay nor the manufactured mold is a finished substance; they are operations. In the former, one finds an operation of preparation, and in the latter there is an operation of manufacture, neither of which is finished in the prepared clay or in the manufactured mold, because both of those antecedent operations persist in compacting the clay and mold together. In other words, shape is not emergent from the mold as applied to the clay, but as a result of an operant process of compacting of clay *and* mold procuring "prepared clay" and "manufactured mold." Mediation in Simondon's account is thus a process of transformation of heterogeneous entities rather than an operation of shaping between a dominant and active form and a submissive and passive matter.[36]

   The example of mold and clay are, of course, a reference to Aristotle's famous treatment of bronze molds in his *Metaphysics*, and Simondon explicitly reworks these in his articulation of a dispositional account of mediation, one that does not take substances (like mold and clay) as pre-given but are in themselves *in*-formation. Rather, what he offers is a dynamic technical operation of molding ("*l'opération technique de moulage*") that, he explains, is not dependent on a determinant metaphysics of linear causality but is one developed from dispositional powers of individuation. Mediation is thus not a linear operation oriented toward a resolution between two antagonistic substances (i.e., identity/difference; form/matter); it is a complex of participation and transformation, perpetually operant within any entity that is, itself, a metastable dephasing. In short, mediation is difference-in-itself conceived as independent to and undetermined by Being qua substance. Simondon's account of mediation is fundamentally different from Aristotle's mimetic account of the technical object. Rather than representation, recognition, and imitation of identity, Simondonian mediation isolates an operation of individuation whose dispositional powers generate a "more-than-a-unity."

With this account of radical mediation in mind, we are now in a position to appreciate Simondon's contributions to the analysis of technical media, how this analysis is different from traditional accounts of technics as derived from Aristotle's theory of forms, and how Simondon's account of technical objects contributes to postwar French sentimental empiricism.[37] Recall that Simondon wrote his two works simultaneously, and both were submitted as part of his *Doctorat d'État* requirements (however, the first part of the *Individuation* book (the part that works out his critique of Aristotelian hylomorphism and explains his philosophy of individuation in detail) isn't published until 1964 (the completed three-part edition of the *Individuation* isn't published in France until 2005), whereas *On the Mode of Existence of Technical Objects* is published in 1958. My point is that within the context we're discussing, the *Technical Objects* book would have been available for wider readership, whereas the *Individuation* book was not. Hence its importance and relevance not just to understanding Simondon's philosophical project or, for that matter to the study of media, but for his contributions to sentimental empiricism. For the remainder of this chapter, then, I will focus on the first part of the *Technical Objects* book (the section entitled "Genesis and Evolution of Technical Objects") because it is in these pages that we find the crux of Simondon's technical thinking in relation to his critique of Aristotelian hylomorphism.

A Sentimental Empiricist Philosophy of Technical Objects

In the Introduction to *On the Mode of Existence of Technical Objects*, as a prelude to his account of the ontogenesis of technical objects, Simondon sets out his task thusly: to conceive of the relation between humans, technics, and culture anew. He will understand that new relation as one of pluri-participation rather than one of the hierarchical domination of form onto matter.[38] This is enabled by his having shown how the Aristotelian account of mediation in hylomorphism (the one that subjects matter to form) is not determinative of the operant conditions of mediation as such. Simondon thus begins by asserting that the rigid distinction between technics and culture is a false one, that it is "a facile humanism" that "masks a reality rich in human efforts and natural forces, and which constitutes a world of technical objects as mediators between man and nature."[39] Recalling that Heidegger's *The Question Concerning Technology* essay was published just four years prior to Simondon's book, it is difficult not to read his castigation of facile humanisms as anything other than a rejection of Heidegger's account of enframing.[40] Simondon doubles down on distancing himself from the pervasive "misoneism directed against machines" by asserting that the real condition of alienation in the world resides "in this misunderstanding of the machine, which is not an alienation caused by the machine, but by the non-knowledge of its nature and its essence, by way of its absence from the world of significations, and its omission from the table of values and concepts that make up culture."[41] He further affirms that "the machine is the stranger; it is the stranger inside which something human is locked up, misunderstood, materialized, enslaved, and yet which nevertheless remains human all the same."[42]

As we have noted, one of the characteristics of the tradition of sentimental empiricism is a rejection of the Eleatic and Hegelian postulate that difference is negation. We see this emphasis expressed in Simondon's reconceptualization of the relation between human and technics beyond the precepts of Aristotelian hylomorphism. Simondon will thus refuse the account of technicity as a mode of alienation or negation of being. Instead he will show that by not reducing technical objects and their operations to a facile instrumentalism, we can better appreciate how technical objects exist in a participatory relation to humans, but also how the technical object is not an object in the substantialist sense, but an association of human, environment, and machine (what he calls an "associated milieu").[43] Hence his ambition to "reintroduce an awareness of the nature of machines, of their mutual relations and of their relations with man, and of the values implied in these relations."[44] This, for Simondon, is what it means to define the technical object "through its genesis," thereby showing why the technical object "cannot be considered as a mere utensil."[45]

The process of technical evolution and concretization to which the first part of the book is dedicated is likened to a "phylogenetic lineage, a definite stage of evolution [that] contains dynamic structures and schemas within itself that partake in the principal stages of an evolution of forms."[46] Simondon's main example—the engine—will provide the basis for his analyses throughout the book. In a now familiar sentimental empiricist move, Simondon does not treat the engine as a substance or a fixed structure. The steam engine, the diesel engine, and the gasoline engine—each of these engines exist independent of each other and in relation to the specificity of their own forms of individuation. That is, each of these is part of a phylogenetic lineage of dynamics that partakes in the dispositional arrangement of the technical object:

> The unity of the technical object, its individuality, and its specificity are the characteristics of consistency and convergence in its genesis. The genesis of the technical object partakes in its being. The technical object is that which is not anterior to its becoming, but is present at each stage of its becoming; the technical object in its oneness is a unit of becoming. The gasoline engine is not this or that engine given in time and space, but the fact that there is a succession, a continuity that runs through the first engines to those we currently know and which are still evolving.[47]

Notice the emphasis in this passage on treating processes of continuity not as individual instances or atomistic data: there is unity, but the unity of the technical object is metastable. Thus the affirmation that "the technical object in its oneness is a unit of becoming" that emerges as a convergence of functions and operations. To the naked eye, in other words, an engine, a canvas, or a film—that is, any technical object—presents as a unity. But as we have seen, Simondon invites us to think these as a plural and dynamic entity, one that is characterized both by movement and displacement. This is the lesson of his metaphysics of individuation that forces us to rethink the objecthood of technical objects and the participatory dynamics of mediation. Simondon will affirm that the medium's existence is its forms of mediation or participation within a phylogenetic (or networked) lineage of transformations and convergences that remain in various phases of individuation (i.e., *in*formation): "The technical object thus exists as a specific type obtained at the end of a convergent series. This series goes from the abstract to the concrete mode: it tends toward a state which would turn the technical being into a system that is entirely coherent within itself and entirely unified."[48]

At this point we might wonder whether we haven't returned to some kind of Aristotelian unity of form and matter. Isn't the whole point of Aristotle's treatment of dramatic poetry in *Poetics* just this: to offer an account of a coherent and unified system that constitutes the criteria for what a good work is? This would be a correct conclusion drawn from Simondon's statement if we did not give full weight to the powers of dispositionality at work in his account of technical objects. There is a unity of the technical object, but it is a metastable ensemble accomplished at a point in a convergent series. Indeed, the "concrete mode" that the technical object tends toward is dispositional as a "process of concretization" that is more-than-a-unity. Here, aspects of Jean Wahl's empirico-criticism are very much present in Simondon who, like Wahl, insists that concretization is a process rather than a thing. "Each piece, in the concrete object," Simondon explains, "is no longer simply that which essentially corresponds to the accomplishment of a function desired by the builder, but part of a system where a multitude of forces act and produce effects that are independent of the fabricating intention."[49] "Therefore," he continues, "it is not enough to say that the technical object is that for which there is a specific genesis proceeding from the abstract to the concrete; the point has to be made that this genesis occurs because of essential, discontinuous improvements, as a result of which the internal schema of the technical object is modified in leaps rather than following a continuous line."[50]

Beyond noting the overlaps between the project of the *Individuation* book and that of the *Technical Objects* book, we are at a point where we might now draw some conclusions regarding Simondon's contributions to postwar French sentimental empiricism. But before we do, I would like to add one final commentary to Simondon's discussion: "We can therefore affirm," he says,

> that the individualization of technical beings is the condition of technical progress. This individualization is made possible by the recurrence of causality within a milieu that the technical object creates around itself and that conditions it, just as it is conditioned by it. This simultaneously technical and natural milieu can be called an associated milieu. It is that through which the technical object conditions itself in its functioning. This milieu is not fabricated, or at least not fabricated in its totality; it is a certain regime of natural elements surrounding the technical being, linked to a certain regime of elements that constitute the technical being. The associated milieu mediates the relation between technical, fabricated elements and natural elements, at the heart of which the technical being functions.[51]

A fundamental difference between Simondon's account of the individuation of technical objects and Aristotle's account of the unity of poetic form lies in the fact that for Simondon there can be no subject/object distinction between human and technical being. A technical object is indistinguishable from its associated milieu—in fact, it *is* the associated milieu that is engendered by the dispositional powers of adjacency at work in the metastable concretization (i.e., the engine); this because the technical being is a plural formation that transforms according to the interaction between fabricated and natural elements. Hence the assertion that the associated milieu "mediates" the relation

of elements. To further illustrate this, Simondon will refer to a classic sentimental empiricist trope that becomes a cornerstone of the interaction of
organs in the human body: "An individual is not made up of a collection of organs combined with one another into systems; an individual is also made up
of that which is neither organ nor structure of living matter, insofar as it constitutes an associated milieu for the organs; living matter is the content of the
organs; it is what allows them to relate to each other and become an organism;
it is what maintains the fundamental thermal and chemical equilibriums
upon which the organs deliver brisk, but limited, variations: the organs participate in the body."[52]

Two conclusions need to be drawn from this account of mediation that are
fundamental to Simondon's contributions to sentimental empiricism: (1) As
already noted, the human/technical object partition is not determined (or,
indeed, conceived of) in terms of the subject/object relation implicit in philosophies of identity and recognition. The human and technical do not stand
apart from one another but partake and participate with one another like the
organs in a body participate to maintain thermal and chemical equilibriums.
Rather than distinct terms that associate with one another, the human and
the technical are processes of concretization in the associated milieu. (2) The
second—and perhaps most dramatic and arresting—consideration given traditional accounts of mediation is that the mode of relation of mediation is
neither negation nor overcoming. Individuation and mediation for Simondon
are dispositional powers that precede the actualization of technical objects. To
conclude from this that technical objects are instrumental tools of alienation
or enframing is not a sustainable conclusion, given the pluralist and non-
substantialist nature of the technical object.[53] The genesis of a technical object, Simondon will thus assert, "is very different from the dialectical schema
because it implies neither necessary succession, nor the intervention of nega-
tivity as a motor of progress; furthermore, opposition, within the schema of
phases, only exists in the particular case of a two-phased structure."[54]

For the purposes of this study, the preceding passage is the clearest formulation of the sentimental empiricist rejection of a metaphysics of negation
that is available. For Simondon there is no inherent relation of the technical
object that determines its organization, including dialectical negation. The
account of the organism as complex system is exemplary and assists in enforc-
ing this insight: An organism is not simply an organization of organs that
constitutes an ordered system; it is, rather, a dynamic of system of dispositional
powers that enables the participation of parts. These parts exist as active elements in an associated milieu that disposes organs.[55] Thus he affirms that "all
these elements . . . participate in a content that gives them direction, a ho-

meostatic unity, and that acts as a vehicle for informed energy from one to the other and among all of them. One could say that the content is axiomatic; in it new systems of forms are elaborated. . . . We can create technical beings because we have within us a play of relations and a matter-form relation that is highly analogous to the one we constitute in the technical object."[56]

Gilbert Simondon's philosophy of individuation is uncannily familiar to us, despite perhaps our encountering it for the first time. We've read many of his ideas before, though perhaps not expressed in the manner in which he expresses them, and certainly not in relationship to the ontology of technical objects he articulates. The critique of substances, the anti-essentialism, the pluralism, the emphasis on the undetermined participation of parts, the resistance toward dialectical negation as the inherent principal of all critique—all these elements are, dare we say, recognizable positions typically associated with the post-structural critique of identity politics. But part of my ambition in this book, and in this chapter especially, is to show that our recognition of these positions and our identification of them with the arrival of French theory in North America come at the cost of acknowledging the aspects of sentimental empiricism with which these positions participate and, I would say further, to which they are indebted.

There is no doubt that Simondon is a sentimental empiricist thinker. Like Wahl before him, Simondon begins by turning to the world of physics (especially) to assert that our metaphysical assumptions, rooted as they are in Aristotelian hylomorphism, need to be refigured. Hence his development of a philosophy of individuation. Simondon believes that metaphysical existence is a metastable phase for the partaking of form. But this form-taking or, becoming-form, does not happen as a result of preformed elements or atoms coming together according to various specified causal modes. With neither substantialism nor atomism at his disposal, a sentimental empiricist metaphysics needs to be articulated and with it a new mode of thinking the relationship of parts and the dispositional powers that assemble and dephase entities.

I wish to conclude this chapter by specifying the ways in which Simondon's philosophy of individuation contributes to the minor tradition of sentimental empiricism that we explore further in the subsequent pages. As we have noted, there are certain specific elements of this minor tradition that one sees appearing throughout the authors and works we examine. Two of those major features appear in Simondon's work: the critique of substances and the pluralist ontology of relations. What Simondon's philosophy of individuation allows for is an account of the dispositional powers of collective participation. As I have presented it, Simondon's thinking is wholly and unabashedly anti-authoritarian and anti-totalitarian. His realism rejects the possibility of unity/totality as something that is at once physically and metaphysically real. Any unity/totality that might be named as such can only exist as a metastable equilibrium in an associated milieu comprised of dispositional powers. In light of this, and of his influence in the works of such other thinkers as Michel Foucault, Gilles Deleuze, Bruno Latour, and contemporary new materialists, it is not surprising to see his ideas extended directly to discussions of political organization and participation in everyday life. In short, the minor tradition of sentimental empiricism that emerges from an engagement with Simondon offers the French postwar period a way of rethinking political participation and political organization beyond the hylomorphic reduction of the identity/difference binary. By doing away with the law of non-contradiction as inherent to thinking as such, Simondon makes it possible to think pluralism as the simultaneity of differences and to think political participation as a transformation of relations.

6

Gilles Deleuze

Displacing Reflection

By "displacing" I actually mean "overthrowing," and by "reflection" I mean "mimesis." This is how I understand the political stakes of Gilles Deleuze's philosophical enterprise when, in *The Logic of Sense*, he characterizes thinkers of nonsense as the ones who "displace all reflection."[1] My focus in this chapter will be Gilles Deleuze's single-authored works, and specifically the works that predate his collaborations with Félix Guattari in the 1970s. Those later collaborations, *A Thousand Plateaus* chief among these, have received substantial attention by political theorists in recent years, especially with regard to such concepts as deterritorialization, rhizomes, assemblage theory, and lines of flight.[2] These ideas also find expression in works of political theory that extend Deleuze and Guattari's oeuvre to other fields of inquiry. I'm thinking here of Neil Roberts's articulation of freedom as *marronage*, Christina Beltrán's queering of a unified Latino political identity, and Jane Bennett's account of "influence" as something other than a linear causal relation.[3] There is also a well-established tradition of scholars who mine Deleuze and Guattari's writings for inventive new ways of thinking about contemporary democratic life.[4] Finally, there is much work on Deleuze's contributions to metaphysics and the history of philosophy, from which I draw extensively.[5]

In continuation with the project of this book, however, I depart from these engagements with Deleuze's work and focus on two things: (1) how Deleuze's pre-1970s works establish the centrality of sentimental empiricism to his philosophical and political project; and (2) how his philosophical oeuvre—that is, the philosophical ideas he innovates and develops, the authors he relies on for his innovations, *and* the conceptual transformations he advances—are the locus of a sentimental empiricism that undermines the historico-philosophical commitment to mimesis and understanding as first philosophy. This political project of displacing reflection is, as I understand it, what Deleuze means by the "overturning of Platonism."[6] But here we must be careful: Platonism is not reducible to Plato's ideas and/or works. The term Platonism is, for Deleuze, a synecdoche for a system of selection and participation grounded in the Eleatic ideal of non-contradiction.

Gilles Deleuze is a sentimental empiricist thinker who wishes to challenge the Eleatic/Parmenidean rejection of difference-in-itself and its intellectual inheritance in the history of Western thought. This is as much a political project as it is a philosophical one. Or, better put, Deleuze's work will show that the philosophy of difference-in-itself is crucial to a non-essentialist and non-hylomorphic account of collective political participation. For Deleuze, radical democratic thinking and radical democratic participation cannot be thought of in terms of the unification of individual will or the unification of collective wills. Indeed, the identitarian impulse to unification in philosophy and political thinking must be substituted with a metaphysics of difference-in-itself. This involves many steps. But the most fundamental step Deleuze takes is a sentimental empiricist one: like (and via) Hume he will affirm that a mental or physical representation is not a substance (pace Aristotle and Kant); it is an association of impressions (i.e., between word and object, between thought and world, between image and nature). The associated milieu is not premised on an inherent relation that anticipates the existence of something but is an event of individuation (Simondon) or concretization (Wahl) that Deleuze will variously articulate as an assemblage, the Body-without-Organs, or in his work with Guattari, as the rhizomatic and deterritorialization. The basic premise, however, is a critique of power as attributable to any unified substance, whether individual, group, or sovereign state. Put differently, there is no being of the subject that predates the processes of formation of subjectivity that are dispositional and not teleological. This fundamental commitment to sentimental empiricism (as expressed in his 1953 monograph on Hume and sustained in *Difference and Repetition* and *The Logic of Sense*) allows him to displace the privilege of mimesis as a necessary relation for collective life. But this also means that understanding (or sense, or meaning) is not an anterior or inherent relation for existence. By turning to Hume's empiricism, Deleuze will refute the priority of Being and understanding, or what he also refers to as "the dogmatic image of thought."[7] This then allows him to revisit the Eleatic reduction of difference to negation (i.e., non-Being) and propose a metaphysics of difference-in-itself. The project of a metaphysics of difference-in-itself and that of displacing of reflection constitute the sentimental empiricist core of Deleuze's political thinking.

How are these philosophical contributions *political*? That is, how is the project of a metaphysics of difference-in-itself a political theory of sentimental empiricism? To provide the framework for answering this and other related questions is the task of this chapter. I focus on two of Deleuze's works: his 1953 monograph on Hume and an Appendix to his 1969 *The Logic of Sense* entitled "The Simulacra and Ancient Philosophy." Though made available in 1969, the "The Simulacra and Ancient Philosophy" appendix is a reworked version of an essay entitled "Lucrèce et le naturalisme" originally published in 1961 in the journal *Études philosophiques*.[8] As I have noted throughout, my wish is to explore the development of a labile series of minoritarian aesthetic and political innovations of those authors whose intellectual formation and writing career took shape in France immediately after the war. For this reason, this chapter deals primarily with Deleuze's first monograph as well as the 1961 essay, though I will make occasional references to some parts of *The Logic of Sense*.

In my discussion of Deleuze's sentimental empiricism I will keep the following political context in mind (one that, I trust, will be familiar to readers at this point): For many postwar denizens of the Latin Quarter, the modern French state is a bourgeois colonial state whose practices of settler colonial violence continue well into the Fifth Republic. The national education system—and the expectations of its institutions of reading (especially the *explication des textes*)—make this palpable. When Deleuze declares, in his 1962 book on Nietzsche, that "philosophy does not serve the State or the Church, who have other concerns,"[9] he is referring to the political ontology of mimesis as situated in the relationship between knowledge and state/ecclesiastical domination in France.[10] A mode of political thinking and criticism that responds to a political ontology of mimesis can't be one that recuperates and rehabilitates the dogmas of the image of thought. The point is not simply the development of an epistemological rupture, as Bachelard and Althusser might conceive of it, but a metaphysical one. Thus, the motivating question for our sentimental empiricist authors: what is the nature of criticism if and when mimesis is not prioritized as the inherent relation of all thinking and when understanding is not considered the telos of all critical activity?

As we shall see, the philosophical and political task for Deleuze isn't to critique—in the sense of "negate"—the dogmatic image of thought, but to turn it inside out that is, to overturn or displace it. Deleuze's development of an inversive operation will introduce a sentimental empiricist mode of criticism that doesn't negate propositions but rather disjoins adjacencies by proposing a logic of *renversements* or inversions that stand as non-sense.[11] This critical operation begins by not accepting a metaphysics of substances as *le bon sens* of critical thinking and, in its stead, considering all apparent continuities as a series of adjacencies. A critical philosophy of inversion means operating at the junctures of adjacencies that hold things together. Political power, then, is conceived not simply as a form of domination that keeps things in order; it is also a dispositional power that arranges relations.

Deleuze's project begins with a radical revisiting of Hume's philosophy and (especially) of Hume's dismantling of Aristotle's metaphysics of substances that—from both a classical and Catholic humanist standpoint—is the foundation of state thinking.[12] In this chapter I analyze the following elements of Deleuze's sentimental empiricism that I treat as among his most compelling contributions to political theory:

1. The empiricist critique of Aristotelian substances: Substances exist because of a logical and metaphysical system that understands the necessity of cause and effect as prior to all relations and the determinative of existence as such. The dismantling of substances results in the dismantling of causality and necessity as principles of inherent relation, but also the dismantling of a system of logic based on chrono-time and the law of non-contradiction. This operation of dismantling inherent relations comes through the articulation of political and philosophical critique as an operation of inversion (i.e., *renverser*).

2. Relations are thus not inherent but external. This makes it so that one may treat any unity or totality as a system of external (and invertible) adjacencies. This proposition is explicit as a mode of political and aesthetic critique in Deleuze's work, but we also recall that it had already been fully formulated by Jean Wahl in *The Pluralist Philosophies of England and America*.

3. A political ontology of change or "difference-in-itself." This is part of what Deleuze refers to as the overturning of Platonism.

4. A metaphysics of difference-in-itself will ground a critical theory not beholden to negation as the inherent principle of critique.

5. Deleuze develops a political theory of sentimental empiricism, but also a political physics of dispositional powers: The "sentiments" in sentimental empiricism do not name specific feelings but rather describe a domain of forces (i.e., affections) that move bodies in space and time. This movement of bodies in space and time, their arrangement and disposability, are what makes sentimental empiricism political. In short, sentimental empiricism denotes a political physics of disposability.

6. If sentimental empiricism offers a political philosophy of difference-in-itself, then the central unit of analysis is no longer the subject but

the series. A series, however, does not imply sequence (i.e., understood as an external system for organizing succession according to chrono-time).

My analysis of these themes begins with an engagement of Deleuze's first monograph, *Empiricism and Subjectivity* (1953). Specifically, I will show how Deleuze reads Hume's empiricism and sentimentalism *together* and as part of the same collection of ideas. By examining these features of Hume's thought, Deleuze is able to establish some foundational commitments to sentimental empiricism that will remain with him throughout his oeuvre. From here I proceed to offer a close reading of Deleuze's essay "The Simulacrum and Ancient Philosophy." Here my focus will be on the critical operation of inversion as a sentimental empiricist mode of critical political thinking.[13]

Deleuze, Reader of Hume

Deleuze offers a highly original account of Hume's empiricism that seems to draw quite substantially from Jean Wahl's contributions. I say "seems to" because Deleuze's work doesn't cite Wahl, though, as we have noted, it is possible to see substantial parallels between their works. This is not surprising, of course, since we also noted that Wahl was likely the person who encouraged Deleuze to write on Hume.[14] The originality of Deleuze's reading of Hume is in its departure from post-Kantian engagements with his epistemology. For Deleuze empiricism does not refer simply to a theory of knowledge, but to a practice of life in and through which worlds emerge.[15] He will thus emphasize how Hume is a thinker of difference and a dismantler of the priority of representation. Central to this reading is what Deleuze will refer to as Hume's logic of relations, which affirms that relations are not dependent on the quality or the nature of substances. This means that for Deleuze, Hume allows us to think difference as a relation, thereby concluding that Hume's empiricism a philosophy of difference.

One of the most notable features of Deleuze's engagement with Hume is how Deleuze does not present Hume either as a dialectical thinker or as a thinker of contradictions. For Deleuze, Hume's contributions to critical thinking do not require negation. A contradiction implies a metaphysical apparatus that confirms the existence of substance/being/identity and its negation (i.e., non-Being). In this system both Being and non-Being are substances; non-Being, however, is a contradiction as a substance because the negation of something cannot be anything. Hence the privilege of negation as the operant of critique. But Hume's dismantling of identity negates the Eleatic metaphysics of

Being. Hume's empiricism turns to experience and impressions and emphasizes the operations of relation in the imagination because it does not presuppose contradiction (and thus reason) as the inherent and exclusive law of thinking and understanding. For the sentimental empiricist critique cannot be reducible to overcoming contradictions, because any entity or event is the locus of multiple relations and impressions.

From a Humean perspective, then, philosophy can only be an exercise of conceptual creation in the imagination, as Deleuze notes in the Preface to the English edition of *Empiricism and Subjectivity*. By the time of his composing this Preface, Deleuze had dedicated his career to such an enterprise: that is, he understood and practiced the study of philosophy as an experimentation with impressions and ideas. For instance, in Claire Parnet's philosophical documentary *Abécédaire*, she arrives at the letter K and asks, "K is for Kant"? His response is revealing. He knows very well that he is known as a critic of Kant's normative ethics and of his epistemology. Indeed, his 1967 book entitled *Kant's Critical Philosophy* offers a compelling and influential inversion of Kant's legislative theory of the faculties as a foundation for common sense. But his reply in the *Abécédaire* shows how his critique of a Kantian system of facultative legislation stems from Kant's own magisterial conceptual invention: the idea of the tribunal as a mode of philosophical engagement. Kant, he says, is the thinker of judgment who articulated the practice of philosophy as a "tribunal of reason" that is "inseparable from his critical method."[16]

From this answer we sense a political provocation. Deleuze is a state-sanctioned teacher of philosophy who must teach the history of philosophy within a national education program designed to conserve and reproduce knowledge. The tradition of mimesis that grounds the French education system seeks imitation from the history of philosophy. One reads authors to imitate their ideas, their ways of thinking, their forms of thought, their ways of asking questions, and—most crucially—their ways of solving problems. These authors have been selected as worthy of imitation; they are the *Maîtres* of thought because through their writings one develops a *sens d'État*. But this is not how Deleuze begins. He is not interested in the history of philosophy as another occasion for the imitation of the derivation of proofs; rather, his approach will be to show how new concepts are invented as a result of various processes of conceptual individuation. In other words, his critique of state authority comes through his inversion (i.e., *renverser*) of the history of philosophy.

We can extrapolate how Deleuze might have developed his approach to concept creation from Hume's own work. For Hume, thinking does not involve the derivation of truths. Rather, the mind artifices ideas by associating impressions. Impressions are the felt impact of an external world upon the body; they are the immediate residue of experience. Hume wants us to appreciate the extent to which we think with our bodies. Whatever happens in the mind simultaneously happens in and through the body, and vice versa. But neither mind nor body is a substance that precedes experience. Rather, whatever mind or body may be, its coming to be is spontaneous. Deleuze explains that for Hume, "the mechanism of the body cannot explain the spontaneity of the subject."[17] This means that both body and subject are not reducible to one another; *in* the imagination the subject is artificed of the body, which means that *in* the imagination a spontaneous relation is created between body and subject. This is what Hume calls "personal identity," which, he famously asserts, is not a substance but a composite or series of impressions. The continuous repetition of associations between serial impressions creates a habit of associations that generates a sense of integrity and continuity; that habit of associations is a subject. Thus, Deleuze warns, "one must always avoid endowing, in the beginning, the organism with an organization, an organization that will come about only when the subject itself comes to mind, that is, an organization that depends on the same principles as the subject."[18] The subject is not a substance; it is a spontaneous organization of forces. But the subject's form of organization does not precede the power of organization itself: the organism does not determine the form the organization takes. Rather, any existing organism is a metastable formation generated by the dispositional powers of the imagination.

It is in this sense that we speak of the freedom of the imagination. But freedom here is not a liberty born of a will. The imagination is free because it is unwilled and automatic. This is what Hume means by "human nature." "Nature" for Hume is not an essence or a core value; it is an autonomous and free operation. The imagination is human nature because it is not legislated by any external power or concept; it is a fully automated system whose operation is one of associating differences—different impressions, different sensations, different experiences. This is why neither substances nor selves exist as anything other than differential relations generated *in* the imagination. The Aristotelian conjoining of form and matter, in other words, does not indicate Being; it indicates adjacency. It's as simple as that: hylomorphism does not produce a substance; it is the name given to processes of adjacency that relate form and matter. But it's also as radical as that: neither form nor matter has an inherent causal power because dispositional adjacencies (fr. *agencement*) are at once external and non-purposive: Any substance, including that substance we call a self, is a dispositional adjacency *in* the imagination.

If ideas are adjacencies forged in the imagination, then the history of philosophy is not a progressive unveiling of reason. It is a discontinuous history of practices of solidarity qua dispositional adjacencies. Hume iterates the fact that ideas emerge *in* the imagination. And Deleuze reiterates it: "Nothing is done *by* the imagination," Deleuze explains; "everything is done *in* the imagination."[19] The imagination doesn't even form ideas. The philosophy of techne that affirms essence as a kind of molding (i.e., Aristotle's discussion of bronzes in the *Physics*) is wholly out of place and off the mark for our sentimental empiricist authors. The imagination is not a willful power that imposes form upon impressions to produce innate ideas. On the contrary, the imagination is an operant where automatic processes of repetition adjoin impressions to one another. Nothing is formed or molded; everything is in process and emergent. Thus, Deleuze affirms, "we are indeed capable of stating what the idea of subjectivity is. The subject is not a quality but rather the qualification of a collection of ideas."[20] In very curt terms: "the subject" is an entanglement generated from the dispositional powers of intermediality.[21]

Much of Deleuze's treatment of Hume in *Empiricism and Subjectivity* is an attempt to account for a dynamic theory of habit that he famously reprises in his discussion of the contractile power of habit in *Difference and Repetition*.[22] Typically when we think of a habit, we assume something that is done at once tacitly, passively, and unreflectively—like biting one's nails or smoking. We oppose habit to reflection. Habit in this sense is a kind of repetition compulsion that makes humans unfree by denying us a critical understanding of our own actions and, more importantly, by denying us access to a dimension of willful agency that would allow us to do things otherwise. A classic example here is Augustine's account of sin articulated in his *Confessions*. Sin is an appetitive compulsion that habituates the subject to turn away from God's love. This movement of turning away from God's love grounds Augustine's definition of evil. Therein lies the paradox of original sin: God didn't create evil. God created free creatures. Humans will evil freely by turning toward themselves and thus turning away from God. In the end, the *Confessions* narrates a series of repetitive acts of turning away that Augustine articulates as the life-narrative of the sinner that, as it turns out, is also the narrative arch of human history until Jesus's redemptive act of sacrifice. The Paulinian Christology at the heart of Augustine's theology introduces the figure of a redemptive Christ (qua incarnation of God's love) as the only source of critical rupture from the human compulsion to sin. Augustine is ultimately converted through an act of transformation that he describes as a turning *toward* God's love.

This is not how either Hume or Deleuze understands habit. For these thinkers, habit is a force of contraction; it is passive, but not in a conformist way.[23]

Habit is a contractile power of mind that adjoins (i.e., contracts) impressions. In *Difference and Repetition*, Deleuze calls habit a passive synthesis. Here is how he explains it: "In essence, habit is contraction. Language testifies to this in allowing us to speak of 'contracting' a habit, and in allowing the verb 'to contract' only in conjunction with a complement capable of constituting a habitude. . . . This is no mystical or barbarous hypothesis. On the contrary, habit here manifests its full generality: it concerns not only the sensory-motor habits that we have (psychologically), but also, before these, the primary habits that we are; the thousands of passive syntheses of which we are organically composed. It is simultaneously through contraction that we are habits, but through contemplation that we contract. We are contemplations, we are imaginations, we are generalities, claims and satisfactions."[24] In short, humans do not have selves; or, better put, a self is not a qualitative substance but a series of repetitions, contractions, adjacencies, and recurrences: "Selves are larval subjects," Deleuze famously concludes; "the world of passive synthesis constitutes the system of the self, under conditions yet to be determined, but it is the system of a dissolved self."[25]

What we can observe in Deleuze's development of Humean habit is, as in the account of the imagination, a techne (i.e., "the system of self") independent of will or legislation. Habit here is a wholly impersonal force that, through its powers of contraction (i.e., its passive syntheses), participates in the formation of what Hume calls character, and it is impersonal because it is a force that precedes personhood.[26]

The same holds for the power of the sentiments. These are not qualities of human beings; they are dispositional powers that affect bodies. A sentiment like sympathy is not a virtue; it is an impersonal affection that attracts bodies to one another and in so doing partially concretizes the composition of character. My capacity for sympathy is not a marker of good character in the sense that it is not a quality I possess because there is no "I" that precedes that power of sympathy to compose character. Sympathy is felicitous to the extent that it is a dispositional power that extends bodies outward and provides occasions for character to acquire reputation. But it is not a quality, nor is it a determined virtue. The sentiments are thus both natural and impersonal operants that precede subjectivity because they are dispositional powers that adjoin impressions and ideas. The sentiment of sympathy is thus an expression of human partiality because subjectivity can only be partial. The concatenation of my partialities doesn't result from a will but from a series of forces that operate to conditionally concretize my sense of self.

Moreover, no human has the capacity to overcome one's partiality; the best that we can do is move beyond our particular sympathies (those attractions grounded on our capacity to experience immediate pleasure and pain) and extend outward. This, at its core, is the challenge of sentimental empiricism: how might bodies extend sympathy beyond the immediacy of their partiality. The impersonal power to relate and to arrange is how Deleuze understands sentimentalism, which is (once again) neither feeling nor affection but refers to forces of adjacency that disposes bodies in space and time. Such dispositional arrangements are a provisional composition.

What, then, is empiricism according to Deleuze's Hume? It is the discovery of a world of difference and repetition: "Empiricism begins from the experience of a collection, or from an animated succession of distinct perceptions. . . . This is the principle of difference . . . experience is succession, or the movement of separable ideas insofar as they are different, and different insofar as they are separable. We must begin with *this* experience because it is *the* experience. It does not presuppose anything else and nothing else precedes it."[27] The human subject is thus not a substance—not in the Aristotelian sense of *ousia* or "essence/soul." Human subjectivity is always a plural repetition of differences. What is key in this empiricist account of subjectivity is the interstitial space between the differences that separate distinct perceptions. To the perennial question "what is existence?" the Eleatics had affirmed the totalizing virtues of purpose and meaning; to wit, meaning is life's purpose. The availability of meaning is a mimetic operation, as we saw in our discussion of Aristotle's metaphysics of mimesis, whereas criticism and judgment are those operations of mind that when used correctly provide a sense that is proper.

By showing how all substances and unities are systems of adjacency, the sentimental empiricist will turn away from a mimetic concept of criticism. Their answer to the question "what is existence?" is not meaning, but the activities of association and the modes of participation that adjoin and disjoin experiences. Existence, in short, is the creation of worlds. The turn away from an idealist metaphysics of mimesis also marks a turn toward a materialist physics of dispositional powers—of bodies, of elements, of events, and so forth. What holds all these things together is not an ontology of being but dispositional powers of adjacency.

"Hume's philosophy," Deleuze affirms, "is a sharp critique of representation. It does not elaborate a critique of relations but rather a critique of representations, precisely because representations *cannot* present relations. By making representation into a criterion and by placing ideas within reason, rationalism expects ideas to stand for something which cannot be constituted within experience or be given in an idea without contradiction."[28] If impressions are serial repetitions that the imagination adjoins automatically, then we can't say that the mind is a substance with an inherent power of representation, nor can we say that representation is a property of mind. Hume has shown us otherwise. His philosophy offers a trenchant critique of mimesis qua property because it insists on the interstitial space between experiences as autonomous and un-regulated interstices of difference-in-itself. This is the radical innovation that Hume's thinking contributes to sentimental empiricism and that distinguishes it sharply from the dogmatic image of thought. Hume shows us how the subject is a probability and not a necessity.

This point needs further clarification, so let us turn briefly to a relevant pas-sage in Hume's *Treatise* (Part I, Section IV) for some assistance:

> The idea of a substance as well as that of a mode is nothing but a collection of simple ideas, that are united by the imagination, and have a particular name assigned them, by which we are able to recall, either to ourselves or others, that collection. But the difference betwixt these ideas consists in this, that the particular qualities, which form a substance, are commonly refer'd to an unknown something, in which they are supposed to inhere; or granting this fiction should not take place, are at least supposed to be closely and inseparably connected by the relations of contiguity and causation. The effect of this is, that whatever new simple quality we discover to have the same connexion with the rest, we immediately comprehend it among them, even tho' it did not enter into the first conception of the substance. Thus our idea of gold may at first be a yellow colour, weight, malleableness, fusibility; but upon the discovery of its dissolubility in aqua regia, we join that to the other qualities, and suppose it to belong to the substance as much as if its idea had from the beginning made a part of the compound one. The principle of union being regarded as the chief part of the complex idea, gives entrance to whatever quality afterwards occurs, and is equally comprehended by it, as are the others, which first presented themselves.[29]

We know that Hume's point of reference in this section of the *Treatise* is the scholastic commitment to Aristotelian substances. But it is the principle of in-herent adjacency in the idea of substance that Hume will unravel. His criti-cism points out the painfully obvious: whenever we think of something as a substance or an identity—say, "the nation" or "gender"—we are *thinking* of it; that is, we have an idea of it. And an idea is a probability—*not* in the sense of something that isn't true; but in the sense of something that might otherwise be the case. In order for there to be such things as Aristotelian substances, there must be the guarantee of a force of association that perpetuates through time. However, the stochastic nature of impressions is such that we cannot confirm or guarantee the force of necessity in all possible permutations of future outcomes. It is in this sense that an adjacency is an actualized probability, or what Hume will also call a fiction. An actualized probability will feel like a substance—"an unknown something in which they are supposed to inhere"—but this unknown something is nothing other than a repetition, a power of recurrence holding impressions together *in* the imagination.

When Hume says that "the idea of a substance as well as that of a mode, is nothing but a collection of simple ideas, that are united by the imagination, and have a particular name assigned them" and then proceeds to call this operation "fiction," he is describing the mechanics of the imagination where experiences are conjoined to produce the instantaneity of an impression. Most importantly, the forces of adjacency in the imagination betray a simple fact: no association is necessary; all associations are probabilities. For Hume unities are unities out of habit, and habit is a process of the repetition of difference. This is what I take him to mean when he concludes that "the principle of union being regarded as the chief part of the complex idea, gives entrance to whatever quality afterwards occurs, and is equally comprehended by it, as are the others, which first presented themselves."

This is a powerful statement and a powerfully devastating principle of criticism. It puts on display the radical pluralism of sentimental empiricism by affirming that we have no way of guaranteeing what properly belongs to any system of associations. At its core, Hume's conclusion suggests that sentimental empiricist criticism is uninterested in what we can know but *is* interested in what and how things participate (i.e., enjoin) with one another. *This* is the sentimentalist part of sentimental empiricist criticism, by which I mean the associationist and pluralist dimensions that treat criticism as a power of adjacency without qualities or qualifications. That power of enjoining is what Hume calls "the principle of union" that cannot be read as an a priori principle, but as a felt and observed—or sensed—one. The principle of union is not something that precedes that moment of union; it is that which is actualized in the process of adjacency. It is an emulsifying agent rather than a binding agent; it occurs independent of an external source that would or could legitimate the fact of union. Hence the power of the imagination that deploys forces like cause, contiguity, analogy, and the like. The principle of union is the "chief part" of a complex idea because it gives "entrance to whatever quality afterwards occurs." Importantly, we must read the appeal to comprehension as something other than the mind's capacity to understand. By "comprehension" Hume means "include" or "pull into its orbit," a *prehension with*. The principle of union is a centripetal power that "gives entrance" to (i.e., prehends with) a "whatever quality."

I read the word "whatever" as crucial to Hume's critique of causal necessity and, *ceteris paribus*, to his rejection of an Aristotelian metaphysics of mimesis; but I also read it as crucial to his development of sentimental empiricist criticism. The "whatever quality" of what follows is an undetermined (and undeterminable) property, in the same way that Hume famously characterizes sunrises, which are probable but not certain. (Recall: *"That the sun will not rise to-morrow* is no less intelligible a proposition, and implies no more contradiction than the affirmation, *that it will rise.* We should in vain, therefore, attempt to demonstrate its falsehood. Were it demonstratively false, it would imply a contradiction, and could never be distinctly conceived by the mind.")[30] Hume's "whatever quality" is thus not a relativism, but a probability. More than a statistical likelihood, a Humean probability refers to a pluralist disposition toward potential actualities that are not yet occurrent. In other words, Hume's "whatever quality" names his appreciation of the experimental method that, Jacqueline Taylor has argued, "allows him to create a *new* discourse of human nature, one emphasizing the origin of certain mental perceptions (most notably, belief, the indirect passions, and the moral sentiments) within the framework of the theory of association."[31] In doing so Hume is able to displace all explanations that rely on final causes and thus all appeals to understanding as beholden to a mimetic a priori.

What then is the critical operation in sentimental empiricism? It is not the negation of an identity but the pluralization of adjacencies and probabilities of future entrances of whatever qualities. Sentimental empiricist criticism is not related to the negation of an opinion but to the proliferation of world relations. The orientation toward "experience" thus does not determine the concrete facts qua data but, instead, signals events of relation that artifice worlds. It is possible to believe in the world not because we can prove its existence, but because the dispositional powers of the sentiments extend bodies outward to produce new—metastable—relations. This, for Deleuze's Hume, is sentimental empiricism's principle of difference that, in the end, is also a principle of criticism: "Hume often talks about a critique of relations. Actually, *it is not the relation that is subject to critique, but rather representation. Hume shows that representation cannot be a criterion for the relations. Relations are not the object of a representation, but the means of an activity.* . . . What is denounced and criticized is the idea that a subject can be a knowing subject."[32]

I read this last passage, which concludes Deleuze's *Empiricism and Subjectivity*, not only as the foundation for his critique of Aristotelian scholasticism and Cartesian consciousness, but also as a political critique of the system of selection that qualifies participation in political activity on the basis of a mimetic theory of the self. Within the political milieu of state-authorized systems of mimetic belonging, the "knowing subject" is not simply an abstract philosophical category: it is the foundation—indeed the quality—for citizenship. We saw how France's education system is designed to produce a knowing subject whose mode of political action is mimesis (i.e., representation and imitation). The knowing subject is thus an agent of the State; that is why—to repeat a passage already cited—"philosophy does not serve the State or the church, who have other concerns."[33] In order for philosophy not to serve the State, it must innovate a new set of relations between thinking and the world that inverts the system of privileges of the dogmatic image of thought. Deleuze's experimentation in concept creation develops a political metaphysics of difference-in-itself that is wholly indebted and ensconced in the tradition of sentimental empiricism he uncovers in Hume's writings. From this, he will develop a critical theory of inversions (i.e., *renversements*) that attempts to do away with the privileged status of contradiction as the form of all criticism.

Inversions

One of the claims I make in the previous section is that Deleuze's turn to Hume, and the account of sentimental empiricism that he offers in turning to Hume, are political. Unlike Anglophone readers of Hume who do not acknowledge Hume's philosophical writings (and especially the *Treatise*) as works of political theory (turning instead to either his *History of England* or his *Essays*), Deleuze focuses wholly on the *Treatise* and the *Enquiry*, and from these he extracts a radical critique of subjectivity, identity, and substance that *is* a political critique of authority and innate property. Moreover, Hume's dismantling of an Aristotelian metaphysics of substances also offers Deleuze a new approach to critical theorizing—one that is not beholden to the identity/difference relation. This innovation in criticism lies in the following precept: order is emergent from a system of adjacencies that organizes bodies, perceptions, and experiences; it is not an external power that commands and authorizes social, cultural, political, and metaphysical belonging. A. W. Moore explains this insight well: "For Deleuze difference is not to be thought of derivatively. It is to be thought of as the fundamental character of what is given, indeed as the Being of what is given. This is not to say that difference is *itself* given. It is not. But it is that *by that* what is given is given. What is given includes discrete entities and their various features, as well as assemblages in that discrete entities are interconnected in various ways. But it also includes something more basic, a multiplicity of differences, in terms of which everything that is given must ultimately be explained. Any such explanation must therefore eschew appeal to the subject, to God, to Platonic forms, to a transcendental structure holding everything together, even to persisting physical objects."[34]

This metaphysics of difference-in-itself is explicitly expressed as a political problem in "The Simulcrum and Ancient Philosophy." In this essay Deleuze tasks himself with showing how the Eleatic denunciation of difference-in-itself and the subsequent privileging of a theory of Ideas are the result of a process of selection rooted in mimesis: "The motivation of the theory of Ideas," he says, "must be sought in a will to select and to choose."[35] "Platonism" is a dispositional system of domination that selects participants by attending to their capacity for claim-making. In this respect, it is difficult not to read Deleuze's efforts at inverting Platonism as anything other than a political critique of the mimetic relationship between philosophy and the State. In other words, Platonism is "the method of division" that enables the partitions that create categories for selection.[36] Thus, to negate Platonism is insufficient to the political task of inverting the system of selection and participation precisely because Platonism treats the capacity to think negation as its principle of selection. For Plato's Socrates, what distinguishes the sophist from the philosopher is the latter's capacity to think the negative: "To distinguish pretenders; to distinguish the pure from the impure, the authentic from the inauthentic . . . the Platonic dialectic is neither a dialectic of contradiction nor of contrariety, but a dialectic of rivalry (*aphisbetesis*), a dialectic of rivals and suitors. The essence of division does not appear in its breadth, in the determination of the species of a genus, but in its depth, in the selection of the lineage. It is to screen the claims (*pretensions*) and to distinguish the true pretender from the false one."[37] The theory of Ideas that grounds the history of Western thought is inseparable from the mode of dialectical thinking that selects pretenders. The first order of the theory of Ideas is thus not that of determining a truth, but of partitioning claimants, of selecting between true and false pretenders. Hence the originary power of the dialectic: to select lineages. The political stakes of Deleuze's philosophical analysis are immediately given: the problem with Platonism is the relationship it establishes between selection, lineage, and state power that is precisely the political dilemma of equality and democratic participation at the heart of the French education system.

Let us clarify something further: The French word for "claim-making" is *prétendre*, which also means "to pretend," as in to have a pretense or to lay a claim on something.[38] A *prétendant* is a candidate or suitor who has pretenses. To pretend in this sense is to put something forward "as an assertion or statement; to allege, assert, contend, claim, declare."[39] That Platonism distinguishes between true and false pretenders means that the task of this system of thought is to select between the good claimant and false one, as a young woman and her family might select a good suitor for marriage. The familial metaphor works here because we are talking about a kind of sacred union, one that produces a pure line of inheritance: Platonism creates a lineage of resemblances or, if you will, a kinship of future selections and privileges that is, of *legitimate claims*.

"Il s'agit de faire la différence," Deleuze says (the English text translates this as, "It is a question of making a difference").[40] This originary difference is created in the way that all ideas are (as Deleuze's Hume tells us)—*in* the imagination. Deleuze, the sentimental empiricist, thus wishes to emphasize at once the creational and relational elements that found the operational dynamics of a system of thought. The power of Platonism is its ability to transform a division (i.e., a *stoicheion*) into a lineage of true claimants (i.e., *muthos*).[41] In this logic of sense one discovers another logic, that of natural relations and privileged selections. The task of sentimental empiricism is thus not to contradict the statement of the claimant and thus verify the truth of the matter; rather, it is to dismantle the entire chain of adjacencies that enables the legitimacy—and the political authority—of this system of selection. "As a consequence of searching in the direction of the simulacrum," Deleuze affirms, "Plato discovers, in the flash of an instant, that the simulacrum is not simply a false copy, but that it places in question the very notations of copy and model."[42] This activity of placing into question the system of relations that establishes the "and" of "copy *and* model" is the task of sentimental empiricist criticism.

That Plato "discovers" this "in the flash of an instant" is about as Humean of an assertion as one can make. Platonism doesn't actually discover anything in the flash of an instant because discovery requires the long, difficult, and laborious work of reflection and derivation. But Deleuze tells us that Plato is struck by the impression that the simulacra queers the copy/model relation. The simulacra, in other words, is a critical *dispositif* not because it is the hidden truth of mimesis, but because it "places in question" the adjacencies that hold together the system of mimesis and its privileged processes of selection: "If we say of the simulacrum that it is a copy of a copy, an infinitely degraded icon, an infinitely loose resemblance, we then miss the essential, that is, the difference in nature between simulacrum and copy, or the aspect by that they form the two halves of a single division. The copy is an image endowed with resemblance, the simulacrum is an image without resemblance."[43] To think image without resemblance/mimesis is what Deleuze's sentimental empiricism affords.

His project, in other words, is one that refuses "the model of the Idea," because, as he affirms, "the same and the similar no longer have an essence except as simulated, that is as expressing the function of the simulacrum. There is no longer any possible selection. The non-hierarchical work is a condensation of coexistences and the simultaneity of events."[44] The simulacrum is thus not a conceptual edifice, nor is it a principle of criticism; it is a form of adjacency that concretizes coexistences and simultaneities; the simulacrum is the domain of seriality without either sequence or *muthos*. It is in this sense, then, that we must understand Deleuze's claim that the "overturning (*renversement*) of Platonism" is an activity of displacement. But what does it displace? It displaces the systems of relations that ensure the exclusivity of privileged procedures of selection and participation: "The simulacrum is not a degraded copy. It harbors a positive power that denies *the original and the copy, the model and the reproduction.*"[45]

Deleuze's critical project "is inspired in its entirety by empiricism. Only empiricism knows how to transcend the experiential dimensions of the visible without falling into Ideas, and how to track down, invoke, and perhaps produce a phantom at the limit of lengthened or unfolded experience."[46] The same can be said of his political metaphysics of difference-in-itself. Unlike his Anglophone contemporaries, Deleuze is thoroughly dissuaded by a faith in the powers of mimesis to legitimate justice. The liberal commitment to consensus is, for him, the central political problem of postwar France. There already *is* a political common sense (*le bon sens*)—as well as an entire educational, cultural, and philosophical apparatus—committed to the reproduction of *une pensée d'État*. Deleuze's intervention stands as an effort to provide and account for metaphysical difference that is not tethered or reducible to the reproduction of state domination. In this respect, for Deleuze, political and aesthetic criticism is not oriented toward the sharing of meanings among participants admitted to the conversation of justice. Sentimental empiricist criticism unravels the political and aesthetic adjacencies that make selection and participation possible. These adjacencies, moreover, are neither subjects nor substances but concretizations. If the Image of Thought gives us a metaphysics of mimesis, Deleuze's minoritarian proposal offers a metaphysics of political thinking rooted in the sentimental powers that adjoin differences. Impressions are composed *in* the imagination "insofar as the collection designates not a faculty but rather an assemblage of things, in the most vague sense of the term: things as they are appear—a collection without an album, a play without a stage, a flux of perceptions."[47] And the same holds for a political society—that is, not a unity derived from an external authority (whether God, history, or nature) that organizes bodies in space and time so as to determine the legitimacy of selection and participation in the system of hierarchies; a political society is a dynamic process of associations and dissociations.

7

Michel Foucault and the Political Ontology of the *Dispositif*

At an otherwise innocuous moment during his January 18, 1978, lecture at the Collège de France, Michel Foucault stumbles just when he is about to resume his discussion of "apparatuses of security" (*dispositifs de sécurité*, fr.).[1] In both the English and French editions of the lecture, the interruption is footnoted in the text. Apparently, Foucault had bumped into the microphone of the device recording his lecture. As he recovers and before resuming his discussion he says this: "I am not against any apparatuses (*les appareils*, fr.), but I don't know—forgive me for saying so—I'm just a bit allergic. . . ."[2] The English doesn't render what's notable in the comment because the language is unable to mark the lexical shift, as the translation of *dispositif* is, conventionally, "apparatus."[3] Whereas there are multiple terms in French, we tend to use "apparatus" in English. But by 1978, Foucault had fully adopted and adapted the language of the *dispositif* to discuss the technical media of discipline, security, and governmentality, and he had done so—I will argue—by making an explicit political and aesthetic decision to substitute the conceptual architecture and term apparatus (*appareil*, fr.) with that of the *dispositif*.[4]

To chart this substitution and its political morphology, I look to Michel Foucault's extension of 1950s sentimental empiricism in the philosophical, political, and aesthetic innovations of his 1970s studies on the dispositional powers of governmentality, which, as I understand it, is a general term referring to an associated milieu of technologies of governance. My attention is on his shift away from a dialectical and negative account of technical objects that he identifies in the language of the *appareil* and toward an account of *dispositifs* of power. This articulation of the *dispositifs* of power offers a sentimental empiricist account of technical objects. In this period of Foucault's work, we find resonances of Wahl's account of concretization as well as Beauvoir's treatment of the dispositional powers of patriarchy as a technology that arranges bodies to produce the right order of things. Foucault's contribution to the study of political technologies is, I would suggest, also wholly aligned with Simondon's critique of hylomorphism and his reconceptualization of technical objects as an associated milieu of forces and perceptibilities. Finally, and not surprisingly, we see in Foucault's works strong affinities with Deleuze's reversal of Platonism and overturning of the exclusivity of negative critique. All of this results in a sentimental empiricist account of technologies of social and political arrangement that Foucault deems necessary to appreciate the dispositional powers of domination at work in everyday life.

A central theme of this book is to show how the philosophical projects elaborated in our authors' works contribute to a political theory of sentimental empiricist criticism. This approach to criticism is neither dialectical, nor teleological, nor sovereigntist. It is associationist, pluralist, and radically participatory. It begins by looking at the forces of association that coordinate relations. As a philosophy of criticism, sentimental empiricism is committed to the Humean critique of substances and thus of the principle that there are no inherent relations or innate powers of unity. This means that the principles of linear causality that guarantee a continuous succession of power, or the inheritance of privilege, or the reproduction of elite rule are the focus of sentimental empiricist criticism. As a mode of criticism, it is oriented to exploring how such causal relations might be fragmented and disjoined to break the momentum of the reproduction of the same.

In this chapter, I wish to show how Foucault picks up on these concerns, elaborated in France in the 1950s, and develops them with a specific focus on the political technologies implemented to dispose peoples, perceptibilities, and bodily movement in Western democratic societies. As is well known, one of Foucault's principal concerns throughout his lectures of the 1970s is to articulate a political theory of dispositional power that looks beyond the hierarchical model of sovereignty that accounts for how social value is concretized and distributed. In short, and as I read him, Foucault's efforts in the 1970s amount to providing his readers with a reworking and a rethinking of the conceptual arsenal of modern power in light of the fact that one of the features of modern Western democracies is that they are systems of social valuation and judgment and that these are skills and competencies that do not belong exclusively to authorized structures of juridical or sovereign authority.[5] As subjects within such political societies (indeed, as readers taught to assess the value of what we read) we are not just judged and evaluated by a juridical entity like a tribunal or by the fiat of a pontiff or a king; we are also judged and evaluated by one another in the classroom, on the playground, in an office, or (today) by an algorithm; and unlike the occasional fiat of sovereign and juridical judgment, evaluation in modern democratic societies is permanent and incessant.

This chapter focuses on Foucault's development of the language of the *dispositif*, but my interest extends beyond a scholium on Foucaultian terminology. My larger concerns regard how we might develop a sentimental empiricist account of media that looks to their dispositional powers. The reason Foucault's development of the *dispositif* is especially rich for such an investigation is that his terminology marks a shift from an instrumentalist view of technical objects as substances and toward a consideration of them as systems that arrange dispositions, attentions, and perceptibilities that is, as sentiments. This is a move that finds strong affinities with the work of Simondon, which offers a rethinking and reformulation of the forces of causality of modern technical media. The matter of the *dispositif* is, indeed, an issue of causality and, specifically, of the causal relationship between technology and influence that is said to produce a condition of alienation. For the sentimental empiricist Foucault, the account of direct causal influence implied in Louis Althusser's invocation of ideological recognition is insufficient (both historically and ontologically) to account for the dispositional powers of technical objects like the Panopticon (see Figure 3). Direct causality is equally insufficient in accounting for the work of collectivization that accompanies the *dispositif*'s capacity to distribute relations between spaces and sights, persons and things. In essence, Foucault's turn to the language of *dispositif* insists on thinking political mediation as a series of relational dynamics between entities rather than as a singular power of coercion or alienation upon subjects. The *dispositif* doesn't alienate or coerce, like the apparatus does; nor does it trigger a dynamic of recognition, as in the case of the interpellation scenario. It can't. Interpellation and recognition presume a sense of identity that for the sentimental empiricist is not available. Moreover, both of those related moral and medial psychologies exist in a metaphysical world of Aristotelian substances where objects have inherent qualities. The *dispositif*, on the other hand, articulates bodily arrangements and adjacencies where neither recognition nor substance is presupposed as necessary for the functioning of a technical milieu. The *dispositif* thus disposes, arranges, and assembles in exactly the way that Foucault appreciates Guillaume de La Perrière's definition of government as "the right disposition of things."[6] It is a dispositional modality of governance that aligns itself with a capacity for arranging, for doing, for crafting, and it implies a milieu of associated participation not available in the metaphysical universe of the apparatus.[7]

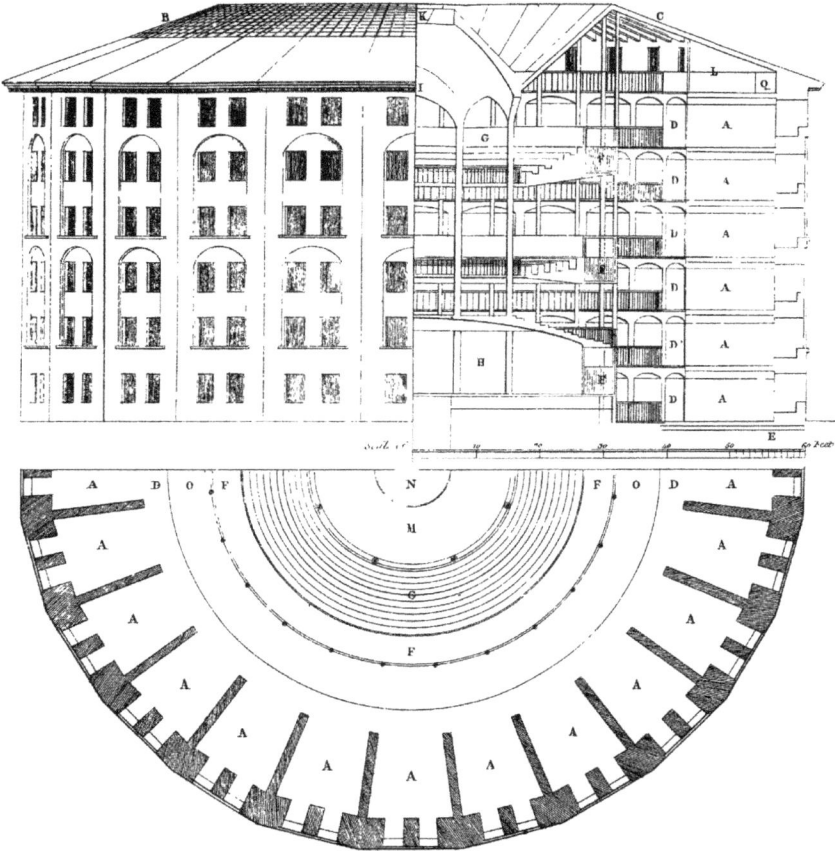

Figure 3. Jeremy Bentham's *Panopticon Penitentiary*, drawn by Willey Reveley, 1791 (*The works of Jeremy Bentham*, vol. IV, 172–73)

Unlike previous treatments of Foucault's *dispositif* that focus on his work from the mid-1970s onward (and especially his often-cited 1977 interview "Le jeu de Michel Foucault"),[8] I will show how Foucault begins with and never abandons the formal aesthetic insights he develops in his lectures on Édouard Manet's paintings. I will thus forward a sentimental empiricist reading of Foucault's Manet lectures (emphasizing his treatment of the *tableau-objet*) that argues that the distributions of visibilities he enlists in his (and our) viewings become the structuring visual mode that informs both his shift from the language of apparatus to *dispositif* and his formalist accounts of modern works of political theory. While it is true that Foucault offers a reading of Manet's paintings in his late 1960s lectures, it is also true that he develops a way of reading by means of the paintings. In his accounts of disciplinary *dispositifs* of governmentality (and the Panopticon chief among these), what matters is an attention to a *dispositif*'s capacity to arrange spatialities and visibilities. The Manet canvas also allows Foucault to appreciate Bentham's architectural drawings of the Panopticon *as* drawings on a flat surface and read his writings as if they were tableau-like objects that render available perceptibilities. This because his viewings of Manet's paintings and his account of the *tableau-objet* therein enable a perceptual mode that is attentive to the formal aesthetics of the canvas, to the formal dynamics of the Panopticon, and ultimately to the formal distributions in Bentham's own writings. In short, Foucault's viewings of Manet's *tableaux* and his discovery of the *tableau-objet* offer us an instance of sentimental empiricist criticism as a practice of reading that he deploys when reading and lecturing on the works of governmentality he explores in the 1970s.

The first section of the chapter discusses some studies on Foucault's *dispositif* in recent years, while the second section constructs the parallels between Foucault's treatment of Manet's canvasses and his subsequent readings of the Panopticon. By constructing these parallels, I not only want to draw the relevant insights of Foucault's aesthetic and political innovations; I also want to emphasize the sentimental empiricist critical reading practices Foucault develops in his Manet lectures that he then enlists in his 1970s Collège de France lectures and, of course, throughout *Discipline and Punish*. What will become evident, and what will seem to go against the grain of many Anglophone receptions of this period of Foucault's work, is that there is a decisive resistance to drawing normative conclusions from the formal analyses he provides. Instead, Foucault shows us the extent to which the cognitive model of recognition implied (and made famous by) Althusser's account of an apparatus's sovereigntist power of interpellation is inadequate to the operational dynamics of the *dispositif*. The final section of this chapter draws out the political stakes of this shift.

A Political Morphology of the *Dispositif*

Matteo Pasquinelli shows that there is little in Giorgio Agamben's account of the *dispositif* that is persuasive.[9] For Agamben, the term *dispositif* "designates that in which, and through which, one realizes a pure activity of governance devoid of any foundation in being," and he ties this claim to the translation by the Latin fathers of the Christian church of the Greek *oikonomia* as *dispositio* (i.e., the source of the French *dispositif*).[10] In his essay, however, Pasquinelli convinces us that Foucault's adoption of the term *dispositif* is actually indebted to his mentor Georges Canguilhem, who introduces it in his essay "Machine and Organism."[11] For Pasquinelli the connection that matters between Foucault's and Canguilhem's treatment of the *dispositif* regards the importance of the concept of normalization that Foucault inherits from Canguilhem. But more than this, it is the fact that the mechanical language to which the *dispositif* is tethered is, as he says, "first tributary to the emerging mechanical craftsmanship of the 17th century and to a technological view of power rather than to a Hegelian translation of the paradigm of positive religion."[12] The result of Foucault's innovation is to abstract the *dispositif* from the domain of Canguilhem's bio-philosophy and adapt it to this technological view of power in the modern period. Rather than a secularized form of divine power, as Agamben would have us believe, the *dispositif* is for Foucault a kind of automated force—in the most mechanical sense of the term—for the distribution and arrangement of bodies.

In a more generous reading of Agamben's disquisition, Jeffrey Bussolini recuperates something helpful in the etymology of *dispositif* from the Latin *dispositio* and shows how it relates to the verb *dispone*, which "concerns placing here and there, setting in different places, arranging, distributing (regularly), disposing; it also addresses specifically setting in order, arraying, or settling and determining (in the military sense)."[13] I would further add that the etymological root of *dispositif* from *dispositio* ties the activities of Foucault's intermedial objects to the ancient rhetorical tradition of *dispositio*, or the order and organization of oration. The classical sources here are Aristotle's *Rhetoric*, Cicero's *De Oratore*, and Quintillian's *Institutio Oratoria*, all of which delineate in their own specific manner the parts of a speech, from *exordium* to *peroratio*, and the importance of the arrangement of the parts.[14] As Perelman and Olbrechts-Tyteca note, the order of the parts of a speech are essential to persuasion, where "in choosing the order in which arguments are to be presented in persuasive discourse, account should be taken of all the factors capable of furthering acceptance of the arguments by the hearers."[15] There is no doubt that the orator must know her audience so as to best arrange her words accordingly. But this ambition differs in both matter and form from the activity of demonstration that, in the case of oration, is not an objective of speech.

Following the classical authors, Perelman and Olbrechts-Tyteca distinguish the *dispositio* of an argument from the demonstration of a proof. In the demonstration everything is given, and (as the word implies) what is given needs only be shown. "In argumentation, on the other hand, the premises are labile. They can be enriched as argument proceeds, but they always remain precarious, and they are adhered to with a shifting intensity. The order of the arguments will accordingly be dedicated in large measure by the desire to bring forward new premises, to confer presence on certain elements, and to extract certain agreements from the interlocutor."[16] Premises "remain precarious," in other words, because arguments are not demonstrative proofs but are constituent forms and thus "labile."[17] Such sensibilities of the *dispositio* suggest that the *dispositif* is not reducible to a medium of communication where demonstrable propositions are enunciated, represented, and can be clearly identified, analyzed, and transmitted. Quite the contrary. Communication has little to do with the practices of *disposition*, because *dispositio* is not a matter of transmission of information but rather of formal arrangements emergent from the dynamism between orator, audience, and the ornament of parts.[18] In *dispositio* the transparency of meaning is not what matters but how what is said is posed (and poised) so as to call attention and bestow notice: *dispositio* is a modality of collective participation. Hence the importance of the *dispono* of the *dispositif*—the active placing upon of parts, one in relation to the other, resting between and among each other.[19]

Another way of saying this, the way Canguilhem expresses it in "Machine and Organism," is that a *dispositif* is a "configuration of solids in motion such that the motion does not abolish the configuration. The mechanism is thus an assemblage of deformable parts, with periodic restoration of the relations between them. The assemblage consists in a system of connections with a degree of freedom: for example, a pendulum and a cam valve each have one degree of freedom; a threaded screw has two. . . . In any machine, movement is thus a function of the assemblage, and mechanism is a function of configuration."[20] Like the practices of *dispositio* in classical rhetoric, the *dispositif*'s role is not that of transmission of meaning but of arranging moving parts. Canguilhem's emphasis is on dispositional activities, or what he will call the "*cinématique*"[21] principles (translated in English as "the elementary concepts of kinematics")[22] of the *dispositif* that enable adjacency. Just as the order of premises needs to be labile to move an audience, so is the order of parts in a *dispositif* labile to produce a "configuration of solids in motion." These *cinématique*/kinematic elements raise the problem of machinic vitalism—an old problem that dates back (for Canguilhem) to Descartes but really, as he notes, to Aristotle's ontology of movement and the latter's likening of "the organs of animal motion to *organa*—that is, to the parts of war machines (e.g., the arm of a catapult, which launches a projectile), and he compares the course of their movement to that of machines capable of releasing, after being set off, a stored-up energy, automatic machines, of which catapults were the typical example in his period."[23]

Whereas Pasquinelli notes the aspects of the *dispositif* that connect Foucault's use of the term to Canguilhem's, I want to emphasize the kinematics of the *dispositif*, and specifically Canguilhem's central observation that "movement is thus a function of the assemblage, and mechanism is a function of configuration"—an observation that remains pressing in Foucault's adoption of the term. The *dispositif*, in other words, is a device of disposition, arrangement, and movement and precisely not an instrument of representation and alienation. What Canguilhem's formulation allows Foucault to do is to develop his critical analytics of power on the basis of the motility of things rather than on what will appear as a static and linear reflex function implicit in the model of recognition that the apparatus will exploit (i.e., the stimulus-response of interpellation). From an analytic perspective, then, this is the great shift that the *dispositif* enables, allowing Foucault to distance himself from what Knox Peden rightly notes as the perceived "conceptual poverty of the 'State apparatus,' in either its repressive or ideological incarnations."[24]

The dilemma, however, is more severe than even Peden's formulation implies. The problem isn't just the conceptual poverty of the State apparatus and the political stakes that follow from this. The real issue regards the political ontology of the Ideological State Apparatus and its inability to register any form of interactivity other than a call/response dynamic of recognition. The issue, in other words, regards whether the political function of media is always reducible to forms of alienation that demand the existence of a subject of recognition. For Foucault, Althusser's account of Ideological State Apparatuses is too committed to the private/public division in selfhood (recall that for Althusser the Ideological State Apparatus is a private relation that differs from the Repressive State Apparatus and its application of violence upon publics);[25] moreover, this model is equally too enmeshed within the causal logic of recognition as the engine of ideological coercion/influence. The ideological apparatus operates via a call and response feedback loop; this much is clear from the infamous interpellation scenario such that for something to "function by ideology"[26] means that from the perspective of causal powers, it is an automated, linear, call-response influence machine.

With these brief remarks, I suggest that the shift from apparatus to *dispositif* in the work of Foucault is (in part) invested in a dissatisfaction with the idea that political life operates on the model of the "reflex circuit."[27] In light of this we can begin to rethink Foucault's work of the 1970s as an attempt to recalibrate the commitment of ideology-critique to representing social and political domination exclusively on the behavioral mechanics of stimulus/response. Thus, it's not just the case that the Ideological State Apparatus is insufficiently attentive to the microphysics of power that Foucault will analyze throughout the 1970s, nor is it the case that such models of analysis have yet to cut off the head of the king, as he famously quips.[28] In fact, there is nothing in Althusser's account of Ideological State Apparatuses that would prevent an analysis of the microphysics of power, and—notably—all of Althusser's ideological institutions (i.e., schools, the military, prisons, and the police) are the same institutions that Foucault will examine in his treatment of disciplinary *dispositifs*.

For Foucault, the problem is greater than the issue of an image of power; it's an ontological one. The apparatus and its commitment to the call-response reflex circuit of recognition cannot consider complex participation and thus reduce political and aesthetic power to a model of linear causality. This is because the model of the apparatus (as we shall soon see) retains all the vestiges of a representational regime of perception like the one outlined in Foucault's reading of the mirror function in *Las Meninas* (see Figure 4). In contradistinction, the *dispositif* will be a site of complex movement of perceptibilities and actions that queer the private/public dividing line of the classical episteme. Hence the notable importance, for Foucault, of Manet's *tableau-objet*.

The status of the complex in perception and action is also the tenor of Gilles Deleuze's observations on Foucault's *dispositif*. In his short essay Deleuze describes the *dispositif* complex as a "multilinear ensemble" that holds "curves of visibility," "curves of enunciation," and "lines of force."[29] It is neither a specific device nor a linear function, but an ontology of entanglement; it is a relational mechanism, a complex of adjacency. We exist within *dispositifs*. In this respect they share with Ideological State Apparatuses the fact that there is no outside to them: "lines of visibility and enunciation, lines of force, lines of subjectification, lines of splitting, breakage, fracture, all of which criss-cross and mingle together, some lines reproducing or giving rise to others, by means of variations or even changes in the way they are grouped."[30] The ontology of the reflex constitutive of the apparatus can't grasp the complex ensemble of associations that the *dispositif* makes available—movements that, I should add, are not beholden to the subject/object dualism implicit in an ontology of the reflex. One senses this distinction (between the private individualism of the reflex and the associationism of the complex) when Foucault explicitly addresses the term *dispositif* in his January 15, 1975, lecture for the first time: "The eighteenth century, or the Classical Age, also set up a State Apparatus [*appareil*] that extended into and was supported by different institutions. And then—and it is on this that I would like to focus, or that I would like to serve as background to my analysis of the normalization of sexuality—it refined a general technique of the exercise of power that can be transferred to many different institutions and apparatuses [*appareils*]. This technique constitutes the other side of the juridical and political structures of representation and

Figure 4. Diego Vélazquez, *Las Menminas*, 1656, Museo del Prado (ArtStor)

is the condition of their functioning and effectiveness. This general technique of the government of men comprises a typical ~~apparatus~~ [*dispositif*], which is the disciplinary organization I spoke to you about last year. To what end is this ~~apparatus~~ [*dispositif*] directed? It is, I think, something that we can call "normalization." This year, then, instead of considering the mechanics of the disciplinary apparatus [*appareils disciplinaires*], I will be looking at their effects of normalization, at what they are directed toward, the effects they can achieve and that can be grouped under the rubric of 'normalization.'"[31]

The *dispositif* is "a general technique of the exercise of power" (or a "general technique of the government of men") that is also—and this is crucial to our appreciation of the aesthetics and politics of the *dispositif*—"the other side of the juridical and political structures of representation." So now we have a complex of dispositional powers for the "configuration of solids in motion" (Canguilhem), that is the "other side" of juridical and political structures of representations.[32] In short, as a power for the arrangement and disposition of elements and their relations (i.e., a power of governance) the *dispositif* is not a device of representation (like, say, a constitution might be a device of representation, or a Velazquez canvas). The power of governance is not reducible to the power of representation; in fact, as we learn throughout the 1970s, governmentality has little to do with representation.[33] This is why Foucault turns to modern tactics of discipline—not, that is, because discipline identifies the coercive and oppressive modes of domination in modern state forms, but because discipline is a complex dispositional modality not reducible to the privacy of the reflex circuit. In this regard, consider this earlier (November 28, 1973) invocation of "*dispositifs disciplinaires*": "This triple function, this triple aspect of the techniques of the accumulation of men and of the forces of work, is, I think, the reason why the different disciplinary ~~apparatuses~~ [*dispositifs*] were deployed, tried out, developed, and refined. The extension, movement, and migration of the disciplines from their lateral function to the central and general function they exercise from the eighteenth century are linked to this accumulation of men and to the role of the accumulation of men in capitalist society."[34] What the political ontology of the *dispositif* offers Foucault is a complex dynamic of vectors and forces (i.e., a "triple function") that is foreclosed by the apparatus and its ontology of linear causality.

Under the preceding summary, Foucault's descriptions of the *dispositif* and his attributions of its formal elements start to look and feel decidedly like descriptions and attributions of the formal elements of a modernist canvas. All the elements are there: it is a nonrepresentational surface, it is an entangle of multiple vectors of perceptibility, it is a medium of adjacencies and dispositions, and it is a site of dispositional powers and practices. The *dispositif* is also a domain where lines of visibility and invisibility, flatness, straightness, and curvature intermingle. It is a plateau wherein linearity itself—the capacity of lines (of sight, of writing, of drawing, of narrative, of agency) to hold shape, form, and representation—is placed under duress and rendered "precarious." The *dispositif*, in other words, shares an undeniable family resemblance to the *tableau-objet* that Foucault discovers in his viewing of Manet's paintings; it is a dispositional power in a world where the traditional logics of mimesis (which sustained the authority of sovereignty) no longer hold sway.

A Political Aesthetics of Foucault's *Dispositif*

One of the most remarkable things about Foucault's treatment of Manet is how decidedly acute it is in relation to his analysis of *Las Meninas*. This shouldn't surprise us, of course, because he is dealing with two very different painters in two very different historical periods; and one of the virtues of Foucault's study of *Las Meninas* in *The Order of Things* (however accurate or debatable it might be) is his attention to its status as a representational object and (more importantly) its archetypal stature as a painting that is of and about representation. Hence the lines of looking move us in and out of the painting and are consistently inflected by a desire to explain how representation qua reflection works therein. Of course, all of Foucault's descriptions about the inner mimetics of the painting are directed at bringing us toward the missing spectacle, outside the painting, but reflected in the painting by the gaze of the figures looking out: "A condition of pure reciprocity," as he affirms, "manifested by the observing and observed mirror."[35] In short, the painting confers upon the mimetic operation a reflex function: The reflection "restores, as if by magic, what is lacking in every gaze."[36]

In contrast, Foucault's treatment of Manet moves us across the viewing surfaces of the canvasses, not in and out of them. From his perspective, Manet's tableaux are a completely different object from Velazquez's, since the reflex dynamic of representation is wholly absent. The latter would likely not recognize the former's works as painting at all, because Manet's works seem to have little to do with the reflexive power of representation. Foucault is explicit about this in his introductory remarks when he discusses a general set of ambitions of painting that, since the *quattrocento*, typically revolve around the reflexive circuit of representational perspective and that create in painting an illusory space, "a represented space which denies, in a sense, the space on which it is painted."[37] But Manet breaks with this ambition; he interrupts representation: "The rectangular surface, the large vertical and horizontal axes, the real lighting of the canvas, the possibility for the viewer of looking one way or another, all of this is present in Manet's pictures, and given back, restored in Manet's pictures. And Manet reinvents (or perhaps he invents) the picture-object (*tableau-objet*, fr.), the picture as materiality, the picture as something colored that clarifies an external light and in front of which, or about which, the viewer revolves. This invention of the picture-object (*tableau-objet*, fr.), this reinsertion of the materiality of the canvas in that which is represented, this I believe is at the heart of the great change wrought by Manet to painting, and it is in this sense that one could say that Manet really turned upside-down, beyond what could have foreshadowed Impressionism, all that was fundamental in Western painting since the quattrocento."[38]

In this section, I want to pick up on Foucault's viewing practices when looking at Manet's paintings and on his insistence that Manet's canvasses move the
viewer "about." In doing so I want to recreate the mood, the "curves of visibility," the "regimes of light," and "the lines of force" (Deleuze) that enable Foucault to attend to and develop his attentions to the *dispositif* as a medium of
modern political life.[39] In short, what I wish to put on display is Foucault's development of the *tableau-objet* as a transmedial consonant of the *dispositif* and
show that what he says about Manet's tableaux becomes a portmanteau for a
set of formal aesthetic and political concerns that inform his analysis of politics
in the modern period (and especially his analyses of governmentality in the
1970s).[40] It becomes clear that after Manet, Foucault will no longer be interested in looking at the function of representation in works (of art, of writing, of
political theory) but will instead look for the practices of organization and arrangement that constitute a formal political aesthetics of the modern period.

We know that in 1967 Foucault had signed a contract with Éditions de Min-
uit for a book on Manet entitled *Le noir et la couleur* (The Black and the Color).
But all that remains from this are a series of student notes of a 1971 lecture on
Manet's paintings delivered in Tunisia, where Foucault had been living and
teaching since September of 1966, and where he penned *The Archeology of
Knowledge* (first published in France in 1969).[41] We are assured, by Foucault's
life-long partner and estate manager Daniel Defert, that nothing else exists of
Foucault's extended study of Manet; all notes and the hundred or so pages of the
book that Foucault is said to have written have been destroyed. The text of
the lecture, however, is enough to go on, given its richness, and recent writings
by Joseph Tanke, Gary Shapiro, and Catherine Soussloff have also added much
to our appreciation of Foucault's interest in Manet.[42]

Foucault's lecture focuses on three aspects of Manet's reversal of representational painting: the space of the canvas, lighting, and the place of the viewer.
Many points Foucault raises throughout the lecture, and especially his discussion of the flatness of Manet's paintings, align him with some of Manet's contemporary American interpreters—Stanley Cavell, Clement Greenberg, and
Michael Fried chief among these—all of whom affirm that an important dimension of Manet's contributions to modernist painting is an acknowledgment
of the fact of painting can be something other than a representational art.[43] To
quote Greenberg, "All through the 1860s it was as though each picture (save for
the still lifes and the seascapes) confronted Manet with a new problem. It was as
though he could accumulate nothing from experience. . . . Each painting was a
one-time thing. A new start, and by the same token completely individual."[44]

Foucault's lecture seems to want to address Manet's confrontation with the
problem(s) of painting by focusing on the three elements mentioned earlier.

The discussion of space, and specifically the space of the canvas, deals with the problem of what painting is once the *quattrocento* dependence on Brunelleschi's vanishing point disappears as a necessary element of the pictorial arts. That disappearance, Foucault has already indicated in his introductory remarks, is a principal site of the break that Manet introduces. The result is the displacement of the effect of depth in the canvas, foreshortening the space of the canvas and, of course, rendering it flat. "Not only is the effect of depth effaced," he will detail referencing Manet's *The Masked Ball at the Opera* (1873–74; see Figure 5), "but the distance between the edge of the picture and the back is relatively short such that all the figures find themselves projected forward." And then he will affirm, "You do not really have space per se, you have only something like packages of space, packages of volumes and surfaces which are projected forwards, towards the viewer's eyes."[45]

In other words, it's not so much that Manet is, for Foucault, dealing with a problem of conviction in the pictorial arts (as Fried and Cavell have affirmed), though that is indeed part of it. Foucault's Manet is attacking the problem of "the reproduction of the perception of everyday life" when the reflex function of representation no longer convinces as a pictorial achievement.[46] The problem, then, is how to paint the force of perception rather than representing the world. Foucault finds a possible answer to this question in Manet's treatment of the surface of the canvas as a space of pictorial perception. Thus, referencing *The Execution of Maximilien* (1868; see Figure 6), Foucault will note that "what Manet was using, what he was playing with in his representation, was above all the fact that the canvas was vertical, that it was a surface in two dimensions, that it had no depth; and in a way Manet was trying to represent this absence of depth by diminishing as far as possible the very thickness of the scene which he represents."[47] In short, rather than trying to trump l'oeil, Manet's paintings will paint perception tout court.

To clarify: *quattrocento* painting made perception a condition of perspectivism and thus required the viewer to occupy a specific position to view the painting as a representational object. This fact conditions the viewer's access to the painting in Foucault's discussion of *Las Meninas*. That entire discussion revolves around an in-and-out movement of perception that consolidates the sense of the canvass's depth. This, ultimately, is the interpellative work of representation that will later be considered a "theatrical" ambition: the work requires that the beholder occupy a situation to experience the painting as it ought to be experienced.[48] But Manet eliminates depth of field, and he compresses the canvas, absolving the viewer from the conditioning of "the situation" and the normative demands of looking. The canvas, in other words, stops being a reflex(ive) surface. Rather than lines of entry and exit, Foucault's viewing of

Figure 5. Édouard Manet, *A Masked Ball at the Opera*, 1873, National Gallery of Art (ArtStor)

Manet's canvasses emphasize vectors of visibility, verticalities, horizontalities, and repetitions. What Manet's canvasses thus offer Foucault is "the interior architecture of the picture."[49]

Attention to the tableau's interior architecture is the formal aesthetic insight that will allow Foucault to present Bentham's political writings and architectural drawings as he does; that is, not as normative spaces of ideological positioning (i.e., the apparatus qua alienation) but as surfaces upon which dispositional powers do their work of arranging and adjoining (i.e., the *dispositif* qua complex of adjacency): "There is a circular building, the periphery of the Panopticon, within which cells are set, opening both onto the inner side of the ring through an iron grate door and onto the outside through a window. Around the inner circumference of this ring is a gallery, allowing one to walk around the building, passing each cell. Then there is an empty space and, at its center, a tower, a kind of cylindrical construction of several levels at the top of which is a sort of lantern, that is to say, a large open room, which is such that from this central site one can observe everything happening in each cell, just by turning around. This is the schema."[50]

Figure 6. Édouard Manet, *The Execution of Maximilien*, 1868, Kunsthalle Mannheim (ArtStor)

What interests me in this famous account is less the specifics of Foucault's description than his schematic mode of hovering over the surface of the drawing. In the original French lecture, he doesn't so much conclude that "this is the schema" but affirms "Voilà le schema," as if we were frontally facing the entirety of the tableau. And it is this sense of facingness that makes the description so striking. We are facing an architectural drawing and thus can traverse (and *trans*verse) its surface, hover here and there, along and across its vectors, curves, lines, and forces. But more importantly, and again as in the case of Manet's canvas, Foucault's description of looking at the Panopticon drawing offers no hint of depth, of entering or exiting the space. It is a flat surface where (at least in the account he gives) "the effect of depth" is "effaced."

The second thematic Foucault raises is lighting. Recent studies of Manet (not available to Foucault at the time of his lectures) have remarked on the unusualness of Manet's use of light in his canvasses. Manet's are works lit in atypical ways and (once more) in a manner decidedly acute to traditional chiaroscuro, *quattrocento* painting. Rather than representing light from a position interior and above the painting, Manet's light is frontal and external to the painting. The suggestion that has been forwarded by some scholars is that frontal lighting might indicate, indeed *does* indicate to Beatrice Farwell, Manet's adoption of photographic lighting techniques and perhaps his adoption of the practice of using daguerreotypes as models for his paintings—a practice, I should add, famously disparaged by Charles Baudelaire (in "The Modern Public and Photography") but also famously in vogue during Manet's time.[51] There is much that can be said about such transmedial consonances in Manet's canvasses, and Alexi Worth's perspicuous account of Manet's "counter-photographic style" is a tour de force in this respect.[52] But once again for matters of space I want to focus on how Foucault portrays lighting as an intensity that provides a stark superficiality to the tableau in his treatment of Manet's *The Fifer* (1866; see Figure 7):

> Here, on the contrary, you see that there is absolutely no light coming from above or from below, or from outside the canvas; or rather all the light comes from outside of the canvas, but strikes it absolutely at the perpendicular. You see that the face presents absolutely no modelling, simply two little hollows either side of the nose to indicate the eyebrows and the hollows of the eyes. You notice, however, that the shadow, practically the only shadow which is presented in this picture, is this tiny little shadow here under the hand of the fifer and which indicates that in effect the lighting comes from absolutely opposite since it is behind the fifer, in the hollow of the hand, that the only shadow of the picture is drawn, with this one [under his left foot] which assures stability, as you see, this tiny little shadow, which is the indication of the rhythm that the fifer prints on his music in tapping his foot: as you see, he lightly raises his foot which gives, from this shadow [under the left foot] to this one [in the right hand] the large diagonal which is reproduced clearly here by the fifer's flute case. So we have an entirely perpendicular lighting, a lighting which is the real lighting of the canvas if the canvas in its materiality was to be exposed to an open window, in front of an open window.[53]

Foucault didn't have the advantage of having read Farwell's study or Worth's development of its suggestive insights, and so he assumes that the light upon the canvas of *The Fifer* was coming as if from an open window—in fact, "in front" of an open window. And though Foucault's analogy may turn out to be technically inaccurate, it is also visually exact because what it suggests is that the canvas itself is totally exposed to light precisely *like* a silver plate is

Figure 7. Édouard Manet, *The Fifer*, 1866, Musée D'Orsay (ArtStor)

exposed to light in a daguerreotype. The frontality of light in *The Fifer* also produces the sense of uprightness and thus facingness of the canvas, the fact that—as Foucault says—the lighting renders the perpendicularity of the canvas and, indeed, of the fifer's image. In Foucault's account we also have the matter of the slight shadow of the front left foot that, for him, doesn't indicate an angle of light (as a shadow typically might) but rhythm, the rhythm of the beat of the music to which the fifer is playing. This, to me, is an astounding observation that returns us to the description of the Panopticon cited earlier from the November 28, 1973, lecture. In both the Manet and the Panopticon descriptions we are given a sense of facingness (and thus beforeness) of these objects that refuses the ideal of entry and exit available to *quattrocento* accounts of representational perception and, *ceteris paribus*, to the interpellation scenario of the apparatus. The viewer of the painting and of the architectural drawing is decidedly in front of it, viewing it, but not in it or even drawn into it. In Manet's works, this is accomplished by the canvas's flatness and the frontal lighting effects.

The aforementioned observations allow us to begin to raise some suspicions regarding the general reception of Foucault's interpretation of Bentham's Panopticon writings, a reception that wants to view the example of the architectural form as an archetype of interpellation, indeed as an Ideological State Apparatus. But as my reconstruction of the dynamics of surface viewing suggests, this interpretation of Foucault's descriptions (assisted by the ease with which English translations substitute "*dispositif*" with "apparatus") are not consonant with the formal aesthetic operations available in Foucault's descriptions of these modern (or better, modern*ist*) political media.[54] Indeed, Foucault's insistence that the viewer of Manet's canvas and/or the Panopticon drawing is before (and thus not in) the object seems to suggest, at the very least, that such institutions don't function on the interpellation model of a reflex circuit.[55] Rather, they are technical objects that coordinate and distribute dynamical forces that arrange and dispose bodies in precisely the way that Manet's canvas is a surface upon which forces, intensities, visibilities, and spatialities are disposed. What becomes most effective about *dispositifs*, then, is their way of distributing power without imposing themselves upon bodies or demanding a point of view. This is explicit in Foucault's rendering of the Panopticon's scopic field. It is true that the Panopticon can be used as an architectural form for all the institutions Althusser had listed as belonging to the Ideological State Apparatus. But whereas the structure of visibility in the dynamics of Ideological State Apparatuses is necessarily hierarchical and vertical so that lines of sight penetrate (i.e., move in and out of) the privacy of the subject (which confers the account of influence as alienation), the scopic field of the *dispositif* is horizontal and flat. For the Panopticon to work, in other words, the lines of visibility between the viewer and the object viewed are planar, such that the object of visibility is fully frontal and totally there. It is the exact same line of visibility that we find in Manet's canvas, with exactly the same light exposure: "The panoptic ~~mechanism~~ (*dispositif*) arranges spatial unities that make it possible to see constantly and to recognize immediately." And this, Foucault adds, is enabled by "full lighting."[56]

As an aside, I should remark that my interpretation of the relation between Manet and Bentham in Foucault is at odds with Gary Shapiro when he suggests that the Manet canvas "becomes the inverse of the Panopticon. The 'central lodge' of the latter is the undisputed point of view for the inspector, a position from which every prisoner appears in the window of his or her cell."[57] It should be clear by now that I believe the opposite to be the case: the Manet canvas and Bentham's Panopticon are two exempla of the sentimental empiricist *dispositif*. In both cases the viewer (whether painterly beholder or guard) is equally absolved from having to occupy any one position to look and see what is there: that is, in both cases the viewer is before the canvas/structure. This renders visibility totally there in exactly the manner that Bentham suggests when he claims that (to cite Shapiro's paraphrase) "the activity of the inspectors is like the common occupation of looking out the window."[58]

Recall that Foucault had placed Manet's canvas in front of a window to explain the sense of total lighting. This total exposure to light is Foucault's way of suggesting that there is no specific norm of attention vis-à-vis the *dispositif*. The *dispositif* is an antirepresentational medium that doesn't demand a point of view. This is as true of the Manet canvas as it is of the Panopticon: the canvas doesn't demand a specific angle of viewership in the way that *quattrocento* representational painting does, and the Panopticon doesn't require a specific individual to go to a determined place and look inside, like the early modern dungeon did. With both Manet and Bentham we have "axial" lines of visibility and an "automatic functioning" of dispositional powers that radically undermine any reliance on a metaphysics of substances because no representation of subjectivity is necessary in order to determine who or how to look.[59] Foucault's ambition in turning to the language and political ontology of the *dispositif*, then, is not only a political and aesthetic retort to Althusser's theory of ideology and his commitment to alienation; it also raises the problem of how to account for, explain, and critically engage the proliferation of *dispositifs* in the modern period—that is, the proliferation of media that don't wield powers of representation but dispose, organize, and assemble bodies, visibilities, and enunciations.

Figure 8. Édouard Manet, *A Bar at the Folies-Bergère*, 1882, Courtland Gallery, London (ArtStor)

The aspects of the Manet canvas discussed thus far build toward the final element Foucault will address—namely, the *tableau-objet* (i.e., "picture-object" in the English translation). The last painting considered in the lecture is *A Bar at the Folies-Bergère* (1881–82; see Figure 8). In his description of it, Foucault brings to bear the aesthetic insights he has already raised. He will show that like *The Masked Ball at the Opera* "there is not really any depth," and as with *The Fifer*, the lighting is "entirely frontal" and "strikes the woman in full shot."[60] The French transcription has Foucault affirming that the light strikes the woman *"de plein fouet."*[61] The metaphor is a nineteenth-century French military expression, and it refers to the horizontality of a direct shot of a pistol or a rifle toward a visible target, *fouet* also being the French word for "whip," thereby suggesting that light strikes the canvas directly or in a fully frontal manner in the way that a whip or the shot of a pistol strikes its victim directly.

The most significant part of Foucault's treatment of this painting is his discussion of the three systems of incompatibility that appear (or are implied) on the surface of the canvas: "The painter must be here and he must be there; he must have someone here and he must have no-one there; there is a descending gaze and there is an ascending gaze."[62] This "triple impossibility"

emerges from the discontinuities between the representation of light, the failure of the mirror's reflection, and the odd disposition of the figures in the
canvas—all features, I want to say, that insist on the canvas's being a complex
rather than a reflex and thus an anti-mimetic surface. It's in his recounting
of these incompatibilities that Foucault is almost explicit about the acute relation of the Manet canvas to *Las Meninas*. [And crucial to this is the different
function of the mirror in *Las Meninas* vis-à-vis *A Bar at the Folies-Bergère*.
For reasons of space, I am unable to provide a comparative analysis of these
differences, though as one might expect, in the latter painting the mirror is
not a reflexive surface.] Whereas his reading of the *Las Meninas* had focused
almost obsessively on the empty space of the canvas and the plunging that
takes you into the painting (or, indeed, situates the viewer in the empty space
of the painting as if they were always already in its depths), in his reading of
A Bar at the Folies-Bergère he will affirm that there is no empty space at all.[63]

However limited (because of its shortness) the reading of this painting may
be, what matters to our purposes is a final insight upon which the entirety of
Foucault's viewing will rest—namely, the claim that Manet's canvas is decidedly not a normative space:

> This triple impossibility, whereby we know where we must place
> ourselves to see the spectacle as we see it, this exclusion, if you will, of
> every stable and defined place where we locate the viewer, is evidently
> one of the fundamental properties of this picture and explains at once
> the enchantment and the malaise that one feels in looking at it. While
> all classical painting, by its system of lines, of perspective, of vanishing
> point, etc., had assigned to the viewer and to the painter a certain precise
> place, fixed, constant, from where the spectacle was seen, so that in
> looking at a picture one very clearly saw from where it was seen, if it
> was from above or from below, from an angle or from opposite. Here,
> on the contrary, in a picture like this one, or in any case in this one, it
> is not possible to know where the painter has placed himself in order to
> paint the picture as he has done it, and where we must place ourselves
> in order to see a spectacle such as this. And you see that with this last
> technique, Manet plays with the picture's property of being not in the
> least a normative space whereby the representation fixes us or fixes
> the viewer to a point, a unique point from which to look. The picture
> appears like a space in front of which and by rapport with which one
> can move around: the viewer mobile before the picture, real light
> striking head on, verticals and horizontals perpetually doubled, sup-
> pression of depth. So you see the canvas in which there is something

real, material, in some ways physical, is about to appear and to play with all its properties in representation.[64]

This is the dynamic that will form the crux of what, in the subsequent paragraph, he calls the *tableau-objet*.[65] What the *tableau-objet* does is generate rather than fix movement. Viewing is moving, here and there, up and down; hence the assertion that not only is the canvas decidedly not a normative space (by which he means a space that establishes an ideal point from which to view it) but that there is an exclusion that is neither absence nor a lack, but an unavailability "of every stable and defined place where we locate the viewer." This is how Manet's canvasses paint modern perception: as movement. In other words, it's not that viewership is impossible, but that there is no form of subjectivity assigned to it. Manet's canvas is not a normative space because there is no one place or perspective from which to view it, thereby denuding viewership of the qualifications of positionality and thus subjectivity.

Now, from one perspective (the perspective I wish to dispel), this account of motility around and about the *tableau-objet* might seem counter or even anathema to the claim I made earlier that Manet and Bentham were not opposing exempla for Foucault, but that they stand in transmedial consonance with one another, and that both the *dispositifs* of the *tableau-objet* and the Panopticon source Foucault's discovery (or invention, or reinvention) of dispositional powers of adjacency in governmentality. But in reality, there is no such contradiction.

Recall two things about Foucault's treatment of the architectural drawing. First, and most obviously, during his lectures he's talking about a drawing that is (likely) projected upon the flat surface of a screen from the light of a slide projector. Architectural drawings are flat surfaces whose flatness is rendered perspicuous when projected upon the scrim of a screen.[66] And they are totally in view in part as a result of their flatness but also because they are fully lit. Moreover, the way Foucault talks about these structures, there is never the sense that (again in contrast to *Las Meninas*) he is interested in placing his audience inside them. In other words, the language is never one of "depth" or "entering" the structure; it is, as I suggested, one of hovering about. Secondly, there is the matter of some of the central features of the Panopticon itself: it is round and curved, there is a central tower, and though the occupancy of that tower could be vacant, no specific qualification for its occupancy is assigned. Indeed, for the scenario to work at all, the assumption of a ubiquitous visibility must be in place (i.e., total everywhereness), which is decidedly not a fixed, normative point of view. The tower does exist, just like there is a space of visibility in front of the canvas, but the guard inside the tower is expected to move about and look everywhere, and indeed, the scenario can only work if and when the expectation of visibility is constant—which means in constant movement here and there, up and down. No doubt the tower is a fixed structure; but the viewer inside the tower is not fixed and is constantly moving. If the prisoners or school children had any clue that someone were either normatively fixed, facing only in one direction, or (and what amounts to the same thing) absent, then the entire raison d'être of the *dispositif* would fall apart. The Panopticon works, in other words, like the surface of *A Bar at the Folies-Bergère*; that is, because it arranges visibility, movement, and lines rather than fixing them "so that finally one day we can get rid of representation itself and allow space to play with its pure and simple properties, its material properties."[67] In fact, Foucault does note that by removing a normative space of viewership the Panopticon did just that: it got rid of "representation itself": "The efficiency of power, its constraining force have, in a sense, passed over to the other side—to the side of its surface of application." And "by this very fact, the external power may throw off its physical weight; it tends to the non-corporal; and the more it approaches this limit, the more constant, profound and permanent are its effects: it is a perpetual victory that avoids any physical confrontation, and which is always decided in advance."[68] The ubiquity of total visibility denies a normative place of viewership as well as the confrontation of interpellation.

Though potentially normalizing, this is decidedly not a normative space, nor is it a normative play of powers. In front of the *dispositif* you are totally exposed, and it is totally exposed to you. That's the point of the anti-representational move: to radically uproot the idea that there might be a normative space from which to view and be viewed, and that that is a good space, or the right space, or the expert place of viewership. Herein also we find the implicit critique of the apparatus; the *dispositif* doesn't simply point to a different kind of power, but it removes the private/public distinction implicit in Althusser's account of Ideological State Apparatuses and with that, the propriety of ownership that accompanies the private, situated viewing of the *quattrocento* vanishing point (and *ceteris paribus*, of the dungeon).

Now, none of what I have offered up thus far suggests that we need to reconsider Foucault's disciplinary *dispositifs* as normatively good objects and/or operations. This would be outlandish for more reasons than one, the most important of which is that these are not normative structures but normalizing ones (as Pasquinelli's reading of Foucault's debt to Canguilhem reminds us). What I am proposing is that the *dispositif*'s powers are not the same as the powers of the apparatus, that the *dispositif* is not an instrument of alienation, and that the dispositional powers of domination operate in dispersive ways not susceptible to dialectical critique. It is, rather, a site and source for the distribution of powers and intensities made empirically manifest through lines of visibilities, forms of enunciation, forces of adjacency, events of discontinuity, and practices of assembly-formation. Instead of a normative instrument of domination, therefore, Foucault's *dispositif* is best considered (as James Chandler rightly reminds us) an intermedial form that offers "ways of ordering works and organizing worlds."[69] It is, I want to assert, a sentimental empiricist technology of collectivization.

Conclusion

By means of bringing this chapter to a conclusion I want to raise, however briefly, some further considerations on the ontological stakes of my claim that the *dispositif* is not an influence machine or an apparatus of alienation but an intermedial dynamic of dispositional powers. Recall that one of my ambitions in this chapter is to show how Foucault's adoption and development of the term *dispositif* betrays his sentimental empiricist commitments to forms of political power not reducible to the dualism implicit in the sovereigntist model of domination.[70] My ambition in showing the intermedial resonance between the Manet *tableau-objet* and Bentham's Panopticon in Foucault's thinking is to put on display an aesthetic-political nexus of problems around the idea of the *dispositif* that involve an attempt to rethink the nature of technological subjection beyond or perhaps even against the standard twentieth-century model of communication, transmission, causal influence, and alienation. The *dispositif* is explicitly not a normative apparatus that ensures subjection; it is also not an instrument of meaning-transmission on the model of a linguistic utterance or on the model of an Aristotelian account of understanding. Perhaps the most radically modernist aspect of Foucault's *dispositif* is his implicit claim that it does not function like (nor does it belong to the function of) a mimesis. Regardless, the *dispositif* is said *to do* something; what is, then, the nature of this medium's doing if it's explicitly not subjection through alienation?

   I hint at the answer throughout by enlisting the etymology of the term *dispositif* from the Roman rhetorical tradition of the *dispositio* and its further relation to an aesthetics of ornament (i.e., the *dispono* of *dispositio*), to the practices of arrangement and placing and subsequent forms of attention that the tradition of sentimental empiricism studied throughout these pages. My point is to make explicit the claim that the *dispositif* is not reducible to the instrumentalist view of technology but that it offers a new view of political media as dispositional powers of adjacency that concretize diverse associational modes and forms (including solidarity, equality, discipline, and comparison), but that it determines neither the shape nor the inherent structure of any such arrangements. In short, the political ontology of the *dispositif* lies in the dispositional powers it makes manifest.

"Dispositions," Stephen Mumford reminds us, "are properties, and properties play causal roles in a thing's interaction with the world about it."[71] Though a dispositional power is oriented toward what tends to be, it is also not purely contingent. What a dispositional power makes possible is limited to (in our case) the associated milieu of the *dispositif.* "What it is that makes certain artefacts the things that they are is that they have a particular set of dispositions."[72] This doesn't mean that a *dispositif* has an inherent function (as both Aristotle's *Poetics* and Althusser's ISA commend) or that what they do is determined by the internal mechanism of the thing. That's precisely the point of the *dispositif*: what it is doesn't determine what it can do but that the technical object's concretization emerges from the spontaneous manifestation of its dispositional powers.[73] Manet's reinvention of painting is, according to Foucault, a radical break with previous painting because Manet made available the dispositional powers of the canvas in a manner heretofore unappreciated. There was nothing necessary about the canvas that compelled Manet to make its surface flatness available to the experience of viewing a painting, nor was Manet's *tableau-objet* an ideal representation. The *tableau-objet* was a dispositional power of the pictorial canvas actualized by Manet's ways of rethinking the technical activities of painting beyond (or alongside) representation. And so we can say that the *tableau-objet* was neither a necessary condition of the canvas nor an ideal possibility but something in between, an "intermediate modality."[74] "Dispositionality," Stephen Mumford and Rani Lill Anjum argue, "is a primitive modality that is intermediate between pure possibility and necessity."[75] Dispositionality helps explain how we might appreciate the causal powers of the *dispositif* as neither necessary nor inherent, but as potential forces that may, but need not, actualize.

What the study of the *dispositif* in Foucault shows is not only a concerted effort to rethink modern social and political power beyond the image of sovereignty, nor exclusively an attempt to offer a political alternative to Althusserian conceptions of ideology-critique. Foucault's studies of the dispositional powers of *dispositifs* in his lectures on Manet and his 1970s lectures at the Collège de France represent an ambition to develop a sentimental empiricist theory of political media not beholden to a causal ontology of influence as coercion. This novel critical theory of media is rooted in an attempt to explore the physics of medial movement; the forces, intensities, and associations constituent of those movements; and the emergent political and aesthetic forms of such intermediary modalities. A sentimental empiricist paradigm of intermedial causality, and nothing less, is what is at stake in the political ontology of the *dispositif.*

Epilogue

The bulk of the writing for this book took place in Los Angeles, California, during the COVID-19 pandemic lockdown. Needless to say, these were not felicitous times for any of us. Besides the death drive of a viral unknown, in the summer of 2020 Los Angeles experienced some of the most devastating forest fires in recent decades, accompanied by some of the most intense civic unrest since the 1992 Los Angeles Riots, as well as an (ongoing) international humanitarian refugee crisis only 200 kilometers away. The cracks in the American social safety filament (one can't call it a "safety net," since it actually doesn't save people from falling) became apparent within days of the lockdown. Besides not being able to go to school and lacking basic internet access, a majority of children in the Los Angeles Unified School District (LAUSD) were at risk of starvation because their main source of sustenance was the LAUSD lunch programs. As a response, on March 18, 2020, LAUSD opened sixty-three Grab-and-Go Food Centers across the city, distributing an average of about 700,000 meals per day. By May 28, 2020, the food centers had distributed over 25 million free meals to 80 percent of its students' families, all of whom live below the poverty line.[1] California has the largest economy of any state in the United States, with an annual GDP of three trillion dollars.[2] It is the fifth-largest economy in the world. Yet the largest school district in the state, which is also the second-largest public school district in the country, boasts an unfathomable poverty rate. What remains stunning to me as an immigrant and foreign observer is that American exceptionalism remains unwavering and unchanged on both the so-called U.S. left and the emboldened U.S. right in the face of persistent racial, environmental, and socioeconomic devastation.[3]

As I continued to work on this manuscript in between home schooling, Zoom teaching, and lock-down co-parenting, it became apparent that the period I was studying and the thinkers whose intellectual project I was attracted to were asking a question current to my own: is political change thinkable? The manner in which they posed this question involved an exploration into the political metaphysics of difference-in-itself as a critical intervention on various mimetic operations that had operated to ensure an intergenerational reproduction of the same. These thinkers asked how it is that systems of value reproduce themselves, and what are the forces that ensure mimetic repetition at the cultural, state-institutional, political-economic, racial, gender, and social levels? Furthermore, they queried as to what were the conceptual and philosophical sources for the reproduction of power.

The emergent critical explorations, theoretical innovations, and conceptual creations participated in a minoritarian tradition of political and critical thinking I call "sentimental empiricism" that, though diverse and fluid, retains three predominant aspects:

The first is the rejection of a metaphysics of substances. This expresses itself in various forms: as a critique of Cartesian dualism, a critique of Hegelian consciousness, or most concertedly as a critique of Aristotelian hylomorphism and the Eleatic conceit that Being (and thus identity) precedes Becoming (i.e., difference-in-itself). Each of the thinkers we have studied develop their own versions of this critique: Jean Wahl does so by turning directly to the tradition of radical empiricism and specifically to the pluralist philosophies of William James and Alfred North Whitehead; Beauvoir does so in her critique of patriarchy, showing it to be a dispositional power of domination; Simondon is explicit in his critique of Aristotelian hylomorphism, which is the foundation of his philosophy of individuation and his philosophy of technology; Deleuze extends Wahl's turn to radical empiricism and develops a philosophical project that begins with a political metaphysics of difference-in-itself independent of any idea (or ideal) of identity; and finally, Foucault's political and aesthetic turn to thinking the dispositional powers of technical objects offers us a sentimental empiricist practice of media criticism that is not exclusively indebted to a sovereigntist model of domination.

A second aspect of sentimental empiricist thinking: criticism is not reducible to dialectics. Dialectical thinking, in this view, implies a metaphysics of inherent relations between identity and difference that presupposes what Jean Wahl, borrowing from Alfred North Whitehead, refers to as the bifurcation of nature.[4] The sentimental empiricist thinkers we've studied are metaphysical pluralists who reject the idea of inherent relations and insist, instead, on a dynamic multiplicity of associations as the basis of existence. Critique for the sentimental empiricist does not involve a negation of antagonistic identity but a dismantling of the relational dynamics in any emergent adjacency. Difference-in-itself thus does not name a substance, a concept, or a quality; it refers to a relational form—or dispositional power—in and through which processes of dynamic concretization occur.

The emphasis on dispositional powers and relational modes brings us to a third aspect: the reconsideration of empiricism as a political and aesthetic orientation that cannot exclude the role of the sentiments. Sentimental empiricism is not analogous to anglophone logical positivism: it is sensationist. This modality of empiricism asserts that there are no inherent relations that govern the composition of bodies or their movement in worlds. To experience anything is evidence of our having been moved by a world. Said evidence does not come as an atomistic datum, nor as an inherent fact about the world, but as a spontaneous and undetermined sensation. All the sentimental empiricist authors we've studied take the sentimentalist aspects of empiricism as foundational to human life, and they understand the primacy of relations over substances to emerge as a result of a body's dispositions. Crucial to these thinkers is the fact that the sentiments are not reducible to specific feelings nor to determined representations of experience. Rather, the word "sentiments" and the names given to various sentiments refer us to a multiplicity of forces that activate lived relations between bodies. That there are bodies, of this there is no doubt for our sentimental empiricist authors; but what is in doubt is the extent to which we may confirm the integrity of bodies and the inherent order and organization of body, of self, of experience; to wit, *le bon sens* of propriety. In this respect also, one cannot underappreciate the extent to which sentimental empiricist criticism is materialist through and through. Once again, however, matter does not point to a stable substance but to the dynamism of the sentiments, the dynamism of relations, and the dynamism of interactivity. Reflection on and inclusion of the sentiments in our critical thinking is crucial to the sentimental empiricist thinkers in this study because it is in and through the dispositional powers of the sentiments that difference-in-itself manifests.

Throughout this study I focus on the qualification of literary competence and the missed reception of diverse styles of theoretical writing. In doing so, I rely on John Guillory's claim that the general system of modern academic scholarship comprises diverse elements, including "the conventions and techniques that govern how scholars write and how they read."[5] My research design emphasizes the role and function of the reading practices of postwar anglophone political theory, their partitions of the sensible, their expectations of epistemic excellence, and their own unacknowledged stylistics. The contributions to political and aesthetic theory made by our sentimental empiricist thinkers were misheard (*mésentente*, fr.) upon their arrival to anglophone shores in part as a result of the techniques and conventions governing the reading and writing of theory in the anglophone social sciences and humanities.

Part of the ambition of this book is to show how and why metaphysics played such a pivotal role in the political and aesthetic theories of postwar French thought. In this respect, several features were unique to the French context: (1) the dominance of French Catholicism and Catholic theology in twentieth-century political life that disseminated the dogma of the unity of substances as well as the unity of the heterosexual family as necessary to political stability; (2) the political concern with the reproduction of the same and the system of intergenerational inheritance that ensures elite privilege; and (3) an appreciation that any system of political power relies on metaphysical principles like causation, essence, and identity and thus that the State is a metaphysical entity. In the case of our study, we focused on the metaphysics of mimesis as the theory of the State.

These considerations were unavailable to a generation of social science readers in postwar America who had been instructed to disregard metaphysical inquiry from their scholarly pursuits for fear that these would produce the kind of value relativism that would open the door for various forms of illiberal tendencies, and especially Soviet Communism. To make these available, I show how the development of sentimental empiricist criticism dovetails with concerns over a political metaphysics of mimesis that coordinates meaning and understanding as an inherent relation and that binds this inherent relation to academic excellence that selects for access to elite offices and institutions of power. Archetypal, in this regard, is the *explication de texte* that we learned is a state-instituted aesthetic medium of formal literary criticism across the disciplines and that communicates and enforces *le sens d'état*. The sentimental empiricist critics we studied challenged the metaphysics of mimesis and understanding and the system of political authority and state power tethered to it by challenging the idea of natural and inherent relations and thus natural and inherent criteria of selection for elites. Their metaphysical assertion is unequivocal on this point: There is no inherent relation between mimesis and state power. But more than this, there is no inherent relation tout court. If this is accurate, then the relationship between masculinity and power in patriarchy is not inherent, and neither is the relation between organs of perception and perceptible experience in judgments of taste, nor is the relation between taste and socioeconomic standing, or the relation between epistemic competence and colonial rule, and so forth. In other words, sentimental empiricism offers a critique of political authority by showing how relations are not founded on a metaphysics of identity but on a metaphysics of difference-in-itself.

Finally, sentimental empiricist criticism is concerned with the problem of political solidarity as a problem of relation or, to use the French term, *agencement*. The issue here is one of thinking *agencement* and difference-in-itself together. If relations are independent of their terms, and if the political authority of mimesis is under scrutiny, what are the modes of association enabled by a metaphysics of difference-in-itself? Clearly, institutions like the political party are an insufficient response to this query. The modern party form works when there is a unifying principle, *le bon sens*, that can guarantee the party's identity through time. But appeals to *le bon sens* and perhaps even *le bon sens d'état* return us to a political metaphysics of mimesis as a grounding postulate of belonging. The sentimental empiricist thinkers we have studied are not satisfied with a classical account of solidarity rooted in the unifying principles of Aristotelian mimesis, including such unifying principles as common sense. This is especially the case throughout the 1950s and 1960s, when the reigning metaphors of mimetic association and their appeal to natural unions—chief among these the marriage metaphor—were readily deployed to argue the case that Algerian independence and decolonialization were a direct attack on the French nation because the two nations shared a holy union.[6] This dissatisfaction led to a series of experiments—at once practical and theoretical—that offered occasions for thinking political solidarity and difference-in-itself beyond the conceits of commonness and the demands of a political metaphysics of mimesis.[7]

This book argues that extant anglophone interpretations of postwar French thought tell a partial story, one that overlooks the tradition of sentimental empiricism that proved crucial to the political and aesthetic innovations that would eventually come to be associated with what anglophone readers would call "French theory." At once a genealogy, a polemic, and an exercise in dispositional reading practices, the preceding pages fill in some of the gaps of this missed understanding (*mésentente*, fr.). In doing so, I argue that the developments of postwar French political and aesthetic theory and criticism cannot be fully appreciated without considering the forms of instruction and the expectations of literary competence that accompanied the credentialing standards that would forge the intellectual landscape of the period. Moreover, an appreciation of these institutionalized forms of aesthetic and political judgments must be viewed alongside the geopolitical concerns that dominated French academic life, chief among these being the dismantling of French colonialism. It is my contention that the anti-mimetic thrust of sentimental empiricism I outline in these pages is central to the postwar French critique of colonial power that was premised on an ideal of imitation and repetition of the French nation throughout its colonial holdings. In short, French imperialism and colonialism—and thus the founding and expansion of the modern French state—could not have taken place without a political and aesthetic privileging of the metaphysics of mimesis as the inherent form of unity. For the sentimental empiricist thinkers we have studied, mimesis is not simply an aesthetic form; it is first and foremost a mode of relating considered inherent to all forms of political and social belonging. This commitment to mimesis demands a theory of understanding that establishes who or what counts as participants in political and social belonging. For the sentimental empiricist thinkers, we've studied a critique of political power that focuses exclusively on formal state institutions, and state behavior is insufficient in dealing with the persistent function of mimesis as a dispositional power of domination. Their ambition would thus be to develop new forms of critical interrogation that focused on the system of relations that arranged social and political participation and belonging. This requires a shift in the analysis of hierarchical domination of the centralized state to a critical mode that focuses on the dispositional powers that arrange adjacencies in everyday life. This shift in analysis—from substance to relation and from coercion to disposition—is a major contribution of the political and aesthetic critical philosophies of sentimental empiricism in postwar France.

The first issue of *Tel Quel*, the small literary magazine that would leave a larger-than-life footprint, appeared in France in March 1960. The previous month, the French military had tested its first atomic bomb in the Adrar Province of Algerian Sahara. By early December of the same year Charles de Gaulle's visit to Algeria resulted in nationwide protests and insurrections; and by the end of that same month France would perform its third nuclear test, once again in the Algerian province of Adrar. That the height of the Algerian struggle for independence was book-ended by France's entry into the nuclear race was no innocent coincidence.

As a wholly artificial heuristic, I mark the year 1960—and the publication of the first issue of *Tel Quel*—as the end point of my study. By this point, cultural anthropology, structural linguistics, and Saussurean semiology had become important methods of political and aesthetic criticism in France that would find equally compelling retorts and challenges. Crucial to these developments was the idea that any system of value operates on the basis of a network of relations that are at once pervasive and recalcitrant, but nevertheless arbitrary. Relying on Saussure's insight that the relation between signifier and signified is not inherent to the meaning of a sign, these critical approaches analyzed how the social function of value occurs through powers of reproduction and circulation that produce a seemingly natural *bon sens*.[8] The crucial

task of criticism from now on would not be to produce analyses of the legitimacy or truthfulness of *le bon sens* but an interrogation of the forms of power
that enable the reproduction of the relations of *le bon sens*, as well as the modes
of dissension and forms of discontinuity that could procure fracture therein.
What resulted from the germ of this insight was a series of innovative and radical interventions in the humanities and social sciences that we continue to
engage to this day. The possibility for these political and aesthetic investigations
to gain the purchase they did was due in no small part to the innovations of
sentimental empiricist criticism I discuss throughout.

Acknowledgments

This book has not benefited from the engagement of many audiences. Most of it was written on my balcony during the COVID-19 lockdown period when it was not possible to travel and present research at conferences and other academic venues. As such, the book could not have been researched and written without the availability of various open-access research repositories and libraries. My sincere gratitude to all the librarians, digital laborers, open-access publishers, and grey hats who made this possible.

The only part of the book that did benefit from a live audience was a preliminary version of the introductory chapter presented the week before lockdown at a workshop on *Power, Society, and the Senses* at Arizona State University, Tempe (March 6 & 7, 2020). Thank you to Richard Newhauser for inviting me and to everyone who participated in that workshop—especially to David Howes of Concordia University, who provided me with characteristically generous and encouraging comments and criticisms.

At the other end of the COVID-19 experience I had the occasion to present a talk based on Chapter 1 of the book at the 2023 meeting of the Modern Languages Association in San Francisco. Thank you to my UCLA comrade in all that is David Hume and eighteenth-century moral sentimentalism, Sarah Kareem, and to Vivasvan Soni for inviting me to participate in the Aesthetics and Democracy panel they organized. Thank you also to the USC-Huntington Early Modern Studies Institute for their invitation to present on sentimental empiricist literary criticism at their Long Eighteenth-Century Seminar (January 29, 2021). Prior to lockdown, a version of Chapter 7 was presented at the Western Political Science Association (San Francisco, 2018), The International Conference for the Study of Social and Political Thought (Yale, 2018), the

American Political Science Association (Boston, 2018), and as a public talk at UC-Berkeley's Rhetoric Department. Thank you especially to the Rhetoric Department's Pheng Cheah, James Porter, and Hans Sluga for their hospitality and critical engagement. This chapter also appeared as "On the Political Ontology of the Dispositif" in *Critical Inquiry* (vol. 45, no. 3 [Spring 2019]). I thank the reviewers and editors of the journal for their helpful comments and criticisms and for permission to reprint a version of that chapter here.

Though I did not present much of this work publicly, I did benefit from the grace of many friends and colleagues who discussed parts of the project over email, Facebook, on the phone, and on Zoom, including: Arash Abizadeh, Ira Allen, Libby Anker, Banu Bargu, Kye Barker, Jane Bennett, Ziyaad Bhorat, Emanuela Bianchi, Constantin Boundas (whose initial encouragement way back when to work steadily on Deleuze and Hume has made all the difference), William Connolly, Stephen Cucharo, Helen Deutsch, Alex Diones, Lisa Ellis, Naomi Ellis, Kathy Ferguson, Kennan Ferguson, Rachel Forgash, Jason Frank, Jill Frank, Jairus Grove, Bonnie Honig, Sarah Kareem, Eleanor Kauffman (and all the members of her fabulous Althusser Reading Group), Colin Koopman, Jacob Levy, Nancy Luxon, Naveed Mansoori, James Martel, John McCumber, Alison McQueen, Daniel Morgan, Nicholas Muench, Aamir Mufti, David Owen, Jaeyoon Park, Michael Raeber, Roey Reichert, Duane Rousselle, Mort Schoolman, Michael Shapiro, Claire Sagan (whose mention of the *explication de texte* on a Facebook post ushered me into one of those research rabbit holes that made all the difference), Lucas Swaine, Kyla Wazana Tomkins, Cody Trojan, Stefania Tutino, Dimitris Vardoulakis, and Yves Winter.

One friend, colleague, and mentor who perennially entertains my requests to "take a look at something I wrote," to take my calls, and who is always ready to share her searing intelligence, is Frances Ferguson. To say that I am indebted to her is in every respect an understatement. My friendship with Melvin Rogers is a privilege and an honor. Melvin and I have shared many moments of reflection on how the sentiments shape our dispositions to the inequalities that envelop political life. Each of these moments is a treasure I cherish and hold dear. Lori Marso has been a steadfast companion throughout the writing of this, and many other, projects. Her work, her intellect, and her skills in close reading are a treasure from which I consistently benefit. Joshua Foa Dienstag and I couldn't disagree more on so many things, which is perhaps why he is such a close and dear friend and why my trust and admiration for him are intractable. Paul Vogt has been a stalwart counselor and brilliant friend since my college days at the University of Manitoba. Despite his obligations as president of the College of the Rockies, Paul is always willing to talk political theory with me. Theo Davis and I have been thinking together since our time in grad school, sharing readings, ideas, and aesthetic reflections. Her study of ornamental aesthetics and her verbing of ornament therein inspired my own theorizing of the *ponere* of dispositionality in these pages. In recent years, her treasury of compassion has shepherded me through the frictions and beauties of *dukkha*. May my gratitude be witness to her brilliance.

It goes without saying—but it must also be said—that the Department of Political Science at UCLA remains a charmed place to study and teach political theory. Thank you to all my colleagues for their continued support, encouragement, and especially for their trust. A special note of gratitude goes to my political theory colleagues and friends at UCLA—Anthony Pagden, Tejas Parasher, Natasha Piano, Giulia Sissa, and Juliet Williams—whose respect and thoughtful provocations sustain me.

On December 21, 2023, my esteemed UCLA colleague, friend, and former grad school professor Kirstie McClure passed away. As many readers are no doubt aware, Kirstie's work helped inaugurate and commend to a whole generation of political theory scholars an interdisciplinary perspective in political theory research, especially as regards the pluralization of reading and writing practices. In many respects, this work is testament to her influence on my intellectual trajectory. In the last year of her life, she asked to read the manuscript that became this book, and I shared it with her with fond trepidation of her readerly acumen. She did not disappoint. Her critical attentions sourced the final intellectual exchanges I was able to enjoy with her. For this, I will always be grateful.

Mackenzie Eason, also of UCLA's Department of Political Science, graciously accepted my invitation to help edit, revise, and talk through various drafts. He tried his best to correct my inconsistencies and obfuscations, but, alas, not even his gifted editorial hand could curb my worst writerly inclinations. Praise to him for his efforts; *mea maxima culpa* for my failures.

Tom Lay of Fordham University Press is simply fabulous. The manuscript I first submitted benefited enormously from his wisdom, his patience, and his command of the many research areas I touch upon. Thank you also to the two anonymous reviewers of the manuscript. One of those reviewers, Jeffrey A. Bell, outed himself to me, and I couldn't be happier that he did, because in many respects, he was an ideal reader.

Finally, a special and heartfelt shout-out to my friends in the Summer 2020 lockdown reading group (which quickly morphed into a support group)—Judith

Grant, Deme Kasimis, and Robyn Marasco. I don't think I'll be able to thank you enough for those months of support and sustenance. Starting lockdown with the anticipation of our weekly meetings made everything so much better.

Most importantly I wish to express my everything to my family: Lisanna, Ali, and Elisa. Somehow, we got through it all, and continue to get through it all . . . stumbling together with love.

Notes

Introduction

1. On the epistemic ontologies of camera movement, see Daniel Morgan, "Where Are We?": Camera Movements and the Problem of Point of View," *New Review of Film and Television Studies* 14, no. 2 (April 2, 2016): 222–48, https://doi.org /10.1080/17400309.2015.1125702; also see Lori Marso, "Camerawork as Motherwork," *Theory & Event* 24, no. 3 (2021): 730–57, for a compelling discussion of Chantal Ackerman's use of camera movement as a formal aesthetic-political *dispositif* of encounter-making.

2. François Truffaut, "A Certain Tendency of the French Cinema," in *Movies and Methods: An Anthology*, ed. Bill Nichols (Berkeley: University of California Press, 1976), 224–36.

3. Jessica Riskin, *Science in the Age of Sensibility: The Sentimental Empiricists of the French Enlightenment* (Chicago: University of Chicago Press, 2002).

4. Robbie Shilliam, *Decolonizing Politics: An Introduction* (Hoboken, N.J.: John Wiley & Sons, 2021); Linda Tuhiwai Smith, *Decolonizing Methodologies: Research and Indigenous Peoples* (London: Zed, 2013); Melvin L. Rogers and Jack Turner, *African American Political Thought: A Collected History* (Chicago: University of Chicago Press, 2021); James Tully, *Public Philosophy in a New Key*, vol. 1, *Democracy and Civic Freedom* (Cambridge and New York: Cambridge University Press, 2008); Cristina Beltrán, *The Trouble with Unity: Latino Politics and the Creation of Identity* (Oxford and New York: Oxford University Press, 2010); Robert Nichols, "Theft Is Property! The Recursive Logic of Dispossession," *Political Theory* 46, no. 1 (April 2, 2017): 3–28, https://doi.org/10.1177/0090591717701709; Robert Young, *White Mythologies: Writing History and the West* (London and New York: Routledge, 2004); Jill Doerfler, Niigaanwewidam James Sinclair, and Heidi Kiiwetinepinesiik Stark, *Centering Anishinaabeg Studies: Understanding the World through Stories*

(East Lansing: Michigan State University Press, 2013); Saidiya V. Hartman, *Scenes of Subjection: Terror, Slavery, and Self-Making in Nineteenth-Century America* (New York: Oxford University Press, 1997).

5. Pierre Bourdieu, *Distinction: A Social Critique of the Judgement of Taste* (Cambridge, Mass.: Harvard University Press, 1984); John Guillory, *Cultural Capital: The Problem of Literary Canon Formation* (Chicago: University of Chicago Press, 2013).

6. I take this to be one of the central insights of Edward W. Said's *Orientalism* (New York: Knopf Doubleday, 2014), which offers a postcolonial critique of the mimetic episteme.

7. It is one of the distinctive contributions of Edward Said's foundational study *Orientalism*, as well as his important introductory essay in the recent edition of Auerbach's *Mimesis*, to note the importance of the system of mimesis as one of the political powers of domination in the colonial world; see Said, *Orientalism*; Erich Auerbach and Edward W. Said, *Mimesis: The Representation of Reality in Western Literature*, new and expanded ed. (Princeton, N.J.: Princeton University Press, 2013). On dispossession, mimesis, and the problem of contradiction, see Robert Nichols, *Theft Is Property!: Dispossession and Critical Theory* (Durham, N.C.: Duke University Press, 2019), 1–16.

8. Cornelia Vismann, *Files: Law and Media Technology* (Stanford, Calif.: Stanford University Press, 2008), 26–32.

9. See Gilles Deleuze's essay "Bartleby; Or, the Formula," in *Essays Critical and Clinical*, 1st ed. (Minneapolis: University of Minnesota Press, 1997), and Jacques Rancière's critique "Deleuze, Bartleby, and the Literary Formula," in *The Flesh of Words: The Politics of Writing* (Stanford, Calif: Stanford University Press, 2004).

10. Sophia Rosenfeld, *Common Sense: A Political History* (Cambridge, Mass.: Harvard University Press, 2014), 90–135.

11. René Descartes, *Discours de la méthode* (2004), https://www.gutenberg.org/ebooks/13846.

12. Rosenfeld, *Common Sense*, 186.

13. Jacques Rancière, *The Names of History: On the Poetics of Knowledge*, 1st ed. (Minneapolis: University of Minnesota Press, 1994).

14. Carla Hesse, "Enlightenment Epistemology and the Laws of Authorship in Revolutionary France, 1777–1793," *Representations*, no. 30 (1990): 109–37, https://doi.org/10.2307/2928448.

15. Rosenfeld, *Common Sense*, 198. In a recent work on late twentieth-century American conservatism, Antti Lepistö charts very similar developments in America: "At a time when ruling conceptions of American values were seriously challenged, key theorists of the neoconservative movement invoked this natural 'moral sense' and some of its variants, especially 'moral sentiments' and 'common sense,' as essentially conservative instruments: they were shields from a dangerous moral relativism and perceived moral decline and a means to define in conservative terms what it means to be an ethical American citizen. In doing so, the neoconservatives employed, in a

culture wars context, a vocabulary that derived from Hutcheson, Smith, and Reid, one that had been used for conformist purposes already in eighteenth-century Europe and America"; Lepistö, *The Rise of Common-Sense Conservatism: The American Right and the Reinvention of the Scottish Enlightenment* (Chicago: University of Chicago Press, 2021), 4–5.

16. Kristin Ross, *May '68 and Its Afterlives*, 1st ed. (Chicago: University of Chicago Press, 2004); Camille Robcis, *The Law of Kinship: Anthropology, Psychoanalysis, and the Family in France* (Ithaca, N.Y.: Cornell University Press, 2013), 190.

17. A note on my terminology: Throughout the book, I have chosen to retain the proper name "State" as well as "Ideological State Apparatus." Within the context in which I am writing (i.e., postwar French political philosophy and aesthetics), "State" is a proper noun like "Being" or "God."

18. On the political theory of formats in modern times, see Colin Koopman, *How We Became Our Data: A Genealogy of the Informational Person* (Chicago: University of Chicago Press, 2019).

19. Pierre Bourdieu, "Systems of Education and Systems of Thought," *International Social Science Journal* 19, no. 3 (1967): 351.

20. Giovanni Della Casa and Victoria University (Toronto Studies Ontario) Centre for Reformation and Renaissance, *Galateo: A Renaissance Treatise on Manners* (Toronto: Centre for Reformation and Renaissance Studies, 1994).

21. Though I discuss this at length in Chapter 1, this point about the relationship between politics and philosophy is a notable and significant difference between conceptions of the enterprise of philosophy in France and those that developed in the Anglophone world in the postwar period.

22. Ezra N. Suleiman's *Elites in French Society* provides the best account of France's state-run educational structures tasked, as he explains throughout, with the formation and selection of elites for the purposes of political stability; Suleiman, *Elites in French Society: The Politics of Survival* (Princeton, N.J.: Princeton University Press, 2015), 19.

23. In this respect it is little surprise that from the 1950s onward—but especially in his critical writings of the late 1960s—Roland Barthes would champion a new science of criticism counter to the extant "Lansonisme" that he defines as "une psychologie conformiste de l'homme normal" ("a conformist psychology of the normal human"); Barthes, "Les Deux Critiques," *MLN* 78, no. 5 (1963): 451, https://doi.org/10.2307/3042755.

24. Knox Peden, *Spinoza Contra Phenomenology: French Rationalism from Cavaillès to Deleuze* (Stanford, Calif.: Stanford University Press, 2014); Eleanor Kaufman, *Deleuze, The Dark Precursor: Dialectic, Structure, Being* (Baltimore: Johns Hopkins University Press, 2012); Warren Montag, *Althusser and His Contemporaries: Philosophy's Perpetual War* (Durham, N.C.: Duke University Press, 2013).

25. I am grateful to the important work of Alan Schrift, who in no small part inspired the work I develop throughout; see especially "The Effects of the Agrégation

de Philosophie on Twentieth-Century French Philosophy," *Journal of the History of Philosophy* 46, no. 3 (July 18, 2008): 449–73, https://doi.org/10.1353/hph.0.0033, and "Is There Such a Thing as 'French Philosophy'? Or Why Do We Read the French So Badly?," in *After the Deluge: New Perspectives on the Intellectual and Cultural History of Postwar France*, ed. Julian Bourg (Lanham, Md.: Lexington, 2004), 21–47.

26. There are many examples, but for a helpful recent one, see Jacques Rancière, *The Method of Equality: Interviews with Laurent Jeanpierre and Dork Zabunyan* (Hoboken, N.J.: John Wiley & Sons, 2016).

27. I am here indebted to Aamir R. Mufti's analysis of "the *cultural system* of English"; though my focus is not that of world literature and remains well ensconced in a North Atlantic and French colonial imaginary that Frantz Fanon and Eduard Glissant rightly took to task, my emphasis on English as a political and cultural system of reading and reception shares with Mufti's critical impulse; Mufti, *Forget English!* (Cambridge, Mass.: Harvard University Press, 2016).

28. Emily Apter, *Against World Literature* (London and New York: Verso, 2013), 65.

29. Kathy E. Ferguson offers a compelling challenge to neurotypical assumptions about reading and understanding in Ferguson, "Dyslexia Manifesto," in *Disability and Political Theory*, ed. Barbara Arneil and Nancy J. Hirschmann (Cambridge and New York: Cambridge University Press, 2016), 144–68.

30. Please refer to the following publications that outline my approach to the study of political theory and media: Davide Panagia, "A Theory of Aspects: Media Participation and Political Theory," *New Literary History* 45, no. 4 (2014): 527–48; "On the Possibilities of a Political Theory of Algorithms," *Political Theory*, September 24, 2020, https://doi.org/10.1177/0090591720959853.

31. John Guillory, "The Memo and Modernity," *Critical Inquiry* 31, no. 1 (2004): 108–32, https://doi.org/10.1086/427304.

32. See Gaston Bachelard, *The Formation of the Scientific Mind: A Contribution to a Psychoanalysis of Objective Knowledge* (Manchester, UK: Clinamen, 2002).

33. Louis Althusser, *For Marx*, trans. Ben Brewster (London and New York: Verso, 2006). The idea of the epistemological rupture derives from Althusser's explicit debt to his professors Gaston Bachelard and Georges Canguilhem, both of whom were influential logicians and historians of science.

34. Frances Ferguson, "Our I. A. Richards Moment: The Machine and Its Adjustments," in *Theory Aside*, ed. Jason Potts and Daniel Stout (Durham, N.C., and London: Duke University Press, 2014), 261–85. See especially Ferguson's discussion of I. A. Richards's project with his students that became *Practical Criticism*.

35. Roger Chartier, *The Order of Books: Readers, Authors, and Libraries in Europe between the Fourteenth and Eighteenth Centuries* (Stanford, Calif.: Stanford University Press, 1994).

36. See Davide Panagia, *Impressions of Hume: Cinematic Thinking and the Politics of Discontinuity* (Landham, Md.: Rowman & Littlefield, 2013).

37. Though drawing inspiration from Jean-Paul Sartre, Iris Marion Young offers a wholly Humean account of the serialized nature of gender in Young, "Gender as Seriality: Thinking about Women as a Social Collective," *Signs* 19, no. 3 (1994): 713–38.

38. David Hume, *A Treatise of Human Nature*, ed. David Fate Norton and Mary J. Norton (New York: Oxford University Press, 2000), 1.4.2.21.

39. The most important work that details the connections between the *Tel Quel* writers and postcolonial theory remains Young, *White Mythologies*. Here I note one difference: Young's work is firmly rooted in the 1960–80s, whereas my interest is in the 1950s. Also see Jill Jarvis, *Decolonizing Memory: Algeria and the Politics of Testimony* (Durham, N.C.: Duke University Press, 2021); Simon Gikandi, "Poststructuralism and Postcolonial Discourse," in *The Cambridge Companion to Postcolonial Literary Studies*, ed. Neil Lazarus (Cambridge and New York: Cambridge University Press, 2004).

40. Most recently, Arash Abizadeh has forwarded a similar line of argument in his studies on minoritarian democracies; Abizadeh, "Counter-Majoritarian Democracy: Persistent Minorities, Federalism, and the Power of Numbers," *American Political Science Review*, undefined/ed., 1–15, https://doi.org/10.1017/S0003055421000198; "The Power of Numbers: On Agential Power-with-Others without Power-over-Others," *Philosophy & Public Affairs* (Forthcoming, n.d).

41. On this point, see the important study by Knox Peden, *Spinoza Contra Phenomenology.*

42. David Easton, *The Political System: An Inquiry into the State of Political Science* (New York: A. A. Knopf, 1967); John G. Gunnell, "The Reconstitution of Political Theory: David Easton, Behavioralism, and the Long Road to System," *Journal of the History of the Behavioral Sciences* 49, no. 2 (2013): 190–210, https://doi.org/10.1002/jhbs.21593; David Easton, "An Approach to the Analysis of Political Systems," *World Politics* 9, no. 3 (1957): 383–400, https://doi.org/10.2307/2008920.

43. Forrester, *In the Shadow of Justice.*

44. Thomas Medvetz, *Think Tanks in America* (Chicago: University of Chicago Press, 2012); Pamela M. Lee, *Think Tank Aesthetics: Midcentury Modernism, the Cold War, and the Neoliberal Present* (Cambridge, Mass.: MIT Press, 2020).

45. Louis Althusser, *On the Reproduction of Capitalism: Ideology and Ideological State Apparatuses* (London and New York: Verso, 2014).

46. See, for instance, Richard Wolin's unfortunate work *The Seduction of Unreason: The Intellectual Romance with Fascism from Nietzsche to Postmodernism*, 2nd ed. (Princeton, N.J.: Princeton University Press, 2019).

47. Schrift, "The Effects of the Agrégation de Philosophie on Twentieth-Century French Philosophy," 464–69. Gilles Deleuze in *Difference and Repetition* (trans. Paul Patton [New York: Columbia University Press, 1995]) credits Klossowki's essay for renewing France's interest in Nietzsche. More noteworthy is the fact that Heidegger's multivolume study of Nietzsche was not translated and published in France until 1971 by Klossowski (Schrift, 468nn57,58).

48. Schrift reminds us that an exception here is the interest in Nietzsche sustained and developed by the members of the *College de Sociologie*, including Georges Bataille and Jean Wahl.

49. Schrift, "The Effects of the Agrégation de Philosophie on Twentieth-Century French Philosophy." Some evidence from Schrift is worth citing directly: "Turning to the empiricists, I will simply note that, while Locke is, in the American context, at least as canonical a figure as Hume, and while both are viewed as exceeding Berkeley in terms of philosophical importance, Hume and Berkeley more than double Locke's appearances on the written exam (19 and 16 to 8), and they nearly double Locke's total number of appearances (53 and 50 to 27), with the number of Locke's appearances being less than the appearances of philosophers who would be considered much less significant in an American context like Malebranche (35 total, 15 written) or Plotinus (28 total, 11 written)" (461).

And: "In the thirteen years following the resumption of the agrégation after World War II, an empiricist's work appears on the oral examination in French translation every year but three (and in two of these years, Hume appears on the written Programme), and on the Programme for the written examination in eight of these thirteen years" (461).

50. Schrift, 461, 470, 472.

51. On morphology, see Michael Freeden, "Political Concepts and Ideological Morphology," *Journal of Political Philosophy* 2, no. 2 (June 1, 1994): 140–64, https://doi.org/10.1111/j.1467-9760.1994.tb00019.x; my modification of Freeden's morphological approach is explored in Panagia, *Rancière's Sentiments* (Durham, N.C.: Duke University Press, 2018), 35–39.

52. Riskin, *Science in the Age of Sensibility*, 7.

53. Roger Maioli, *Empiricism and the Early Theory of the Novel: Fielding to Austen* (Cham, Switzerland: Springer, 2017), 5–6.

54. Anthony Pagden, *The Enlightenment: And Why It Still Matters* (New York: Random House, 2013), 65–96.

55. In this regard, I follow Jessica Riskin's use of the term "sensibility" and "sentiment" "to describe an emotional 'movement' of the sensible creature"; Riskin, *Science in the Age of Sensibility*, 1.

56. Though my articulation will prove more demanding, it shares deep affinities with Sharon Krause's vitalist account of social transformation in *Freedom Beyond Sovereignty: Reconstructing Liberal Individualism* (Chicago: University of Chicago Press, 2015), 124–32. Where the style of empiricism I elaborate departs from Krause's is in the retained reliance on regulative ideals for political agency, even when Krause shifts the emphasis from regulative ideals to communicative practices in her analysis of non-sovereign agency.

57. Rani Lill Anjum and Stephen Mumford, "A Powerful Theory of Causation," in *The Metaphysics of Powers: Their Grounding and Their Manifestations*, ed. Anna Marmodoro (New York: Routledge, 2010), 143–59.

58. Stephen Mumford and Rani Lill Anjum, "Dispositional Modality," in *Lebenswelt und Wissenschaft, Deutsches Jahrbuch Philosophie 2*, ed. C. F. Gethmann (Hamburg: Meiner Verlag, 2011), 380. Importantly, Anjum and Mumford take Hume to task for his contingency and thus his critique of necessary powers. And they are right to do so. My addition to their innovative account of dispositional modalities is to suggest that Hume does have an account of dispositional powers in his account of the moral sentiments that act precisely as Anjum and Mumford describe the powers of dispositional modalities as "something in between what is merely possible and what *has* to be the case" (381). In short, I read the empiricist commitment to the moral sentiments (and relationality tout court) as a commitment to dispositional powers. But I add an inflection to Anjum and Mumford's use of the term "disposition" from the world of ancient rhetoric and its account of the *dispositio* of oration, which refers to the compositional arrangement of an order of speech.

59. On the idea of empiricism and external relations, see Bertrand Russell, "On the Nature of Acquaintance: Preliminary Description of Experience," *Monist* 24, no. 1 (1914): 1–16; Deleuze, *Difference and Repetition*; Gilles Deleuze, *Empiricism and Subjectivity: An Essay on Hume's Theory of Human Nature* (New York: Columbia University Press, 1991); Jean André Wahl, *L'expérience métaphysique* (Paris: Flammarion, 1965); also see Daniel W. Smith's discussion of "pure relations" or "the differential relation," in his *Essays on Deleuze* (Edinburgh: Edinburgh University Press, 2012, *passim*); and, finally, A. W. Moore's discussion of Hume's treatment of independent ideas in A. W. Moore's *The Evolution of Modern Metaphysics: Making Sense of Things* (Cambridge and New York: Cambridge University Press, 2012, 100–104).

60. Nancy Fraser, *Feminist Contentions: A Philosophical Exchange* (New York: Routledge, 2017), 18.

61. Carolyn Eichner, *Surmounting the Barricades* (Bloomington: Indiana University Press, 2004), https://iupress.org/9780253217059/surmounting-the -barricades/, 5.

62. Kevin Duong, *The Virtues of Violence: Democracy against Disintegration in Modern France* (New York: Oxford University Press, 2020), 86.

63. Duong, *Virtues of Violence*, 16.

64. The exemplary instance of this is Sheldon S. Wolin's stunningly uninformed and surprisingly anachronistic treatment of Nietzsche and his influence on postwar French thought; Wolin, *Politics and Vision: Continuity and Innovation in Western Political Thought* (Princeton, N.J.: Princeton University Press, 2009), 454–95.

65. Jason Frank, *The Democratic Sublime: On Aesthetics and Popular Assembly* (Oxford and New York: Oxford University Press, 2021), 151.

66. Camille Robcis, *Disalienation: Politics, Philosophy, and Radical Psychiatry in Postwar France* (Chicago: University of Chicago Press, 2021), 5–6.

67. The best account I have read of this is Katrina Forrester, *In the Shadow of Justice: Postwar Liberalism and the Remaking of Political Philosophy* (Princeton, N.J.: Princeton University Press, 2019).

68. Russell Ford, *Experience and Empiricism: Hegel, Hume, and the Early Deleuze* (Evanston, Ill.: Northwestern University Press, 2022), 23. Ford also (and rightly) notes the importance of the externality of relations thesis in sentimental empiricism, "whose core is the claim that there is no property of a thing from which its relations can be deduced." This, he explains, "strikes directly at an equally central tenet of monism: that knowledge of any part implies knowledge of the whole (and vice versa). For the pluralist," Ford continues, "experience can only ever be known empirically; for the monist, the structure of experience, at the very least, can be deduced from any experience by analyzing its constituent elements." (23)

69. Alan D. Schrift, "The Effects of the Agrégation de Philosophie on Twentieth-Century French Philosophy"; Schrift, "Is There Such a Thing as 'French Philosophy'?"; Schrift, *Twentieth-Century French Philosophy: Key Themes and Thinkers* (Hoboken, N.J.: John Wiley & Sons, 2009).

70. My gratitude to Lori Marso for inviting me to be explicit in acknowledging this debt.

71. Judith Grant, *Fundamental Feminism: Contesting the Core Concepts of Feminist Theory* (New York: Routledge, 2013), 28.

72. Emanuela Bianchi, *The Feminine Symptom: Aleatory Matter in the Aristotelian Cosmos* (New York: Fordham University Press, 2014); Bonnie Honig, *Shell-Shocked: Feminist Criticism after Trump* (New York: Fordham University Press, 2021).

73. Here, my debt goes to Rachel Forgash for raising this objection more than once and for insisting that I account for it.

74. The best account of this system of elite formation and power is Suleiman, *Elites in French Society*, passim but especially 3–56.

1. Reading Political Theory in Postwar America and Postwar France

1. On "missed understandings" (*mésentente*) and the scenographic as mode of writing and thinking, see Davide Panagia, "Introduction," in *Rancière's Sentiments* (Durham, N.C.: Duke University Press, 2018).

2. John Guillory, "How Scholars Read," *ADE Bulletin*, no. 146 (Fall 2008): 8.

3. John G. Gunnell, *The Descent of Political Theory: The Genealogy of an American Vocation* (Chicago: University of Chicago Press, 1993), 3; also see Jeremy Arnold, *Across the Great Divide: Between Analytic and Continental Political Theory* (Stanford, Calif.: Stanford University Press, 2020); Eric Lee Goodfield, *Hegel and the Metaphysical Frontiers of Political Theory* (London and New York: Routledge, 2014).

4. Rudolf Carnap, "The Elimination of Metaphysics through Logical Analysis of Language," *Erkenntnis* (1932): 60–81.

5. Here I invoke Stanley Cavell's sense of avoidance as that which we instinctively rule out in our responses to an other's expression of sensation. See especially Cavell, *The Claim of Reason: Wittgenstein, Skepticism, Morality, and Tragedy*, 1st ed. (New York: Oxford University Press, 1999), 338–43.

6. Sheldon S. Wolin, "Political Theory as a Vocation," *American Political Science Review* 63, no. 4 (December 1969): 1062–82, https://doi.org/10.1017/S000305540026320X.

7. In the United States a similar blow would be dealt to logical empiricism by Willard V. O. Quine's essay, "Two Dogmas of Empiricism" (*Philosophical Review* 60, no. 1 [1951]: 20–43, https://doi.org/10.2307/2266637), though that paper had little influence in political science and political theory.

8. Jean Cavaillès, *On Logic and the Theory of Science* (Cambridge, Mass.: MIT Press, 2021), 38.

9. Richard A. Macksey and Eugenio Donato, *The Structuralist Controversy: The Languages of Criticism and the Sciences of Man* (Baltimore: Johns Hopkins University Press, 2007).

10. "From the Editor," *Political Theory* 13, no. 1 (February 1, 1985): 3–4, https://doi.org/10.1177/0090591785013001001, 3–4.

11. Mark Philp, "Foucault on Power: A Problem in Radical Translation?," *Political Theory* 11, no. 1 (February 1, 1983): 29–52, https://doi.org/10.1177/0090591783011001003; William E. Connolly, "Discipline, Politics, and Ambiguity," *Political Theory* 11, no. 3 (August 1, 1983); Charles Taylor, "Foucault on Freedom and Truth," *Political Theory* 12, no. 2 (May 1, 1984): 152–83, https://doi.org/10.1177/0090591784012002002; Fred R. Dallmayr, "Ontology of Freedom: Heidegger and Political Philosophy," *Political Theory* 12, no. 2 (May 1, 1984): 204–34, https://doi.org/10.1177/0090591784012002004.

12. A further notable node in this institutional network history of reading and reception is the establishment of the School of Criticism and Theory (SCT) in 1976 by Murray Krieger at the University of California, Irvine. Currently hosted at Cornell University and having been also hosted by Northwestern University and Dartmouth College, SCT is a summer program for graduate students and early-career academics offering the opportunity to study with prominent theory and criticism scholars in the social sciences and humanities for a six-week period. The focus of SCT's mission is to provide an interdisciplinary and experimental program in theory and criticism. The current director is Hent de Vries. Past directors include Stanley Fish, Amanda Anderson, and Dominick LaCapra. See https://sct.cornell.edu.

13. Sage was also the publisher of the journal *Political Theory*; the current publishers of the series are Rowman and Littlefield. Kennan Ferguson, a former editor of journal *Theory & Event*, is now a co-editor of that series.

14. Barry Smith, "The Derrida Controversy Letter," *Times*, May 9, 1992, http://ontology.buffalo.edu/smith/varia/Derrida_Letter.htm. Here is the full list of signatories: Hans Albert (University of Mannheim), David Armstrong (Sydney), Ruth Barcan Marcus (Yale), Keith Campbell (Sydney), Richard Glauser (Neuchâtel), Rudolf Haller (Graz), Massimo Mugnai (Florence), Kevin Mulligan (Geneva), Lorenzo Peña (Madrid), Willard van Orman Quine (Harvard), Wolfgang Röd (Innsbruck), Karl Schuhmann (Utrecht), Daniel Schulthess (Neuchâtel), Peter Simons (Salzburg), René Thom (Burs-sur-Yvette), Dallas Willard (Los Angeles), Jan Wolenski (Cracow).

15. Barry Smith and Jeffrey Sims, "Revisiting the Derrida Affair with Barry Smith," *Sophia* 38, no. 2 (September 1, 1999): 155–56, https://doi.org/10.1007 /BF02786336.

16. Sara Rimer, "Rejection from Leader Who Vows Diversity," *New York Times*, May 19, 1997, https://www.nytimes.com/1997/05/19/us/rejection-from-leader-who -vows-diversity.html.

17. Rimer, "Rejection from Leader Who Vows Diversity."

18. Jal Mehta, "Tenure Denial Raises Concerns," *Harvard Crimson*, May 9, 1997, https://cyber.harvard.edu/eon/evidence/tdrc5997.html.

19. Rimer, "Rejection from Leader Who Vows Diversity."

20. Rimer.

21. Gunnell, *Descent of Political Theory*, 277.

22. Gunnell, 277.

23. Jeffrey C. Isaac, "The Strange Silence of Political Theory," *Political Theory* 23, no. 4 (1995): 636–52.

24. Isaac, "Strange Silence of Political Theory," 646–47.

25. Isaac, 647.

26. Pierre Bourdieu, *Reproduction in Education, Society and Culture* (London and Beverly Hills: SAGE, 1990), 117.

27. Sheldon S. Wolin, *Politics and Vision: Continuity and Innovation in Western Political Thought* (Princeton, N.J.: Princeton University Press, 2009), 585–87; Martha Nussbaum, "The Professor of Parody: The Hip Defeatism of Judith Butler," *New Republic* 22 (1999): 38; Alan D. Sokal, *The Sokal Hoax: The Sham That Shook the Academy* (Lincoln: University of Nebraska Press, 2000); John Guillory, "The Sokal Affair and the History of Criticism," *Critical Inquiry* 28, no. 2 (2002): 470–508, https://doi.org/10.1086/449049; Johns Hopkins University Press, "Philosophy and Literature," accessed July 27, 2020, https://www.press.jhu.edu/journals/philosophy-and -literature. *Philosophy and Literature*'s website Overview page reads as follows: "For more than forty years, *Philosophy and Literature* has explored the dialogue between literary and philosophical studies. The journal offers fresh, stimulating ideas in the aesthetics of literature, theory of criticism, philosophical interpretation of literature, and literary treatment of philosophy. *Philosophy and Literature* challenges the cant and pretensions of academic priesthoods through its assortment of lively, wide-ranging essays, notes, and reviews that are written in clear, jargon-free prose."

28. Gunnell, *Descent of Political Theory*, 3.

29. My account of this history is limited and is intended to focus our attentions on the postwar period and the scholarly practices of reading that are by this point consolidated after a century of epistemic disciplinary formation of American social science. Dorothy Ross's work shows the complicity of the rise of positivism and scientism with American exceptionalism from the period of the Civil War to the 1930s. Her conclusion is unequivocal: "What my history shows is that American social science has consistently constructed models of the world that embody the values and follow the logic of the national ideology of American exceptionalism. . . .

The most striking outcome of exceptionalist history has been scientism itself. The aim of scientism has been to establish prediction and control of the historical world and perhaps its most conspicuous accomplishment has been a set of quantitative techniques of information gathering and analysis that are used to manipulate such things as the money supply, consumer choices, votes, and remedial social therapies"; Ross, *The Origins of American Social Science* (Cambridge and New York: Cambridge University Press, 1992), 471–72.

30. Peter Galison, "Epistemic Virtues: A Talk by Peter Galison (8.21.19)," Edge .org., accessed July 31, 2020, https://www.edge.org/conversation/peter_galison -epistemic-virtues; Lorraine Daston and Peter Galison, *Objectivity* (Princeton, N.J.: Princeton University Press, 2021), 18–19.

31. Galison, "Epistemic Virtues."

32. Raymond Fosdick, "Passing of the Bertillon System of Identification," *Journal of Criminal Law and Criminology* 6, no. 3 (January 1, 1915): 363.

33. In March 30, 1858, Hymen Lipman registered a patent that combined the lead pencil with an India rubber tip: "What I do claim as my invention, and desire to secure by Letters Patent, is: The combination of the lead and India-rubber or other erasing substance in the holder of a drawing-pencil, the whole being constructed and arranged substantially in the manner and for the purposes set forth"; Lipman, Combination of lead-pencil and eraser, United States Patent Office 19783, n.d.

34. A. W. Moore, *The Evolution of Modern Metaphysics: Making Sense of Things* (Cambridge and New York: Cambridge University Press, 2012), 5–7.

35. Rudolf Carnap, *The Philosophy of Rudolf Carnap*, ed. Paul Arthur Schilpp, rev. ed. (La Salle, Ill.: Open Court, 1999), 11:32.

36. Michael Friedman, "Carnap, Cassirer, and Heidegger: The Davos Disputation and Twentieth Century Philosophy," *European Journal of Philosophy* 10, no. 3 (2002): 263–74, https://doi.org/10.1111/1468-0378.00162; Jimena Canales, *The Physicist and the Philosopher: Einstein, Bergson, and the Debate That Changed Our Understanding of Time* (Princeton, N.J.: Princeton University Press, 2015).

37. Canales, *Physicist and the Philosopher*, 5.

38. Carnap, "The Elimination of Metaphysics through Logical Analysis of Language, " *Erkenntnis* (1932): 60–81.

39. Michael LeMahieu, *Fictions of Fact and Value: The Erasure of Logical Positivism in American Literature, 1945–1975* (New York: Oxford University Press, 2016), 25.

40. Ray Monk and Richard C. Monk, *Ludwig Wittgenstein: The Duty of Genius* (New York: Free Press, 1990), 243.

41. Monk and Monk, *Ludwig Wittgenstein*, 244–45.

42. As a fair warning to the reader, I do not discuss Carnap's essay to assess its truth or falsity, its relative merits vis-à-vis Heidegger's ideas; nor, for that matter, do I wish to engage in a defense of Heidegger's ontology. None of those approaches are of interest to me, especially since more than enough ink has been spilled in these regards. My interest, on the contrary, is to extract the claims of empiricism from

Carnap's essay and to attend to how his elimination of metaphysics is instrumental in articulating logical empiricism as a theoretical *dispositif* for the verification and transcription of meaning.

43. Carnap, "Elimination of Metaphysics through Logical Analysis of Language," 61.

44. Peter Galison, "Aufbau/Bauhaus: Logical Positivism and Architectural Modernism," *Critical Inquiry* 16, no. 4 (1990): 749.

45. Galison, 749–50.

46. Galison, 750.

47. Carnap, "Elimination of Metaphysics through Logical Analysis of Language," 61.

48. Carnap, 63.

49. Carnap, 67.

50. Carnap, 74.

51. Carnap, 79.

52. Carnap, 79.

53. Carnap, 80.

54. Carnap, 80.

55. Carnap, 80.

56. For such an endeavor, see A. W. Moore's excellent chapter on Carnap in Moore, *Evolution of Modern Metaphysics*, 279–301.

57. Charles Taylor, "Interpretations and the Sciences of Man," in *Philosophical Papers*, vol. 2, *Philosophy and the Human Sciences* (Cambridge and New York: Cambridge University Press, 1985), 15–57.

58. David Hume, *An Enquiry Concerning Human Understanding: And Other Writings*, ed. Stephen Buckle (Cambridge and New York: Cambridge University Press, 2011), Section 12, Part 3.

59. Friedrich Stadler, *The Vienna Circle: Studies in the Origins, Development, and Influence of Logical Empiricism*, (2015; repr. New York: Springer, 2016), 869–909.

60. Arnold, *Across the Great Divide*, 8.

61. Katrina Forrester, *In the Shadow of Justice: Postwar Liberalism and the Remaking of Political Philosophy* (Princeton, N.J.: Princeton University Press, 2019), 5.

62. Gunnell, *Descent of Political Theory*, 195.

63. Eugene Miller, "David Easton's Political Theory," *Political Science Reviewer* 1 (July 1, 1971), https://politicalsciencereviewer.wisc.edu/index.php/psr/article/view/75, 187–88.

64. Gunnell, *Descent of Political Theory*, 236.

65. Consider that two years prior to the publication of *The Political System*, Arendt had published *The Origins of Totalitarianism* (1951), and 1952 saw the publication of Leo Strauss's *Natural Law and History*.

66. Norbert Wiener, *Cybernetics; Or, Control and Communication in the Animal and the Machine* (Cambridge, Mass.: MIT Press, 1961).

67. I discuss cybernetics in greater detail here: Davide Panagia, "The Algorithm *Dispositif*: Risk and Automation in the Age of #datapoliti," in *The Routledge Companion to Media and Risk*, ed. Bhaskar Sarkar and Bishnupriya Ghosh (New York: Routledge, 2020).

68. Ernst Kantorowicz, *The King's Two Bodies: A Study in Medieval Political Theology* (Princeton, N.J.: Princeton University Press, 2016).

69. Forrester, *In the Shadow of Justice*, 5.

70. Thomas Medvetz, *Think Tanks in America* (Chicago: University of Chicago Press, 2012).

71. Fred Kaplan, *The Wizards of Armageddon* (Stanford, Calif.: Stanford University Press, 1991), 111.

72. Kaplan, *Wizards of Armageddon*, 109.

73. John Douglass and John Thomas, "The Loyalty Oath Controversy, University of California, 1949–1951," University of California History Digital Archives, accessed August 6, 2020, https://www.lib.berkeley.edu/uchistory/archives _exhibits/loyaltyoath/index.html.

74. Wolin, "Political Theory as a Vocation," 1075.

75. Gunnell, *Descent of Political Theory*, 277.

76. For a very helpful cultural and intellectual history between 1946 and 1960, see M. Kelly, *The Cultural and Intellectual Rebuilding of France after the Second World War* (New York: Palgrave Mcmillan, 2004), 155–79.

77. "From the Editor," *Political Theory* 13, no. 1 (1985): 3–4, JSTOR, http://www .jstor.org/stable/191626, accessed 10 January 10, 2024.

78. Carla Alison Hesse, *Publishing and Cultural Politics in Revolutionary Paris, 1789–1810* (Berkeley: University of California Press, 1991), 125–26.

79. Anne Mccauley, "'Merely Mechanical': On the Origins of Photographic Copyright in France and Great Britain," *Art History* 31, no. 1 (2008): 61, https://doi .org/10.1111/j.1467-8365.2008.00583.x.

80. "La lecture linéaire au lycée—Lettres—Éduscol," accessed August 10, 2020, https://eduscol.education.fr/lettres/actualites/actualites/article/la-lecture-lineaire-au -lycee.html.

81. George James Ranson, "The Method of Literary History by Gustave Lanson" (thesis, University of Kansas, 1929), https://kuscholarworks.ku.edu/handle/1808 /23659.

82. Jean-Albert Bédé, "Gustave Lanson," *American Scholar* 4, no. 3 (1935): 286.

83. John Gerassi, *Jean-Paul Sartre: Hated Conscience of His Century; Protestant or Protester?* (Chicago: University of Chicago Press, 1989), 76–77.

84. Alan D. Schrift, "The Effects of the Agrégation de Philosophie on Twentieth-Century French Philosophy," *Journal of the History of Philosophy* 46, no. 3 (July 18, 2008): 450–51.

85. Bourdieu, *Reproduction in Education, Society and Culture*, 108–14.

86. Schrift, "Effects of the Agrégation de Philosophie on Twentieth-Century French Philosophy," 451.

87. Alan D. Schrift, "Is There Such a Thing as 'French Philosophy'? Or Why Do We Read The French So Badly?," in *After the Deluge: New Perspectives on the Intellectual and Cultural History of Postwar France*, ed. Julian Bourg (Lanham, Md.: Lexington, 2004), 24.

88. Schrift, "Effects of the Agrégation de Philosophie on Twentieth-Century French Philosophy," 455.

89. "Hence I believe I have good reasons for thinking that behind the scenes of its political Ideological State Apparatus, which occupies the front of the stage, what the bourgeoisie has installed as its number-one, i.e., as its dominant Ideological State Apparatus, is the educational apparatus, which has in fact replaced in its functions the previously dominant Ideological State Apparatus, the Church. One might even add: the school-family couple has replaced the Church-family couple"; Louis Althusser, *On the Reproduction of Capitalism: Ideology and Ideological State Apparatuses* (London and New York: Verso, 2014), 250.

90. Schrift, "Effects of the Agrégation de Philosophie on Twentieth-Century French Philosophy," 452–53. The original passage is in Jacques Derrida, "When a Teaching Body Begins," in *Who's Afraid of Philosophy? Right to Philosophy I*, trans. Jan Plug (Stanford, Calif.: Stanford University Press, 2002), 75, which first appeared in *Politiques de la Philosophie*, ed. Dominique-Antoine Grisoni (Paris: Grasset, 1976).

91. Gilles Deleuze and Félix Guattari, *What Is Philosophy?* (New York: Verso, 1994), 2.

92. Among the list of students who have gone through the École's training program, Alan Schrift notes the freshman class of 1924 faculty of Arts and Letters that included Raymond Aron, Georges Canguilhem, and Jean-Paul Sartre, while Jean Hyppolite would enter in 1925 and Maurice Merleau-Ponty would join in 1926. Schrift also notes that of significance are two Latin Quarter high schools (or *lycées*), Louis-le-Grand and Henri-IV, where many of these scholars were students and prepared for admittance to the ENS. These included Derrida, Lyotard, Alain Badiou, Merleau-Ponty, Sartre, Jean Wahl, Gilles Deleuze, Michel Foucault, and Georges Canguilhem.

93. Schrift, "Effects of the Agrégation de Philosophie on Twentieth-Century French Philosophy," 458. There is a complete list of twentieth-century *agrégation* authors available in Schrift's essay.

94. Schrift, "Is There Such a Thing as 'French Philosophy'? Or Why Do We Read the French So Badly?," 25; Schrift, "Effects of the Agrégation de Philosophie on Twentieth-Century French Philosophy," 464–69.

95. Nicholas Hewitt, ed., *The Cambridge Companion to Modern French Culture* (Cambridge and New York: Cambridge University Press, 2003), 46.

96. Howard Davies, *Sartre and "Les Temps Modernes"* (Cambridge and New York: Cambridge University Press, 1987), 1–2.

97. Kristin Ross, *Fast Cars, Clean Bodies: Decolonization and the Reordering of French Culture*, 4th ed. (Cambridge, Mass.: MIT Press, 1996), 124.

98. D. Drake, *Intellectuals and Politics in Post-War France* (Cham, Switzerland: Springer, 2001), 97–127.

99. Paul Ricoeur, *The Rule of Metaphor: Multi-Disciplinary Studies of the Creation of Meaning in Language* (Toronto: University of Toronto Press, 1981).

100. Ross, *Fast Cars, Clean Bodies*, 126.

101. Ross, 124.

102. Philip Nord, "Catholic Culture in Interwar France," *French Politics, Culture & Society* 21, no. 3 (2003): 5.

103. Forrester, *In the Shadow of Justice*, 5–10.

104. Nord, "Catholic Culture in Interwar France," 11.

105. Nord, 11.

106. Pierre Assouline, *Herge: The Man Who Created Tintin* (Oxford and New York: Oxford University Press, 2009), 13–15.

107. Assouline, *Herge*, 14.

108. Nord, "Catholic Culture in Interwar France," 15.

109. Nord, 17.

110. Reinhard Hutter, *Aquinas on Transubstantiation: The Real Presence of Christ in the Eucharist* (Washington, D.C.: The Catholic University of America Press, 2019), 8.

111. "Library: Decree of Excommunication," accessed August 13, 2020, https://www.catholicculture.org/culture/library/view.cfm?recnum=1222; John Paul II, "Ecclesia Dei (July 2, 1988)."

112. Pius XII, "Fidei Donum" (April 21, 1957).

113. Pius XII, "Fidei Donum."

114. David Hume, *A Treatise of Human Nature*, ed. David Fate Norton and Mary J. Norton (New York: Oxford University Press, 2000), Book I, Section VI, *Of Modes and Substances*.

115. On this matter, also see Pamela M. Lee, *Think Tank Aesthetics: Midcentury Modernism, the Cold War, and the Neoliberal Present* (Cambridge, Mass.: MIT Press, 2020), 49–85.

116. Anna Boschetti, *The Intellectual Enterprise: Sartre and Les Temps Modernes* (Evanston, Ill.: Northwestern University Press, 1988), 171–83.

117. Ross, *Fast Cars, Clean Bodies*, 5.

118. See Judith Butler, *Subjects of Desire: Hegelian Reflections in Twentieth-Century France* (New York: Columbia University Press, 2012); Knox Peden, *Spinoza Contra Phenomenology: French Rationalism from Cavaillès to Deleuze* (Stanford, Calif.: Stanford University Press, 2014); Warren Montag, *Althusser and His Contemporaries: Philosophy's Perpetual War* (Durham, N.C.: Duke University Press, 2013); Barry Cooper, *Merleau-Ponty and Marxism: From Terror to Reform* (Toronto: University of Toronto Press, 1979).

119. Ted Toadvine, "Maurice Merleau-Ponty," in *The Stanford Encyclopedia of Philosophy*, ed. Edward N. Zalta (Stanford, Calif.: Stanford University Metaphysics Research Lab, 2019, https://plato.stanford.edu/archives/spr2019/entries/merleau-ponty/.

120. Michel Foucault, *The Order of Things* (London and New York: Routledge), 1994.

2. Mimesis, the *explication de texte*, and State Thinking

1. Ezra N. Suleiman, *Elites in French Society: The Politics of Survival* (Princeton, N.J.: Princeton University Press, 2015). Suleiman's study is to my mind essential reading for any student of political and aesthetic theory and criticism interested in the political dimensions of these theoretical and critical enterprises. His central thesis—that since Napoleonic times, the French education system is a state-run institution of elite formation for the purposes of political stability—is crucial to my own analysis of the political metaphysics of mimesis.

2. I offer an account of the political ontology of the *dispositif* in the Epilogue to this book.

3. Georges Canguilhem gives a lucid account of this system in Canguilhem, "The Teaching of Philosophy in France," in *The Teaching of Philosophy: An International Inquiry of Unesco* (Paris: UNESCO, 1953), 53–55. Perhaps because of the fact that this was an address given to an international audience (and thus not the place for self-criticism), Canguilhem's account (published in 1953) wholly embraces and defends the greatness of France's philosophy program: "Thanks to the tacit but effective collaboration between the board, the competent university professors and the administrative authorities responsible for secondary education, the agrégation in philosophy is thus exceptionally important, for, so far as most students are concerned, it establishes and maintains the high standard of philosophical studies. There may well be a possible danger in this: it may impart to philosophical studies too strong an element of competition, too narrow and utilitarian an outlook, both of which would militate against the true spirit of philosophical research and theory. The real advantage of the system, however, which no one denies, is that it rules out the amateur approach and demands of students both wide knowledge and serious work" (54). His students—Althusser, Bourdieu, Foucault, and Deleuze chief among these—would eventually express dissenting sentiments.

4. Suleiman, *Elites in French Society*, passim.

5. M. Martin Guiney, *Literature, Pedagogy, and Curriculum in Secondary Education: Examples from France* (Cham, Switzerland: Springer, 2017), 119.

6. Cited from De Lozère's collection of *Opinions de Napoléon* in Suleiman, *Elites in French Society*, 19.

7. Suleiman, *Elites in French Society*, 41.

8. Suleiman, 29.

9. Suleiman, 37.

10. Pierre Bourdieu, "Reading, Readers, the Literate, Literature," in *In Other Words: Essays Towards a Reflexive Sociology* (Stanford, Calif.: Stanford University Press, 1990), 95.

11. John Guillory, "Close Reading: Prologue and Epilogue," *ADE Bulletin* 149 (2010): 8–14.

12. Roland Barthes, *Critical Essays* (Evanston, Ill.: Northwestern University Press, 1972), 249–54.

13. The centrality of the work of Gaston Bachelard in the theorization of epistemic ruptures is indisputable. In this regard, see especially Bachelard, *The Formation of the Scientific Mind: A Contribution to a Psychoanalysis of Objective Knowledge* (Manchester, UK: Clinamen, 2002); Tiles, *Bachelard* (Cambridge and New York: Cambridge University Press, 1984).

14. Alan D. Schrift, "The Effects of the Agrégation de Philosophie on Twentieth-Century French Philosophy," *Journal of the History of Philosophy* 46, no. 3 (July 18, 2008): 449–73, https://doi.org/10.1353/hph.0.0033; Kristin Ross, *May '68 and Its Afterlives*, 1st ed. (Chicago: University of Chicago Press, 2004); John Guillory, *Cultural Capital: The Problem of Literary Canon Formation* (Chicago: University of Chicago Press, 2013); Pierre Bourdieu, *Reproduction in Education, Society and Culture* (London and Beverly Hills: SAGE, 1990).

15. On the influence of Jean Cavaillès to the postwar generation of Spinozism in France, see Knox Peden, *Spinoza Contra Phenomenology: French Rationalism from Cavaillès to Deleuze* (Stanford, Calif.: Stanford University Press, 2014); Jean Cavaillès, *On Logic and the Theory of Science* (Cambridge, Mass.: MIT Press, 2021).

16. Carla Alison Hesse, *Publishing and Cultural Politics in Revolutionary Paris, 1789–1810* (Berkeley: University of California Press, 1991), 120. It is within this context, I would add, that we might better appreciate Michel Foucault's "What Is an Author?" essay, as well as Roland Barthes's "Death of an Author" essay.

17. Terry Nichols Clark, *Prophets and Patrons: The French University and the Emergence of the Social Sciences* (Cambridge, Mass.: Harvard University Press, 1973), 20.

18. D. R. Watson, "The Politics of Educational Reform in France during the Third Republic 1900–1940," *Past & Present* 34, no. 1 (July 1, 1966): 83, https://doi.org/10.1093/past/34.1.81.

19. Bourdieu, *Reproduction in Education, Society and Culture*, 141–76.

20. Watson, "The Politics of Educational Reform in France during the Third Republic 1900–1940," 86.

21. I take one of Aamir Mufti's claims in his *Forget English* to be that the English language is a credentialing standard for Global Literatures in much the same way that Latin and Greek, in the French context, were credentialing standards of political and cultural capital; see Mufti, *Forget English!* (Cambridge, Mass.: Harvard University Press, 2016).

22. Glenn H. Roe, *The Passion of Charles Péguy: Literature, Modernity, and the Crisis of Historicism* (Oxford and New York: Oxford University Press, 2014), 137.

23. Guiney, *Literature, Pedagogy, and Curriculum in Secondary Education*, 89.

24. Allan Peter Farrell, *The Jesuit Code of Liberal Education: Development and Scope of the Ratio Studiorum* (Milwaukee: Bruce, 1938), vii.

25. Frederic Ernest Farrington, *French Secondary Schools: An Account of the Origin, Development and Present Organization of Secondary Education in France* (New York: Longmans, Green, 1910), 49.

26. Farrell, *Jesuit Code of Liberal Education*, 403.

27. Pierre Bourdieu, "Esprits d'État," *Actes de la Recherche en Sciences Sociales* 96, no. 1 (1993): 49.

28. Farrell, *Jesuit Code of Liberal Education*, 298–99.

29. I elaborate this further in Chapter 3.

30. Farrell, *Jesuit Code of Liberal Education*, 403.

31. Jean-Jacques Rousseau, *The Government of Poland* (Indianapolis: Hackett, 1985), 19.

32. Louis Althusser, *On the Reproduction of Capitalism: Ideology and Ideological State Apparatuses* (London and New York: Verso, 2014); Michel Foucault, *Discipline & Punish: The Birth of the Prison* (New York: Knopf Doubleday, 2012).

33. David Funt, "Roland Barthes and the Nouvelle Critique," *Journal of Aesthetics and Art Criticism* 26, no. 3 (1968): 331, https://doi.org/10.2307/429117.

34. The words are a direct citation from an article by Gustave Lanson, "Dix-septième ou dix-huitième siècle?," in *L'enseignement du français* (Paris: F. Alean, 1903); and in Martine Jey, "The Literature of the Enlightenment: An Impossible Legacy for the Republican School," trans. Antoine Krieger, *Yale French Studies*, no. 113 (2008): 46.

35. Jey, "Literature of the Enlightenment," 48.

36. Jey, 51.

37. D. R. Watson, "The Politics of Educational Reform in France during the Third Republic 1900–1940," *Past & Present* 34, no. 1 (July 1, 1966): 82, https://doi.org/10.1093/past/34.1.81.

38. Guiney, *Literature, Pedagogy, and Curriculum in Secondary Education*, 94.

39. Étienne Karabétian, *Histoire des stylistiques* (Paris: A. Colin, 2000), 152.

40. Mark Wolff, "Individuality and l'Esprit Français: On Gustave Lanson's Pedagogy," *Modern Language Quarterly* 62, no. 3 (September 1, 2001): 248, https://doi.org/10.1215/00267929-62-3-239.

41. Wolff, "Individuality and l'Esprit Français," 244. Cited in Gustave Lanson, "Un nouveau genre de critique littéraire: La critique évolutioniste," *Revue de l'enseignement secondaire et de l'enseignement supérieur* (August 15, 1890): 135–36.

42. The only edition of this text I could find is online and thus has no pagination: Lanson, "Méthodes de l'histoire Littéraire—Critique Littéraire," accessed March 2, 2021, https://obvil.sorbonne-universite.fr/corpus/critique/lanson_methodes/#body-3. However, it is a passage also cited in Jean-Jacques Briu and Étienne Karabétian, *Leo Spitzer: Etudes sur le style; Analyse de textes littéraires français (1918–1931)* (Paris: Editions Ophrys, 2009), 80, who note the original publication as *Études françaises* (Paris: Les Belles Lettres, 1925), 52.

43. Cited in Briu and Karabétian, *Leo Spitzer*, 80.

44. Lanson, "Méthodes de l'histoire Littéraire—Critique Littéraire"; Briu and Karabétian, *Leo Spitzer*, 81.

45. Roe, *Passion of Charles Péguy*, 145.

46. Roe, 153–69.

47. John Gerassi, *Jean-Paul Sartre: Hated Conscience of His Century; Protestant or Protester?* (Chicago: University of Chicago Press, 1989), 76.

48. Kristin Ross, *Communal Luxury: The Political Imaginary of the Paris Commune* (London: Verso, 2015), 49.

49. Barthes, *Critical Essays*, 254.

50. Rae Beth Gordon, "From Charcot to Charlot: Unconscious Imitation and Spectatorship in French Cabaret and Early Cinema," *Critical Inquiry* 27, no. 3 (2001): 515–49. In this study, Gordon develops a cinematic argument about movement, public spectatorship, imitation, and the aesthetic avant-garde that helps us appreciate how uncontrolled and automatic bodily movements (associated in the early twentieth century with hysteria) were viewed as a threat to bodily integrity and social reproducibility and how the viewing of moving bodies on a cinematic screen was considered dangerous because of a fear of hysterical contagion through the imitation of bodily gyrations.

3. Jean Wahl, Empirico-Criticism, and the Concrete

1. Gilles Deleuze, *The Logic of Sense* (New York: Columbia University Press, 1990), 3.

2. Jean André Wahl, *Transcendence and the Concrete: Selected Writings* (New York: Fordham University Press, 2017), 13.

3. Wahl, *Transcendence and the Concrete*, 13.

4. We are fortunate that the introductions written by Ian Alexander Moore and Alan D. Schrift, Sean Bowden, Mathias Girel, William C. Hackett, and Giulio Piatti for the following volumes provide us with a rich and comprehensive account of Wahl's life and works: Wahl, *Transcendence and the Concrete*; Sean Bowden, "Jean Wahl," in *Deleuze's Philosophical Lineage II*, ed. Graham Jones and Jon Roffe (Edinburgh: Edinburgh University Press, 2019), 183–206; Wahl, *Vers le concret: Études d'histoire de la philosophie contemporaine; William James, Whitehead, Gabriel Marcel* (Paris: Vrin, 2004); Wahl, *Human Existence and Transcendence* (Notre Dame, Ind.: University of Notre Dame Press, 2016); Wahl, *Verso il concreto: Studi di filosofia contemporanea William James, Whitehead, Gabriel Marcel* (Sesto San Giovanni: Mimesis, 2020). Most recently Russell Ford's important study, *Experience and Empiricism*, dedicates much needed elaboration of Wahl's philosophy and his intellectual contributions; see Ford, *Experience and Empiricism: Hegel, Hume, and the Early Deleuze* (Evanston, Ill.: Northwestern University Press, 2022).

5. François Dosse, *Gilles Deleuze and Félix Guattari: Intersecting Lives* (New York: Columbia University Press, 2011), 110; Bowden, "Jean Wahl," 185.

6. Kennan Ferguson, "La Philosophie Americaine: James, Bergson, and the Century of Intercontinental Pluralism," *Theory & Event* 9, no. 1 (March 27, 2006), https://doi.org/10.1353/tae.2006.0014; Melvin L. Rogers, *The Undiscovered Dewey:*

Religion, Morality, and the Ethos of Democracy (New York: Columbia University Press, 2008); Erin Manning, *Always More Than One: Individuation's Dance* (Durham, N.C.: Duke University Press, 2013); Alexander Livingston, *Damn Great Empires!: William James and the Politics of Pragmatism* (New York: Oxford University Press, 2016); Jane Bennett, *Vibrant Matter: A Political Ecology of Things* (Durham, N.C.: Duke University Press, 2009); William E. Connolly, *A World of Becoming* (Durham, N.C.: Duke University Press, 2011); Brian Massumi, *Ontopower: War, Powers, and the State of Perception* (Durham, N.C.: Duke University Press, 2015); Jairus Victor Grove, *Savage Ecology: War and Geopolitics at the End of the World* (Durham, N.C.: Duke University Press, 2019); Antoine Bousquet, *The Eye of War: Military Perception from the Telescope to the Drone* (Minneapolis: University of Minnesota Press, 2018); Steven Shaviro, *Without Criteria: Kant, Whitehead, Deleuze, and Aesthetics* (Cambridge, Mass.: MIT Press, 2012).

7. Bruno Latour, *Reassembling the Social: An Introduction to Actor-Network-Theory* (Oxford and New York: Oxford University Press, 2007); Isabelle Stengers, *Thinking with Whitehead: A Free and Wild Creation of Concepts* (Cambridge, Mass.: Harvard University Press, 2014); David Lapoujade, *William James: Empiricism and Pragmatism* (Durham, N.C.: Duke University Press, 2019).

8. Wahl, *Transcendence and the Concrete*, 34. Please note that when citing from the Preface of *Vers le concret*, I will use this translated version. When citing from the rest of the work, I will provide my own translations of the original French.

9. Wahl, 34.

10. Wahl, 38.

11. Wahl, 39.

12. Wahl, 39.

13. For a more sustained analysis of Wahl, see Ford, *Experience and Empiricism*.

14. Emmanuel Levinas, Xavier Tilliette, and Paul Ricoeur, *Jean Wahl et Gabriel Marcel* (Paris: Beauchesne, 1976), 16.

15. Wahl, *Transcendence and the Concrete*, 3.

16. Wahl, *Verso il concreto*, 267.

17. Levinas, Tilliette, and Ricoeur, *Jean Wahl et Gabriel Marcel*, 15 and 17.

18. Wahl, *Transcendence and the Concrete*, 16.

19. Wahl, 3.

20. Hamilton Basso, "Profiles: Philosopher," *New Yorker*, May 12, 1945, 31, http://www.newyorker.com/magazine/1945/05/12/philosopher-3.

21. Wahl, *Transcendence and the Concrete*, 4.

22. Jean André Wahl, *Voices in the Dark: Fifteen Poems of the Prison & the Camp* (Kirkwood, Mo.: Printery, 1974).

23. Basso, "Profiles: Philosopher," 35.

24. Wahl, *Transcendence and the Concrete*, 5.

25. Basso, "Profiles: Philosopher," 41.

26. Wahl, *Transcendence and the Concrete*, 15.

27. Levinas, Tilliette, and Ricoeur, *Jean Wahl et Gabriel Marcel*, 18.

28. Levinas, Tilliette, and Ricoeur, 24.

29. Wahl, *Transcendence and the Concrete*, 35.

30. Wahl, 35.

31. Wahl, 35n9.

32. Wahl, 36.

33. Wahl, 51.

34. Wahl, 51.

35. Wahl, 52.

36. The first French translation of *Process and Reality* is published by Gallimard in France in 1995: Alfred North Whitehead, *Procès et réalité: Essai de cosmologie* (Paris: Gallimard, 1995).

37. Wahl, *Transcendence and the Concrete*, 39.

38. Wahl, *Vers le concret*, 131. NB: "C.N." refers to Whitehead's "Concept of Nature," first published in French in 1998, and "N. Kn" refers to Whitehead's as yet untranslated *An Enquiry Concerning the Principles of Natural Knowledge.*

39. We will see a different account of Hume—though one thoroughly influenced by Wahl's account of empiricism—when we discuss Gilles Deleuze's sentimental empiricism in Chapter 7. Deleuze recuperates a radical empiricist Hume by moving beyond Wahl's reading and showing how if we read Hume as both an empiricist and a sentimentalist, then we find in Hume's writings what Wahl discovers in James's and Whitehead's radical empiricism.

40. This may seem counterintuitive, given our inherited understandings of empiricism that one finds throughout the social sciences; see Charles Taylor, "Interpretations and the Sciences of Man," in *Philosophical Papers*, vol. 2, *Philosophy and the Human Sciences* (Cambridge and New York: Cambridge University Press, 1985), 15–57; Sheldon S. Wolin, "Political Theory as a Vocation," *American Political Science Review* 63, no. 4 (December 1969): 1062–82, https://doi.org/10.1017/S0003 05540026320X; David Easton, *The Political System: An Inquiry into the State of Political Science* (New York: A. A. Knopf, 1967). However, that account of empiricism is indebted to a specific interpretation inherited from logical positivism that doesn't consider the sentimentalist aspects of experience and assumes, wrongly, the substance of "datum" as a pre-experiential classification adequate to all experience.

41. Wahl, *Vers le concret*, 131.

42. Wahl, 131.

43. Wahl, *Transcendence and the Concrete*, 45.

44. Wahl, 46.

45. This is, importantly, something Kennan Ferguson also identifies in his study of William James's metaphysical pluralism by distinguishing James's pluralism from the sense of pluralism in postwar American political science; see Ferguson, *William James: Politics in the Pluriverse* (Lanham, Md.: Rowman & Littlefield, 2007).

46. Wahl, *Vers le concret*, 61. The French "chevauchement" can be translated literally as "overlapping," but it also holds the sense of superimposition, adjacency, or a disjointed connection of lines (in the case of the disposition of railroads); see Éditions Larousse, "Définitions: chevauchement—Dictionnaire de français Larousse," accessed November 5, 2021, https://www.larousse.fr/dictionnaires/francais /chevauchement/15189.

47. Wahl, *Transcendence and the Concrete*, 52.

48. Wahl, 40.

49. Ferguson, *William James*. See especially Chapter 4.

50. Jean Wahl, *The Pluralist Philosophies of England and America*, trans. Fred Rothwell (London: Open Court, 1925), 154.

51. Wahl, *Pluralist Philosophies of England and America*, 154.

52. Wahl, 246. Wahl's chapter on Russell is a sustained discussion of his doctrine of external relations, taken from Russell's 1911 paper "The Basis of Realism." From this, Wahl cites the following directly from Russell's paper: "(1) relatedness does not imply any corresponding complexity in the *relata*; (2) any given entity is a constituent of many different complexes" (244).

53. Wahl, *Pluralist Philosophies of England and America*, 255.

54. Gilles Deleuze, *Empiricism and Subjectivity: An Essay on Hume's Theory of Human Nature* (New York: Columbia University Press, 1991), 98–99. "Let us examine the problem of relations. We should not debate futile points; we do not have to ask: on the assumption that relations do not depend upon ideas, is it *eo ipso* certain that they depend on the subject? This is obvious. If relations do not have as their causes the properties of the ideas between which they are established, that is, if they have other causes, then these other causes determine a subject which alone establishes relations. The relation of truth to subjectivity is manifested in the affirmation that a true judgment is not a tautology. Thus, the truly fundamental proposition is that relations are external to ideas. And if they are external, the problem of the subject, as it is formulated in empiricism, follows. It is necessary, in fact, to know upon what other causes these notions depend, that is, how the subject is constituted in the collection of ideas. Relations are external to their terms. When James calls himself a pluralist, he does not say, in principle, anything else. This is also the case when Russell calls himself a realist. We see in this statement the point common to all empiricisms." Reading between the lines, in his Hume book Deleuze shows how Wahl's acceptance of Whitehead's attribution of naïve empiricism to Hume is too quick, especially since the naïve empiricism to which Whitehead refers is not Hume's but that of the post-Kantian interpretation of Hume that does not acknowledge the importance of the moral sentiments (sympathy chief among these) as oscillating with the claim of immediate experience.

55. Wahl, *The Pluralist Philosophies of England and America*, 134.

56. Wahl, 140.

57. Wahl, 139.

58. Wahl, 255.

4. Simone de Beauvoir and the Elementary Structures of Patriarchy

1. The English translation is collected in Simone de Beauvoir and Margaret A. Simons, *Philosophical Writings* (Champaign: University of Illinois Press, 2005). The original French is "Litterature et Metaphysique," *Les Temps Modernes* 7 (1946): 1153–63.

2. Jo Bogaerts, "Beauvoir's Lecture on the Metaphysics of the Novel and Its Contemporary Critiques," *Simone de Beauvoir Studies* 29 (2013): 20–32; Toril Moi, "What Can Literature Do? Simone de Beauvoir as a Literary Theorist," *PMLA* 124, no. 1 (2009): 189–98. Moi's engagement with the question of Beauvoir and literary theory focuses on her participation and contribution to the 1964 *Que peut la littérature?* meeting in Paris.

3. Beauvoir and Simons, *Philosophical Writings*, 269.

4. Beauvoir and Simons, 270.

5. Beauvoir and Simons, 275.

6. Alexandre Kojève, *Introduction to the Reading of Hegel* (Ithaca, N.Y.: Cornell University Press, 1980).

7. Here is one way Beauvoir expresses her disdain of abstract idealism: "If one imagines that through the colorful and living paste of things he sees only desiccated essences, one can fear that the author will hand over to us a dead universe, as foreign to the one we breathe in as an X-ray picture is different from a fleshed body. But this fear is well founded only in regard to philosophers who, separating essence from existence, disdain appearance in favor of the hidden reality; fortunately, they are not tempted to write novels"; Beauvoir and Simons, *Philosophical Writings*, 275.

8. Meryl Altman, "Beauvoir, Hegel, War," *Hypatia* 22, no. 3 (2007): 71, https://doi.org/10.1111/j.1527–2001.2007.tb01091.x.

9. Altman, "Beauvoir, Hegel, War," 72.

10. Bruce Baugh, "Hegel in Modern French Philosophy: The Unhappy Consciousness," *Laval Théologique et Philosophique* 49, no. 3 (1993): 431, https://doi.org/10.7202/400791ar.

11. Lori Jo Marso, *Politics with Beauvoir: Freedom in the Encounter* (Durham, N.C.: Duke University Press, 2017), 24.

12. Annette C. Baier, *A Progress of Sentiments: Reflections on Hume's Treatise* (Cambridge, Mass.: Harvard University Press, 2009), 25.

13. Jacqueline Anne Taylor, *Reflecting Subjects: Passion, Sympathy, and Society in Hume's Philosophy* (Oxford: Oxford University Press, 2015), 11. Citing a capacious bibliography of sources, Taylor notes that "by the eighteenth century, it was widely accepted within the academy, and particularly in Scotland, that the new experimental methodologies could be adapted to the science of human nature."

14. Ezra N. Suleiman, *Elites in French Society: The Politics of Survival* (Princeton, N.J.: Princeton University Press, 2015), 41.

15. In this respect, we see Beauvoir anticipating Gayle Rubin's concerns vis-à-vis her reading of Lévi-Strauss; see Gayle Rubin, "The Traffic in Women: Notes on the

'Political Economy' of Sex," in *Toward an Anthropology of Women*, ed. Rayna R. Reiter (New York: Monthly Review Press, 1975), 157–210.

16. Lori Marso, "Thinking Politically with Simone de Beauvoir in The Second Sex," *Theory & Event* 15, no. 2 (2012), https://muse.jhu.edu/article/478359"; Toril Moi, *What Is a Woman? And Other Essays* (Oxford and New York: Oxford University Press, 2001); see especially "I Am a Woman: The Personal and the Philosophical."

17. Moi, *What Is a Woman?*; Marso, *Politics with Beauvoir*; Elaine Stavro, *Emancipatory Thinking: Simone de Beauvoir and Contemporary Political Thought* (Montreal: McGill-Queen's University Press, 2018); Marso, "Thinking Politically with Simone de Beauvoir in The Second Sex." I was especially shocked in this respect by the first sentence of Marso's *Theory & Event* essay: "Simone de Beauvoir is seldom recognized by critics as a political thinker."

18. Lori Marso, "Simone de Beauvoir, The Second Sex," *The Oxford Handbook of Classics in Contemporary Political Theory* (December 10, 2015), 1, https://doi.org/10 .1093/oxfordhb/9780198717133.013.31.

19. Toril Moi, *Simone de Beauvoir: The Making of an Intellectual Woman* (Oxford and New York: Oxford University Press, 2008), 203.

20. Moi, *Simone de Beauvoir*, 218.

21. Stavro, *Emancipatory Thinking*, 4.

22. It is important to Beauvoir's argument that the sexual relation is oriented to procreation and is thus heterosexual. This is the case for many reasons, not the least of which is her reliance on Lévi-Strauss's anthropology of the incest taboo, but also because of the importance of Family Code (*Code de Famille*) to the history of French politics in the nineteenth and twentieth centuries.

23. David Hume, *A Treatise of Human Nature*, ed. David Fate Norton and Mary J. Norton (New York: Oxford University Press, 2000), 2.1.1.3. Following convention, citations from Hume's *Treatise* will hereafter appear as parenthetical references in the main text, listing first the Book (2), then the part (1), then the section (1), and finally the paragraph (3).

24. Jaeyoon Park, "Does Power 'Spread'? Foucault on the Generalization of Power," *Political Theory* (October 11, 2021), 00905917211046576, https://doi.org/10.1177 /00905917211046576. I am grateful to Jaeyoon Park for our discussions regarding the theme of generalized power in postwar French thought and for his critical provocations throughout those discussions.

25. Marso, *Politics with Beauvoir*, 24.

26. Davide Panagia, *Impressions of Hume: Cinematic Thinking and the Politics of Discontinuity* (Landham, Md.: Rowman & Littlefield, 2013).

27. Dennis C. Rasmussen, *The Infidel and the Professor: David Hume, Adam Smith, and the Friendship That Shaped Modern Thought* (Princeton, N.J.: Princeton University Press, 2019), 46.

28. I note that by "everyday" I do not intend it in the ableist sense of "normal."

29. Taylor, *Reflecting Subjects*, 39.

30. Marso, *Politics with Beauvoir*, 2.

31. Simone de Beauvoir, *Memoirs of a Dutiful Daughter* (New York: HarperCollins, 2016), 82.

32. Simone de Beauvoir, *Memoirs of a Dutiful Daughter* (New York: HarperCollins, 2016), 82.

33. Jules Ferry, "Lettre aux instituteurs–17 novembre 1883," *Académie de Paris*, November 17, 1883, https://www.ac-paris.fr/portail/jcms/p1_; 1153893/lettre-aux -instituteurs-jules-ferry-17-novembre-1883. The original French reads as follows: "Sans doute il a eu pour premier objet de séparer l'école de l'Église, d'assurer la liberté de conscience et des maîtres et des élèves, de distinguer enfin deux domaines trop longtemps confondus: celui des croyances, qui sont personnelles, libres et variables, et celui des connaissances, qui sont communes et indispensables à tous, de l'aveu de tous."

34. Ferry: "Elle affirme la volonté de fonder chez nous une éducation nationale, et de la fonder sur des notions du devoir et du droit que le législateur n'hésite pas à inscrire au nombre des premières vérités que nul ne peut ignorer. Pour cette partie capitale de l'éducation, c'est sur vous, Monsieur, que les pouvoirs publics ont compté. En vous dispensant de l'enseignement religieux, on n'a pas songé à vous décharger de l'enseignement moral; c'eût été vous enlever ce qui fait la dignité de votre profession. Au contraire, il a paru tout naturel que l'instituteur, en même temps qu'il apprend aux enfants à lire et à écrire, leur enseigne aussi ces règles élémentaires de la vie morale qui ne sont pas moins universellement acceptées que celles du langage ou du calcul."

35. Ferry.

36. Ferry: "Le livre est fait pour vous, et non vous pour le livre, il est votre conseiller et votre guide, mais c'est vous qui devez rester le guide et le conseiller par excellence de vos élèves."

37. Delphine Mercier, "L'enseignement de la morale au quotidien: Le rôle des inspecteurs primaires, 1880–1914," *Histoire de l'education* 105, no. 1 (2005): 2–2.

38. Mercier, "L'enseignement de la morale au quotidien," 51, translated from the original French by the author.

39. A. Poignet and H. Bernat, *Le Livre Unique de Morale et d'instruction Civique*, 10th ed. (Paris: Auguste Godchaux, 1911). The title page also indicates that Poignet is the principal inspector and officer of public instruction, while Bernat is an instituteur.

40. Poignet and Bernat, *Le Livre Unique*: "Bien choisis, les exemples peuvent à la rigueur suffire pour former la conscience morale de l'enfante e le conduire à la vertu."

41. Poignet and Bernat: "L'heure viendra où vous devrez quitter définitivement l'école. Si, à ce moment là, vous avex bien appris les trois paragraphes de chaque leçon, si vous êtes intimement pénétrés des préceptes qu'ils renferment si enfin vous vous sentez disposés à imiter les bons exemples contenu dans les lectures, ce livre aura contribué à faire de vous des bons fils, de bons citoyens, de bons Français."

42. Deirdre Bair, *Simone de Beauvoir: A Biography* (New York: Simon and Schuster, 1991), 64.

43. Bair, *Simone de Beauvoir*, 64.

44. Camille Robcis, *The Law of Kinship: Anthropology, Psychoanalysis, and the Family in France* (Ithaca, N.Y.: Cornell University Press, 2013), Chapter 1.

45. Robcis, *Law of Kinship*, 60.

46. Pierre Rosanvallon, *Le sacre du citoyen: Histoire du suffrage universel en France* (Paris: Gallimard, 1992), 39; quoted in Robcis, *Law of Kinship*, 40.

47. On this point, see Giulia Sissa's discussion of St. Thomas's treatment of heterosexuality in *I generi e la storia* (Bologna, Italy: Il Mulino, 2024), 94–99.

48. Claude Lévi-Strauss, *The Elementary Structures of Kinship*, rev. ed. (Boston: Beacon Press, 1969), 480.

49. Simone de Beauvoir, *Memoirs of a Dutiful Daughter* (New York: HarperCollins, 2016), e-book.

50. Simone de Beauvoir, *The Second Sex* (New York: Knopf Doubleday, 2012), 7. By "the second part" Beauvoir is referring to chapter 2 of volume 1, entitled "History."

51. Quoted in Simone de Beauvoir, *Feminist Writings* (Champaign: University of Illinois Press, 2015), 52; Beauvoir, *Feminist Writings*.

52. Beauvoir, *Feminist Writings*, 58.

53. Beauvoir, 59.

54. Beauvoir, 59.

55. Beauvoir, 60.

56. Beauvoir, 61.

57. Beauvoir, 64.

58. Beauvoir, 64.

59. Beauvoir, 60.

60. Beauvoir, *Second Sex*, 85.

61. Beauvoir, 88.

5. More than a Unity: Gilbert Simondon's Sentimental Empiricism

1. A peculiarity of the French academic system during the first half of the twentieth century requires noting. In fact, both works (Gilbert Simondon, *Du mode d'existence des objets techniques* [Paris: Éditions Aubier, 2012] and *L'individuation à la lumière des notions de forme et d'information* [Grenoble: Éditions Jérôme Millon, 2005]) were required in order to obtain a *Doctorat ès Lettres* (renamed *Doctorat d'État* in the 1950s), and thus, both works count as Simondon's theses for his degree completion. The expectation at the time that a student, in order to obtain a *Doctorat*, submit a *thèse principale* and a *thèse secondaire* or *these complémentaire*. These requirements have changed several times since then, especially in light of the post-'68 reforms to the French university system; Alan D. Schrift, *Twentieth-Century French Philosophy: Key Themes and Thinkers* (Hoboken, N.J.: John Wiley & Sons, 2009), 207–8.

Simondon's *On the Mode of Existence of Technical Objects* (Minneapolis: Univocal, 2016), was first published in 1958, while his *Individuation in the Light of* the *Notions of Form and Information* (Minneapolis: University of Minnesota Press, 2020) is a three-part work, the first part of which was published in Simondon's lifetime in 1964; in 2005 the complete three volumes were published together for the first time. We are currently awaiting the English translation of the complete *Individuation* book, scheduled to appear in May 2020 with the University of Minnesota Press.

2. Recent interest in the work of Simondon has increased, as noted in the following works, which I draw on significantly throughout this essay: Brian Massumi, *Parables for the Virtual: Movement, Affect, Sensation* (Durham, N.C.: Duke University Press, 2002); Alberto Toscano, *Theatre of Production: Philosophy and Individuation between Kant and Deleuze* (Basingstoke and New York: Palgrave Macmillan, 2006); Muriel Combes, *Gilbert Simondon and the Philosophy of the Transindividual* (Cambridge, Mass.: MIT Press, 2013); Andrea Bardin, *Epistemology and Political Philosophy in Gilbert Simondon: Individuation, Technics, Social Systems* (Cham, Switzerland: Springer, 2015); Anne Sauvagnargues, *Artmachines: Deleuze, Guattari, Simondon* (Edinburgh: Edinburgh University Press, 2016); Simon Mills, *Gilbert Simondon: Information, Technology, and Media* (London and New York: Rowman & Littlefield International, 2016). Further, *Philosophy Today* dedicated a special issue: *The Work of Simondon*, ed. Andrea Bardin, Giovanni Carrozzini, and Pablo Rodríguez, 63, no. 3 (Summer 2019).

3. Andrea Bardin, "Philosophy as Political Technē: The Tradition of Invention in Simondon's Political Thought," *Contemporary Political Theory* 17 (2018): 417–36.

4. This may be, in part, because Simondon's writings have only recently been translated into English. The first official translation of his *On the Mode of Existence of Technical Objects*, an expansion on his doctoral thesis first published in 1958, for example, wasn't published until 2012 (though an unofficial translation by Ninian Mellamphy of the first third of that work has been circulating for several decades), and his opus *Individuation in the Light of the Notions of Form and Information* wasn't available in English translation until 2020.

5. Bardin, "Philosophy as Political Technē," 417.

6. In this regard, Alberto Toscano is absolutely correct in giving the title *"Tertium Datur?"* to his chapter on Simondon; Toscano, *Theatre of Production*.

7. Gilbert Simondon, "The Position of the Problem of Ontogenesis," *Parrhesia*, no. 7 (2009): 4–16. My choice in focusing on this is that the English translation of the *Individuation* book has not yet appeared during the time of my writing this chapter and because this selection offers the most succinct and concise account of Simondon's critique of hylomorphism.

8. Gaston Bachelard, *The New Scientific Spirit* (Boston: Beacon Press, 1984), 147–48.

9. Martin Heidegger, "On the Essence and Concept of Φύσις in Aristotle's Physics B, I (1939)," in *Pathmarks*, ed. William McNeil, trans. Thomas Sheehan (Cambridge: Cambridge University Press, 1998), 183–230, https://www.cambridge.org /core/books/pathmarks/on-the-essence-and-concept-of-in-aristotles-physics-b-i-1939/3 BC2B1D9539AD10A8980B4963062337E; Heidegger, "The Question Concerning

Technology," in *Basic Writings*, 2nd ed., rev. and expanded (San Francisco: HarperPerennial, 1993).

10. Heidegger, "Question Concerning Technology," 332.

11. Heidegger, "On the Essence and Concept of Φύσις in Aristotle's Physics B, I (1939)," 190.

12. Bardin, *Epistemology and Political Philosophy in Gilbert Simondon*, 191.

13. Bardin, 6–10.

14. Combes, *Gilbert Simondon and the Philosophy of the Transindividual*, 2.

15. Combes, 2.

16. Taylor Adkins, "A Short List of Gilbert Simondon's Vocabulary," *Fractal Ontology*, accessed April 22, 2020, https://fractalontology.wordpress.com/2007/11/28/a -short-list-of-gilbert-simondons-vocabulary/.

17. Simondon, *L'individuation à la lumière des notions de forme et d'information*, 48 (my translation). Here is the original French: "Le véritable principe d'individuation est la genèse elle-même en train de s'opérer, c'est-à-dire le système en train de devenir, pendant que l'énergie s'actualise. . . . Le principe d'individuation est une opération."

18. Simondon, "Position of the Problem of Ontogenesis," 4.

19. Simondon, 5–6.

20. In an interview simultaneous with the publication of this translation of Simondon's Introduction, Brian Massumi makes this point thusly: "For Simondon, all transition, all change, all becoming, is quantum"; Massumi, "'Technical Mentality' Revisited: Brian Massumi on Gilbert Simondon," *Parrhesia Journal* 7 (2009): 41.

21. Simondon, "The Position of the Problem of Ontogenesis," 6.

22. Simondon, 6.

23. Bardin, *Epistemology and Political Philosophy in Gilbert Simondon*, 6.

24. Simondon, "The Position of the Problem of Ontogenesis," 8. For the purposes of parsing the meaning of the paragraph, I insert numbers between sentences.

25. Simondon, *L'individuation à la lumière des notions de forme et d'information*, 56.

26. Simondon, 10. I take "transductive unity" to be a synonym for the "more than a unity" of individuation.

27. Simondon, 12.

28. Mills, *Gilbert Simondon*, 217–24. Though it is beyond the scope of this chapter to discuss this further, Simon Mills rightly (I believe) connects Simondon's account of individuation and transduction to the dispositional monism elaborated by Stephen Mumford and Rani Lill Anjum's *Getting Causes from Powers* (Oxford and New York: Oxford University Press, 2011).

29. Simondon, *L'individuation à la lumière des notions de forme et d'information*, 12.

30. Combes, *Gilbert Simondon and the Philosophy of the Transindividual*, 5.

31. Simondon, *L'individuation à la lumière des notions de forme et d'information*, 10.

32. Simondon, 13.

33. Sauvagnargues, *Artmachines*, 64–65.

34. Toscano, *Theatre of Production*, 141.

35. Simondon, *L'individuation à la lumière des notions de forme et d'information*, 40; my translation. The original is as follows: "La médiation est préparée par deux chaînes d'opérations préalables qui font converger matière et forme vers une opération commune. Donner une forme à de l'argile, ce n'est pas imposer la forme parallélépipédique à l'argile brute: c'est tasser de l'argile préparée dans un moule fabriqué. Si on part des deux bouts de la chaîne technologique, le parallélépipédique et l'argile dans la carrière, on éprouve l'impression de réaliser, dans l'opération technique, une rencontre entre deux réalités de domaines hétérogènese, et d'instituer une médiation, par communication, entre un ordre interéleementaire, macrophysique, plus grand que l'individu, et un ordre intra-élémentaire, microphysique, plus petit que l'individu."

36. This is an important insight also developed by Emanuela Bianchi in *The Feminine Symptom: Aleatory Matter in the Aristotelian Cosmos* (New York: Fordham University Press, 2014). For Bianchi the authority of telos (and hence necessity and determinism) is genetic to substance. Telos thus "provides the justification for a rigorously hierarchical cosmological system encompassing the physical world, the biological world, and the human world of ethics and politics" (1). This system hinges on the fact of sexual differentiation vis-à-vis movement (or, in Frank's terms, action/ activity). Bianchi identifies that the "central problem of motion and that of gender are profoundly connected. . . . Aristotle identifies the female as the source of matter for the offspring, while the male provides the principle of motion, generation, soul-principle, logos, and form" (2). Female matter, in other words, is not substance and teleology; it is *sumptōma*, or "the inexplicable *coincidence (sumptōma)* of causal orders, and aleatory matter is the site at which the symptom arises" (4). Bianchi does not deploy the figure of the feminine symptom in Aristotle's text to either undermine or reject his enterprise. In developing a critical intimacy with Aristotle's work, her study elaborates the ontological status of the feminine symptom in and of itself, and this means a construal of feminine matter as "an obscure site of unaccountable movements, as a site of the possibility that A *as such* might not come to be exactly as expected, but that A', A+, A-, or perhaps even B, C, Q, or X might emerge, that is, as a site with potentials for all sorts of unforeseen monstrosities, deformations, and creative revolutions" (17). In short, what Bianchi shows is that (at least in Aristotle) matter *is* difference *is* female *sumptōma*. Furthermore, the distinction between form and matter that structures Aristotle's ousiatic ontology rests on attributing activity, directedness, and causality to *ousia* (i.e., form) as the power of composition and arrangement. Ousia gives coherence and thus unity to parts, rendering the whole available for intelligibility.

37. I borrow the term "radical mediation" from Richard Grusin's theorization of it and, in this context, especially his emphasis on its anti-representational (or, I

would say for the purposes of consistency with the language of this chapter, anti-mimetic) dimension; see Grusin, "Radical Mediation," *Critical Inquiry* 42, no. 1 (September 1, 2015): 128.

38. For a recent treatment of twentieth-century media participation, see Christopher M. Kelty, *The Participant*; Kelty: *A Century of Participation in Four Stories* (Chicago: University of Chicago Press, 2020).

39. Simondon, *On the Mode of Existence of Technical Objects*, 15.

40. Bardin, *Epistemology and Political Philosophy in Gilbert Simondon*, 14.

41. Simondon, *On the Mode of Existence of Technical Objects*, 15. To this I would like to draw the obvious connection to Bruno Latour's developments of actor-network theory and his discussion of the agentialism of objects in *Reassembling the Social: An Introduction to Actor-Network-Theory* (Oxford and New York: Oxford University Press, 2007) 63–86; and, finally, Jane Bennett's discussion of "thing-power," in *Vibrant Matter: A Political Ecology of Things* (Durham, N.C.: Duke University Press, 2009).

42. Simondon, *On the Mode of Existence of Technical Objects*, 15. For a Parisian readership, the not-so-subtle reference to Camus's *L'Étrangèr* would not have been lost in Simondon's declaration that "la machine est l'étrangèr, c'est l'étrangèr en laquelle est enfermé de l'humaine"; Simondon, *Du mode d'existence des objets techniques*, 9.

43. There are, I believe, strong parallels here between Simondon's rejection of a facile instrumentalism and Dimitris Vardoulakis's recent rethinking of an Epicurean *phronesis*; Dimitris Vardoulakis, *Spinoza, the Epicurean: Authority and Utility in Materialism* (Edinburgh: Edinburgh University Press, 2022).

44. Simondon, *On the Mode of Existence of Technical Objects*, 19.

45. Simondon, 20.

46. Simondon, 26.

47. Simondon, 26.

48. Simondon, 29.

49. Simondon, 39.

50. Simondon, 43. It begins to be clear how Simondon's work is a decided precursor to recent theorizations of new materialism. See especially Bennett, *Vibrant Matter*.

51. Simondon, *On the Mode of Existence of Technical Objects*, 70.

52. Simondon, 62; also see Georges Canguilhem, "Machine and Organism," in *Knowledge of Life* (New York: Fordham University Press, 2008). It is unclear of the extent to which Gilles Deleuze's Body-without-Organs thesis, first articulated in *Empiricism and Subjectivity: An Essay on Hume's Theory of Human Nature* (New York: Columbia University Press, 1991), and then further elaborated in Deleuze and Felix Guattari, *A Thousand Plateaus: Capitalism and Schizophrenia*, trans. Brian Massumi, 1st ed. (Minneapolis: University of Minnesota Press, 1987), originates from Simondon's formulation or to what extent it is part of the materialist/machinic aspects of empiricism tout court (see Hobbes's Introduction to *Leviathan*). That said, the parallels are striking.

53. Simondon, *On the Mode of Existence of Technical Objects*, 16. In this regard, Simondon asserts the following: "The most powerful cause of alienation in the contemporary world resides in this misunderstanding of the machine, which is not an alienation caused by the machine, but by the non-knowledge of its nature and its essence, by way of its absence from the world of signification, and its omission from the table of values and concepts that make up culture."

54. Simondon, 173.

55. In this respect, there is a strong family resemblance between Simondon's account of the associated milieu that regulates the dynamism of forms and Samantha Frost's recent account of biocultural creatures that, as she defines it, "encapsulates the mutual constitution of body and environment, of biology and habitat"; Samantha Frost, *Biocultural Creatures: Toward a New Theory of the Human* (Durham, N.C.: Duke University Press, 2016), 4.

56. Simondon, *On the Mode of Existence of Technical Objects*, 74.

6. Gilles Deleuze: Displacing Reflection

1. Gilles Deleuze, *The Logic of Sense* (New York: Columbia University Press, 1990), 6.

2. Paul Patton, *Deleuzian Concepts: Philosophy, Colonization, Politics* (Stanford, Calif.: Stanford University Press, 2010); Patton, *Deleuze and the Political* (London and New York: Routledge, 2000); Nicholas Tampio, *Deleuze's Political Vision* (Lanham, Md.: Rowman & Littlefield, 2015); Nathan Widder, *Political Theory after Deleuze* (London: A & C Black, 2012); William E. Connolly, *The Ethos of Pluralization* (Minneapolis: University of Minnesota Press, 1995); Connolly, *Neuropolitics: Thinking, Culture, Speed* (Minneapolis: University of Minnesota Press, 2002); Connolly, *Pluralism* (Durham, N.C.: Duke University Press, 2005); Connolly, *A World of Becoming* (Durham, N.C.: Duke University Press, 2011).

3. Neil Roberts, *Freedom as Marronage* (Chicago: University of Chicago Press, 2015); Cristina Beltrán, *The Trouble with Unity: Latino Politics and the Creation of Identity* (Oxford and New York: Oxford University Press, 2010); Jane Bennett, *Influx and Efflux: Writing Up with Walt Whitman* (Durham, N.C.: Duke University Press, 2020).

4. Here I'm thinking of the seminal work of Connolly, *World of Becoming*; Michael J. Shapiro, *Studies in Trans-Disciplinary Method: After the Aesthetic Turn* (London and New York: Routledge, 2013); Rosi Braidotti, *Transpositions: On Nomadic Ethics* (Cambridge and Malden, Mass.: Polity, 2006); Braidotti, *Nomadic Subjects: Embodiment and Sexual Difference in Contemporary Feminist Theory* (New York: Columbia University Press, 2011); Elizabeth Grosz, *The Incorporeal: Ontology, Ethics, and the Limits of Materialism* (New York: Columbia University Press, 2017); Grosz, *Chaos, Territory, Art: Deleuze and the Framing of the Earth* (New York: Columbia University Press, 2008); and Morton Schoolman, *A Democratic Enlightenment: The Reconciliation Image, Aesthetic Education, Possible Politics* (Durham, N.C.: Duke University Press, 2020).

5. Eleanor Kaufman, *Deleuze, The Dark Precursor: Dialectic, Structure, Being* (Baltimore: Johns Hopkins University Press, 2012); Daniel Smith, *Essays on Deleuze* (Edinburgh: Edinburgh University Press, 2012); A. W. Moore, *The Evolution of Modern Metaphysics: Making Sense of Things* (Cambridge and New York: Cambridge University Press, 2012); Peter Hallward, *Out of This World: Deleuze and the Philosophy of Creation* (London and New York: Verso, 2006); Knox Peden, *Spinoza Contra Phenomenology: French Rationalism from Cavaillès to Deleuze* (Stanford, Calif.: Stanford University Press, 2014); Ronald Bogue, *Deleuze on Cinema* (New York: Routledge, 2003); Marc Rölli, *Gilles Deleuze's Transcendental Empiricism: From Tradition to Difference* (Edinburgh: Edinburgh University Press, 2016); Felicity Colman, *Deleuze and Cinema: The Film Concepts* (Oxford and New York: Berg, 2011).

6. Deleuze, *Logic of Sense*; Gilles Deleuze, *Difference and Repetition*, trans. Paul Patton (New York: Columbia University Press, 1995).

7. Deleuze, *Difference and Repetition*, 167.

8. Warren Montag, "From Clinamen to Conatus: Deleuze, Lucretius, Spinoza," in *Lucretius and Modernity: Epicurean Encounters across Time and Disciplines*, ed. Jacques Lezra and Liza Blake (Basingstoke and New York: Palgrave Macmillan, 2016). Montag is more precise than I can be in detailing the work's provenance: "In 1961, Gilles Deleuze published a short essay titled 'Lucrèce et le naturalisme' in the journal *Études philosophiques*. At the end of the sixties, a version of the essay, approximately two pages longer, which included the entirety of the earlier version (with the exception of a diagram), appeared as one of five appendices to *The Logic of Sense*. It was presented under the heading "The Simulacrum and Ancient Philosophy," where it was preceded and, in a certain sense, introduced by an essay on Plato, "Plato and the Simulacrum," which was also a revised version of an earlier essay originally published under the title "Renverser le platonisme" (Les Simulacres) ("To Reverse Platonism") in the *Revue de métaphysique et de morale* 71, no. 4, (1966): 426–38.

9. Gilles Deleuze, *Nietzsche and Philosophy* (New York: Columbia University Press, 2006), 106.

10. In a related way, Michel Foucault would (in 1966) describe a similar problematic: "The Classical theory of the sign and the word had to show how representations, which succeeded one another in a chain so narrow and so tightly knit that distinctions did not appear, with the result that they were all, in short, alike, could be spread out to form a permanent table of stable differences and limited identities"; Foucault, *The Order of Things* (London and New York: Routledge, 2005), 369.

11. Gilles Deleuze and Rosalind Krauss, "Plato and the Simulacrum," *October* 27 (Winter 1983): 45–56, https://doi.org/10.2307/778495; Deleuze, *Logique du sens*, Éditions Minuit (Paris: Gallimard, 1969), 292; Montag, "From Clinamen to Conatus: Deleuze, Lucretius, Spinoza," 163. As Montag notes, part of the revisions done to "The Simulacra and Ancient Philosophy" Appendix was to include a second essay written in 1967 entitled "Renverser le platonisme." The English translation of the

Appendix in *The Logic of Sense* translates *renverser* as "reverse." But that is not the best translation of the term, given the sense of "reverse" as a moving backward. In 1983 Rosalind Krauss translated the essay for an issue of *October*, and her translation (which is different from the one in *The Logic of Sense*) renders the original French *"renversement"* as "overthrow." I retain Krauss's term "overthrow." But I also use my own term, "invert" or inversion, in the sense of turning something inside out. The French *"renverser"* retains this sense of inverting, as it is a verb also used to describe, for instance, the act of turning clothes inside out, as one might when hanging them to dry in the sun; that is, an overturning as a turning over. Other resonant translations of the verb include being knocked down or knocking something over. I am grateful to Emanuela Bianchi, Claire Sagan, and Antoine Bousquet for their reminder of this matter of translation on a Facebook post (dated 3.25.21, 10:42 A.M.).

12. In a cultural politics that counts the Catholic Church as a major presence, Aristotle's metaphysics of substances remains central to the doctrine of transubstantiation and the spiritual and divine powers of the church, who, through the Catholic sacrament of Holy Orders (i.e., the investiture of the priesthood), gives priests the power and authority to enact and celebrate five sacraments: Baptism, Reconciliation, Consecration of the Eucharist (i.e., celebrate the Mass), Matrimony, and the Anointing of the Sick. All of these are essential to participation in the Catholic Church and to salvation. The most important of these is the sacramental power of consecration of the Eucharist that transubstantiates the bread and wine into the body and blook of Christ. The Catholic doctrine of transubstantiation is founded on St. Thomas's adoption and Christianization of Aristotle's metaphysics of *ousia*, or substances.

13. Eleanor Kaufman, *Deleuze, The Dark Precursor: Dialectic, Structure, Being* (Baltimore: Johns Hopkins University Press, 2012); Daniel Smith, *Essays on Deleuze* (Edinburgh: Edinburgh University Press, 2012); John Protevi, *Life, War, Earth: Deleuze and the Sciences* (Minneapolis: University of Minnesota Press, 2013); Moore, *Evolution of Modern Metaphysics*; Todd May, *Gilles Deleuze: An Introduction* (New York: Cambridge University Press, 2005); John Rajchman, *The Deleuze Connections* (Cambridge, Mass.: MIT Press, 2000); Braidotti, *Transpositions*; Hallward, *Out of This World*; Protevi, "Deleuze and Guattari," accessed March 16, 2021, http://www.protevi.com/john/DG/.

14. François Dosse, *Gilles Deleuze and Félix Guattari: Intersecting Lives* (New York: Columbia University Press, 2011), 110; Sean Bowden, "Jean Wahl," in *Deleuze's Philosophical Lineage II*, ed. Graham Jones and Jon Roffe (Edinburgh: Edinburgh University Press, 2019), 185.

15. Gilles Deleuze, *Empiricism and Subjectivity: An Essay on Hume's Theory of Human Nature* (New York: Columbia University Press, 1991), 107. Here is what Deleuze says: "The classical definition proposed by the Kantian tradition is this: empiricism is the theory according to which knowledge not only begins with experience but is derived from it. But *why* would the empiricist say that? and as the result of which question? . . . The fact is, though, that the definition is in no way

satisfactory: first of all, because knowledge is not the most important thing for empiricism, but only the means to some practical activity. Next, because experience for the empiricist, and for Hume in particular, does not have this univocal and constitutive aspect that we give it. Experience has two senses which are rigorously defined by Hume, and in neither of these senses is it constitutive. According to the first, if we call 'experience' a collection of distinct perceptions, we should next realize that relations are not derived from experience. They are the effect of the principles of association, namely of the principle of human nature, which, within experience, constitute a subject capable of transcending experience. And if we use the word in the second sense, in order to denote various conjunctions of past objects, we should again realize that principles do not come from experience since, on the contrary, experience itself must be understood as a principle."

16. For verification of this, see "K is for Kant," in *Gilles Deleuze from A to Z*.

17. Deleuze, *Empiricism and Subjectivity*, 89. Please note that for the purposes of this discussion, I take "subject" to be Deleuze's term for consciousness.

18. Deleuze, 89.

19. Deleuze, 23.

20. Deleuze, 64.

21. On intermediality and sentimental empiricism see Davide Panagia, *Intermedialities: Political Theory and Cinematic Experience* (Evanston: Northwestern University Press, 2024).

22. Deleuze, *Difference and Repetition*, 70–80.

23. For an excellent treatment of the concept of habit in modern political theory, see Alexander Diones, "'The Vivacity of Our Ideas': Habit in Modern Political Thought," *UCLA* (2022), https://escholarship.org/uc/item/68z8worw.

24. Deleuze, *Difference and Repetition*, 74.

25. Deleuze, 78.

26. Here I rely on Sharon Cameron's articulation of impersonality as disintegrative and outside the logic of property and propriety to which both personhood and impersonality are conventionally assigned; Sharon Cameron, *Impersonality: Seven Essays* (Chicago: University of Chicago Press, 2009).

27. Deleuze, *Empiricism and Subjectivity*, 87–88.

28. Deleuze, 30.

29. Hume, *A Treatise of Human Nature*, I.iv.

30. Hume, *An Enquiry Concerning Human Understanding: And Other Writings*, Section IV, Part I, 26.

31. Jacqueline Anne Taylor, *Reflecting Subjects: Passion, Sympathy, and Society in Hume's Philosophy* (Oxford: Oxford University Press, 2015), 2.

32. Deleuze, *Empiricism and Subjectivity*, 120.

33. Deleuze, *Nietzsche and Philosophy*, 106.

34. Moore, *Evolution of Modern Metaphysics*, 555–56.

35. Deleuze, *Logic of Sense*, 253.

36. Deleuze, 253.

37. Deleuze, 254.

38. Éditions Larousse, "Prétendre/pretender," *Dictionnaire de français Larousse*, accessed July 1, 2021, https://www.larousse.fr/dictionnaires/francais/pr%C3%A9tendre /63813.

39. Oxford English Dictionary, "'pretend, v.'"

40. Deleuze, *Logique du sens*, 292.

41. James I. Porter, *The Origins of Aesthetic Thought in Ancient Greece: Matter, Sensation, and Experience* (Cambridge and New York: Cambridge University Press, 2010), 112–13, 242.

42. Deleuze, *Logic of Sense*, 256.

43. Deleuze, 257.

44. Deleuze, 262.

45. Deleuze, 262.

46. Deleuze, 20.

47. Deleuze, *Empiricism and Subjectivity*, 22.

7. Michel Foucault and the Political Ontology of the *Dispositif*

1. Michel Foucault, *Security, Territory, Population: Lectures at the Collège de France 1977–1978* (Basingstoke and New York: Macmillan, 2009), 30. In this regard, it is worth citing from the French language edition of the lecture: Prior to bumping into the mic, Foucault says this: "Je voudrais maintenant reprendre cette même analyse des dispositifs de sécurité à partir d'un autre example et pour essayer de cerner un peu autre chose: non plus le rapport à l'espace et au milieu, mais le rapport du gourvernement à l'événement." And then the interruption brought upon by Foucault's clumsiness: "Je ne suis pas contre les appareils quelqonques, mais je ne sais pas—je m'excuse de vous dire ça—, j'ai un petite allergie comme ça. . . ." The apparatus got in his way, and he's allergic to it, but not to the dispositive; Michel Foucault, *Sécurité, territoire, population: Cours au Collège de France, 1977–1978* (Paris: Gallimard, 2004), 32.

2. Foucault, *Security, Territory, Population*, 30.

3. A note on the text: I will, from this point onward, cross out the mistranslations of "dispositive" as "apparatus" in the English translations of Foucault's texts I cite from and insert in parentheses the word *dispositif*.

4. I am not the first to note this. See also Giorgio Agamben, *"What Is an Apparatus?" and Other Essays* (Stanford, Calif.: Stanford University Press, 2009); Louis Althusser, *Machiavelli and Us* (London and New York: Verso, 2001); Alain Brossat, "La notion de dispositif chez Michel Foucault," in *Miroir, appareils et autres dispositifs*, ed. Soko Phay-Vakalis (Paris: Éditions L'Harmattan, 2009); Jeffrey Bussolini, "What Is a Dispositive?," *Foucault Studies*, no. 10 (November 1, 2010): 85–107, https://doi.org/10.22439/fs.v0i10.3120; Gilles Deleuze, "What Is a Dispositif?," in *Michel Foucault, Philosopher: Essays*, ed. Timothy J. Armstrong (New York: Routledge, 1992), 159–68; Gregg Lambert, "What Is a Dispositif?," *Religious Theory*, accessed September 14, 2017, http://jcrt.org/religioustheory/2016/07/11/what-is-a -dispositif-part-1/; Matteo Pasquinelli, "What an Apparatus Is Not: On the Archeology

of the Norm in Foucault, Canguilhem, and Goldstein," *Parrhesia Journal* 22
(May 2015): 79–89; Knox Peden, "Truth and Consequences: Political Judgment and
Historical Knowledge in Foucault and Althusser," *Zinbun*, no. 47 (2016): 33–47;
Michael J. Shapiro, "Foucault and Method," In *Foucault and the Modern
International: Silences and Legacies for the Study of World Politics*, ed. Philippe
Bonditti, Didier Bigo, and Frédéric Gros, 1st ed. (New York: Palgrave Macmillan,
2017). Moreover, there is a Wikipedia page entry dedicated to *dispositifs*.

5. The point about Foucault's concerns regarding social valuation is wholly
indebted to Frances Ferguson's account of Benthamite utilitarianism in Frances
Ferguson, *Pornography, the Theory: What Utilitarianism Did to Action* (Chicago:
University of Chicago Press, 2004); see especially pages 1–33.

6. Michel Foucault, "Governmentality," in *The Foucault Effect: Studies in
Governmentality*, ed. Graham Burchell, Colin Gordon, and Peter Miller, 1st ed.
(Chicago: University of Chicago Press, 1991), 93.

7. To refer to such techne of collectivization we can adopt the French
agencement, a term conventionally translated as "assemblage" but that also means
connecting or adjoining or, again, disposing or ordering; John Phillips,
"Agencement/Assemblage," *Theory, Culture & Society* 23, no. 2–3 (May 1, 2006):
108–9, https://doi.org/10.1177/0263276406062300219. The *Dictionnaire de la Langue
Française* defines *agencement* as "Action d'agencer" (trans. "the activity of
connecting"), as well as "Ajuster, mettre en arrangement" (trans. "to adjust," "to
place in an arrangement"), and finally, "En termes de peinture, arranger des groups,
des figures, adjuster les draperies, disposer les accessoires" (trans. in terms of
painting, "to arrange groups, figures, adjust draperies, and dispose accessories");
"Dictionnaire de La Langue Française. Tome 1 A–C (Éd.1873–1874) / Hachette
BNF," Accessed September 18, 2017, http://www.hachettebnf.fr/dictionnaire-de-la
-langue-francaise-tome-1-c-ed1873-1874–9782012539358. Whereas the dictionary of
the Académie Française defines *agencement* as "Manière d'arranger, de mettre en
ordre" (trans. a "manner of arranging or placing in order") as well as, in architecture,
"dispositions et rapport des différentes parties d'un edifice: l'arrangement, les
proportions relatives des divisions d'un plan, d'une façade, d'une décoration" (trans.
"dispositions and relations of the different parts of an edifice: the arrangement, or
the proportions of the relative divisions of a plan, a façade, or a decoration)";
(*agencement* entry, "Dictionnaire de l'Académie Française, Neuvième Édition,"
accessed September 18, 2017, http://atilf.atilf.fr/academie9.htm.

8. Translated as "The Confession of the Flesh," in Michel Foucault, *Power/
Knowledge: Selected Interviews and Other Writings, 1972–1977* (New York: Pantheon,
1980). Here Foucault famously affirms the following (N.B.: Though I have retained
the original translation from the text, I have put the translator's term "apparatus"
under erasure and substituted with the more correct and untranslatable *dispositif* for
reasons thus far explained): "What I'm trying to pick out with this term is, firstly, a
thoroughly heterogeneous ensemble consisting of discourses, institutions,
architectural forms, regulatory decisions, laws, administrative measures, scientific
statements, philosophical, moral and philanthropic propositions—in short, the said

as much as the unsaid. Such are the elements of the apparatus. The ~~apparatus~~ [*dispositif*] itself is the system of relations that can be established between these elements. Secondly, what I am trying to identify in this ~~apparatus~~ [*dispositif*] is precisely the nature of the connection that can exist between these heterogeneous elements. Thus, a particular discourse can figure at one time as the programme of an institution, and at another it can function as a means of justifying or masking a practice which itself remains silent, or as a secondary re-interpretation of this practice, opening out for it a new field of rationality. In short, between these elements, whether discursive or non-discursive, there is a sort of interplay of shifts of position and modifications of function which can also vary very widely. Thirdly, I understand by the term '~~apparatus~~' [*dispositif*] a sort of—shall we say formation which has as its major function at a given historical moment that of responding to an urgent need. The ~~apparatus~~ [*dispositif*] thus has a dominant strategic function. This may have been, for example, the assimilation of a floating population found to be burdensome for an essentially mercantilist economy: there was a strategic imperative acting here as the matrix for an apparatus which gradually undertook the control or subjection of madness, mental illness and neurosis."

Here is the original French from "Le jeu de Michel Foucault" (entretien avec D. Colas, A. Grosrichard, G. Le Gaufey, J. Livi, G. Miller, J. Miller, J.-A. Miller, C, Millot, G. Wajeman), Ornicar, Bulletin Périodique du champ freudien, no 10, juillet 1977, pp. 62–93, reprinted in Foucault, Michel. *Dits et Ecrits, tome 2: 1976–1988.* French and European Publications Inc, 2013: "Ce que j'essaie de repérer sous ce nom, c'est, premièrement, un ensemble résolument hétérogène, comportant des discours, des institutions, des aménagements architecturaux, des décisions réglementaires, des lois, des mesures administratives, des énoncés scientifiques, des propositions philosophiques, morales, philanthropiques, bref: du dit, aussi bien que du non-dit, voilà les éléments du dispositif. Le dispositif lui-même, c'est le réseau qu'on peut établir entre ces éléments. Deuxièmement, ce que je voudrais repérer dans le dispositif, c'est justement la nature du lien qui peut exister entre ces éléments hétérogènes. Ainsi, tel discours peut apparaître tantôt comme programme d'une institution, tantôt au contraire comme un élément qui permet de justifier et de masquer une pratique qui, elle, reste muette, ou fonctionner comme réinterprétation seconde de cette pratique, lui donner accès à un champ nouveau de rationalité. Bref, entre ces éléments, discursifs ou non, il y a comme un jeu, des changements de position, des modifications de fonctions, qui peuvent, eux aussi, être très différents. Troisièmement, par dispositif, j'entends une sorte -disons -de formation, qui, à un moment historique donné, a eu pour fonction majeure de répondre à une urgence. Le dispositif a donc une fonction stratégique dominante. Cela a pu être, par exemple, la résorption d'une masse de population flottante qu'une société à économie de type essentiellement mercantiliste trouvait encombrante: il y a eu là un impératif stratégique, jouant comme matrice d'un dispositif, qui est devenu peu à peu le dispositif de contrôle-assujettissement de la folie, de la maladie mentale, de la névrose."

9. Pasquinelli, "What an Apparatus Is Not."

10. Agamben, *"What Is an Apparatus?"* 11.

11. Georges Canguilhem, "Machine and Organism," in *Knowledge of Life* (New York: Fordham University Press, 2008); also see Ian Hacking, "Canguilhem amid the Cyborgs," *Economy and Society* 27, no. 2–3 (May 1, 1998): 202–16, https://doi.org /10.1080/03085149800000014.

12. Pasquinelli, "What an Apparatus Is Not," 85.

13. Bussolini, "What Is a Dispositive?," 96.

14. This connection is also made by James Chandler in his preface to his *An Archeology of Sympathy: The Sentimental Mode in Literature and Cinema* (Chicago: University of Chicago Press, 2013), xiv–xviii.

15. Chaïm Perelman and Lucie Olbrechts-Tyteca, *The New Rhetoric: A Treatise on Argumentation* (Notre Dame, Ind.: University of Notre Dame Press, 1971), 491.

16. Perelman and Olbrechts-Tyteca, *New Rhetoric*, 492.

17. One of the compelling ambitions of logical positivism in the twentieth century is to reorient the rhetorical status of argument away from its liable precarity and toward the demonstrable proof. For more on this nexus within the context of postwar fiction, see Chapter 1, Michael LeMahieu, "'Indigestible Residues': Ludwig Wittgenstein, Aesthetic Negativism, and the Incompleteness of Logical Positivism" (Chapter 1), in his *Fictions of Fact and Value: The Erasure of Logical Positivism in American Literature, 1945–1975* (New York: Oxford University Press, 2016).

18. Relevant to this part of my argument is John Guillory's point that "the communication concept emerged in early modernity as an explicit challenge to the system of rhetoric. . . . Rhetoric assumed that the speaker occupied a forensic position, in which his own thoughts and feelings were best kept to himself. Communication by contrast posited the transfer of the speaker's thoughts and feelings accurately to the mind of the auditor"; John Guillory, "Genesis of the Media Concept," *Critical Inquiry* no. 2 (2010): 321, JSTOR, https://doi.org/10.1086/648528.

19. In this regard, I would want to begin considering the *dispositio* of the *dispositif* in relation to Theo Davis's discussion of ornamental aesthetics, where she contends that "ornamentation is about how one object rests upon and in relation to another; how an object carries and even carries out human attention (one approaches and touches something by ornamenting it, which is quite different from expressing an idea about it); how both writers and readers work with and among objects of attention; and how objects both shed and receive notice, light, and value"; Theo Davis, *Ornamental Aesthetics: The Poetry of Attending in Thoreau, Dickinson, and Whitman* (New York: Oxford University Press, 2016), 19.

20. Canguilhem, "Machine and Organism," 76–77.

21. Georges Canguilhem, *La connaissance de la vie* (Paris: Vrin, 1992).

22. Canguilhem, "Machine and Organism," 76.

23. Canguilhem, 79; also see Jessica Riskin, *The Restless Clock: A History of the Centuries-Long Argument over What Makes Living Things Tick* (Chicago: University of Chicago Press, 2016), 51–53.

24. Peden, "Truth and Consequences," 37. Peden is critical of this move by Foucault, which he considers "a central move in his effort to develop a mode of

historical analysis that would not be a form of political judgment in itself." (37) And Peden continues: "In a word, Foucault seeks to de-politicize the account of history grounded in the concept of the 'mode of production' on offer from Althusser, while retaining many of its relational and structural components." (38) And thus, Peden concludes, "what does seem clear is that Foucault's denial of relations of production as primary in any sense, political or otherwise, is not a matter of disproof or a demonstration of theoretical inconsistency. It is rather a denial that is political in its essentials, which means that any critical take on Foucault's writings and lectures of the 1970s—the years in which the Foucaultian concept of power was forged—will bear an unavoidably political character as well." (47)

25. Louis Althusser, *On the Reproduction of Capitalism: Ideology and Ideological State Apparatuses* (London and New York: Verso, 2014). Importantly, though it is beyond the purview of this essay to expand upon this point, Althusser's later writings on aleatory materialism, and especially his book on Machiavelli, stop deploying the language of apparatus and instead adopt the term *dispositif*. See especially Althusser, *Machiavelli and Us*; Louis Althusser, *Philosophy of the Encounter: Later Writings, 1978–87* (London and New York: Verso, 2006).

26. Althusser, *On the Reproduction of Capitalism*, 24. A further discussion needs to be developed about the inheritance and responses to the theory of the reflex in postwar French thought and its relationship to theories of ideology, and especially to the critique of Cartesian automation and Pavlovian stimulus-response therein. Key thinkers here are Georges Canguilhem and Maurice Merleau-Ponty (see especially Merleau-Ponty, *The Structure of Behavior* [Pittsburgh, Pa.: Duquesne University Press, 1963]). Due to spatial constrains, I'm unable to pursue that discussion in these pages. For a helpful initial foray and historiography of the reflex, see Riskin, *Restless Clock*.

27. In this respect, one could read much of Foucault's research from 1970 onward as returned engagement not just with Canguilhem, but also with Maurice Merleau-Ponty's critique of behaviorism, in Merleau-Ponty, *Structure of Behavior*. For a contemporary engagement with Merleau-Ponty's critical phenomenological account of the reflex circuit and behavior modification, see Lisa Guenther, *Solitary Confinement: Social Death and Its Afterlives* (Minneapolis: University of Minnesota Press, 2013) 101–23.

28. Michel Foucault, *The History of Sexuality: An Introduction* (New York: Knopf Doubleday, 2012), 89.

29. Deleuze, "What Is a Dispositif?," 159–60.

30. Deleuze.

31. Pasquinelli, "What an Apparatus Is Not," 81; I cite from Pasquinelli, as he's done the work of noting, in the text, the distinction between the two relevant terms (apparatus/*dispositif*). The original source of the passage is Michel Foucault, *Abnormal: Lectures at the Collège de France, 1974–1975* (New York: Macmillan, 2004), 49. Here is the original French passage: "Le XVIIIe siècle, ou l'Âge classique, a mis en place tout un appareil d'État, avec ses prolongements et ses appuis dans des

institutions diverses. Et puis—c'est à cela que je voudrais un petit peu m'attacher, ou qui devrait me server d'arrière-plan à l'analyse de la normalisation de la sexualité—il a mis au point une technique générale d'exercice du pouvoir, technique transférable à des institutions et à des appareils nombreux et divers. Cette technique constitue l'envers des structures juridiques et politiques de la représentation, et la condition de fonctionnement et d'efficacité de ces appareils. Cette technique générale du gouvernement des hommes comporte un dispositif type, qui est l'organisation disciplinaire dont je vous ai parlé l'an dernier16. Ce dispositif type est finalisé par quoi? Par quelque chose qu'on peut appeler, je crois, la 'normalisation.' Cette année, je me consacrerai donc non plus à la mécanique même des appareils disciplinaires, mais à leurs effets de normalisation, à ce vers quoi ils sont finalisés, aux effets qu'ils obtiennent et que l'on peut mettre sous la rubrique de la 'normalisation'"; Foucault, *Les anormaux: Cours au Collège de France (1974–1975)* (Paris: Seuil, 1999), 45.

32. Georges Canguilhem, "Machine and Organism," in *Knowledge of Life* (New York: Fordham University Press, 2008), 76–77.

33. This is an insight indebted to Kirstie M. McClure, "Taking Liberties in Foucault's Triangle: Sovereignty, Discipline, Governmentality, and the Subject of Rights," in *Identities, Politics, and Rights*, ed. Austin Sarat and Thomas R. Kearns (Ann Arbor: University of Michigan Press, 1997).

34. Michel Foucault, *Psychiatric Power: Lectures at the Collège de France, 1973–1974* (Basingstoke and New York: Palgrave Macmillan, 2008), 72.

35. Michel Foucault, *The Order of Things: An Archaeology of the Human Sciences*, reissue ed. (New York: Vintage, 1994), 14.

36. Foucault, *Order of Things*, 15.

37. Michel Foucault, *Manet and the Object of Painting* (New York: Harry N. Abrams, 2012), 28.

38. Foucault, 31.

39. Gilles Deleuze, *Foucault*. (Minneapolis: University of Minnesota Press, 1988).

40. On transmedial consonances, see Brent Hayes Edwards, *Epistrophies: Jazz and the Literary Imagination* (Cambridge, Mass.: Harvard University Press, 2017), 7.

41. Joseph J. Tanke, *Foucault's Philosophy of Art: A Genealogy of Modernity* (London and New York: Continuum, 2009).

42. Tanke, *Foucault's Philosophy of Art*; Gary Shapiro, *Archaeologies of Vision: Foucault and Nietzsche on Seeing and Saying* (Chicago: University of Chicago Press, 2003); Catherine M. Soussloff, *Foucault on Painting*, 1st ed. (Minneapolis: University of Minnesota Press, 2017).

43. Shapiro, *Archaeologies of Vision*, 302–4; Michael Fried, *Art and Objecthood: Essays and Reviews* (Chicago: University of Chicago Press, 1998), 37; Stanley Cavell, *The World Viewed: Reflections on the Ontology of Film* (Cambridge, Mass.: Harvard University Press, 1979), 103; Clement Greenberg, *The Collected Essays and Criticism*, vol. 4, *Modernism with a Vengeance, 1957–1969* (Chicago: University of Chicago Press, 1995), 85–93. The importance of "acknowledgment" here cannot be

explored in great detail, though I do want to signal that acknowledgment for Fried and Cavell (and, I also want to say, for Foucault) is a complex and not a reflex.

44. Greenberg, *Collected Essays and Criticism*, 4:243.

45. Foucault, *Manet and the Object of Painting*, 36.

46. Foucault, 41.

47. Foucault, 42. I should note that though I cannot develop it at great length in this essay, to me this account of Manet's canvas comes closest to Foucault describing his commitment to a kind of formal reading when dealing with the matter of discipline in Bentham's architectural drawings and Panopticon writings.

48. Fried, *Art and Objecthood*. It is for this reason that, in the first lines of Fried's "Art and Objecthood" essay, he effectively affirms that the enterprise of objecthood is "ideological" because theatrical, as "it seeks to declare and occupy a position" (148). This fact of positionality that, in turn, compels the viewer to have to spatially occupy a position in order to view the work as a work (i.e., that demands a subjection of the viewer to the work) is what allows Fried to argue that "the literalist espousal of objecthood amounts to nothing other than a plea for a new genre of theater, and theater now is the negation of art" (153). This, of course, is not surprising, since Manet becomes, for Fried, a central figure in the history of anti-theatricality. See especially Michael Fried, *Manet's Modernism: Or, The Face of Painting in the 1860s* (Chicago: University of Chicago Press, 1996).

49. Foucault, *Manet and the Object of Painting*, 48.

50. Foucault, *Psychiatric Power*, 74–75.

51. Alexi Worth, "The Lost Photographs of Edouard Manet," *Art in America* (January 2007); Beatrice Farwell, *Manet and the Nude: A Study in Iconography in the Second Empire* (New York: Garland, 1981).

52. Worth, "Lost Photographs of Edouard Manet," 60–61.

53. Foucault, *Manet and the Object of Painting*, 58.

54. Jonathan Crary, *Techniques of the Observer: On Vision and Modernity in the Nineteenth Century* (Cambridge, Mass.: MIT Press, 1992). In this regard, my account of Foucault's concerns with disciplinary *dispositifs* and their relationship to looking in the modern period goes against the grain of Jonathan Crary's treatment of modernist vision as acts of a detached observer. From Crary's perspective, my account is clearly too enamored with the ruptural "fanfare" (4) of traditional accounts of the modernist avant-garde. But from my perspective, Crary's account of the observer is too invested in collapsing the distinction between the normative and normalization and thus treating a regime of vision as if it were exclusively a system of domination. Hence the normative sense of the operative term "techniques" in his title that wants to look at optical devices "as sites of both knowledge and power that operate directly on the body of the individual" (7). I remain indebted to Crary's important work, though I also acknowledge that that work does not appreciate the extent to which Foucault's own assessment of vision in the modern period remains tethered to Manet's aesthetic achievements and to their ruptural fanfare.

55. My argument is indebted to Frances Ferguson's reconstruction of the structures of perceptibility and value ranking that Bentham's utilitarian architectures and techniques sought to develop. In this regard, I wholeheartedly agree with her formulation that "Foucault captured Bentham's interest in creating social structures that displayed the actions individuals performed and that systematized this display to make it possible to see the relative value of those actions instantaneously"; Ferguson, *Pornography, the Theory: What Utilitarianism Did to Action* (Chicago: University of Chicago Press, 2004), 17. I differ from Ferguson in two ways: One is to expand this insight by showing how Foucault's experiences of instantaneity in perceptibility are emergent from his viewership of Manet's tableaux. Secondly, I differ from Ferguson by downplaying the normative weight of complicity and coercion in Foucault's descriptions (see Ferguson's objection to Foucault's account of utilitarian social structures in *Pornography, the Theory*, 18–21). Also like Ferguson, I will acknowledge the perversity (to use her word) of the seemingly Quixotic endeavor of detailing the limitations of Anglo-American receptions of Foucault's readings of Bentham that conflate disciplinary structures with ideological coercion; *Pornography, the Theory*, 18.

56. Michel Foucault, *Discipline & Punish: The Birth of the Prison* (New York: Knopf Doubleday, 2012), 200.

57. Shapiro, *Archaeologies of Vision*, 315.

58. Shapiro.

59. Foucault, *Discipline & Punish*, 200–202. As is well known, one of the great criticisms of Manet's canvasses was that his figures were too ordinary, that they had no specific qualifications, and that they could be easily accessible to an ordinary (i.e. non-specialized) audience; the same absence of qualification is built into the ubiquitous applicability of the Panopticon that could be used for anything and by anyone (indeed, the design of the building is such that if there were a prison riot the inmates could just as easily operate the disciplinary *dispositif* as the inspectors, and the inspectors could just as easily be inmates).

60. Foucault, *Manet and the Object of Painting*, 74.

61. Maryvonne Saison, *La peinture de Manet, suivi de "Michel Foucault, un regard"* (Paris: Seuil, 2004), 44. The expression *de plein fouet* is a nineteenth-century French military expression; it refers to the horizontality of a direct shot of a pistol or a rifle toward a visible target.

62. Foucault, *Manet and the Object of Painting*, 78.

63. Foucault, 77.

64. Foucault, 78–79.

65. For discussions of the tableau form, see Fried, *Manet's Modernism*, 267–80; Jean-François Chevrier, "The Adventures of the Picture Form in the History of Photography," in *The Last Picture Show: Artists Using Photography, 1960–1982*, ed. Douglas Fogle (Minneapolis: Walker Art Center, 2003); Michael Fried, *Why Photography Matters as Art as Never Before* (New Haven, Conn.: Yale University Press, 2008).

66. At this point, it's difficult not to recall Cavell's observation that the screen "holds a projection, as light as light"; Stanley Cavell, *The World Viewed: Reflections on the Ontology of Film* (Cambridge, Mass.: Harvard University Press, 1979), 71.

67. Foucault, *Manet and the Object of Painting*, 79.

68. Foucault, *Discipline & Punish*, 202, 203.

69. Chandler, *Archaeology of Sympathy*, xiv.

70. Brossat, "La notion de dispositif chez Michel Foucault."

71. Stephen Mumford, *Dispositions* (Oxford and New York: Oxford University Press, 2003), 118.

72. Mumford, *Dispositions*, 8–9.

73. Here, I am reminded of Stanley Cavell once again and his definition of modernism: "Modernism signifies not that the powers of the arts are exhausted, but on the contrary that it has become the immediate task of the artist to achieve in his art the muse of the art itself—to declare, from itself, the art as a whole for which it speaks, to become a present of that art. One might say that the task is no longer to produce another instance of an art but a new medium within it"; Cavell, *World Viewed*, 103.

74. Stephen Mumford and Rani Lill Anjum, *Getting Causes from Powers* (Oxford and New York: Oxford University Press, 2011), 189.

75. Mumford and Anjum, *Getting Causes from Powers*, 193.

Epilogue

1. "Los Angeles Unified Crosses 25 Million Meal Milestone In Country's Largest Food Relief Effort (05-28-20)," *Los Angeles Unified*, accessed December 6, 2021, https://achieve.lausd.net/site/http%3A%2F%2Fachieve.lausd.net%2Fsite%2Fdefault.as px%3FPageType%3D3%26DomainID%3D4%26ModuleInstanceID%3D4466%26Vie wID%3D6446EE88-D30C-497E-9316-3F8874B3E108%26RenderLoc%3D0%26Flex DataID%3D89355%26PageID%3D1.

2. State of California, "ICYMI: California Poised to Become World's 4th Biggest Economy," Office of Governor Gavin Newsom, October 24, 2022, https://www.gov .ca.gov/2022/10/24/icymi-california-poised-to-become-worlds-4th-biggest-economy/.

3. My observations of these phenomena were at a distance, given the legal limitations placed on resident aliens in the United States by the "crimes involving moral turpitude" clause to which all legal immigrants are subject and that risks rendering immigrants inadmissible, deported, or detained; see "All Those Rules About Crimes Involving Moral Turpitude (June 2021), Immigrant Legal Resource Center, ILRC," accessed December 7, 2021, https://www.ilrc.org/all-those-rules -about-crimes-involving-moral-turpitude.

4. Wahl, *Vers le concret*, 155.

5. John Guillory, "How Scholars Read," *ADE Bulletin*, no. 146 (Fall 2008): 8.

6. Kristin Ross, *Fast Cars, Clean Bodies: Decolonization and the Reordering of French Culture*, 4th ed. (Cambridge, Mass.: MIT Press, 1996), 124–25.

7. On this point, see the Epilogue of Camille Robcis, *Disalienation: Politics, Philosophy, and Radical Psychiatry in Postwar France* (Chicago: University of Chicago Press, 2021).

8. A parallel and noteworthy genealogy to my own is available in Bernard Geoghegan's *Code*. Here Geoghegan traces the development of "French modernization from the 1950s to the 1970s (including the rise of laboratories, centers, and seminars as a centerpiece of French intellectual life) and how it figured in key French intellectuals' reception of cybernetics, information theory, and communication theory. Against the backdrop of decolonization, modernization, and ascendant technocracy, theorists including psychoanalysts Jacques Lacan and Luce Irigaray, literary semiologist Roland Barthes, and philosopher Michel Foucault thematized the material and political operations responsible for cultural codes"; see Bernard Dionysius Geoghegan, *Code: From Information Theory to French Theory* (Durham, N.C.: Duke University Press, 2023), 4.

Bibliography

Abizadeh, Arash. "Counter-Majoritarian Democracy: Persistent Minorities, Federalism, and the Power of Numbers." *American Political Science Review*, undefined/ed., 1–15. https://doi.org/10.1017/S0003055421000198.

———. "The Power of Numbers: On Agential Power-with-Others without Power-over-Others." *Philosophy & Public Affairs*, forthcoming (n.d.).

Adkins, Taylor. "A Short List of Gilbert Simondon's Vocabulary." *Fractal Ontology*. Accessed April 22, 2020. https://fractalontology.wordpress.com/2007/11/28/a-short-list-of-gilbert-simondons-vocabulary/.

Agamben, Giorgio. *"What Is an Apparatus?" And Other Essays*. Stanford, Calif.: Stanford University Press, 2009.

"All Those Rules About Crimes Involving Moral Turpitude (June 2021). Immigrant Legal Resource Center, ILRC." Accessed December 7, 2021. https://www.ilrc.org/all-those-rules-about-crimes-involving-moral-turpitude.

Althusser, Louis. *For Marx*. Translated by Ben Brewster. London and New York: Verso, 2006.

———. *Machiavelli and Us*. London and New York: Verso, 2001.

———. *On the Reproduction of Capitalism: Ideology and Ideological State Apparatuses*. London and New York: Verso, 2014.

———. *Philosophy of the Encounter: Later Writings, 1978–87*. London and New York: Verso, 2006.

Altman, Meryl. "Beauvoir, Hegel, War." *Hypatia* 22, no. 3 (2007): 66–91. https://doi.org/10.1111/j.1527–2001.2007.tb01091.x.

Anjum, Rani Lill, and Stephen Mumford. "A Powerful Theory of Causation." In *The Metaphysics of Powers: Their Grounding and Their Manifestations*, edited by Anna Marmodoro, 143–59. New York: Routledge, 2010.

Apter, Emily. *Against World Literature: On the Politics of Untranslatability*. London and New York: Verso, 2013.

Arnold, Jeremy. *Across the Great Divide: Between Analytic and Continental Political Theory.* Stanford, Calif.: Stanford University Press, 2020.

Assouline, Pierre. *Herge: The Man Who Created Tintin.* Oxford and New York: Oxford University Press, 2009.

Auerbach, Erich, and Edward W. Said. *Mimesis: The Representation of Reality in Western Literature.* New and Expanded ed. Princeton, N.J.: Princeton University Press, 2013.

Bachelard, Gaston. *The Formation of the Scientific Mind: A Contribution to a Psychoanalysis of Objective Knowledge.* Manchester, UK: Clinamen, 2002.

———. *The New Scientific Spirit.* Boston: Beacon Press, 1984.

Baier, Annette C. *A Progress of Sentiments: Reflections on Hume's Treatise.* Cambridge, Mass.: Harvard University Press, 2009.

Bair, Deirdre. *Simone de Beauvoir: A Biography.* New York: Simon and Schuster, 1991.

Bardin, Andrea. *Epistemology and Political Philosophy in Gilbert Simondon: Individuation, Technics, Social Systems.* Cham, Switzerland: Springer, 2015.

———. "Philosophy as Political Technē: The Tradition of Invention in Simondon's Political Thought." *Contemporary Political Theory* 17 (2018): 417–36.

Barthes, Roland. *Critical Essays.* Evanston, Ill.: Northwestern University Press, 1972.

———. "Les Deux Critiques." *MLN* 78, no. 5 (1963): 447–52. https://doi.org/10.2307/3042755.

Basso, Hamilton. "Profiles: Philosopher." *New Yorker,* May 12, 1945. http://www.newyorker.com/magazine/1945/05/12/philosopher-3.

Baugh, Bruce. "Hegel in Modern French Philosophy: The Unhappy Consciousness." *Laval Théologique et Philosophique* 49, no. 3 (1993): 423–38. https://doi.org/10.7202/400791ar.

Beauvoir, Simone de. *Feminist Writings.* Champaign: University of Illinois Press, 2015.

———. *Memoirs of a Dutiful Daughter.* New York: HarperCollins, 2016.

———. *The Second Sex.* New York: Knopf Doubleday, 2012.

Beauvoir, Simone de, and Margaret A. Simons. *Philosophical Writings.* Champaign: University of Illinois Press, 2005.

Bédé, Jean-Albert. "Gustave Lanson." *American Scholar* 4, no. 3 (1935): 286–91.

Beltrán, Cristina. *The Trouble with Unity: Latino Politics and the Creation of Identity.* Oxford and New York: Oxford University Press, 2010.

Benhabib, Seyla. "L'Affaire du Foulard (The Scarf Affair)." *Yearbook of the National Society for the Study of Education* 107, no. 1 (2008): 100–111. https://doi.org/10.1111/j.1744-7984.2008.00134.x.

Bennett, Jane. *Influx and Efflux: Writing Up with Walt Whitman.* Durham, N.C.: Duke University Press, 2020.

———. *Vibrant Matter: A Political Ecology of Things.* Durham, N.C.: Duke University Press, 2009.

Bianchi, Emanuela. *The Feminine Symptom: Aleatory Matter in the Aristotelian Cosmos.* New York: Fordham University Press, 2014.

Bogaerts, Jo. "Beauvoir's Lecture on the Metaphysics of the Novel and Its Contemporary Critiques." *Simone de Beauvoir Studies* 29 (2013): 20–32.

Bogue, Ronald. *Deleuze on Cinema.* New York: Routledge, 2003.

Boschetti, Anna. *The Intellectual Enterprise: Sartre and Les Temps Modernes.*
Evanston, Ill.: Northwestern University Press, 1988.

Bourdieu, Pierre. *Distinction: A Social Critique of the Judgement of Taste.* Cambridge, Mass.: Harvard University Press, 1984.

———. "Esprits d'État." *Actes de la Recherche en Sciences Sociales* 96, no. 1 (1993):
49–62. https://doi.org/10.3406/arss.1993.3040.

———. "Reading, Readers, the Literate, Literature." In *In Other Words: Essays
Towards a Reflexive Sociology.* Stanford, Calif.: Stanford University Press, 1990.

———. *Reproduction in Education, Society and Culture.* London and Beverly Hills:
SAGE, 1990.

———. "Systems of Education and Systems of Thought." *International Social
Science Journal* 19, no. 3 (1967): 338–58.

Bousquet, Antoine. *The Eye of War: Military Perception from the Telescope to the
Drone.* Minneapolis: University of Minnesota Press, 2018.

Bowden, Sean. "Jean Wahl." In *Deleuze's Philosophical Lineage II*, edited by
Graham Jones and Jon Roffe, 183–206. Edinburgh: Edinburgh University Press,
2019.

Braidotti, Rosi. *Nomadic Subjects: Embodiment and Sexual Difference in Contemporary Feminist Theory.* New York: Columbia University Press, 2011.

———. *Transpositions: On Nomadic Ethics.* Cambridge and Malden, Mass.: Polity,
2006.

Briu, Jean-Jacques, and Étienne Karabétian. *Leo Spitzer: Études sur le style; Analyse
de textes littéraires français (1918–1931).* Paris: Editions Ophrys, 2009.

Brossat, Alain. "La notion de dispositif chez Michel Foucault." In *Miroir, appareils
et autres dispositifs,* edited by Soko Phay-Vakalis. Paris: Éditions L'Harmattan,
2009.

Bussolini, Jeffrey. "What Is a Dispositive?" *Foucault Studies,* no. 10 (November 1,
2010): 85–107. https://doi.org/10.22439/fs.v0i10.3120.

Butler, Judith. *Subjects of Desire: Hegelian Reflections in Twentieth-Century France.*
New York: Columbia University Press, 2012.

California, State of. "ICYMI: California Poised to Become World's 4th Biggest
Economy." Office of Governor Gavin Newsom, October 24, 2022. https://www
.gov.ca.gov/2022/10/24/icymi-california-poised-to-become-worlds-4th-biggest
-economy/.

Cameron, Sharon. *Impersonality: Seven Essays.* Chicago: University of Chicago
Press, 2009.

Canales, Jimena. *The Physicist and the Philosopher: Einstein, Bergson, and the
Debate That Changed Our Understanding of Time.* Princeton, N.J.: Princeton
University Press, 2015.

Canguilhem, Georges. *La connaissance de la vie.* Paris: Vrin, 1992.

———. "Machine and Organism." In *Knowledge of Life*. New York: Fordham University Press, 2008.

———. "The Teaching of Philosophy in France." In *The Teaching of Philosophy: An International Inquiry of Unesco*, 53–72. Paris: UNESCO, 1953.

Carnap, Rudolf. "The Elimination of Metaphysics through Logical Analysis of Language." *Erkenntnis* (1932): 60–81.

———. "The Elimination of Metaphysics through Logical Analysis of Language." In *Logical Positivism*, edited by A. J. Ayer, 60–81. New York: Simon and Schuster, 1959.

———. *The Philosophy of Rudolf Carnap*. Vol. 11. Edited by Paul Arthur Schilpp. Rev. ed. La Salle, Ill.: Open Court, 1999.

Casa, Giovanni Della, and Victoria University (Toronto Studies Ontario) Centre for Reformation and Renaissance. *Galateo: A Renaissance Treatise on Manners*. Toronto: Centre for Reformation and Renaissance Studies, 1994.

Cavaillès, Jean. *On Logic and the Theory of Science*. Cambridge, Mass.: MIT Press, 2021.

Cavell, Stanley. *The Claim of Reason: Wittgenstein, Skepticism, Morality, and Tragedy*. 1st ed. New York: Oxford University Press, 1999.

———. *The World Viewed: Reflections on the Ontology of Film*. Cambridge, Mass.: Harvard University Press, 1979.

Chandler, James. *An Archaeology of Sympathy: The Sentimental Mode in Literature and Cinema*. Chicago: University of Chicago Press, 2013.

Chartier, Roger. *The Order of Books: Readers, Authors, and Libraries in Europe between the Fourteenth and Eighteenth Centuries*. Stanford, Calif.: Stanford University Press, 1994.

Chevrier, Jean-François. "The Adventures of the Picture Form in the History of Photography." In *The Last Picture Show: Artists Using Photography, 1960–1982*, edited by Douglas Fogle. Minneapolis: Walker Art Center, 2003.

Clark, Terry Nichols. *Prophets and Patrons: The French University and the Emergence of the Social Sciences*. Cambridge, Mass.: Harvard University Press, 1973.

Colman, Felicity. *Deleuze and Cinema: The Film Concepts*. Oxford and New York: Berg, 2011.

Combes, Muriel. *Gilbert Simondon and the Philosophy of the Transindividual*. Cambridge, Mass.: MIT Press, 2013.

Connolly, William E. "Discipline, Politics, and Ambiguity." *Political Theory* 11, no. 3 (August 1, 1983): 325–41. https://doi.org/10.1177/0090591783011003002.

———. *The Ethos of Pluralization*. Minneapolis: University of Minnesota Press, 1995.

———. *Neuropolitics: Thinking, Culture, Speed*. Minneapolis: University of Minnesota Press, 2002.

———. *Pluralism*. Durham, N.C.: Duke University Press, 2005.

———. *A World of Becoming*. Durham, N.C.: Duke University Press, 2011.

Cooper, Barry. *Merleau-Ponty and Marxism: From Terror to Reform*. Toronto: University of Toronto Press, 1979.

Crary, Jonathan. *Techniques of the Observer: On Vision and Modernity in the Nineteenth Century.* Cambridge, Mass.: MIT Press, 1992.

Dallmayr, Fred R. "Ontology of Freedom: Heidegger and Political Philosophy." *Political Theory* 12, no. 2 (May 1, 1984): 204–34. https://doi.org/10.1177 /0090591784012002004.

Daston, Lorraine, and Peter Galison. *Objectivity.* Princeton, N.J.: Princeton University Press, 2021.

Davies, Howard. *Sartre and "Les Temps Modernes."* Cambridge and New York: Cambridge University Press, 1987.

Davis, Theo. *Ornamental Aesthetics: The Poetry of Attending in Thoreau, Dickinson, and Whitman.* New York: Oxford University Press, 2016.

Deleuze, Gilles. *Difference and Repetition.* Translated by Paul Patton. New York: Columbia University Press, 1995.

———. *Empiricism and Subjectivity: An Essay on Hume's Theory of Human Nature.* New York: Columbia University Press, 1991.

———. *Essays Critical and Clinical.* 1st ed. Minneapolis: University of Minnesota Press, 1997.

———. *The Logic of Sense.* New York: Columbia University Press, 1990.

———. *Logique du sens.* Éditions Minuit. Paris: Gallimard, 1969.

———. *Nietzsche and Philosophy.* New York: Columbia University Press, 2006.

———. "Renverser Le Platonisme (Les Simulacres)." *Revue de Métaphysique et de Morale* 71, no. 4 (1966): 426–38.

———. "What Is a Dispositif?" In *Michel Foucault, Philosopher: Essays,* edited by Timothy J. Armstrong, 159–68. New York: Routledge, 1992.

Deleuze, Gilles, and Félix Guattari. *A Thousand Plateaus: Capitalism and Schizophrenia.* Translated by Brian Massumi. 1st ed. Minneapolis: University of Minnesota Press, 1987.

———. *What Is Philosophy?* New York: Verso, 1994.

Deleuze, Gilles, and Rosalind Krauss. "Plato and the Simulacrum." *October* 27 (1983): 45–56. https://doi.org/10.2307/778495.

Derrida, Jacques. "When a Teaching Body Begins." In *Who's Afraid of Philosophy? Right to Philosophy I,* translated by Jan Plug. Stanford, Calif.: Stanford University Press, 2002.

Descartes, René. *Discours de la méthode.* 2004. https://www.gutenberg.org/ebooks /13846.

Diones, Alexander. "'The Vivacity of Our Ideas': Habit in Modern Political Thought." *UCLA* (2022). https://escholarship.org/uc/item/68z8worw.

Doerfler, Jill, Niigaanwewidam James Sinclair, and Heidi Kiiwetinepinesiik Stark. *Centering Anishinaabeg Studies: Understanding the World through Stories.* East Lansing: Michigan State University Press, 2013.

Dosse, François. *Gilles Deleuze and Félix Guattari: Intersecting Lives.* New York: Columbia University Press, 2011.

Douglass, John, and Sally Thomas. "The Loyalty Oath Controversy, University of California, 1949–1951." Text. University of California Digital Archives. Accessed

August 6, 2020. https://www.lib.berkeley.edu/uchistory/archives_exhibits
/loyaltyoath/index.html.

Drake, D. *Intellectuals and Politics in Post-War France*. Cham, Switzerland:
Springer, 2001.

Duong, Kevin. *The Virtues of Violence: Democracy against Disintegration in
Modern France*. New York: Oxford University Press, 2020.

Easton, David. "An Approach to the Analysis of Political Systems." *World Politics* 9,
no. 3 (1957): 383–400. https://doi.org/10.2307/2008920.

———. *The Political System: An Inquiry into the State of Political Science*. New York:
A. A. Knopf, 1967.

Edwards, Brent Hayes. *Epistrophies: Jazz and the Literary Imagination*. Cambridge,
Mass.: Harvard University Press, 2017.

Eichner, Carolyn. *Surmounting the Barricades*. Bloomington: Indiana University
Press, 2004. https://iupress.org/9780253217059/surmounting-the-barricades/.

Miller, Eugene. "David Easton's Political Theory." *Political Science Reviewer* 1 (July 1,
1971). https://politicalsciencereviewer.wisc.edu/index.php/psr/article/view/75.

Farrell, Allan Peter. *The Jesuit Code of Liberal Education: Development and Scope
of the Ratio Studiorum*. Milwaukee: Bruce, 1938.

Farrington, Frederic Ernest. *French Secondary Schools: An Account of the Origin,
Development and Present Organization of Secondary Education in France*. New
York: Longmans, Green, 1910.

Farwell, Beatrice. *Manet and the Nude: A Study in Iconography in the Second
Empire*. New York: Garland, 1981.

Ferguson, Frances. "Our I. A. Richards Moment: The Machine and Its Adjustments." In *Theory Aside*, edited by Jason Potts and Daniel Stout, 261–85.
Durham, N.C., and London: Duke University Press, 2014.

———. *Pornography, the Theory: What Utilitarianism Did to Action*. Chicago:
University of Chicago Press, 2004.

Ferguson, Kathy E. "Dyslexia Manifesto." In *Disability and Political Theory*, edited
by Barbara Arneil and Nancy J. Hirschmann, 144–68. Cambridge and New York:
Cambridge University Press, 2016.

Ferguson, Kennan. "La Philosophie Americaine: James, Bergson, and the Century
of Intercontinental Pluralism." *Theory & Event* 9, no. 1 (March 27, 2006).
https://doi.org/10.1353/tae.2006.0014.

———. *William James: Politics in the Pluriverse*. Lanham, Md.: Rowman & Littlefield, 2007.

Ferry, Jules. "Lettre aux instituteurs–17 novembre 1883." *Académie de Paris*, November 17, 1883. https://www.ac-paris.fr/portail/jcms/p1_1153893/lettre-aux-instituteurs
-jules-ferry-17-novembre-1883.

Ford, Russell. *Experience and Empiricism: Hegel, Hume, and the Early Deleuze*.
Evanston, Ill.: Northwestern University Press, 2022.

Forrester, Katrina. *In the Shadow of Justice: Postwar Liberalism and the Remaking of
Political Philosophy*. Princeton, N.J.: Princeton University Press, 2019.

Fosdick, Raymond. "Passing of the Bertillon System of Identification." *Journal of Criminal Law and Criminology* 6, no. 3 (January 1, 1915): 363.

Foucault, Michel. *Abnormal: Lectures at the Collège de France, 1974–1975*. New York: Macmillan, 2004.

———. *Discipline & Punish: The Birth of the Prison*. New York: Knopf Doubleday, 2012.

———. "Governmentality." In *The Foucault Effect: Studies in Governmentality*, edited by Graham Burchell, Colin Gordon, and Peter Miller. 1st ed. Chicago: University of Chicago Press, 1991.

———. *The History of Sexuality: An Introduction*. New York: Knopf Doubleday, 2012.

———. *Les anormaux: Cours au Collège de France (1974–1975)*. Paris: Seuil, 1999.

———. *Manet and the Object of Painting*. New York: Harry N. Abrams, 2012.

———. *The Order of Things*. London and New York: Routledge, 1994.

———. *The Order of Things: An Archaeology of the Human Sciences*. Reissue ed. New York: Vintage, 1994.

———. *Power/Knowledge: Selected Interviews and Other Writings, 1972–1977*. New York: Pantheon, 1980.

———. *Psychiatric Power: Lectures at the Collège de France, 1973–1974*. Basingstoke and New York: Palgrave Macmillan, 2008.

———. *Sécurité, territoire, population: Cours au Collège de France, 1977–1978*. Paris: Gallimard, 2004.

———. *Security, Territory, Population: Lectures at the Collège de France 1977–1978*. Basingstoke and New York: Macmillan, 2009.

Frank, Jason. *The Democratic Sublime: On Aesthetics and Popular Assembly*. Oxford and New York: Oxford University Press, 2021.

Fraser, Nancy. *Feminist Contentions: A Philosophical Exchange*. New York: Routledge, 2017.

Freeden, Michael. "Political Concepts and Ideological Morphology." *Journal of Political Philosophy* 2, no. 2 (June 1, 1994): 140–64. https://doi.org/10.1111/j.1467-9760.1994.tb00019.x.

Fried, Michael. *Art and Objecthood: Essays and Reviews*. Chicago: University of Chicago Press, 1998.

———. *Manet's Modernism: Or, The Face of Painting in the 1860s*. Chicago: University of Chicago Press, 1996.

———. *Why Photography Matters as Art as Never Before*. New Haven, Conn.: Yale University Press, 2008.

Friedman, Michael. "Carnap, Cassirer, and Heidegger: The Davos Disputation and Twentieth Century Philosophy." *European Journal of Philosophy* 10, no. 3 (2002): 263–74. https://doi.org/10.1111/1468-0378.00162.

"From the Editor." *Political Theory* 13, no. 1 (February 1, 1985): 3–4. https://doi.org/10.1177/0090591785013001001.

Frost, Samantha. *Biocultural Creatures: Toward a New Theory of the Human*. Durham, N.C.: Duke University Press, 2016.

Funt, David. "Roland Barthes and the Nouvelle Critique." *Journal of Aesthetics and Art Criticism* 26, no. 3 (1968): 329–40. https://doi.org/10.2307/429117.

Galison, Peter. "Aufbau/Bauhaus: Logical Positivism and Architectural Modernism." *Critical Inquiry* 16, no. 4 (1990): 709–52.

——. "Epistemic Virtues: A Talk by Peter Galison (8.21.19)." Edge.org. Accessed July 31, 2020. https://www.edge.org/conversation/peter_galison-epistemic-virtues.

Geoghegan, Bernard Dionysius. *Code: From Information Theory to French Theory*. Durham, N.C.: Duke University Press, 2023.

Gerassi, John. *Jean-Paul Sartre: Hated Conscience of His Century; Protestant or Protester?* Chicago: University of Chicago Press, 1989.

Gikandi, Simon. "Poststructuralism and Postcolonial Discourse." In *The Cambridge Companion to Postcolonial Literary Studies*, edited by Neil Lazarus. Cambridge and New York: Cambridge University Press, 2004.

Gilles Deleuze from A to Z. DVD. Cambridge, Mass.: MIT Press, n.d.

Goodfield, Eric Lee. *Hegel and the Metaphysical Frontiers of Political Theory*. London and New York: Routledge, 2014.

Gordon, Rae Beth. "From Charcot to Charlot: Unconscious Imitation and Spectatorship in French Cabaret and Early Cinema." *Critical Inquiry* 27, no. 3 (2001): 515–49.

Grant, Judith. *Fundamental Feminism: Contesting the Core Concepts of Feminist Theory*. New York: Routledge, 2013.

Greenberg, Clement. *The Collected Essays and Criticism*. Vol. 4, *Modernism with a Vengeance, 1957–1969*. Chicago: University of Chicago Press, 1995.

Grisoni, Dominique-Antoine, ed. *Politiques de la Philosophie*. Paris: Grasset, 1976.

Grosz, Elizabeth. *Chaos, Territory, Art: Deleuze and the Framing of the Earth*. New York: Columbia University Press, 2008.

——. *The Incorporeal: Ontology, Ethics, and the Limits of Materialism*. New York: Columbia University Press, 2017.

Grove, Jairus Victor. *Savage Ecology: War and Geopolitics at the End of the World*. Durham, N.C.: Duke University Press, 2019.

Grusin, Richard. "Radical Mediation." *Critical Inquiry* 42, no. 1 (September 1, 2015): 124–48.

Guenther, Lisa. *Solitary Confinement: Social Death and Its Afterlives*. Minneapolis: University of Minnesota Press, 2013.

Guillory, John. "Close Reading: Prologue and Epilogue." *ADE Bulletin* 149 (2010): 8–14.

——. *Cultural Capital: The Problem of Literary Canon Formation*. Chicago: University of Chicago Press, 2013.

——. "How Scholars Read." *ADE Bulletin*, no. 146 (Fall 2008): 8–17.

——. "The Memo and Modernity." *Critical Inquiry* 31, no. 1 (2004): 108–32. https://doi.org/10.1086/427304.

——. "The Sokal Affair and the History of Criticism." *Critical Inquiry* 28, no. 2 (2002): 470–508. https://doi.org/10.1086/449049.

Guiney, M. Martin. *Literature, Pedagogy, and Curriculum in Secondary Education: Examples from France.* Cham, Switzerland: Springer, 2017.

Gunnell, John G. *The Descent of Political Theory: The Genealogy of an American Vocation.* Chicago: University of Chicago Press, 1993.

———. "The Reconstitution of Political Theory: David Easton, Behavioralism, and the Long Road to System." *Journal of the History of the Behavioral Sciences* 49, no. 2 (2013): 190–210. https://doi.org/10.1002/jhbs.21593.

Hacking, Ian. "Canguilhem amid the Cyborgs." *Economy and Society* 27, no. 2–3 (May 1, 1998): 202–16. https://doi.org/10.1080/03085149800000014.

Hallward, Peter. *Out of This World: Deleuze and the Philosophy of Creation.* London and New York: Verso, 2006.

Hartman, Saidiya V. *Scenes of Subjection: Terror, Slavery, and Self-Making in Nineteenth-Century America.* New York: Oxford University Press, 1997.

Heidegger, Martin. "On the Essence and Concept of Φύσις in Aristotle's Physics B, I (1939)." In *Pathmarks*, edited by William McNeil, translated by Thomas Sheehan, 183–230. Cambridge: Cambridge University Press, 1998. https://www.cambridge.org/core/books/pathmarks/on-the-essence-and-concept-of-in-aristotles-physics-b-i-1939/3BC2B1D9539AD10A8980B4963062337E.

———. "The Question Concerning Technology." In *Basic Writings*, 2nd ed. Rev. and expanded. San Francisco: Harper Perennial, 1993.

Hesse, Carla (Alison). "Enlightenment Epistemology and the Laws of Authorship in Revolutionary France, 1777–1793." *Representations*, no. 30 (1990): 109–37. https://doi.org/10.2307/2928448.

———. *Publishing and Cultural Politics in Revolutionary Paris, 1789–1810.* Berkeley: University of California Press, 1991.

Hewitt, Nicholas, ed. *The Cambridge Companion to Modern French Culture.* Cambridge and New York: Cambridge University Press, 2003.

Honig, Bonnie. *Shell-Shocked: Feminist Criticism after Trump.* New York: Fordham University Press, 2021.

Hume, David. *An Enquiry Concerning Human Understanding: And Other Writings.* Edited by Stephen Buckle. Cambridge and New York: Cambridge University Press, 2011.

———. *A Treatise of Human Nature.* Edited by David Fate Norton and Mary J. Norton. New York: Oxford University Press, 2000.

Hutter, Reinhard. *Aquinas on Transubstantiation: The Real Presence of Christ in the Eucharist.* Washington, D.C.: The Catholic University of America Press, 2019.

Isaac, Jeffrey C. "The Strange Silence of Political Theory." *Political Theory* 23, no. 4 (1995): 636–52.

Jarvis, Jill. *Decolonizing Memory: Algeria and the Politics of Testimony.* Durham, N.C.: Duke University Press, 2021.

Jey, Martine. "The Literature of the Enlightenment: An Impossible Legacy for the Republican School." Translated by Antoine Krieger. *Yale French Studies*, no. 113 (2008): 46–59.

John Paul II. "Ecclesia Dei (July 2, 1988)." Accessed August 13, 2020. http://www
    .vatican.va/content/john-paul-ii/en/motu_proprio/documents/hf_jp-ii_motu
    -proprio_02071988_ecclesia-dei.html.
Johns Hopkins University Press. "Philosophy and Literature." Accessed July 27, 2020.
    https://www.press.jhu.edu/journals/philosophy-and-literature.
Kantorowicz, Ernst. The King's Two Bodies: A Study in Medieval Political Theology.
    Princeton, N.J.: Princeton University Press, 2016.
Kaplan, Fred. The Wizards of Armageddon. Stanford, Calif.: Stanford University
    Press, 1991.
Karabétian, Étienne. Histoire des stylistiques. Paris: A. Colin, 2000.
Kaufman, Eleanor. Deleuze, The Dark Precursor: Dialectic, Structure, Being.
    Baltimore: Johns Hopkins University Press, 2012.
Kelly, M. The Cultural and Intellectual Rebuilding of France after the Second World
    War. New York: Palgrave Macmillan, 2004.
Kelty, Christopher M. The Participant: A Century of Participation in Four Stories.
    Chicago: University of Chicago Press, 2020.
Kojève, Alexandre. Introduction to the Reading of Hegel. Ithaca, N.Y.: Cornell
    University Press, 1980.
Koopman, Colin. How We Became Our Data: A Genealogy of the Informational
    Person. Chicago: University of Chicago Press, 2019.
Krause, Sharon R. Freedom beyond Sovereignty: Reconstructing Liberal Individualism.
    Chicago: University of Chicago Press, 2015.
"La lecture linéaire au lycée—Lettres—Éduscol." Accessed August 10, 2020.
    https://eduscol.education.fr/lettres/actualites/actualites/article/la-lecture-lineaire
    -au-lycee.html.
Lambert, Gregg. "What Is a Dispositif?" Religious Theory (blog). Accessed Septem-
    ber 14, 2017. http://jcrt.org/religioustheory/2016/07/11/what-is-a-dispositif-part-1/.
Lanson, Gustave. "Dix-septième ou dix-huitième siècle?" In L'enseignement du
    français. Paris: F. Alean, 1903.
——. "Méthodes de l'histoire Littéraire—Critique Littéraire." Accessed March 2,
    2021. https://obvil.sorbonne-universite.fr/corpus/critique/lanson_methodes/#body-3.
——. "Un nouveau genre de critique littéraire: La critique évolutioniste." Revue de
    l'enseignement secondaire et de l'enseignement supérieur (August 15, 1890): 135–36.
Lapoujade, David. William James: Empiricism and Pragmatism. Durham, N.C.:
    Duke University Press, 2019.
Latour, Bruno. Reassembling the Social: An Introduction to Actor-Network-Theory.
    Oxford and New York: Oxford University Press, 2007.
Lee, Pamela M. Think Tank Aesthetics: Midcentury Modernism, the Cold War, and
    the Neoliberal Present. Cambridge, Mass.: MIT Press, 2020.
LeMahieu, Michael. "'Indigestible Residues': Ludwig Wittgenstein, Aesthetic
    Negativism, and the Incompleteness of Logical Positivism." In Fictions of Fact
    and Value: The Erasure of Logical Positivism in American Literature, 1945–1975.
    New York: Oxford University Press, 2016.

Lepistö, Antti. *The Rise of Common-Sense Conservatism: The American Right and the Reinvention of the Scottish Enlightenment.* Chicago: University of Chicago Press, 2021.

Levinas, Emmanuel, Xavier Tilliette, and Paul Ricoeur. *Jean Wahl et Gabriel Marcel.* Paris: Beauchesne, 1976.

Lévi-Strauss, Claude. *The Elementary Structures of Kinship.* Revised ed. Boston: Beacon Press, 1969.

"Library: Decree of Excommunication." Accessed August 13, 2020. https://www.catholicculture.org/culture/library/view.cfm?recnum=1222.

Lipman, Hymen. Combination of lead-pencil and eraser. United States Patent Office 19783, n.d.

Livingston, Alexander. *Damn Great Empires!: William James and the Politics of Pragmatism.* New York: Oxford University Press, 2016.

"Los Angeles Unified Crosses 25 Million Meal Milestone In Country's Largest Food Relief Effort (05-28-20)." *Los Angeles Unified.* Accessed December 6, 2021. https://achieve.lausd.net/site/http%3A%2F%2Fachieve.lausd.net%2Fsite%2Fdefault.aspx%3FPageType%3D3%26DomainID%3D4%26ModuleInstanceID%3D4466%26ViewID%3D6446EE88-D30C-497E-9316-3F8874B3E108%26RenderLoc%3D0%26FlexDataID%3D89355%26PageID%3D1.

Macksey, Richard A., and Eugenio Donato. *The Structuralist Controversy: The Languages of Criticism and the Sciences of Man.* Baltimore: Johns Hopkins University Press, 2007.

Maioli, Roger. *Empiricism and the Early Theory of the Novel: Fielding to Austen.* Cham, Switzerland: Springer, 2017.

Manning, Erin. *Always More Than One: Individuation's Dance.* Durham, N.C.: Duke University Press, 2013.

Marso, Lori. "Camerawork as Motherwork." *Theory & Event* 24, no. 3 (2021): 730–57.

———. "Simone de Beauvoir, The Second Sex." *The Oxford Handbook of Classics in Contemporary Political Theory* (December 10, 2015). https://doi.org/10.1093/oxfordhb/9780198717133.013.31.

———. "Thinking Politically with Simone de Beauvoir in The Second Sex." *Theory & Event* 15, no. 2 (2012). https://muse.jhu.edu/article/478359.

Marso, Lori Jo. *Politics with Beauvoir: Freedom in the Encounter.* Durham, N.C.: Duke University Press, 2017.

Massumi, Brian. *Ontopower: War, Powers, and the State of Perception.* Durham, N.C.: Duke University Press, 2015.

———. *Parables for the Virtual: Movement, Affect, Sensation.* Durham, N.C.: Duke University Press, 2002.

———. "'Technical Mentality' Revisited: Brian Massumi on Gilbert Simondon." *Parrhesia Journal* 7 (2009): 19–36.

May, Todd. *Gilles Deleuze: An Introduction.* New York: Cambridge University Press, 2005.

Mccauley, Anne. "'Merely Mechanical': On the Origins of Photographic Copyright in France and Great Britain." *Art History* 31, no. 1 (2008): 57–78. https://doi.org/10.1111/j.1467-8365.2008.00583.x.

McClure, Kirstie M. "Taking Liberties in Foucault's Triangle: Sovereignty, Discipline, Governmentality, and the Subject of Rights." In *Identities, Politics, and Rights*, edited by Austin Sarat and Thomas R. Kearns. Ann Arbor: University of Michigan Press, 1997.

Medvetz, Thomas. *Think Tanks in America*. Chicago: University of Chicago Press, 2012.

Mehta, Jal. "Tenure Denial Raises Concerns." *Harvard Crimson*, May 9, 1997. https://cyber.harvard.edu/eon/evidence/tdrc5997.html.

Mercier, Delphine. "L'enseignement de la morale au quotidien: Le rôle des inspecteurs primaires, 1880–1914." *Histoire de leducation* 105, no. 1 (2005): 2–2.

Merleau-Ponty, Maurice. *The Structure of Behavior*. Pittsburgh, Pa.: Duquesne University Press, 1963.

Mills, Simon. *Gilbert Simondon: Information, Technology, and Media*. London and New York: Rowman & Littlefield International, 2016.

Moi, Toril. *Simone de Beauvoir: The Making of an Intellectual Woman*. Oxford and New York: Oxford University Press, 2008.

———. "What Can Literature Do? Simone de Beauvoir as a Literary Theorist." *PMLA* 124, no. 1 (2009): 189–98.

———. *What Is a Woman?: And Other Essays*. Oxford and New York: Oxford University Press, 2001.

Monk, Ray, and Richard C. Monk. *Ludwig Wittgenstein: The Duty of Genius*. New York: Free Press, 1990.

Montag, Warren. *Althusser and His Contemporaries: Philosophy's Perpetual War*. Durham, N.C.: Duke University Press, 2013.

———. "From Clinamen to Conatus: Deleuze, Lucretius, Spinoza." In *Lucretius and Modernity: Epicurean Encounters across Time and Disciplines*, edited by Jacques Lezra and Liza Blake, 163–71. Basingstoke and New York: Palgrave Macmillan, 2016.

Moore, A. W. *The Evolution of Modern Metaphysics: Making Sense of Things*. Cambridge and New York: Cambridge University Press, 2012.

Morgan, Daniel. "Where Are We?: Camera Movements and the Problem of Point of View." *New Review of Film and Television Studies* 14, no. 2 (April 2, 2016): 222–48. https://doi.org/10.1080/17400309.2015.1125702.

Mufti, Aamir R. *Forget English!* Cambridge, Mass.: Harvard University Press, 2016.

Mumford, Stephen. *Dispositions*. Oxford and New York: Oxford University Press, 2003.

Mumford, Stephen, and Rani Lill Anjum. "Dispositional Modality." In *Lebenswelt und Wissenschaft, Deutsches Jahrbuch Philosophie 2*, edited by C. F. Gethmann. Hamburg: Meiner Verlag, 2011.

———. *Getting Causes from Powers*. Oxford and New York: Oxford University Press, 2011.

Nichols, Robert. *Theft Is Property!: Dispossession and Critical Theory.* Durham, N.C.: Duke University Press, 2019.

———. "Theft Is Property! The Recursive Logic of Dispossession." *Political Theory* 46, no. 1 (April 2, 2017): 3–28. https://doi.org/10.1177/0090591717701709.

Nord, Philip. "Catholic Culture in Interwar France." *French Politics, Culture & Society* 21, no. 3 (2003): 1–20.

Nussbaum, Martha. "The Professor of Parody: The Hip Defeatism of Judith Butler." *New Republic* 22 (1999): 37–45.

Pagden, Anthony. *The Enlightenment: And Why It Still Matters.* New York: Random House, 2013.

Panagia, Davide. "The Algorithm Dispositif: Risk and Automation in the Age of #datapolitik." In *The Routledge Companion to Media and Risk*, edited by Bhaskar Sarkar and Bishnupriya Ghosh. New York: Routledge Press, 2020.

———. *Impressions of Hume: Cinematic Thinking and the Politics of Discontinuity.* Landham, Md.: Rowman & Littlefield, 2013.

———. *Intermedialities: Political Theory and Cinematic Experience.* Evanston: Northwestern University Press, 2024.

———. "On the Possibilities of a Political Theory of Algorithms." *Political Theory*, September 24, 2020. https://doi.org/10.1177/0090591720959853.

———. *Rancière's Sentiments.* Durham, N.C.: Duke University Press, 2018.

———. "A Theory of Aspects: Media Participation and Political Theory." *New Literary History* 45, no. 4 (2014): 527–48.

Park, Jaeyoon. "Does Power 'Spread'? Foucault on the Generalization of Power." *Political Theory* (October 11, 2021). https://doi.org/10.1177/00905917211046576.

Pasquinelli, Matteo. "What An Apparatus Is Not: On the Archeology of the Norm in Foucault, Canguilhem, and Goldstein." *Parrhesia Journal* 22 (May 2015): 79–89.

Patton, Paul. *Deleuze and the Political.* London and New York: Routledge, 2000.

———. *Deleuzian Concepts: Philosophy, Colonization, Politics.* Stanford, Calif.: Stanford University Press, 2010.

Peden, Knox. *Spinoza Contra Phenomenology: French Rationalism from Cavaillès to Deleuze.* Stanford, Calif.: Stanford University Press, 2014.

———. "Truth and Consequences: Political Judgment and Historical Knowledge in Foucault and Althusser." *Zinbun*, no. 47 (2016): 33–47.

Perelman, Chaïm, and Lucie Olbrechts-Tyteca. *The New Rhetoric: A Treatise on Argumentation.* Notre Dame, Ind.: University of Notre Dame Press, 1971.

Phillips, John. "Agencement/Assemblage." *Theory, Culture & Society* 23, no. 2–3 (May 1, 2006): 108–9. https://doi.org/10.1177/026327640602300219.

Philosophy Today. Special issue: *The Work of Simondon*, edited by Andrea Bardin, Giovanni Carrozzini, and Pablo Rodríguez, 63, no. 3 (Summer 2019).

Philp, Mark. "Foucault on Power: A Problem in Radical Translation?" *Political Theory* 11, no. 1 (February 1, 1983): 29–52. https://doi.org/10.1177/0090591783011001003.

Pius XII. "Fidei Donum (April 21, 1957)." Accessed August 17, 2020. http://www.vatican.va/content/pius-xii/en/encyclicals/documents/hf_p-xii_enc_21041957_fidei-donum.html.

Poignet, A., and H. Bernat. *Le Livre Unique de Morale et d'instruction Civique.* 10th ed. Paris: Auguste Godchaux, 1911.

Political Theory 13, no. 3 (August 1, 1985). Accessed July 29, 2020. https://journals .sagepub.com/toc/ptxa/13/3.

Porter, James I. *The Origins of Aesthetic Thought in Ancient Greece: Matter, Sensation, and Experience.* Cambridge and New York: Cambridge University Press, 2010.

Protevi, John. "Deleuze and Guattari." Accessed March 16, 2021. http://www.protevi .com/john/DG/.

———. *Life, War, Earth: Deleuze and the Sciences.* Minneapolis: University of Minnesota Press, 2013.

Quine, Willard V. O. "Two Dogmas of Empiricism." *Philosophical Review* 60, no. 1 (1951): 20–43. https://doi.org/10.2307/2266637.

Rajchman, John. *The Deleuze Connections.* Cambridge, Mass.: MIT Press, 2000.

Rancière, Jacques. *The Flesh of Words: The Politics of Writing.* Stanford, Calif: Stanford University Press, 2004.

———. *The Method of Equality: Interviews with Laurent Jeanpierre and Dork Zabunyan.* Hoboken, N.J.: John Wiley & Sons, 2016.

———. *The Names of History: On the Poetics of Knowledge.* 1st ed. Minneapolis: University of Minnesota Press, 1994.

Ranson, George James. "The Method of Literary History by Gustave Lanson." Thesis, University of Kansas, 1929. https://kuscholarworks.ku.edu/handle/1808/23659.

Rasmussen, Dennis C. *The Infidel and the Professor: David Hume, Adam Smith, and the Friendship That Shaped Modern Thought.* Princeton, N.J.: Princeton University Press, 2019.

Ricoeur, Paul. *The Rule of Metaphor: Multi-Disciplinary Studies of the Creation of Meaning in Language.* Toronto: University of Toronto Press, 1981.

Rimer, Sara. "Rejection From Leader Who Vows Diversity." *New York Times,* May 19, 1997. https://www.nytimes.com/1997/05/19/us/rejection-from-leader-who -vows-diversity.html.

Riskin, Jessica. *The Restless Clock: A History of the Centuries-Long Argument over What Makes Living Things Tick.* Chicago: University of Chicago Press, 2016.

———. *Science in the Age of Sensibility: The Sentimental Empiricists of the French Enlightenment.* Chicago: University of Chicago Press, 2002.

Robcis, Camille. *Disalienation: Politics, Philosophy, and Radical Psychiatry in Postwar France.* Chicago: University of Chicago Press, 2021.

———. *The Law of Kinship: Anthropology, Psychoanalysis, and the Family in France.* Ithaca, N.Y.: Cornell University Press, 2013.

Roberts, Neil. *Freedom as Marronage.* Chicago: University of Chicago Press, 2015.

Roe, Glenn H. *The Passion of Charles Péguy: Literature, Modernity, and the Crisis of Historicism.* Oxford and New York: Oxford University Press, 2014.

Rogers, Melvin L. *The Undiscovered Dewey: Religion, Morality, and the Ethos of Democracy.* New York: Columbia University Press, 2008.

Rogers, Melvin L., and Jack Turner. *African American Political Thought: A Collected History*. Chicago: University of Chicago Press, 2021.

Rölli, Marc. *Gilles Deleuze's Transcendental Empiricism: From Tradition to Difference*. Edinburgh: Edinburgh University Press, 2016.

Rosanvallon, Pierre. *Le sacre du citoyen: Histoire du suffrage universel en France*. Paris: Gallimard, 1992.

Rosenfeld, Sophia. *Common Sense: A Political History*. Cambridge, Mass.: Harvard University Press, 2014.

Ross, Dorothy. *The Origins of American Social Science*. Cambridge and New York: Cambridge University Press, 1992.

Ross, Kristin. *Communal Luxury: The Political Imaginary of the Paris Commune*. London: Verso, 2015.

——. *Fast Cars, Clean Bodies: Decolonization and the Reordering of French Culture*. 4th ed. Cambridge, Mass.: MIT Press, 1996.

——. *May '68 and Its Afterlives*. 1st ed. Chicago: University of Chicago Press, 2004.

Rousseau, Jean-Jacques. *The Government of Poland*. Indianapolis: Hackett, 1985.

Rubin, Gayle. "The Traffic in Women: Notes on the 'Political Economy' of Sex." In *Toward an Anthropology of Women*, edited by Rayna R. Reiter, 157–210. New York: Monthly Review Press, 1975.

Russell, Bertrand. "On the Nature of Acquaintance: Preliminary Description of Experience." *Monist* 24, no. 1 (1914): 1–16.

Said, Edward W. *Orientalism*. New York: Knopf Doubleday, 2014.

Saison, Maryvonne. *La peinture de Manet, suivi de "Michel Foucault, un regard."* Paris: Seuil, 2004.

Sauvagnargues, Anne. *Artmachines: Deleuze, Guattari, Simondon*. Edinburgh: Edinburgh University Press, 2016.

Schoolman, Morton. *A Democratic Enlightenment: The Reconciliation Image, Aesthetic Education, Possible Politics*. Durham, N.C.: Duke University Press, 2020.

Schrift, Alan D. "The Effects of the Agrégation de Philosophie on Twentieth-Century French Philosophy." *Journal of the History of Philosophy* 46, no. 3 (July 18, 2008): 449–73. https://doi.org/10.1353/hph.0.0033.

——. "Is There Such a Thing as 'French Philosophy'? Or Why Do We Read the French So Badly?" In *After the Deluge: New Perspectives on the Intellectual and Cultural History of Postwar France*, edited by Julian Bourg, 21–47. Lanham, Md.: Lexington, 2004.

——. *Twentieth-Century French Philosophy: Key Themes and Thinkers*. Hoboken, N.J.: John Wiley & Sons, 2009.

Shapiro, Gary. *Archaeologies of Vision: Foucault and Nietzsche on Seeing and Saying*. Chicago: University of Chicago Press, 2003.

Shapiro, Michael J. "Foucault and Method." In *Foucault and the Modern International: Silences and Legacies for the Study of World Politics*, edited by Philippe Bonditti, Didier Bigo, and Frédéric Gros. 1st ed. New York: Palgrave Macmillan, 2017.

————. *Studies in Trans-Disciplinary Method: After the Aesthetic Turn.* London and New York: Routledge, 2013.

Shaviro, Steven. *Without Criteria: Kant, Whitehead, Deleuze, and Aesthetics.* Cambridge, Mass.: MIT Press, 2012.

Shilliam, Robbie. *Decolonizing Politics: An Introduction.* Hoboken, N.J.: John Wiley & Sons, 2021.

Simondon, Gilbert. *Du mode d'existence des objets techniques.* Paris: Éditions Aubier, 2012.

————. *L'individuation à la lumière des notions de forme et d'information.* Grenoble: Éditions Jérôme Millon, 2005.

————. *Individuation in the Light of the Notions of Form and Information.* Minneapolis: University of Minnesota Press, 2020.

————. *On the Mode of Existence of Technical Objects.* Minneapolis: Univocal, 2016.

————. "The Position of the Problem of Ontogenesis." *Parrhesia,* no. 7 (2009): 4–16.

Sissa, Giulia. *I generi e la storia.* Bologna, Italy: Il Mulino, 2024.

Smith, Barry. "The Derrida Controversy Letter." *The Times,* May 9, 1992. http://ontology.buffalo.edu/smith/varia/Derrida_Letter.htm.

Smith, Barry, and Jeffrey Sims. "Revisiting the Derrida Affair with Barry Smith." *Sophia* 38, no. 2 (September 1, 1999): 142–69. https://doi.org/10.1007/BF02786336.

Smith, Daniel. *Essays on Deleuze.* Edinburgh: Edinburgh University Press, 2012.

Smith, Linda Tuhiwai. *Decolonizing Methodologies: Research and Indigenous Peoples.* London: Zed, 2013.

Sokal, Alan D. *The Sokal Hoax: The Sham That Shook the Academy.* Lincoln: University of Nebraska Press, 2000.

Soussloff, Catherine M. *Foucault on Painting.* 1st ed. Minneapolis: University of Minnesota Press, 2017.

Stadler, Friedrich. *The Vienna Circle: Studies in the Origins, Development, and Influence of Logical Empiricism.* New York: Springer, 2016. Originally published in 2015.

Stavro, Elaine. *Emancipatory Thinking: Simone de Beauvoir and Contemporary Political Thought.* Montreal: McGill-Queen's University Press, 2018.

Stengers, Isabelle. *Thinking with Whitehead: A Free and Wild Creation of Concepts.* Cambridge, Mass.: Harvard University Press, 2014.

Suleiman, Ezra N. *Elites in French Society: The Politics of Survival.* Princeton, N.J.: Princeton University Press, 2015.

Tampio, Nicholas. *Deleuze's Political Vision.* Lanham, Md.: Rowman & Littlefield, 2015.

Tanke, Joseph J. *Foucault's Philosophy of Art: A Genealogy of Modernity.* London and New York: Continuum, 2009.

Taylor, Charles. "Foucault on Freedom and Truth." *Political Theory* 12, no. 2 (May 1, 1984): 152–83. https://doi.org/10.1177/0090591784012002002.

————. "Interpretations and the Sciences of Man." In *Philosophical Papers,* Vol. 2, *Philosophy and the Human Sciences,* 15–57. Cambridge and New York: Cambridge University Press, 1985.

Taylor, Jacqueline Anne. *Reflecting Subjects: Passion, Sympathy, and Society in Hume's Philosophy.* Oxford: Oxford University Press, 2015.

Tiles, Mary. *Bachelard: Science and Objectivity.* Cambridge and New York: Cambridge University Press, 1984.

Toadvine, Ted. "Maurice Merleau-Ponty." In *The Stanford Encyclopedia of Philosophy*, edited by Edward N. Zalta. Stanford, Calif.: Stanford University, Metaphysics Research Lab, 2019. https://plato.stanford.edu/archives/spr2019/entries/merleau -ponty/.

Toscano, Alberto. *Theatre of Production: Philosophy and Individuation between Kant and Deleuze.* Basingstoke and New York: Palgrave Macmillan, 2006.

Truffaut, François. "A Certain Tendency of the French Cinema." In *Movies and Methods: An Anthology*, edited by Bill Nichols, 224–36. Berkeley: University of California Press, 1976.

Tully, James. *Public Philosophy in a New Key.* Vol. 1, *Democracy and Civic Freedom.* Cambridge and New York: Cambridge University Press, 2008.

Vardoulakis, Dimitris. *Spinoza, the Epicurean: Authority and Utility in Materialism.* Edinburgh: Edinburgh University Press, 2022.

Vismann, Cornelia. *Files: Law and Media Technology.* Stanford, Calif.: Stanford University Press, 2008.

Wahl, Jean (André). *Human Existence and Transcendence.* Notre Dame, Ind.: University of Notre Dame Press, 2016.

———. *L'expérience métaphysique.* Paris: Flammarion, 1965.

———. *The Pluralist Philosophies of England and America.* Translated by Fred Rothwell. London: Open Court, 1925.

———. *Transcendence and the Concrete: Selected Writings.* New York: Fordham University Press, 2017.

———. *Vers le concret: Études d'histoire de la philosophie contemporaine; William James, Whitehead, Gabriel Marcel.* Paris: Vrin, 2004.

———. *Verso il concreto: Studi di filosofia contemporanea William James, Whitehead, Gabriel Marcel.* Sesto San Giovanni: Mimesis, 2020.

———. *Voices in the Dark: Fifteen Poems of the Prison & the Camp.* Kirkwood, Mo.: Printery, 1974.

Watson, D. R. "The Politics of Educational Reform in France during the Third Republic 1900–1940." *Past & Present* 34, no. 1 (July 1, 1966): 81–99. https://doi.org /10.1093/past/34.1.81.

Whitehead, Alfred North. *Procès et réalité: Essai de cosmologie.* Paris: Gallimard, 1995.

Widder, Nathan. *Political Theory after Deleuze.* London: A. & C. Black, 2012.

Wiener, Norbert. *Cybernetics; Or, Control and Communication in the Animal and the Machine.* Cambridge, Mass.: MIT Press, 1961.

Wolff, Mark. "Individuality and l'Esprit Français: On Gustave Lanson's Pedagogy." *Modern Language Quarterly* 62, no. 3 (September 1, 2001): 239–58. https://doi.org /10.1215/00267929-62-3-239.

Wolin, Richard. *The Seduction of Unreason: The Intellectual Romance with Fascism from Nietzsche to Postmodernism*. 2nd ed. Princeton, N.J.: Princeton University Press, 2019.

Wolin, Sheldon S. "Political Theory as a Vocation." *American Political Science Review* 63, no. 4 (December 1969): 1062–82. https://doi.org/10.1017 /S000305540026320X.

———. *Politics and Vision: Continuity and Innovation in Western Political Thought*. Princeton, N.J.: Princeton University Press, 2009.

Worth, Alexi. "The Lost Photographs of Edouard Manet." *Art in America*, January 2007.

Young, Iris Marion. "Gender as Seriality: Thinking about Women as a Social Collective." *Signs* 19, no. 3 (1994): 713–38.

Young, Robert. *White Mythologies: Writing History and the West*. London and New York: Routledge, 2004.

Index

Abécédaire (Parnet), 172
Abizadeh, Arash, 227n40
abstract idealism, Beauvoir disdaining, 245n7
Ackerman, Chantal, 223n1
Across the Great Divide (Arnold), 51
action, behavior and, 53–55
actual politics, Easton defining, 52
adjacency, 80, 110, 117, 173, 176
"An affectionate Daughter" ("*Une fille affectueuse*"), 135–37
affect theory, 100
Agamben, Giorgio, 188–89
agencement. See assemblage
Agrégation de Philosophie, 17, 26, 74, 102; Catholicism influencing, 70–71; Hume appearing on, 228n49; Schrift emphasizing, 62–63
agrégé-répétiteur (or *caïman*), 63–64
Air Force Intelligence, American, 57
Algeria, 67–68, 71–72, 216
Algerian war, French intellectuals criticizing, 71–72
"L'Algerie n'est pas la France" (article), 67
allagmatics, 152
Althusser, Louis, 186, 191, 226n33, 260n24; *dispositif* adopted by, 261n25; "Ideology and Ideological State Apparatuses" by, 16; *For Marx* by, 13; *Reading Capital* by, 13
Altman, Meryl, 117
America, postwar. *See* postwar America
American exceptionalism, 211, 233n29

American political science, 33–34, 50–51, 55, 58, 61
Anglophone political theory: as national faith, 16–17; in postwar France, 41; postwar French counterapproaches contrasted with, 27; reading practices of, 213
Anglophones, postwar French thought interpreted by, 215–16
Anjum, Rani Lill, 19, 209, 229n58, 250n28
anti-authoritarian, sentimental empiricism as, 24, 148
apparatus (*appareil*), *dispositif* contrasted with, 184–85, 188–89, 191–93
appliance model of theorizing, 58–59
Apter, Emily, 12
Aquinas, Thomas, 71, 73
The Archeology of Knowledge (Foucault), 196
architectural drawings, 188, 206–7, 263n47
Arguing Revolution (Khilnani), 67
Aristotelian substances, 70–71, 152, 170; adjacency in, 117; Catholic Church centering, 255n12; Eleatic law of the excluded middle grounding, 153–54; Hume opposing, 73; media and, 150–51; sentimental empiricism rejecting, 21; Wahl critiquing, 111
Aristotle, 65, 190, 251n36; Aquinas relying on, 71; metaphors warned of by, 67–68; *Metaphysics* by, 153–54, 159; *Physics* by, 151, 153–54; *Poetics* by, 162–63
Arnold, Jeremy, 51

arrangement, sentimental powers of, 129–38, 134, 136
"Art and Objecthood" (Fried), 263n48
assemblage (agencement), 215, 257n3, 258n7
atomism, hylomorphism contrasted with, 152–53
Auerbach, Erich, 224n7
Augustine, 174
The Augustinian Imperative (Connolly), 37
autonomy, verifiability procuring, 48–49

baccalauréat (exam): curriculum of, 89; Latin and Greek requirements removed from, 82–83; reforms to, 81
Bachelard, Gaston, 13, 75, 150, 155, 226n33, 239n14
Baier, Annette, 118
A Bar at the Folies-Bergère (Manet), 204, 205, 207
Bardin, Andrea, 149, 151
Barthes, Roland, 13, 74, 80, 88, 93, 225n23
"The Basis of Realism" (Russell), 244n52
The Battle of Algiers (Pontecorvo), 68
Baudelaire, Charles, 200
Bauhaus (art school), logical empiricism connected with, 47
Baum, Bruce, 118
Bazin, André, 1
Beauvoir, Simone de, 27, 80; abstract idealism disdained by, 245n7; Catholicism influencing, 138; Le deuxième sexe by, 26; The Elementary Structures of Kinship reviewed by, 141–44; La femme et les mythes by, 141–42; The Force of Circumstance by, 117, 141; Lévi-Strauss influencing, 140–42, 147, 246n22; "Literature and Metaphysics" by, 117; Memoirs of a Dutiful Daughter by, 129–30; "The Novel and Metaphysics" by, 116; patriarchy critiqued by, 11, 115, 119, 146; political thought of, 120–23, 144–45, 147; Sartre contrasted with, 26, 87; The Second Sex by, 115–18, 120–21, 123, 135, 139–40, 144; Stavro on, 122
becoming, being and, 153–54
Bédé, Jean-Albert, 62
behavior, action and, 53–55
behavioral social sciences, postwar America turning to, 16
behaviorism, 33; negative feedback enabled by, 53; political science influenced by, 42–43; United States influenced by, 34, 42
being, becoming and, 153–54

"being, pre-individual," 152
Bélgique et Rhénanie (Wallez), 70
Beltrán, Christina, 167
Benhabib, Seyla, 37, 40
Bennett, Jane, 167
Bentham, Jeremy, 187, 188, 198, 202–3, 263n47, 264n55
Bergson, Henri, 45, 65, 100, 102, 109
Berkeley, 228n49
Bernat, H., 119, 133–35, 134, 136, 138, 247n39
Bertillon, Alphonse, 43
"The Better Son" ("Le Meilleur fils"), 135–37
Bianchi, Emanuela, 251n36
bilingualism, precocious, 102
The Black and the Color (Le noir et la couleur) (Foucault), 196
Boas, Frank, 142
bodily movements, Gordon on, 241n51
Bonaparte, Napoleon, 78, 81–82
le bon sens. See common sense
Boschetti, Anna, 73
Bourdieu, Pierre, 8, 41, 79
Bourget, Paul, 130–31
Bousquet, Gilles, 66
Brunatière, M., 90
Bussolini, Jeffrey, 189
Butler, Judith, 37

Cahiers du Cinéma (journal), 1
caïman. See agrégé-répétiteur
camera movement, of Ackerman, 223n1
Cameron, Sharon, 256n25
Camus, 252n42
Canguilhem, Georges, 75, 92, 150, 188–90, 226n33, 238n13
Cannes Film Festival, 66
Carnap, Rudolph, 47, 51; "The Elimination of Metaphysics through Logical Analysis of Language" by, 46; Heidegger analyzed by, 234n42; "Intellectual Autobiography" by, 44; on logical empiricism, 44–45; on pseudo-statements, 48–49
Carroll, Lewis, 96
Cassirer, Ernst, 45
Catholic Church, 71, 73; Aristotelian substances centering, 255n12; education system controlled by, 82, 86–87; in France, 8; the soul saved through, 72; Vichy regime and, 69–70
Catholicism: Agrégation de Philosophie influencing, 70–71; Beauvoir influenced

by, 138; France dominated by, 214; during World War II, 70
causal theory, value theory distinguished from, 52–53
Cavaillès, Jean, 34, 75
Cavell, Stanley, 230n5, 265, 265n66
Centre Universitaire Expérimental de Vincennes. See University of Paris VIII at Vincennes
Chandler, James, 260n14
change, the mind and, 125
Chaplin, Charlie, 94
characteristics, of sentimental empiricism, 2–3
chevauchement. See overlapping
Christian faith, understanding of faith sustaining, 71
civil morals, 119–20, 131–33
claim-making (*prétendre*), 181–82
classical humanism, 90–91
close reading, 59–62
Code (Geoghegan), 266n8
Code de la famille. See Family Code
Cold War, 16–17, 23, 52–54
Cold War universities, American, 55–56, 58, 74–75
Collège de Sociologie, 228n48
Collège Philosophique, 99, 104, 114
colonialism, French, 5
colonies, of France, 67–68
Combes, Muriel, 157
common sense (*le bon sens*), 5–6, 118, 146, 216–17; method needed by, 8; of mimesis, 6–7; paradox destroying, 96; the State and, 9, 15–16
Communal Luxury (Ross, K.), 22, 92
communication, rhetoric challenged by, 260n18
Communist Party, of France, 75
Compayré, 135
Comte, Auguste, 17
Concourse (Davy), 124
the concrete: empiricism and, 110; as energy, 109; idealism rejecting, 105–6; metaphysical experience accessed through, 105; pluralism of, 112
concrete relations, patriarchy analyzed through, 119–20
Confessions (Augustine), 174
Connolly, William E., 36, 37
consciousness, James on, 111
conservatism, American, 224n15

"Contestations" (series), 37
copyright laws, 81
Corlett, William, 36
Cornell University, 231n12
Cornell University Press, 37
Cosmopolis (Bourget), 130–31
Cousin, Victor, 63
COVID-19 pandemic, LAUSD impacted by, 211
Crary, Jonathan, 263n54
criminology, photography and, 43
critical thinking, minor mode of, 17–22
criticism, dialectics contrasted with, 212–13
criticism, literary. *See* literary criticism
criticism, structuralist, 74
Critique of Pure Reason (Kant), 44
cultural capital, 12
cybernetics, 53–55, 235n67

Dallmayr, Fred, 36
Dartmouth College, 231n12
Daston, Lorraine, 43
Davis, Theo, 260n19
Davy, Georges, 17–18, 124
"Declaration of the Rights of Genius" (1793), 6, 60, 81
Defert, Daniel, 196
De la Grammatologie (Derrida), 35
Deleuze, Gilles, 3, 11, 28, 64, 100, 255n15; on difference, 180; *Difference and Repetition* by, 174–75; difference-in-itself prioritized by, 168; *dispositif* described by, 192–93; *Empiricism and Subjectivity* by, 113–14, 171, 172, 174, 179–80; empiricism inspiring, 183; Hume analyzed by, 171–80, 243n39; *The Logic of Sense* by, 95–96, 167, 169, 254n11; "Lucrèce et le naturalisme" by, 169, 254n8; mimesis overthrown by, 167; Montag on, 254n8; *Nietzsche and Philosophy* by, 17; on Plato, 182; on relations, 244n54; sentimental empiricism of, 169–70; Simondon paralleled by, 252n52; "The Simulacrum and Ancient Philosophy" by, 171, 181–83, 254n11; *A Thousand Plateaus* by, 167; Wahl not cited by, 171
Democracy and Difference (Benhabib), 37
The Democratic Sublime (Frank), 23–24
de plein fouet (expression), 264
Der Derian, James, 37
Derrida, Jacques, 59; *agrégé-répétiteur* described by, 64; *De la Grammatologie* by, 35; University of Cambridge honoring, 37–39

Descartes, René, 5–8, 65, 102, 190
Le deuxième sexe (Beauvoir), 26
dialectical movement, universality of, 107
dialectics, 10, 212–13
difference, Deleuze on, 180
Difference and Repetition (Deleuze), 174–75
difference-in-itself, 170, 215; Deleuze prioritizing, 168; metaphysics of, 115, 149, 181; philosophy of, 110
Disalineation (Robcis), 24
Discourse on Method (*Discours de la méthode*) (Descartes), 5–7
dispositif, 257nn3–4, 260n19, 263n54; Althusser adopting, 261n25; apparatus contrasted with, 184–85, 188–89, 191–93; Deleuze describing, 192–93; *dispositio* contrasted with, 189–90, 208; Foucault developing, 186–88, 203, 207–10, 258n8; movement of, 190–91; picture-object contrasted with, 196; political aesthetics of, 195–208, 198, 202, 204; political morphology of, 188–94; representation contrasted with, 194. *See also* theoretical *dispositif*
dispositio, dispositif contrasted with, 189–90, 208
dispositionality, 209
dispositional powers, 2–3, 156; domination of in-between-ness as, 20–21; Hume on, 229n58; indirect passion as, 122–23; Mumford on, 209; patriarchy as, 116–17, 120; political theory of, 185; relations and, 21; sentiments as, 97, 175; sympathies equated with, 119
domination, 10, 116–17
Donato, Eugene, 35
Drancy internment camp, 103
Dreyfus Affair, 81, 82–83
Dumm, Thomas, 36
Duong, Kevin, 22–23
Durkheim, Émile, 142

Easton, David, 52
École Libre des Hautes Études, at New School for Social Research, 103–4
École Normale Supérieure (ENS), 62, 65, 78–79, 102, 236n92
Éditions de Minuit (publisher), 196
Éditions Gallimard (academic press), 99
education system, French, 169, 238n11; Bonaparte reforming, 81–82; Catholic Church controlling, 82, 86–87; Lanson

criticized by, 89; literary criticism and, 8, 11–12; mimesis grounding, 172; political thought innovated by, 80; reforms to, 82–83, 91, 131–32; two-tiers of, 78–79, 82; women lacked in, 26
Eichner, Carolyn, 22–23
Einstein, Albert, 44–46
Eleatic law of the excluded middle, 149–54
The Elementary Structures of Kinship (Lévi-Strauss), 27, 120, 123, 140–42
Eléments d'éducation morale et civique (Compayré), 135
"The Elimination of Metaphysics through Logical Analysis of Language" (Carnap), 46
Elites in French Society (Suleiman), 78, 230n74
empiricism, 17, 243n40; the concrete and, 110; Deleuze inspired by, 183; of Hume, 176; Kantian tradition defining, 255n15; the particular shifted to by, 18–19; radical, 212; transcendental, 115; Wahl defining, 101. *See also* logical empiricism
Empiricism and Subjectivity (Deleuze), 113–14, 171, 172, 174, 179–80
empirico-criticism, 111–13, 163
engines, sentimental empiricism exemplified through, 162–63
English-speaking world, Wahl ignored in, 100
ENS. *See* École Normale Supérieure
epistemic virtue, logical empiricism developing, 43–44
"Epitaph for a Hare" ("*Épitaphe pour un lièvre*") (Richepin), 2
l'esprit Française, 6–7, 89, 90, 93
essentialism, 140
L'Étranger (Camus), 252n42
Études philosophiques (journal), 169, 254n8
the Eucharist, 71–72
Evening in the Walls (Wahl), 103
exceptionalism, American, 211, 233n29
The Execution of Maximilien (Manet), 197, 199
exogamy, 120, 123, 143–44, 147–48
experience, Hume defining, 255n15
Experience and Empiricism (Ford), 24–25
explication des textes, 65, 77, 79, 86, 214; classical humanism demanded by, 90; genealogy of, 27; Lanson and, 62, 87–93; *lecture linéaire* contrasted with, 60; mimesis operationalized in, 80; *Ratio Studiorum* rejected by, 89
expression, in sentimental empiricism, 79

faith, 71
Family Code (*Code de la famille*), 139, 147, 246n22
family law, in France, 138–39
family relations, 135
Fanon, Frantz, 226n27
Farrell, Allan Peter, 84, 85
Farwell, Beatrice, 200
Fast Cars (Ross, K.), 22
Faure, Edgar, 68
feminine symptom, 251n36
feminist scholars, 25–26
Feminists Theorize the Political (Butler and Scott), 37
La femme et les mythes (Beauvoir), 141–42
Ferguson, Frances, 258n5, 264n55
Ferguson, Kathy E., 36, 226n29
Ferguson, Kennan, 243n45
Ferry, Jules, 131, 132
Fidei Donum (Pius XII), 71–72
The Fifer (Manet), 200–202, 201
"*Une fille affectueuse.*" *See* "An affectionate Daughter"
The Force of Circumstance (Beauvoir), 117, 141
Ford, Russell, 24–25, 230n68
Forgash, Rachel, 230n73
Forget English (Mufti), 239n22
form, medium related to, 49–50
For Marx (Althusser), 13
formist, sentimental empiricism as, 79–80
Forrester, Katrina, 16, 51, 55
Foucault, Michel, 11, 17, 28, 123, 254n10, 257n1; *The Archeology of Knowledge* by, 196; architectural drawings lectured on by, 206–7; *A Bar at the Folies-Bergère* analyzed by, 204–5; Bentham interpreted by, 198, 202–3; *The Black and the Color* by, 196; Crary contrasted with, 263n54; *dispositif* developed by, 186–88, 203, 207–10, 258n8; *The Execution of Maximilien* lectured on by, 197; *The Fifer* discussed by, 200–202; *Las Meninas* analyzed by, 195, 197; Merleau-Ponty engaged with by, 261n26; *The Order of Things* by, 35, 195; Peden criticizing, 260n24; reflex circuit rejected by, 191–92; sentimental empiricism extended by, 184–85
The Four Hundred Blows (*Les Quatre cents coups*) (film), 1–2, 66, 88
Fourth Republic, 29
France, 5, 71–72; Catholicism dominating, 214; colonies of, 67–68; Communist Party of, 60–61, 75; family law in, 138–39; Grands Corps of, 78–79, 96; Ministry of Defense of, 78; Ministry of Education of, 78; Ministry of Higher Education, Research, and Innovation of, 87; Ministry of Public Instruction of, 63; totalitarianism rejected by, 66; university system in, 248n1; Wahl escaping, 103–4. *See also* education system, French; postwar France; postwar French thought
Frank, Jason, 23–24
freedom, of imagination, 173
Freedom Beyond Sovereignty (Krause), 228n56
French intellectuals, Algerian war criticized by, 71–72
Fried, Michael, 263n48
Frost, Samantha, Simondon compared with, 253n55
Fundamental Feminism (Grant), 25

Galison, Peter, 43, 47, 50
Gandillac, Maurice de, 102
Gaulle, Charles de, 15, 139, 216
gender, motion connected to, 251n36
gender roles, 135–38
Gender Trouble (Butler), 37
general law of relations, thought not determined by, 107–8
genesis, 152, 161, 164
Geoghegan, Bernard, 266n8
Germany, France invaded by, 102
Getting Causes from Powers (Mumford and Anjum), 250n28
Gilligan, Carol, 40
Glissant, Eduard, 226n27
Goblot, Edmond, 8
good sense. *See* common sense
Gordon, Rae Beth, on bodily movements, 241n51
The Government of Poland (Rousseau), 86
Grab-and-Go Food Centers, 211
grade school, in France, 60–61
grammatical analysis, Lanson on, 91
grandes écoles (elite universities), 78–79
Grands Corps, of France, 78–79, 96
Grant, Judith, 25
Green, Elizabeth Alden, 102
Greenberg, Clement, 196
Grusin, Richard, 251n37
Guattari, Félix, 65, 167
Guillory, John, 33, 213–14, 260n18

Guiney, M. Martin, 78, 83, 89–90
Gunnell, John, 40–41, 51

habits, 14–15, 174–76
Harvard University, 39–40
H-bomb. *See* hydrogen bomb
Hegel, 65, 71, 117–18
Hegelism, French, 75
Heidegger, Martin, 45, 49, 227n47; Carnap
    analyzing, 234n42; *The Question Con-*
    cerning Technology by, 151, 161; Simondon
    contrasted with, 151–52; "What Is Meta-
    physics?" by, 47
Henri-IV (high school), 236
Hesiod, 145
Hesse, Carla, 81
history of philosophy, political values
    transmitted through, 9
Hobbes, 128
Honig, Bonnie, 37, 39–40
humanism, 8, 90–91
Humanities Center of Johns Hopkins
    University, 35
Hume, David, 3, 50, 100, 108, 113–17, 168;
    Agrégation de Philosophie appeared
    on by, 228n49; Aristotelian substances
    opposed by, 73; Deleuze analyzing,
    171–80, 243n39; on dispositional powers,
    229n58; empiricism of, 176; experience
    defined by, 255n15; identity, 124–26; on
    indirect passion, 118–19, 127–28; represen-
    tation critiqued by, 176–77; *A Treatise of*
    Human Nature by, 14, 117, 124, 126–27, 177,
    246n23; on "whatever quality," 178–79
humility, 128
Husserl, Edmund, 75
hydrogen bomb (H-bomb), 56
hylomorphism, 71, 115, 150, 152–53, 160–61, 212
Hyppolite, Jean, 24, 236n92

idealism: abstract, 245n7; the concrete
    rejected by, 105–6; Wahl criticizing, 106
ideas: in imagination, 21, 173–74; oscillation
    of, 107–8, 112; as serialized adjacencies, 14
identity, 37, 124–26, 150
Identity/Difference (Connolly), 37
Ideological State Apparatus, 236n89
"Ideology and Ideological State Appara-
    tuses" (Althusser), 16
imagination, 14, 182; Cold War gripping, 23;
    freedom of, 173; ideas in, 21, 173–74;
    philosophy and, 172

The Imitation of Christ (book), 138
immanence, transcendence and, 113
incest taboo, 140, 142
indirect passion: as dispositional powers,
    122–23; Hume on, 118–19, 127–28; patriar-
    chy and, 123–29, 138–46
individuation: as genesis, 152; without law of
    non-contradiction, 157; metastability and,
    155–58; Simondon on, 154–55, 158, 165
Individuation in the Light of the Notions of
    Form and Information (Simondon),
    149–50, 160, 163, 249n4, 249n7
inner problematic, participation and, 157–58
"Intellectual Autobiography" (Carnap), 44
intellectual formation, 3, 12–15
International/Intertextual Relations
    (Shapiro and Der Derian), 37
"Interpretation and Genealogy in Politics"
    (seminar), 36
Isaac, Jeffrey, 40–41
Istitut Adeline Désir (prep school), 138

Jakobson, Norman, 142
James, William, 27, 107, 111, 243n45
Johns Hopkins University, 35–36
July Monarchy, 63

Kant, Immanuel, 44, 65, 108
Kantian tradition, empiricism defined in,
    255n15
Kant's Critical Philosophy (Deleuze), 172
Kaplan, Fred, 56
Khilnani, Sunil, 67
Klossowski, Pierre, 17, 227n47
Kojève, Alexander, 75, 117
Krause, Sharon, 228n56
Krauss, Rosalind, 254n11
Krieger, Murray, 231n12

La Fontaine, Jean de, 133
"Languages of Criticism and the Sciences
    of Man" symposium, 35
Lanson, Gustave, 27, 61, 83; classical hu-
    manism recapitulated by, 91; education
    system criticized by, 89; *explication des*
    textes and, 62, 87–92; on grammatical
    analysis, 91; literary criticism restructured
    by, 87–88; Sartre ousted by, 62, 92; at
    Sorbonne University, 91
"Lansonisme," 80, 88, 225n23
Latin Quarter, of Paris, 87, 169
Latour, Bruno, 252n41

Laurent, Noël, 104–5
LAUSD. *See* Los Angeles Unified School District
law of non-contradiction (*tertium non datur*), 72, 154, 157
lecture linéaire, 60, 65, 67
Lefebvre, Marcel, 72
Leiris, Michel, 141
Lepistö, Antti, 224n15
Levering Act, UCLA impacted by, 57
Levinas, Emanuel, 99, 101, 105
Lévi-Strauss, Claude: Beauvoir influenced by, 140–42, 147, 246n22; *The Elementary Structures of Kinship* by, 27, 120, 123, 140–42; *Savage Mind* by, 140–41; *Les structures de la parenté* by, 142
Lipman, Hymen, 233n33
literarity, political, 35–42, 59–65
literary criticism, 6; education system and, 8, 11–12; Lanson restructuring, 87–88; without siloing, 79
literature, philosophy contrasted with, 37–39
"Literature and Metaphysics" (Beauvoir), 117
literature programs, postwar French thought propagated through, 81
Le livre unique de morale & d'instruction civique (Poignet and Bernat), 119, 133–35, 134, 136, 138, 146
Locke, 228n49
logical empiricism, 33; within American political science, 61; Bauhaus connected with, 47; Carnap on, 44–45; epistemic virtue developed by, 43–44; political theory influenced by, 42–43; in United States, 51; verifiability offered by, 44, 55
logical positivism, 34, 213, 243n40, 260n17
The Logic of Sense (*La logique du sens*) (Deleuze), 95–96, 167, 169, 254n11
London Times (newspaper), 38–39
Los Angeles Unified School District (LAUSD), COVID-19 pandemic impacting, 211
Louis-le-Grand (high school), 236
Louis XV (king), 63
"Lucrèce et le naturalisme" (Deleuze), 169, 254n8
Lyceé Janson de Sailly (high school), 102

"Machine and Organism" (Canguilhem), 188–90
Macksey, Richard, 35
Maioli, Roger, 18

Mallarmé, Stéphane, 102
Manet, Édouard, 187, 195–96, 199, 263nn47–48, 264n59; *A Bar at the Folies-Bergère* by, 204; Bentham contrasted with, 203; *The Execution of Maximilien* by, 197, 198, 199; *The Fifer* by, 200–202, 201; *The Masked Ball at the Opera* by, 197, 198
Marcel, Gabriel, 102
Marso, Lori, 118, 124, 129, 147, 230n70
Marx, Karl, 13, 36
The Masked Ball at the Opera (Manet), 197, 198
Massumi, Brian, on Simondon, 250n20
Mauss, Marcel, 140
May 1, 1802, decree, 81
McCarthyism, 52
meaning, 43–44, 143–44
media: Aristotelian substances and, 150–51; reproduction of, 43; technical, 12–13
mediation, 159–60, 164, 251n37
medium, form related to, 49–50
Medvetz, Thomas, 56
Mehta, Jal, 40
"*Le Meilleur fils*." *See* "The Better Son"
Mellamphy, Ninian, 249n4
Melville, Herman, 5
Memoirs of a Dutiful Daughter (*Mémoires d'une jeune fille rangée*) (Beauvoir), 129–30, 138
Las Meninas (Vélazquez), 192, 193, 195, 197–98, 205
Mercier, Delphine, 132
Merleau-Ponty, Maurice, 75, 141, 236n92, 261n26
mésentente. *See* missed understanding
metaphors, Aristotle warning of, 67–68
metaphysical experience, the concrete and access to, 105
metaphysics, 49, 71; of difference-in-itself, 115, 149, 181; mimesis and, 7, 77; philosophy eliminating, 47; pluralist, 113–14; postwar America rejecting, 214; postwar France critiquing, 11; postwar French thought influenced by, 214; pseudo-statements and, 50, 58; of substances, 212. *See also specific works*
Metaphysics (Aristotle), 153–54, 159
metaphysics of substances, sentimental empiricism rejecting, 212
metastability, 155–58, 162
method, 8, 50
Miller, E. F., 52

Mills, Simon, 250n28
Mimesis (Auerbach), 224n7
mimesis *"le même"*: common sense of, 6–7; Deleuze overthrowing, 167; education system grounded in, 172; *explication des textes* ope rationalizing, 80; metaphysics and, 7, 77; political authority and, 22; reproduction performed through, 26; sentimental empiricism defined by, 5; the State connected to, 5–7, 24
the mind, change and, 125
Ministry of Defense, of France, 78
Ministry of Education, of France, 78
Ministry of Higher Education, Research, and Innovation, of France, 87
Ministry of Public Instruction, of France, 63
minor tradition, of sentimental empiricism, 3–4, 11, 25, 99, 114, 165–66
Minow, Martha, 40
missed understanding (*mésentente*), 33, 76, 215, 230n1
modernism, Cavell defining, 265n73
Modernity and Political Thought series (Schoolman), 37
Moi, Toril, 121, 147, 245n2
monism, pluralism refuting, 114
Monk, Ray, 46
Montag, Warren, 254n8, 254n10
Moore, A. W., 102, 180
morals, civil, 119–20, 131–33
morals, religious, 131
moral sentimentalism, 17–18
motion, gender connected to, 251n36
Les mots et les choses (Foucault). See *The Order of Things*
Mount Holyoke College, 102, 104
movement: camera, 223n1; *of dispositif*, 190–91; picture-object generating, 206
Mufti, Aamir R., 226n27, 239n22
Mumford, Stephen, 19, 209, 229n58, 250n28
music theory, Western, 3–4
Mythologies (Barthes), 74

Napoleonic Code, 138
negative feedback, behaviorism enabling, 53
Nelböck, Johann, 51
neo-realism, 112–13
new materialism, 252n50
New School for Social Research, 103–4, 142
The New Scientific Spirit (Bachelard), 150

Nietzsche, Friedrich, 17; *On the Genealogy of Morals* by, 65; interest in, 227n47, 228n48; *Thus Spake Zarathustra* by, 50; Wolin on, 229n64
"Nietzsche, le polythéisme et la parodie" (Klossowski), 17
Nietzsche and Philosophy (Deleuze), 17
Nietzsche and the Vicious Circle (Klossowski), 17
Le noir et la couleur (Manet). See *The Black and the Color*
non-sense, 11
Nord, Philip, 69–73
Northwestern University, 231n12
"The Novel and Metaphysics" (Beauvoir), 116
Nussbaum, Martha, 42

objects, technical. *See* technical objects
oeuvre. *See* a work
Olbrechts-Tyteca, Lucie, 189
On the Genealogy of Morals (Nietzsche), 65
On the Mode of Existence of Technical Objects (Simondon), 149, 151, 160, 249n4
The Order of Things (*Les mots et les choses*) (Foucault), 35, 195
Orientalism (Said), 224nn6–7
oscillation, of ideas, 107–8, 112
the Other, women as, 144–45
overlapping (*chevauchement*), 244n46
The Oxford Handbook of Classics in Contemporary Political Theory, 121

Pagden, Anthony, 19
pandemic, COVID-19, 211
Panopticon Penitentiary, 187, 199, 202–3, 206–7, 263n47, 264n59
paradox, common sense destroyed by, 96
Paris, Latin Quarter of, 87, 169
Paris Commune, 22–23
Park, Jaeyoon, 246n24
Parmenides (Plato), 105
Parnet, Claire, 172
participation, 158–59, 166
the particular, 18–19, 105–6
Pasquinelli, Matteo, 188–89, 190–91
passion, indirect. *See* indirect passion
the past, desire to break out of, 66
Patch, Helen Elizabeth, 104
patriarchy (*patriarchie*): Beauvoir critiquing, 11, 115, 119, 140, 146; as dispositional

powers, 116–17, 120; indirect passion and, 123–29, 138–46
Patton, Paul, 227n47
"peculiarly American enterprise," 42
Peden, Knox, 260n24
Péguy, Charles, 92
Perelman, Chaïm, 189
La Perrière, Guillaume de, 186
Pessin, Alain, 66
Le Petit Vingtième (newspaper), 70
Phenomenology of Spirit (Kojève), 75
philosophy: of difference-in-itself, 110; history of, 9; imagination and, 172; literature contrasted with, 37–39; metaphysics eliminated from, 47; politics contrasted with, 58, 76, 168–69, 225n21. See also specific works
Philosophy and Literature (journal), 42, 232n27
Philp, Mark, 36
photography, criminology and, 43
phylogenetic lineage, 161–62
Physics (Aristotle), 151, 153–54
picture-object (tableau-objet), 187–88, 192, 194–96, 206, 209
Pius XII (pope), 71
Plato, 105, 145, 182
Platonism, 181–82
pluralism, 112–14, 178, 230n68, 243n45
Pluralism (Russell), 112–13
pluralist metaphysics, of relations, 113–14
The Pluralist Philosophies of England and America (Wahl), 100, 102, 111, 170
Poèmes de circonstance (Wahl), 103
Poetics (Aristotle), 162–63
Poignet, A., 119, 133–35, 134, 136, 138, 247n39
political ambitions, professional requirements and, 4
political authority, mimesis and, 22
political change, in sentimental empiricism, 80
political literarity, 35–42, 59–65
political relations, 10, 66–69
political science: American, 33–34, 50–51, 55, 58, 61; behaviorism influencing, 42–43; University of Chicago influencing, 51
political solidarity, 215
The Political System (Easton), 52
political theory, 76; American, 33–34, 50–51, 55, 58, 61; of dispositional powers, 185; esoteric verbosity betraying, 41; Gunnell

studying, 40; logical empiricism influencing, 42–43; philosophical projects contributing to, 185; of sentimental empiricism, 95, 170; state thinking equated with, 55–56. See also Anglophone political theory
Political Theory (journal), 36, 40, 59
Political Theory and Postmodernism (White), 37
Political Theory and the Displacement of Politics (Honig), 37
"Political Theory as a Vocation" (Wolin), 57–58
political thought, 80, 120–23, 144–45, 147
political values, history of philosophy transmitting, 9
politics: actual, 52; literarity of, 76; philosophy contrasted with, 58, 76, 168–69, 225n21; Wahl influenced by, 102
Politics and Vision (Wolin), 42
Politics with Beauvoir (Marso), 129
Pompidou, Georges, 79
Pontecorvo, Gillo, 68
"The Position of the Problem of Ontogenesis" (Simondon), 150
positivism, 34, 213, 233n29, 243n40, 260n17
posthumanism, 100
postwar America: behavioral social sciences turned to by, 16; metaphysics rejected in, 214; political literarity in, 35–42; postwar France contrasted with, 33–34, 73–75
postwar France: Anglophone political theory in, 41; metaphysics critiqued in, 11; political and aesthetic criticism in, 2; political literarity in, 59–65; postwar America contrasted with, 33–34, 73–75; symptomatic critique developed in, 13
postwar French counterapproaches, Anglophone political theory contrasted with, 27
postwar French thought: Anglophones interpreting, 215–16; literature programs propagating, 81; metaphysics influencing, 214
poverty rate, in U.S., 211
power relations, representation reproducing, 15
Practical Criticism (Richards), 59
precocious bilingualism, 102
"pre-individual being," Simondon focusing on, 152
prelection, order of, 84–85

prétendre. See claim-making
pride, 128
Principia Mathematica (Whitehead), 45
The Principles of Literary Criticism
  (Richards), 59
Process and Reality (Whitehead), 243n36
professional requirements, political
  ambitions and, 4
Programme (*agrégation* syllabus), 63–65, 99
propriety, 130–31
pseudo-statements: Carnap on, 48–49;
  metaphysics and, 50, 58; statements
  distinguished from, 52–53

*Les Quatre cents coups. See The Four
  Hundred Blows*
The Question Concerning Technology
  (Heidegger), 151, 161
Quine, Willard V. O., 231n7

radical empiricism, Wahl, J., turning to, 212
radical mediation, 160, 251n37
radical pluralism, of sentimental empiricism, 178
Rancière, Jacques, 6
RAND Corporation, 55–57
Ratio Studiorum (1599), 8, 23, 82, 83–86, 89
Rawls, John, 51
reading, 76; civil morals taught through,
  132; close, 59–62; practices of, 13–14,
  61, 213; propriety associated with, 131.
  See also *explication des textes*
Reading Capital (Althusser), 13
Reassembling the Social (Latour), 252n41
recognition, political association based on,
  28–29
Red-Ucators, 52, 57
the reflex, theory of, 261n26
reflex circuit, Foucault rejecting, 191–92
Reichenbach, Hans, 44
relations, 150, 170; concrete, 119–20; Deleuze on, 244n54; dispositional powers
  and, 21; family, 135; general law of, 107–8;
  as independent of terms, 20; participation
  transforming, 166; pluralist metaphysics
  of, 113–14; political, 10, 66–69; power, 15;
  sentimental empiricism thinking of
  entities as, 155; social, 129
religious morals, civil morals separated
  from, 131
Remi, Georges "Hergé," 70

representation: *dispositif* contrasted with, 194;
  Hume critiquing, 176–77; picture-object
  as, 209; power relations reproduced
  through, 15; reproduction and, 64
reproduction: of media, 43; mimesis
  performing, 26; representation and, 64;
  of state authority, 9
resident aliens, in United States, 265
Reveley, Willey, 187
rhetoric, communication challenging,
  260n18
Ribot, Théodule, 88
Richards, I. A., 59
Richepin, Jean, 2
Ricoeur, Paul, 68
Riskin, Jessica, 3, 18, 228n55
Robcis, Camille, 24, 138
Roberts, Neil, 167
Rockefeller Foundation, 103
"The Role of the Idea of the Moment in
  the Philosophy of Descartes" (Wahl), 102
Rosenfeld, Sophia, 6
Ross, Dorothy, 42, 68, 233n29
Ross, Kristin, 22, 67, 74, 92
Rousseau, Jean-Jacques, 65, 86
Rudenstine, Neil L., 39–40
Rue d'Ulm. *See* École Normale Supérieure
Russell, Bertrand, 45, 112–13, 244n52

SAC. *See* Strategic Air Command
Said, Edward W., 224nn6–7
La Santé prison, 102
Sartre, Jean-Paul, 66–67, 227n37; Beauvoir
  contrasted with, 26, 87; Lanson ousted
  by, 62, 92; Wahl contrasted with, 104–5
Savage Mind (Lévi-Strauss), 140–41
Schlick, Moritz, 44, 46, 51
Schoolman, Morton, 37
School of Criticism and Theory (SCT),
  231n12
Schrift, Alan D., 17, 25, 27, 62–63, 102,
  228n48
science, the State and, 55–59
Science in the Age of Sensibility (Riskin), 3
"The Scientific Conception of the World"
  (1929), 46
scientism, 233n29
Scott, Joan W., 37
Scouts de France (SdeF), 69
SCT. *See* School of Criticism and Theory
SdeF. *See* Scouts de France

The Second Sex (Beauvoir), 115–18, 120–21, 123, 135, 139–40, 144
Second Vatican Council, 72
Ségur, Madame de, 130
sensation, 18
sensibility, 18, 228n55
sentimental empiricism. *See specific topics*
sentimental powers of arrangement, 129–38, 134, 136
sentimentalism, moral, 17–18
sentiments, 19, 97, 175, 228n55
sexuality, women repressing, 121–22
sexual relation, social solidarity based in, 143
Shapiro, Gary, 203
Shapiro, Michael, 37
Le siècle de Louis XIV (Voltaire), 89
Simondon, Gilbert, 11, 28, 186; Deleuze paralleling, 252n52; Eleatic law of the excluded middle challenged by, 149–50; Frost compared with, 253n55; Heidegger contrasted with, 151–52; hylomorphism rebutted by, 71, 115, 150, 212; on individuation, 154–55, 158, 165; *Individuation in the Light of the Notions of Form and Information* by, 149–50, 160, 163, 249n4, 249n7; Massumi on, 250n20; on mediation, 159–60; minor tradition contributed to by, 165–66; *On the Mode of Existence of Technical Objects* by, 149, 151, 160, 249n4; "The Position of the Problem of Ontogenesis" by, 150; "pre-individual being" focused on by, 152; sentimental empiricism contributed to by, 150–60, 164; *Technical Objects* by, 160, 163; Vardoulakis paralleling, 252n43
"The Simulacrum and Ancient Philosophy" (Deleuze), 171, 181–83, 254n11
Situating the Self (Benhabib), 37
skepticism, sentimental empiricism and, 21
Skinner, Q. R. B., 53
Skocpol, Theda, 40
Smith, Barry, 37, 39, 59, 79
social relations, sympathies and, 129
social sciences, behavioral, 16
social solidarity, sexual relation as basis of, 143
Social Text (Sokal), 42
the Society of Jesus, 83–84
Sokal, Alan, 42
solidarity, political, 215
Sorbonne University, 87, 91, 142

Sorokin, Natalie, 26
the soul, Catholic Church saving, 72
Soustelle, Jacques, 68
Souvenirs de la Bataille D'Alger (Yacef), 68
Spivak, Gayatri, 35
the State, 191, 225n17, 236n89; common sense and, 9, 15–16; mimesis connected to, 5–7, 24; science and, 55–59; total authority, 6–7
state authority, reproduction of, 9
statements, pseudo-statements distinguished from, 52–53
state thinking, political theory equated with, 55–56
Statute on Jews, Vichy, 102
Stavro, Elaine, 122, 147
"The Strange Silence of Political Theory" (Isaac), 41
Strategic Air Command (SAC), American, 56–57
The Structuralist Controversy (symposium record), 35
structuralist criticism, 74
The Structure of Behavior (Merleau-Ponty), 75
Les structures de la parenté (Lévi-Strauss), 142
substances, Aristotelian. *See* Aristotelian substances
substances, metaphysics of, 212
Suleiman, Ezra, 78, 230n74, 238n1
Surmounting the Barricades (Eichner), 22
sympathies, 119, 129, 175–76
symptomatic critique, postwar France developing, 13

tableau-objet. See picture-object
Tagore, Rabindranath, 46
Taylor, Charles, 36
Taylor, Jacqueline Anne, 129, 179, 245n13
"The Teaching of Philosophy in France" (Canguilhem), 238n3
technical media, intellectual formation participated in by, 12–13
technical objects: analysis of, 74; genesis defining, 161, 164; metastability of, 162; sentimental empiricist philosophy of, 160–66
Technical Objects (Simondon), 160, 163
telos, 251n36
Tel Quel (magazine), 3, 216

Les Temps Modernes (film), 94
Les Temps Modernes (magazine), 67, 73, 94, 141, 144
tertium non datur. See law of non-contradiction
theoretical *dispositif*, 49–50; American, 42; meaning proven through, 44; totalitarianism resisted through, 74–75; validity proven through, 51–52
theorizing, appliance model of, 58–59
"Theory and History of Literature" (series), 35–36
A Theory of Justice (Rawls), 51
Third Republic, 27
Thomist Scholasticism, 108
thought, general law of relations determining, 107–8
A Thousand Plateaus (Deleuze and Guattari), 167
Thus Spake Zarathustra (Nietzsche), 50
Tintin (Hergé), 70
totalitarianism, 52–55; France rejecting, 66; redemptive violence associated with, 23; theoretical *dispositif* resisting, 74–75
Totality and Infinity (Levinas), 99
Tractatus Logico-Philosophicus (Wittgenstein), 46–47
transcendence, immanence and, 113
transcendental empiricism, 115
A Treatise of Human Nature (Hume), 14, 117, 124, 126–27, 177, 246n23
Truffaut, François, 1–2, 5, 9, 10, 15, 66
The Twentieth Century (*Le Vigntième Siècle*) (newspaper), 70
"Two Dogmas of Empiricism" (Quine), 231n7

UCLA. *See* University of California Los Angeles
Ulrich, Laurel Thatcher, 40
understanding of faith (*intellectus fidei*), Christian faith sustained by, 71
unintentional acts, meaning of, 143–44
United States (U.S.), 33, 50, 55, 58, 61, 233n29; behaviorism influencing, 34, 42; logical empiricism in, 51; poverty rate in, 211; resident aliens in, 265. *See also* postwar America
universalism, 140; French republican, 9, 28–29, 83, 147; sentimental empiricism dismantling, 21–22; women excluded from, 139

universality, of dialectical movement, 107
universal suffrage, French, 138
University of Berlin, 44
University of California, 231n12
University of California Los Angeles (UCLA), 51, 57
University of Cambridge, Derrida honored by, 37–39
University of Chicago, political science influenced by, 51
University of Massachusetts, 36
University of Minnesota Press, 35
University of Paris VIII at Vincennes, 7
University of Vienna, 51
university system, in France, 248n1
U.S. *See* United States

Les Vacances (Ségur), 130
validity, theoretical *dispositif* proving, 51–52
value theory, causal theory distinguished from, 52–53
Vardoulakis, Dimitris, Simondon paralleled by, 252n43
Vélazquez, Diego, 193
verifiability, 44, 48–49, 55
Vers le concret (Wahl), 100–101, 102, 105–14, 242n8
Vichy regime, 69–70, 102, 139
Vichy Statute on Jews, 102
Vienna Circle, 44, 46–47, 50
Le Vigntième Siècle (newspaper). See *The Twentieth Century*
The Virtues of Violence (Duong), 22–23
Vismann, Cornelia, 5
Voltaire, 89, 137
voting rights, women lacking, 139
Vries, Hent de, 231n12

Wahl, Barbara, 102, 142
Wahl, Edmund, 102
Wahl, Jean, 27, 80, 99, 155, 165, 243n39; Aristotelian substances critiqued by, 111; Deleuze not citing, 171; empiricism defined by, 101; English-speaking world ignoring, 100; France escaped by, 103–4; Hegel contrasted with, 117–18; idealism criticized by, 106–7; life and works of, 241n4; *The Pluralist Philosophies of England and America* by, 100, 102, 111, 170; *Poèmes de circonstance* by, 103; politics influencing, 102; radical empiricism

turned to by, 212; "The Role of the Idea of the Moment in the Philosophy of Descartes" by, 102; on Russell, 244n52; Sartre contrasted with, 104–5; terms renamed and reformulated by, 110–11; *Vers le concret* by, 100–101, 242n8; Whitehead influencing, 108–9

Wallez, Abbé Norbert, 70

"*Was ist Metaphysik?*" (Heidegger). *See* "What Is Metaphysics?"

Waters, Mary, 40

Western music theory, 3–4

"whatever quality," Hume on, 178–79

"What Is Metaphysics?" ("*Was ist Metaphysik?*") (Heidegger), 47

White, Steven, 36

Whitehead, Alfred North, 27, 107, 155; *Principia Mathematica* by, 45; *Process and Reality* by, 243n36; Wahl influenced by, 108–9

White Mythologies (Young), 227n39

Whitman, Walt, 102

Wiener, Norbert, 53

Wittgenstein, Ludwig, 46–47

Wohlstetter, Albert, 56–57

Wolin, Sheldon S., 42, 57–58, 229n64

women: education system lacking, 26; as the Other, 144–45; sexuality repressed by, 121–22; universalism excluding, 139; voting rights lacked by, 139

a work (*oeuvre*), 60

Works and Days (Hesiod), 145

World War I, 117

World War II, Catholicism during, 70

Worth, Alexi, 200

Yacef, Saadi, 68

Young, Iris Marion, 227n37, 227n39

Zadig (Voltaire), 137

DAVIDE PANAGIA is Professor and Chair of Political Science at UCLA. His books include *The Poetics of Political Thinking* (Duke University Press, 2006), *Ten Theses for an Aesthetics of Politics* (University of Minnesota Press, 2016), and *Intermedialities: Political Theory and Cinematic Experience* (Northwestern University Press, 2024).

www.ingramcontent.com/pod-product-compliance
Lightning Source LLC
Chambersburg PA
CBHW031141020426
42333CB00013B/475